The Blackwell Guide to

Social and Political Philosophy

—— Blackwell Philosophy Guides ——

Series Editor: Steven M. Cahn, City University of New York Graduate School

Written by an international assembly of distinguished philosophers, the *Blackwell Philosophy Guides* create a groundbreaking student resource – a complete critical survey of the central themes and issues of philosophy today. Focusing and advancing key arguments throughout, each essay incorporates essential background material serving to clarify the history and logic of the relevant topic. Accordingly, these volumes will be a valuable resource for a broad range of students and readers, including professional philosophers.

The Blackwell Guide to
Social and Political Philosophy

Edited by

Robert L. Simon

Copyright © Blackwell Publishers Ltd 2002

First published 2002

2 4 6 8 10 9 7 5 3 1

Blackwell Publishers Inc.
350 Main Street
Malden, Massachusetts 02148
USA

Blackwell Publishers Ltd
108 Cowley Road
Oxford OX4 1JF
UK

Library of Congress Cataloging-in-Publication Data has been applied for.

ISBN 0-631-22126-3 (hardback); 0-631-22127-1 (paperback)

British Library Cataloguing in Publication Data
A CIP catalogue record for this book is available from the British Library.

Typeset in 10 on 13 pt Galliard
by Best-set Typesetter Ltd., Hong Kong
Printed in Great Britain by T.J. International, Padstow, Cornwall

This book is printed on acid-free paper.

To Joy, for always being there

Contents

Notes on Contributors

Richard J. Arneson is Professor of Philosophy at the University of California, San Diego, where he was department chair from 1992 to 1996. His research centers on contemporary theories of justice. Since 1990 he has 46 essays in ethics and political philosophy published and forthcoming. In fall, 1996 he was visiting professor of political science at Yale University and in spring, 1999 he was visiting fellow at Australian National University.

Ann E. Cudd is Professor of Philosophy at the University of Kansas. She received her MA in Economics and her Ph.D. in Philosophy from the University of Pittsburgh in 1988. Her research is in the areas of social and political philosophy, feminist theory, game theory, and philosophy of economics. She is currently working on a book on oppression, and future plans include further work on liberal-democratic remedies of oppression.

Christopher J. Eberle is Assistant Professor of Philosophy at Concordia University-River Forest and works in the fields of political philosophy and the philosophy of religion. Among his publications are "What Respect Requires – And What It Does Not" (*Wake Forest Law Review*), "Liberalism and Mysticism" (*Journal of Law and Religion*), "Why Restraint is Religiously Unacceptable" (*Religious Studies*), and "The Autonomy and Explanation of Mystical Perception" (*Religious Studies*).

James S. Fishkin holds the Patterson-Banister Chair at the University of Texas at Austin where he is Professor of Government, Law and Philosophy. He is the author of several works on democratic theory and the theory of justice including *Democracy and Deliberation* (Yale, 1991), *The Dialogue of Justice* (Yale, 1994), and *The Voice of the People* (Yale, 1997).

A. Todd Franklin is Assistant Professor of Philosophy at Hamilton College, where he teaches courses in nineteenth-century continental philosophy, Existentialism, and Cultural Studies. He earned his Ph.D. from Stanford University and is currently editing a collection of essays that focus on the critical affinities between Friedrich Nietzsche and African-American Thought.

Virginia Held is Distinguished Professor of Philosophy at the City University of New York, Graduate School and Hunter College. Among her books are *The Public Interest and Individual Interests* (1970); *Rights and Goods: Justifying Social Action* (1984); *Feminist Morality: Transforming Culture, Society, and Politics* (1993); and the edited collections *Property, Profits, and Economic Justice* (1980); and *Justice and Care: Essential Readings in Feminist Ethics* (1995). She has also taught at Yale, Dartmouth, UCLA, and Hamilton. She is currently working on a number of essays on the ethic of care and the challenge this kind of theory presents to standard moral theories.

Richard W. Miller is Professor of Philosophy at Cornell University. His writings, in social and political philosophy, ethics, epistemology, the philosophy of science, and aesthetics, include *Analyzing Marx* (1984), *Fact and Method* (1987), and *Moral Differences* (1992).

William Nelson is Professor of Philosophy at the University of Houston. He is the author of *On Justifying Democracy* (1980) and *Morality, What's In It for Me: An Historical Introduction to Ethics* (1991). His current interests include liberal political theory and justifications for moral rights.

A. John Simmons is Commonwealth Professor of Philosophy and Professor of Law at the University of Virginia, where he has taught since 1976. He received his BA in Philosophy from Princeton University and his MA and Ph.D. in Philosophy from Cornell University. He is the author of *Moral Principles and Political Obligations* (Princeton, 1979), *The Lockean Theory of Rights* (Princeton, 1992), *On the Edge of Anarchy* (Princeton, 1993), and *Justification and Legitimacy* (Cambridge, 2001).

Robert L. Simon is Professor of Philosophy at Hamilton College. He is the author of numerous articles in social and political philosophy as well as *Fair Play* (1991), *Neutrality and the Academic Ethic* (1994), and (with Norman E. Bowie) *The Individual and the Political Order* (3rd edn., 1998). He currently is working on issues in ethics and athletics, and is a past president of the International Association of the Philosophy of Sport.

James P. Sterba is Professor of Philosophy at the University of Notre Dame. He has written more than 150 articles and published 21 books, including *How to Make People Just* (1998), *Earth Ethics* (2nd edn., 1994), *Feminist Philosophies* (2nd edn., 1998), and *Morality in Practice* (6th edn., 1991). His book *Justice for Here and Now* published with Cambridge University Press was awarded the 1998 Book of the Year Award of the North American Society for Social Philosophy. His most recent book, *Three Challenges to Ethics: Environmentalism, Feminism and Multiculturalism*, was published by Oxford University Press.

Daniel M. Weinstock is an Associate Professor of Philosophy at the Université de Montréal. He has published widely on issues relating to multiculturalism and pluralism and their impact on theories of justice and citizenship. He is presently working on a project dealing with the normative theory of institutional design for multination states.

Christopher Heath Wellman directs the Jean Beer Blumenfeld Center for Ethics and teaches in the Department of Philosophy at Georgia State University. He works in ethics, specializing in political and legal philosophy.

Alan Wertheimer is John G. McCullough Professor of Political Science at the University of Vermont. He is the author of *Coercion* (Princeton University Press, 1987) and *Exploitation* (Princeton University Press, 1996) and numerous articles. He is currently working on a book on consent to sexual relations.

Introduction: Social and Political Philosophy – Sorting Out the Issues

Robert L. Simon

Human beings normally do not live in isolation but interact within a variety of social and political practices and institutions. Many different kinds of issues can be raised about these practices and institutions which include how the organizations or practices actually work, what they are, how they affect people, and how they compare across national and cultural boundaries. However, others are normative and concern disputes over such matters as whether the institutions and the principles underlying them are good or bad, fair or unfair, just or unjust. Moreover, we can ask just how "fairness," "justice," and other criteria used to evaluate the social and the political order are understood themselves.

The purpose of this collection of essays is to provide a comprehensive guide to the major questions that arise within social and political philosophy. Each contribution addresses a major issue or set of issues within the field and provides a conceptual or historical guide to the central arguments and positions that bear on the topic. In addition, each essay offers a defense of a particular approach or conclusion concerning the problems addressed. Thus, each essay provides a guide to the major positions that have been developed in response to the issues it addresses, and then attempts to move the discussion forward from there. That is, not only is each contribution a guide to an area of social and political philosophy but it also contributes to the ongoing discussion of the issues it considers. This collection, then, is a guide in two senses. Not only does it attempt to offer extensive background on the issues discussed, but it also is a contribution toward resolving them, or at least advancing our understanding of them, as well.

In the first section of this introduction, I will attempt to place the major issues discussed within the context of social and political philosophy, and in the second section, I will review the major arguments of each contribution and, in some cases, suggest connections between and among articles.

Major Issues of Social and Political Philosophy

Political and social philosophy is concerned with the moral evaluation of political and social institutions, and the development, clarification, and assessment of proposed principles for evaluation of the political and social order. Different philosophers would draw the line between the political and the social in different places, and, in any case, that line most probably is blurred and shifting. As feminist philosophers among others have reminded us in their discussions of the private vs. the public, this is at best a rough characterization that sometimes can be misleading. Thus, although we may think of issues concerning the proper role of the national government as political, and issues of child rearing as social rather than political, clearly national policies, or failure to make policy, can have significant effects upon the nature and quality of child care. Although some distinction between the social and political probably can be maintained, it may be best not to assign too much weight to it, and to remember that however one draws the boundary, many issues almost surely will cut across it.

Perhaps the most dominant political institution throughout much of human history has been the state. It is not surprising, then, that philosophers concerned with the political order from Plato and Aristotle in ancient Greece until our own day have devoted major attention to this institution. At the most basic level, states have claimed the right to pass laws that limit the freedom of citizens and have maintained that citizens have the duty to obey. That is, states claim to have not just power over their citizens but moral authority as well, and claim that those under that authority have a moral duty to comply. One set of issues concerns whether and under what conditions such claims can be made good.

A second set of issues concerns the proper extent and limit of the state's authority or legitimate exercise of power. Are there some areas that are the proper domain of individual liberty that may not be regulated by the state? For example, almost everyone would agree that the state acts legitimately when it sets speed limits on public highways. However, does the state act legitimately when it requires motorcyclists using those highways to wear helmets? What, if anything, distinguishes the area that government may regulate from that where individuals should be free of such regulation? The famous nineteenth-century philosopher John Stuart Mill maintained that the state may legitimately interfere with the liberty of individuals only to prevent harm to others, but how is "harm" to be understood? May we never interfere with liberty even to prevent displays of behavior highly offensive to almost everyone, for example? So if one set of issues concerns the basis, if any, of claims by the state to exercise power legitimately, or at least with justification, a second set concerns the scope and limits of that authority, or of the defensible use of political power over individuals.

Even if political institutions act within justifiable boundaries or constraints, what criteria should be used to evaluate their behavior? Among the major standards that have been applied to the political order are justice, equality, and democratic choice. But how are these standards best understood? What is justice? What kind of equality, if any, should political institutions foster? We surely do not want equality in the sense of absolute uniformity, for some differences are not only legitimate, but also valuable, while others may arise from the proper exercise of individual liberty. If so, with what form of equality should political and social institutions be concerned? Moreover, we may also believe that political institutions should be democratic, governed ultimately by the will of the people. But democracy itself raises many questions. How is democracy to be understood? What are proper limits of the power of the majority? Can a majority vote, for example, legitimize restrictions on the liberty of those who hold unpopular or even obnoxious views? One of the major undertakings of social and political philosophers, then, is to develop and evaluate conceptions of notions such as justice, fairness, equality, and democracy that are used as standards for assessing political and social institutions alike.

The body of political and social philosophy which endorses limits on the power of the state set according to the value put on the individual, and which emphasizes the importance of such values as liberty, justice, equality, individual rights, and democratic choice, is known as liberal theory. The liberal-democratic tradition has had profound influence, not only on those states in the West which, however imperfectly, try to embody its standards, but on others attempting to develop liberal-democratic institutions, as well. Moreover, opponents of tyranny elsewhere look to liberal-democratic theory as providing those standards to which all states are obligated to conform.

Can free and democratic institutions which value individual liberty and social justice be defended against other forms of political and social organization? Among the more basic approaches to moral theory which philosophers have employed in evaluating the political order are utilitarian and what might be called Kantian approaches to justification. Utilitarianism, which can take many different forms, looks to the consequences of political acts, rules, or practices for all those affected. Sophisticated utilitarians, perhaps following the lead of John Stuart Mill, need appeal not to the direct results of each act, which many fear might lead to a tyranny of the majority, but to indirect results of broad rules or practices. For example, individual rights restricting the power of the majority might be defended on utilitarian grounds, as constituting a system of protections for the individual which, while sometimes producing bad consequences in individual cases, work systematically to promote utility in the long run.

Philosophers more in the tradition of the eighteenth-century philosopher Immanuel Kant, however, appeal not to the consequences of a practice but to such factors as whether it is rationally acceptable to impartial, autonomous agents. For example, in his widely acclaimed work *A Theory of Justice* (1971), John Rawls suggested that the basic structure of society is just only if it conforms to principles acceptable to rational and impartial persons ignorant of the place in society and the personal qualities, such as race, gender, religion, and character, of the society's members. Although Rawls's own views have changed as his theory of justice developed, his theory still constitutes a major alternative to the consequentialism of the utilitarian approach. It remains a major defense of liberal-democratic institutions, which political philosophers must engage, whether or not they end up accepting or rejecting its principal conclusions, or the arguments advanced in support of them.

But, even if, as its philosophic critics generally concede, liberal democracy is a significant moral advance over such forms of political organization as monarchy or dictatorships of various kinds, the liberal-democratic state, and the theoretical approach underlying it, may have deep problems of its own. Many of these issues concern how justice, equality, democracy, and other concepts central to the ideal of liberal democracy are best understood. For example, on libertarian conceptions of justice, the just state is the minimal state, which acts legitimately only when it acts to protect the negative rights of its citizens to be free from coercion. On the other hand, many liberals, such as Rawls, believe that social justice requires some redistributive mechanisms, in some cases quite extensive ones, to promote economic and other forms of equality, or at least keep inequality within fair and reasonable limits.

Moreover, for a variety of reasons, many liberals believe that the state should be neutral in considering various conceptions of the good life. On this view, the state's role is to provide a fair framework in which the fundamental rights of individuals are to be protected, but so long as the rights are not violated and fair principles are in place, individuals should be left free to choose for themselves how to live. The state should not favor, for example, the religious life over the non-religious life, or, say, a life devoted to contemplation of artistic and intellectual works over one of hedonistic indulgence in physical pleasures. The basic idea is that people should be left free to choose for themselves how to live, so long as they do not violate the principles of justice and rights that protect all the citizens of the democratic state.

Although liberals have done much to clarify what they mean by neutrality, and to develop sophisticated accounts of justice, equality, and liberty, liberal political theory has been exposed to serious philosophical challenge. Thus, yet another set of major issues concerns whether liberal theory, including the work of Rawls and other contemporary liberal thinkers, is acceptable or whether liberal theory itself must be rejected or significantly modified.

Communitarians, some feminists, as well as pluralists influenced sometimes by postmodern thought and the "politics of identity," along with humanistically oriented Marxists, recommend modification, alteration, or rejection of some key elements of liberal political thought. For example, communitarians question whether the liberal ideal of the autonomous self, free to step back and evaluate its commitments, ignores the extent to which actual selves are already embedded in and so constituted by various social identities, such as those of culture, race, gender, religion, and class. Communitarians also reject the doctrine they attribute to liberals of the priority of the right over the good; basically the idea that the job of the state is to provide a fair and just framework within which individuals pursue their own conception of the good, rather than to endorse and support an overriding conception of the good itself. Cultural pluralists, on the other hand, question whether liberalism, and its emphasis on individual rights, needs to be modified to make room for the claims of cultural, religious, racial, and ethnic groups. Moreover, some feminists question whether the framework of individual rights and impartial justice is the best one for pursuing many of the complex issues of political and social thought.

The contributors to this volume address many of the issues raised above, as well as related questions and controversies, from a variety of perspectives. In the next section of this introduction, I will provide a guide to each contribution, indicate how the contributions bear on the kinds of issues specified above, and comment briefly on some of the general themes running through the collection.

Summary of Essays

Following the organization of the book, this section is divided into three parts: Part I, Core Principles and the Liberal Democratic State; Part II, Liberalism, Its Critics, and Alternative Approaches; and Part III, Pluralism, Diversity, and Deliberation. While the topics treated in each section clearly bear on the topics in other sections, this division does focus on the main emphasis of the contributions in each division.

Core Principles and the Liberal Democratic State

In the first essay of the collection, A. John Simmons addresses the issue of whether and under what conditions states, especially morally decent states, have authority over their citizens and whether citizens have obligations to obey. Put another way, do states ever have the moral right to rule and citizens the moral duty to obey? Simmons's question is not whether citizens can ever have good reason to comply with the law. For example, we all may have good reason to obey the law prohibiting driving an automobile while intoxicated, because people may be seriously harmed if the law is broken. But, as stated so far, the reason for obeying is to avoid harm to individuals, not simply that the state has passed a law. The question of whether states can claim legitimate authority is not identical with the question of whether there are ever good reasons, even good moral reasons, to obey the state's commands. Rather, it is more akin to the question of whether the fact that the state has commanded or prohibited certain behaviors is in itself a moral reason to obey, and whether failure to obey is at least a prima facie moral wrong or violation of duty.

Simmons considers approaches to justifying claims to political authority. Three arguments from Plato's *Crito* are given special attention, in both their classical and more modern formulations. After examining various formulations of these arguments, including contemporary approaches, Simmons finds that none is strong enough to ground claims to political authority by actual or existing states, although he allows that some conceivable states (ideally free and just contractual democracies) could rightly claim authority over their citizens. He concludes that in the actual world, we should not presume that we have an obligation to obey the commands or laws of even decent states, but judge them on a case by case basis. (Note that this analysis rests not only on a philosophical examination of various theories of authority and obligation but also on an evaluation of whether and to what degree actual states must or do measure up to the criteria these theories lay down.) On his view, no general presumption in favor of a right to rule or a general duty to obey exists, since no actual state satisfies the moral criteria that would generate such obligations in the first place.

In the second essay, Alan Wertheimer discusses the related issue of what grounds might justify the state in interfering with the liberty of its citizens. Wertheimer assumes, at least for the sake of argument, that democratic states are legitimate and asks under what conditions they act properly in restricting individual liberty. However, those readers who, along with Simmons, are skeptical about the claims of states to exercise legitimate authority, can view the essay as asking when legal restrictions on individual liberty are justified, or supported by reasons of sufficient merit to support the restriction.

In *On Liberty* (1859), John Stuart Mill advanced what he claimed to be "one very simple principle" to the effect that society is justified in limiting the liberty of individuals only to prevent them from harming others. Wertheimer brings out, however, the complexity of the issue he considers. In addition to discussing such familiar grounds for limiting liberty as paternalism, prohibition of offensive behavior, and the enforcement of morality, he also considers such grounds for limiting liberty as promotion of social justice, protection of collective goods, or fulfillment of the basic needs of citizens.

On the basis of considering a multitude of different cases that cannot all be easily subsumed under one principle, Wertheimer concludes first that Mill's Harm Principle is not so simple itself, and secondly and of perhaps greater importance, that a plurality of principles that might justify restricting liberty need to be weighed and balanced in complex cases. Since it is not clear there is only one weighing of these principles that alone is reasonable, disagreement over hard cases is at best extremely difficult to avoid. No easy philosophical resolution is immediately available.

The conclusions advanced by Simmons and Wertheimer are not dissimilar. Both seem to end up with a view that might be called *justificatory pluralism*. That is, they seem to suggest that when weighing whether the laws of a state ought to be obeyed (Simmons), or whether legal restrictions on the freedom of individuals are justified (Wertheimer), there are a plurality of factors that need to be assessed. Each, in different ways, questions whether any simple principle or line of argument exists for resolving the issues they discuss.

Perhaps then, political philosophers should focus on fair and just ways for reconciling conflicting claims. What we want are criteria for a just political order, and a just resolution to disputes within it. The topic of social justice is addressed by Christopher Wellman in chapter 3.

Wellman surveys a number of approaches to justice that have been defended by contemporary philosophers, and discusses major criticisms of each one. He first considers utilitarian views of justice. Perhaps the most attractive and plausible utilitarian approach to justice is to see principles of justice as injunctions which, if generally or universally followed, tend to maximize aggregate utility, or the ratio of benefits to harms for all affected. However, as Wellman points out, defenders of this version of utilitarianism have not persuaded critics that their view gives adequate weight to moral rights or gives people what they are due, rather than treating people as if they had rights simply because it is useful to do so.

The principal alternative to utilitarian views of justice is the extremely influential view of justice developed by John Rawls, particularly as expressed in his monumental work *A Theory of Justice*. Although Rawls's work has been extensively discussed, and criticized by many commentators, its significance is such that anyone hoping to contribute in this area must be familiar with and take account of the Rawlsian approach. It is not surprising, therefore, that Rawls's work is discussed by many of the contributors to this collection.

In his essay, Wellman acknowledges that Rawls's theory has many virtues. However, he questions whether it provides a uniquely acceptable approach to issues of social justice. After examining several criticisms of the Rawlsian account, he considers alternative approaches to justice, including those emphasizing communal accounts of justice relativized to different spheres of human interest (Walzer), equality and freedom from oppression (Anderson), and oppression and the politics of recognition and group difference (Young). While he finds Young's approach promising for reasons provided in his essay, he also expresses doubt about whether any one theory or approach by itself will be satisfactory. He too suggests that we consider a kind of what I have called justificatory pluralism in which we combine the best elements of each approach to resolve issues of injustice, perhaps in a piecemeal fashion rather than in an overarching or comprehensive way.

Equality might seem like a simple concept, referring in some way to identity of treatment or distribution, but as Richard J. Arneson suggests, it actually is quite complex. Arneson distinguishes between different conceptions of equality, and offers an assessment of each one. For example, he considers whether we should be concerned with equality of rights, equality of the distribution of some resource, or whether it is actual equality of welfare (since the same package of resources might lead to different levels of welfare for different individuals) that ought to be of concern. His discussion brings out the vast variety of considerations that apply to discussions of equality, and why many issues concerning the nature, scope, and weight to be assigned to equality remain controversial.

Differences of opinion and even of fundamental values, as well as disagreements about how to resolve conflicts among values, suggest that we need a morally sound procedure for resolving such differences. Democracy is often thought to be such a procedure. In her essay, Ann E. Cudd examines different conceptions of democracy, and considers whether democracy is best thought of as a means of aggregating the preferences of individuals in order to reach a collective decision. But, as she asks, over what matters may individual preferences determine outcomes, and how are the preferences of diverse individuals to be aggregated to arrive at a collective decision? Cudd explores theoretical complexities with the notion of aggregating preferences and also considers different versions of democratic theory, such as the idea that individuals should vote for their conception of the common or group good rather than their own individual preferences. Although, like the other authors in this section, she acknowledges that democracy sometimes needs to be balanced against other values with which it can conflict, she suggests that a suitably constrained form of preference-based democracy can be justified.

Taken as a group, the essays in this section clarify and examine some of the basic concepts of political philosophy. Many of these values are central to what was briefly described above as liberal theory (although some authors may not have themselves endorsed typically liberal conclusions about the values they explored). For example, the question of at what point individual liberty should be protected from the state is a major concern of liberals. The essays in the next section consider views which depart from liberal theory in some fundamental respect, and so provide a fuller evaluation of the liberal-democratic approach to political and social theory.

Liberalism, Its Critics, and Alternative Approaches

Marxism has been one of the most influential political philosophies of the twentieth century. Although many identify it with the rule of repressive communist regimes, many scholars have found in the work of the nineteenth-century thinker Karl Marx a humanistic and non-repressive approach to criticism not only of capitalist economic structures but also of much of liberal-democratic thought as well. In his essay, Richard W. Miller asks what is worth retrieving from Marx's thought and how it applies to evaluation of the contemporary political and social order.

For example, Miller suggests that a careful analysis of what Marxists might mean by exploitation can cast doubt on too narrow conceptions of freedom presupposed by liberal philosophers, on liberal conceptions of neutrality toward conceptions of the good life, and on liberal conceptions of equality. Marxists might also challenge the liberal faith in democratic procedures, since if Marxist analyses of exploitation and alienation have even some force, those procedures may contain an inherent bias in favor of the interests of some groups or classes and against the interests of others. Miller also explores Marx's complex views about morality. He considers what can be retrieved from Marx's apparent scornful rejection of basic moral notions, although liberals may question whether what can be saved of morality within Marxism is sufficiently robust as to make any moral critique, let alone a moral critique of liberal-democratic ideology, even possible. Be that as it may, as Miller argues, Marxism casts many assumptions of liberal-democratic political theory into question, and provides a less individualistic alternative than liberalism for understanding and evaluating the political and social order.

Feminism primarily is a movement committed to the equality of women. In social and political theory, feminists have considered such issues as the nature of equality for women, how it may be achieved, the existence and extent of male biases in traditional political theory, and the development of moral theories which reflect the experiences of women and give voice to a wider variety of perspectives than that of traditional approaches.

As Virginia Held indicates in her contribution, feminist theorists differ among themselves on many issues, so feminism should not be thought of as a monolithic approach to social and political thought. For example, Held points out that many feminist theorists work within basic liberal paradigms and argue that a fuller application of liberal principles to such areas as justice within the family, child care, harassment, and economic justice, is what is needed to promote equality for women. Thus, full application of a robust principle of equal opportunity might support the principles of more equitable distribution of burdens between males and females within the family, non-discrimination and perhaps affirmative action in the workplace, and more egalitarian economic policies (perhaps such as comparable pay for work of comparable worth) as well. However, as Held also points out, many other feminists either reject or modify liberal policies, regarding them as too individualistic, and too firmly grounded on notions such as contractualism, which tend to ignore the important role of relationships and personal commitments in human life.

In her discussion, Held explores the role rights should play in achieving justice, and contrasts a rights-based approach with a less individualistic ethics of care grounded in concrete human relationships. The ethics of care explores the moral role our personal ties with one another should play within such institutions as the family, where the approach of impartial consideration of benefits and burdens recommended by many liberal theorists often seems inappropriate. Held also considers extending the ethics of care to the political and even international arena. And while she expresses some suspicion of postmodernist attempts to dismiss such notions as objectivity, impartiality, and rationality as inevitably biased and distorted, she suggests that a more concrete conception of rational discourse, which might involve such traits as listening, empathy, and care for common interests, might lead to an improved conception of reasonable discussion and inquiry. Whether such a conception of discourse can best be carried out without the protective framework of familiar liberal rights, and so to what extent someone who holds Held's view should remain committed to some conception of individual rights, is open to further discussion.

Communitarian philosophers, like Marxists and non-liberal feminists, are troubled by what they regard as the excessive individualism of liberalism. Communitarians have raised questions about what they see as excessive attachment by liberals to the self as an autonomous chooser able to step back from any of its social roles in order to assess existing social arrangements. Instead, they view the self as at least in part constituted by its commitments in concrete communities. Communitarians also have sharply questioned the liberal idea of state neutrality toward the good, arguing instead that only given a conception of the good life can a community avoid arbitrariness in moral decision-making, and provide the kind of communal context in which humans flourish. Communitarians regard liberals as insufficiently sensitive to the importance of communities, which, they suggest, at least partially shape our identities and commitments, and which provide the social framework without which moral judgment is unintelligible. Since neither communitarianism nor liberalism are monolithic philosophies, it is difficult to say just which concrete policies communitarians would favor and liberals oppose. However, to cite some plausible examples of possible differences, communitarians might be more inclined than liberals to limit obscenity as well as brutal and misogynist language in popular music on the grounds that otherwise the community would be degraded and coarsened. Liberals would tend to protect individual liberty to choose, absent concrete evidence of harm to others. (But see Wertheimer's essay on the complexity of this issue.) In short, while communitarians emphasize the value of a shared social and political life based on conceptions of the good, liberals wonder if communities can too easily become repressive without the protections for the individual provided by liberalism.

Many communitarians claim that in spite of protestations of neutrality, liberalism itself rests on a conception of the good, one that communitarians regard as unacknowledged and arbitrary. James P. Sterba, in the course of examining this claim, does concede that contrary to those liberals who claim to base their views on principles neutral with respect to the good, liberalism does rest on a thin theory of the good after all. Following a suggestion made by Rawls, Sterba maintains that liberalism rejects comprehensive or robust conceptions of the good, such as those based solely on the claims of particular religions, which can be reasonably rejected by some citizens of the democratic state. Rather, he suggests liberalism rests only on a partial or thin theory of the good. Sterba argues that this partial conception can be justified by premises that neither libertarians nor communitarians can reasonably reject, and which lead to a demanding (socialist) conception of equality, rather than the more limited welfare state favored by many liberals. Readers, of course, will have to judge for themselves whether this kind of argument is successful. It may be helpful to compare Sterba's approach with Miller's attempt to retrieve elements of Marxism and with Weinstock's consideration in Part III of particularistic moral obligations that arguably may limit the global scope of Sterba's principles.

In "Liberal Theories and their Critics," William Nelson points out that there is no one canonical version of liberalism, and that liberal theorists disagree on a wide variety of questions about the formulation and justification of liberal theory. His account of different forms of liberalism distinguishes not only between Rawls's views in *A Theory of Justice* and his later shift to what he has called "political liberalism," but also between versions of liberalism often identified with some versions of neutralism and approaches, such as those of Raz and Sher, committed to a kind of moderate perfectionism which sanctions limited pursuit of some conceptions of the human good. Nelson considers whether some lines of agreement may be found among these positions, and points out some distinctions that may promote accommodation. For example, he points to the difference, suggested by some liberal theorists, between neutrality at the level of constitutional principle and neutrality in the pursuit of democratically enacted legislative policy. By making room for a wider pursuit of values at the latter level, liberalism may be able to accommodate some of the concerns of its critics, while preserving an insistence that the basic principles of society must be those citizens could not reasonably reject.

While Nelson does not directly address all of the criticisms of liberalism made in other essays in this section, readers may want to ask to what extent some of those criticisms are based on the kind of comprehensive (in the sense explained by Nelson) doctrines that many liberals deny would be freely agreed to by all reasonable citizens in the democratic state. Of course, the importance of the criterion of reasonable agreement, as well as the form it should take, are among the points that liberals themselves, as well as some of their critics, disagree upon.

Pluralism, Diversity, and Deliberation

Liberal-democratic political theorists have tended to focus upon the individual as the primary unit of moral concern. The individual is to be protected from the power of the state, or the tyranny of the majority. It is the individual who has rights, who exercises liberty, and whose preferences are expressed in the democratic process. Of course, a number of liberal-democratic theorists have been sensitive to the role of groups and associations, such as Rawls who at times speaks of the state as a social union of social unions. In fact, the primary motivation for Rawls's defense of political liberalism is his view that it can provide a mutually acceptable framework for diverse groups that disagree among themselves on fundamental issues and values.

If society consists of diverse individuals and groups with conflicting views on many fundamental issues, how are they to relate to one another within the political arena? A number of contributors to this volume (and this Part) refer, often sympathetically, to the idea of deliberation among citizens of the *polis* (or among pluralistic groups), as an alternative to abstract derivation of principles from conceptions of impartial rational choice. James S. Fishkin explores the idea of deliberative democracy in depth. Drawing on historical examples from ancient Athens and from American Constitutional development, he considers whether an emphasis on deliberation is compatible with other democratic values, such as equality and avoidance of tyranny. Is thoughtful deliberation compatible, for example, with mass participation? Fishkin concludes with some suggestions (but compare with Cudd's comments on deliberative democracy) for at least partial reconciliation of what may seem to be competing values within democracy itself.

Recently, a number of contemporary philosophers have raised questions about whether liberalism, even in forms sensitive to group concerns and to fundamental disagreement among citizens on many issues, has paid sufficient attention to the role and importance of cultural, ethnic, religious, and other forms of pluralism within the polity. In his essay, Daniel Weinstock examines these concerns. He considers whether there is a case for group rights within multicultural democratic societies, and the meaning of citizenship in such contexts. For example, does emphasis on groups and what has been called the politics of difference undermine the unity needed for liberal democratic societies to survive? Do pluralism and multiculturalism undermine the belief in a neutral conception of public reason? If not, can conceptions of actual deliberation among groups replace the liberal conception of public reason, or do conceptions of deliberative democracy themselves presuppose some kind of universal procedural norms? In considering questions such as these, Weinstock assesses modifications in liberal conceptions of citizenship and tries to articulate how citizenship might best be understood in pluralistic and multicultural democratic societies.

A. Todd Franklin continues Weinstock's examination of the implications of pluralism and diversity by assessing the significance of race for political and social theory. After considering the historical roots of liberal treatment of race, Franklin explores contemporary liberalism's treatment of it. He endorses the view of some critics of liberalism that liberal reliance on universal principles that reasonable people cannot reject in fact functions to impose the norms of dominant groups under the guise of neutrality. Moreover, he maintains that liberal theory fails to give due weight to the social reality of race as a constitutive element of individual identity. He suggests that a liberalism transformed by elements of what has been called the politics of difference, as developed by such writers as Iris Young (discussed earlier in the collection by Wellman, Held, Nelson, and Weinstock), constitutes a more acceptable response to issues of race than even the political liberalism of the Rawlsians. Liberal theorists might question, however, whether the need to find fundamental principles that reasonable citizens from different groups can all reasonably accept can be so easily avoided. Without fundamental ground rules applying to discourse among groups, more traditional liberals might retort, it is unclear how one could avoid one group's values dominating the conflicting commitments of other groups. Thus, Franklin's concern that appeal to universal and presumably impartial frameworks reinforces the power of the already dominant raises a particularly fundamental question that will continue to be debated both by political theorists and in the larger public arena as well.

In the final contribution, Christoper J. Eberle examines the implications of the idea of public reason, as defended by liberal philosophers such as Rawls, and its implications for the role of religious belief in the political realm. In particular, Eberle considers the question of whether it is appropriate for some citizens to support a law on the basis of their religious convictions, even if the law would coerce other citizens who do not share their religious beliefs. According to many liberal theorists, a citizen should appeal to public reason, and not support coercive laws solely on religious grounds. Eberle concludes that the liberal is partly right in that citizens should certainly *try* to find a non-religious rationale for their views, and they fail to respect their fellow citizens if they do not make such an attempt. However, he questions whether citizens who have conscientiously tried to find a publicly accessible non-religious justification for their views but have failed to do so, should avoid supporting laws for religious reasons alone. Hence, Eberle concludes that religiously grounded reasons do have a proper place in public debate.

The essays in this collection have provided an introduction to major debates in social and political philosophy, and also constitute as a whole an examination of many of the major principles of liberal-democratic thought. Although no collection this size can cover all major issues in social and political philosophy, the bibliographies at the end of each article suggest further readings and discussions.

Many of the essays have raised questions about various aspects of liberalism, including its emphasis on individual rights, and its understanding of such values as justice, equality, and democracy While few, if any, of the writers represented here totally reject liberal thought, many question aspects of it or suggest revisions in our understanding of its core principles or its applications to concrete issues.

In light of these conflicting views, it may prove helpful to keep two points in mind. One is the concern that if we totally reject the very ideas of rationality, such as the objective and impartial consideration of evidence, our own political critiques cannot themselves claim the rational allegiance of those who are committed to the consideration of issues objectively and impartially. This makes it all too easy to dismiss, for example, the claims of victims of injustice as themselves arguing from a biased and subjective perspective. While such a charge may sometimes be true of all of us, an all-encompassing skepticism that denies the very possibility of rational objective argument risks cutting out the very grounds on which it itself tries to stand. Current doubts about whether a universal and neutral conception of rational justification is possible in light of the various forms of pluralism in our society may avoid such a self-defeating skepticism, perhaps through a commitment to reasonable deliberation. Whether liberal arguments that our most fundamental principles, perhaps including those regulating deliberation itself, must be rationally acceptable to all are justified will remain part of the debate between liberal theorists and their critics.

The second point is that the essays in this collection are part of a continuing debate, and aim not only at clarifying the main lines of argument that have been developed that are relevant to the issues considered, but also at advancing the discussion and pointing to a resolution. Perhaps this continuing commitment to open, fair, and rational inquiry is the greatest legacy of political and social philosophy.

Part I

Core Principles and the Liberal Democratic State

Chapter 1

Political Obligation and Authority

A. John Simmons

The Basic Concepts

We know, of course, that much obedience to law and support for established governments is motivated by fear of legal sanctions, by habit, and by various non-rational attachments to community, nation, or state. We know as well, however, that both philosophers and laypersons frequently cite as reasons for obedience and allegiance the legitimate authority of their governments (and the laws they issue) or the general obligations that citizens are thought to be under to comply with and support legitimate government. It is common to suppose, in short, that (some) governments possess more than merely the power to threaten punishment and coerce compliance; they possess as well genuine authority over their subjects, a moral "right to rule" in the ways they do. Similarly, it is common to suppose that citizens in decent states have more than mere prudential reasons and nonrational motivations to obey and support their governments; there are in addition rational moral grounds for demanding from them obedience to and support for government. The philosophical problem of political obligation and authority is the problem of understanding when (if at all) and for what reasons we are morally required to be "good citizens" in these ways, and when (if at all) and for what reasons states and/or their governments possess a moral right to rule.

Political obligations, then, as these are commonly understood, are general moral requirements to obey the laws and support the political institutions of our own states or governments. The requirements are *moral* in the sense that their normative force is supposed to derive from independent moral principles, a force beyond any conventional or institutional "force" that might be thought to flow from the simple facts of institutional requirement (according to existing rules) or general social expectations for conduct. Our question is why (or whether) one ought morally to do what the rules require or what society expects. Political obligations are normally taken to be *general* requirements in the following two senses:

first, they are moral requirements to obey the law (or to support government) because it *is* valid law (or legitimate government) – or because of what its being valid law (or legitimate government) implies – and not because of any further contingent properties particular laws (or governments) might possess. (Being obligated to an authority, it is often claimed, involves a certain kind of "surrender of judgment," with the obligations displaying "content-independence"; it is the source of an authoritative command, not its independent merits, that binds those subject to the authority.) So, for instance, a moral duty to refrain from legally prohibited murders because of murder's independent moral wrongness would not constitute a political obligation (since valid law can prohibit acts which are not independently wrong), nor would a moral obligation to refrain from legally prohibited theft because of a promise made to one's mother to so refrain. Second, political obligations are general requirements in the sense that their justifications are thought to apply to all or most typical citizens of decent states. Most who have addressed the problem of political obligation would regard their accounts as unsuccessful if the obligations they identified bound only a small minority of the citizens of decent states.

There is far less agreement about how we should understand *de jure* political authority or legitimacy, but much of this disagreement is in fact due to theorists confusing questions about the nature or content of legitimate authority (on which we focus here) with far more contentious questions about the grounds or justification of authority (which we will address later). Confusion and disagreement is also generated by differences between accounts focusing on the authority or legitimacy of states (or political societies) and those focusing on the authority or legitimacy of governments (or regimes). The questions here are distinct but not independent, since governments can be illegitimate where the states they govern are not, but illegitimate states cannot have legitimate governments (except in a purely procedural, nonmoral sense of "legitimate"). While I will discuss here both governments and states, my arguments should be understood as concerning in the first instance the authority or legitimacy of states, not governments. Governments, in my view, obtain whatever authority they possess only from the authority that their states possess to empower particular governments.

The most common understanding of political authority or legitimacy sees it as a state's moral *right* to act in the ways central to the conduct of actual decent states, and particularly a right to perform the principal legislative and executive functions of such states. States with legitimate authority possess the "right to rule": the right to make law (within tolerable moral limits) for those in their jurisdictions and to coerce compliance with that law by threatening and (if necessary) applying legal sanctions. The dominant philosophical view of political authority takes the rights in which it consists to be still more extensive. Legitimate states have not only the right to command and coerce; they have the right to command and be obeyed. A legitimate state has not only a claim to discharge its legislative and executive political functions, but also a claim to obedience and support from its subjects. Understood in this way, the rights in which political authority consists are taken to be just the logical correlates of subjects' political obligations (i.e., of their general moral requirements to support and comply with valid laws and political institutions). The justifications for political authority and for political obligation are on such accounts at least in part identical.

This understanding of political authority or legitimacy has not gone unchallenged. Some philosophers argue that political authority and political obligation should not be seen as correlative (e.g., Ladenson in Raz, 1990; Sartorius and Greenawalt in Edmundson, 1999). The rights in which authority consists are said either to be only moral liberties (or privileges), which correlate with no obligations at all, or they are claim rights (i.e., rights that do correlate with others' obligations) that correlate with obligations other than political obligations. The first suggestion – that political authority rights are mere liberties – is implausible, since states which are thought to enjoy legitimate authority surely are thought to possess at least the right to exclude rival provision of legislative and executive services (by, e.g., internal vigilantes or rival states), and so to possess rights that do correlate with others' obligations to refrain from "competitive governing." But the second suggestion – that political authority consists in claim rights not correlating with political obligation – is implausible as well, for we take actual states to have claims on subjects' obedience, not merely rights to use coercion to control people (as we might think zookeepers had rights to use coercion to control the zoo's animals). The traditional claim of states is to their subjects' obedience and support (and even to their loyalty and allegiance), not merely to the means of controlling them. So any "justification of political authority" that fails to justify these further claims will fail in its conservative ambitions (see below), failing to justify the central practices of actual decent states.

I will, as a consequence, concentrate here on accounts of political obligation and authority that treat these as (at least in part) moral correlates. Actual states claiming authority or legitimacy in fact typically make three kinds of rights claims, all of which rights correlate with moral requirements, including the political obligations of their subjects. States claim rights over their subjects (i.e., over those within their claimed legal jurisdictions), rights against aliens (i.e., against those without their jurisdictions), and rights of control over a particular geographical territory. The claimed rights against aliens correlate with the obligations of aliens not to interfere with or usurp the state's right to exercise its legislative and executive functions, while the claimed rights over territory correlate with obligations on all others not to oppose or compete with the state's territorial control. Finally, the claimed rights of legitimate states over subjects correlate with (among other things) citizens' political obligations of obedience and support (including their obligations not to attempt rival provision of central state services and not to resist lawful state coercion).

The Philosophical Problem

The traditional philosophical examination of the problems of political obligation and authority has been conservative in nature. That is, the project has been to show how we can justify the intuitive conviction (of many) that decent states in fact possess legitimate political authority and that citizens of decent states in fact owe those states general obligations of support and compliance (as these notions of authority and obligation have been specified above). It may, of course, be the case that familiar states have far more limited rights than they claim and enforce. It may be that typical citizens of these states have far narrower obligations than they or their governments suppose or that full political obligations apply far less generally than is normally supposed. Or it may be, as anarchists have insisted, that all (possible or actual) states in fact lack all components of the right to rule and that all (possible or actual) citizens lack even limited political obligations. These possibilities have been defended (until very recently) by only a very few serious philosophers; but it is certainly unclear why an otherwise acceptable account of political obligation and authority should be deemed a failure simply because its conclusions fail to conform to our pretheoretical beliefs on the subject. We will, accordingly, examine attempts to provide a positive philosophical case for a conservative conclusion about political obligation and authority, but we will also leave open the possibility that a less conservative result might still be acceptable.

Because answers to questions about political obligation and authority (or legitimacy) appear to have quite immediate practical implications for our political lives, they seem to be the point at which social and political philosophy makes its most salient contact with the concerns of ordinary men and women. Political philosophy, of course, tries to answer not only questions about how we as individuals ought to act qua political persons or qua citizens of particular kinds of states, but also questions about the kinds of political societies we collectively ought to create – and so questions about social justice and the division of property, about forms of government and institutional means for resolving political differences, about the proper extent of individual liberty and the proper influence of cultural identities, etc. Few of us, however, are ever in a position (except in fortuitous concert with many others) to influence decisions about these latter concerns. We may care deeply about justice or liberty, but rarely are we able, individually or in small groups, to make much of a difference to how (or whether) our societies pursue these values. By contrast, we all face, individually and frequently, questions about whether or not to obey the law, support our government, or treat governmental dicta as authoritative: whether to exceed the speed limit or drive while intoxicated, to cheat on our taxes or use illegal recreational substances, to evade jury duty or registering for the military draft, to engage in civil disobedience or even revolutionary activity.

These are questions that are *immediately* addressed (even if not, perhaps, fully resolved) by solutions to the problems of political obligation and authority, in a way that day-to-day questions about conduct are routinely not addressed by solutions to problems about the most just institutional structure or other aspects of "ideal" political philosophy. Showing that a political structure or form of government is just or ideal often has far from immediate practical consequences, since both our individual duties to promote the good and our individual abilities to bring about such political ends are severely limited. Questions about political obligation (and about authority narrowly conceived as its correlate), however, are questions we, perhaps unwittingly, grapple with regularly. Is it really wrong to break this law, even if I can easily get away with it and even if nobody else will be obviously harmed by my disobedience? What portions of the conduct prescribed by political convention are morally compulsory, and what parts are morally optional? The answers to such questions matter to most of us, since most of us take our moral obligations at least reasonably seriously.

Brief History

Like most enduring philosophical problems, the problems of (what we today call) political obligation and political authority (or legitimacy) have gone in and out of fashion during the course of the history of philosophy. Some aspects of the problems, of course, were addressed very early in that history, as Plato's *Crito* attests, while others were touched on by a very few among the other great pre-modern philosophers (such as Aquinas). But pre-modern theorists, though keenly interested in the legitimacy of particular rulers or political institutions, tended to accept as inherently legitimate the general social and political order (which was thought to be instituted by God, nature, or inviolable tradition), and so tended not to raise questions about the legitimacy of their states. Similarly, the worries about individual liberty that prompt questions about our political obligations tended not to be central in pre-modern thought. Only with the breakdown of feudal hierarchies and traditions did concerns about the general legitimacy of the social order become prominent enough to sharply focus theoretical attention on individuals' political obligations and the authority of the state. As a result, concerns about political obligation and authority did not come to have their place near the center of political philosophy until the great early-modern political treatises and the multifarious tradition of social-contract thought that flowed from them – a tradition that includes the classic works of Hobbes, Locke, Rousseau, and Kant. In those works we find the twin challenges of obligation and authority clearly posed and energetically accepted.

To call these "twin" challenges is perhaps misleading, for most of the contract theorists treated the two problems as one problem, with authority and obligation viewed as correlates justified by the same arguments. Citizens have political obligations only if (and for the same reasons that) their political societies (or governments) have authority over or are legitimate with respect to them. The very same social contract – sometimes seen as actual, sometimes hypothetical – both authorized or rendered legitimate political society (or government), and obligated citizens to do their parts in maintaining that society.

The utilitarian and positivist critiques of social-contract theory – best known from the works of Hume, Bentham, and Mill – succeeded in driving the problems of political obligation and authority to the fringes of political philosophy. Indeed, they succeeded so completely that, with a few noteworthy exceptions (such as the work of T. H. Green [Green, 1882]), little serious attention was paid to these problems again until the mid-twentieth century. Hume, who inspired most of these critiques, famously argued (Hume, 1742) that social necessity (or utility) could by itself explain our political obligations and governments' authority, without any need to resort to the artificial (and largely fictional) device of a binding contract or general consent. Our political obligations were simply placed by Hume on the same footing as all of our other obligations. There was no longer any *special* problem of political obligation, to be addressed (as the contract theorists addressed it) *after* our more basic, nonpolitical obligations (such as the obligation to keep a promise or honor a contract) had been established. Instead, we were to treat our political obligations as we treat all of the other moral obligations we have that depend for their force on beneficial sets of social conventions. Nor was the problem of political obligation and authority an especially *hard* problem to solve, in Hume's view. For viewed as a simple question of social necessity, there appears to be an easy case to make on behalf of at least most governments' authority (hence legitimacy) and most citizens' obligatory obedience (or allegiance).

Nearly a century after Hume wrote, we can find J. S. Mill still taking the success of Hume's critique for granted. At the start of chapter 4 of *On Liberty*, for instance, Mill's casual assertions make it plain that he takes it as simply obvious both that no contract is necessary to explain (what he calls) our "social obligations" and that all those protected by society owe to it their shares of the burdens of maintaining the society. The social-contract theorist's version of the problems of political obligation and authority had largely disappeared from the philosophical landscape by the time Mill wrote. And it was not really until the 1950s that it reappeared, the problems revived (as were so many other long neglected problems in their areas) by the most influential legal and political philosophers of their generation, H. L. A. Hart and John Rawls. The American civil rights movement and the Vietnam war both provided practical contexts in which doubts about political obligation and authority were frequently raised, further stimulating the revival of interest in the theoretical problems, which has continued to this day.

Socrates and the Three Strategies

Probably most of us living in reasonably just societies believe in a general obligation to support our governments and comply with our laws, or at least would *say* that we believe in such an obligation (see Green in Edmundson [1999]). But even if most people *feel* obligated in these ways, we should not regard such feelings as justified, or as accurately tracking true obligations, unless we can support them by reference to some intelligible line of moral reasoning. After all, many people feel obligated to act in ways that we cannot comfortably say reflect their true obligations: the housewife who still feels obligated to wait hand and foot on her husband, to fashion no real life of her own; the black man who still feels obligated to defer to whites in both trivial and important matters; the brainwashed political prisoner who finally feels obligated in just the ways his tormentors have so long and so forcefully insisted.

Where relations of domination and subjection are at issue, as they certainly are in all political communities, we should be extremely wary of trying to defend judgments about moral obligation simply by appealing to the "feelings of obligation" of the subjects – feelings that may be simple elements of "false consciousness" or vague sentiments of misplaced loyalty to the only authorities one knows. Resolving the problem of political obligation must involve bypassing questionable appeals to felt obligation and looking instead straight to the recognizable moral arguments that might yield conclusions about our political obligations.

Similarly, defenses of "attitudinal" accounts of political legitimacy or authority, which are dominant in social-scientific literature (see the essays in Connolly, 1984), constitute an unpromising path to justifying judgments of legitimacy. On such accounts, legitimate authority is ascribed to states or regimes whose subjects feel toward them loyalty, allegiance, or other kinds of approval, or to states or regimes with the capacities to generate such feelings. But this kind of account implies, of course, that states can acquire or enhance their legitimate authority by misleading or by indoctrinating their subjects, or on the strength of subjects' extraordinary stupidity, immorality, or imprudence. Any plausible argument that a state (or kind of state) enjoys the rights in which legitimate authority consists will appeal not to the fact of subjects' positive attitudes (or states' capacities to produce those attitudes), but rather to more obviously morally significant features of the state's history, character, or relations with its subjects.

We can begin, then, by identifying these more plausible argumentative strategies for addressing the problems of political obligation and authority. One natural place to start is with a brief examination of Plato's dialogue the *Crito* (in Woozley, 1979), the earliest recorded treatment of these philosophical problems (now nearly 2,400 years old). For in that dialogue we can find hints of each of the three basic strategies for solving the problems of political obligation and authority that I will identify. The *Crito*, of course, is Plato's (probably nonfictional) recounting of Socrates' reasons for refusing to flee Athens after his trial and death sentence. Tried for criminal meddling, corrupting the young, and believing in false gods, Socrates refuses the offer of his friend Crito to assist him in escaping into exile; and in the process, Socrates presents a complex argument to the conclusion that justice (or right) requires him to remain and accept the unjust sentence of the Athenian court, outlined in Socrates' imagined conversation with the Laws of Athens.

How, then, does Socrates identify the ground or justification of his obligations to obey the state's commands? Three arguments, at least, seem to be clearly articulated by the Laws. The first is that the state (the Laws) is like a father and master to Socrates, having "begotten, nurtured, and educated" him. This status requires Socrates to "either persuade it or do what it commands" (50d–51e). The second is that the state, in bringing him up, has given Socrates a "share of all the fine things" that it could (51d). And the third argument is that by remaining in the state without protest, raising children in the state (and so on), even after "seeing the way in which [the Laws] decide [their] cases in court and the other ways in which [they] manage [their] city," Socrates has, "by his act of staying, agreed with [the Laws] to do what [they] demand of him" (51d–52d).

The first argument points to who Socrates *is*, to his identity, by noting a role or status he occupies. Just as a child is said to owe its parents honor and obedience, simply by virtue of the nonvoluntary role ("child" or "offspring") it occupies, so Socrates, having been "begotten" by the state, owes the state honor and obedience. Thus, Socrates' obligations to the state, on this model, are "role obligations," "obligations of status," or "associative obligations." I will hereafter refer to accounts of political obligation that explain the obligation in this way as "*associative* accounts" of political obligation.

The second argument points to what Socrates has *received*: Athens has provided him, as it provides all its citizens, with numerous significant benefits; and the recipients of important benefits owe their benefactors a fair return for them. The third argument points to what Socrates has *done*: he has freely, if only implicitly, consented or agreed to abide by the verdicts of Athens' courts (and, presumably, agreed as well to go along with the other basic ways in which the city is managed).

The second and third arguments employed by Socrates (through the Laws) appeal not to who Socrates is, or to what role he occupies, but rather to the nature of his morally significant interactions or transactions with the state. It has benefited him. He has promised or agreed to obey. While the second of these transactions (the agreement) is necessarily voluntary (if it is to be binding), and the first (the benefaction) need not be, both arguments concern what has been *done by or for* Socrates. I will call accounts of political obligation that appeal to such justifications "*transactional* accounts."

The three arguments specifically individuated by the Laws in the *Crito* all appeal to either associative or transactional obligations to the state, obligations which bind not only Socrates but (presumably) many or all of his fellow citizens as well. But Socrates (through the Laws) does also apparently advance in the dialogue other kinds of considerations that seem to bear on his obligations to the state. For instance, the very first response made by the Laws against Crito's proposal for escape is this: "Do you intend to do anything else by this exploit . . . than to destroy both ourselves the laws and the entire city – at least as far as you can?" (50a–b). If private individuals in the city disregard their courts' lawful verdicts, for instance, the city cannot long survive; and it is this destruction at which Socrates' proposed escape must be taken to aim.

There is a variety of ways in which this argument might be understood. Socrates surely does not want to argue that (aiming at) the destruction of *any* city, in any circumstances, is wrong or unjust. The destruction of (e.g.) deeply unjust cities, of cities involved in genocide, of cities with which one is (legitimately) at war, and so on, may be a good thing to try to accomplish, not a wrong. So it may be that Socrates instead intends for the Laws to argue only that it is wrong to (try to) destroy a city to which one antecedently owes indefeasible obligations of honor and obedience – such as those which Socrates owes to Athens, but which he does not owe to Sparta, and would not (perhaps) owe to an imaginary, genocidal Athens. That would make the "argument from destructiveness" a simple supplement to the three arguments we have already discussed.

But there are other possible ways of reading the "argument from destructiveness" which see it as advancing an approach to the problem which is both freestanding and quite different from the associative and transactional approaches. Two obvious possibilities are to read Socrates' argument either as a direct consequentialist argument or as a consequentialist generalization (a "What if everyone did that?") argument against disobedience. On the direct consequentialist reading, the claim would be that Socrates' escape would be wrong because it would have worse consequences than would his remaining to face his lawful punishment. The escape would contribute incrementally to a quite awful possible result (destruction of the Laws) and might well encourage others to do the same. On the consequentialist generalization reading of the argument, Socrates would be claiming that escaping would be wrong because if others, similarly situated, did the same, the consequences would be far worse than if others, similarly situated, remained to face their punishments. No appeal to the actual, expectable results of Socrates' escaping (as on the direct consequentialist line) is necessary here; the hypothetical consequences of generalized escape in similar circumstances is supposed to be sufficient by itself to establish the wrongness of escape.

Neither of these readings of the text makes the argument convincing, but both readings anticipate later (18th–20th century) attempts to defend utilitarian accounts of political obligation and authority. Direct consequentialist arguments for obedience fail in our day for the same reason they did in Socrates' day: it simply seems empirically false that Socrates' escape would either have made an interesting incremental contribution to a bad end or have encouraged enough others to disobey that Athenian law would have been weakened. More generally, while disobedience may often have worse direct consequences than obedience, there is no guarantee that this will be the case, and we are all familiar with commonplace instances in which it quite plainly is not the case. Similarly, so-called arguments from "necessity" for authority and political obligation – which maintain that authority to act is justified for those who perform "necessary" tasks, such as imposing the rule of law on a society (e.g., Anscombe in Raz, 1990) – seem utterly unable to explain why authority should extend as far as those frequent instances in which compliance with authoritative commands simply is *not* essential to the accomplishment of the state's necessary tasks.

The actual language used by the Laws, of course, looks more like an appeal to consequentialist generalization, but the argument fares no better if we read it that way. For consequentialist generalization arguments are either thoroughly implausible or simply extensionally equivalent to direct consequentialist arguments. If everyone ate lunch at noon, the consequences for society would be far worse than if people ate their lunches at different times. But from this it surely does not follow that it would be wrong for me to eat lunch at noon. If we adjust the example so that the argument yields the desired conclusion – by generalizing over more specific acts, such as eating lunch at noon when doing so would have bad direct consequences – we simply render the argument equivalent to a direct consequentialist argument.

Consequentialist (including utilitarian) theories of obligation and authority can, of course, be advanced in more sophisticated "rule-consequentialist" forms in which they are not equivalent to direct consequentialist arguments. But such approaches face the equally daunting problem of explaining why they do not count as endorsing rule-following in circumstances where it is simply irrational (from a consequentialist viewpoint) to conform one's conduct to the rule. These obstacles, along with the difficulties such theories face on the issue of particularity (see below), seem to me sufficient to render unconvincing all consequentialist (and "necessity") accounts of political obligation and authority, regardless of form.

There is, however, at least one other, *non*consequentialist reading of the "argument from destructiveness" that we might consider here. As already suggested, it seems unlikely that Socrates intends to categorically oppose the destruction of any state on any occasion. Which cities, then, is he saying that we must not (try to) destroy? Perhaps Socrates' idea is not that it is wrong for him to (try to) destroy Athens per se, or that it is wrong for citizens generally to (try to) destroy the states that have begotten and nurtured them, or the states with which they have made agreements, but instead that it is wrong for anyone to (try to) destroy any just or good state. The Laws' speech makes it clear that Socrates has no complaint with Athenian law and government. Perhaps he does not regard Athens as a model city, but he at least seems to regard it as acceptably just or good. The Laws, remember, remind Socrates that "as things stand, you will leave here, if you do, wronged not by us the laws but by men" (54c). On this reading of the argument, then, because Socrates has an obligation never to do an injustice, and because it is unjust to (attempt to) subvert a just city, Socrates has an obligation not to (try to) subvert his own just city. The justice or goodness of cities binds us to respect or support them.

The appropriate reply to such an argument will have to await our consideration of the particularity problem. Here, however, we should notice that, like the consequentialist readings of the "argument from destructiveness," the reading of it as an argument from justice takes the wrongness of Socrates' disobedience to be explained by neither transactional nor associative "facts" about Socrates and Athens. It is not who Socrates is, who the Laws are in relation to him, what

Socrates has done or what has been given to him by Athens that (on this strategy) explains his obligation not to (try to) destroy Athens. It is rather the moral quality of the state and the impartial moral values that his obedience to the state will promote – values such as social happiness or social justice. Our general duties to advance or respect such values, by (in this case) upholding the institutions that embody and promote them, is what explains the wrongness of Socrates' proposed escape, on all of the three readings of the "argument from destructiveness." I will refer to accounts of political obligation that appeal in this way to general duties to promote utility, justice, or other impartial moral values as "*natural duty accounts.*"

I want now to suggest that all of the accounts of political obligation and authority familiar to us from Western political philosophy can be classified as belonging to one of the three general types (or strategies) that we have discovered in (or read into) the argument of the *Crito*. Natural duty accounts, as we have seen, have been advanced by both the classical and contemporary utilitarians. But the "justice" variant of the natural duty approach is also much in evidence, in the work of Kant and the many contemporary Kantians (including Rawls, 1971; Waldron in Edmundson, 1999). Associative accounts of political obligation (and of correlative political authority) are familiar to us from the work of contemporary communitarians, who themselves are routinely inspired by the work of Aristotle, Burke, Hegel, or Wittgenstein. And transactional accounts of political obligation and authority are the most familiar of all, given the centrality, in writings on those topics, of the consent and contract traditions of thought. Consent theory, of course, was given its first clear formulation by Locke and is appealed to in the foundational political documents of many modern nations (including the American Declaration of Independence). But reciprocation theories – which find our obligations (and correlative authority) in our responsibilities to reciprocate for the benefits we receive from our states or governments – are equally transactional in nature; and they both capture much commonsense thinking about political obligation and authority and have been amply represented in the writings of contemporary political philosophy. The details and variants of, along with the problems faced by, the three strategies identified here will be more precisely specified below.

Particularity and Natural Duty Accounts

In order to be clearer about my proposed classification of theories of political obligation – and in order to be clearer about the kind of moral requirement we should be prepared to count as a "political obligation" – it is necessary to make some relatively elementary observations about the nature of moral requirements. Let us say first, that all moral requirements are either general or special requirements, and second, that all moral requirements are either voluntary or nonvoluntary. Moral requirements are general when they bind persons irrespective of their special roles, relationships, or performances. Thus, duties not to murder, assault, or steal count as general requirements, as do duties to promote impartial values like justice or happiness. Such duties are commonly said to be owed to humanity or to persons generally – or not owed to anyone at all. Special requirements, by contrast, arise from (or with) special relationships we have (or create) with particular others or groups; and these special requirements are owed specifically to those others or groups. So promissory or contractual obligations, obligations to cooperate within collective enterprises or groups, and obligations to friends, neighbors, or family members will all be special moral requirements. Even more familiar is the (related, but not identical) division of moral requirements into those we have because of some voluntary performance of our own – such as a promise, the free acceptance of benefits, injuring another, or freely bringing a child into the world – and those that fall on us nonvoluntarily, simply because we are persons or because we occupy some nonvoluntary role or status.

These two exhaustive dichotomies might at first appear to give us four general classes of moral requirements: general, voluntary; general, nonvoluntary; special, voluntary; and special, nonvoluntary. But the first of these suggested classes of moral requirement – the general, voluntary – seems clearly to be empty, indeed self-contradictory. Voluntary acts cannot both ground moral requirements and do so irrespective of our special relationships or performances; morally significant voluntary acts are morally significant precisely by virtue of creating or constituting such special relationships or performances. So I will say that all moral requirements belong to one of three classes: general, nonvoluntary; special, voluntary; or special, nonvoluntary.

It is important to see, I think, that the three strategies for solving the problem of political obligation – the associative, the transactional, and the natural duty – utilize in their accounts quite different kinds of moral requirements. Natural duty approaches, focusing as they do on the requirement to promote impartial values, plainly characterize our political obligations as what I have called general, nonvoluntary moral requirements. Associative approaches, with their emphasis on nonvoluntary roles, clearly identify our political obligations as special, nonvoluntary moral requirements. Finally, transactional approaches may either utilize special, nonvoluntary requirements – as when Socrates points to the debt he owes for benefits he received nonvoluntarily (that is, "nonvoluntarily" in the sense that he had no option of refusing them) – or utilize special, voluntary requirements, such as the obligation Socrates claims he owes Athens by virtue of the implicit agreement he freely made with the state.

From these simple observations about the three strategies, an important point follows. The associative and the transactional strategies have a clear advantage over the natural duty approach, by defending accounts of political obligation that seem to square better with our ordinary conception of that obligation. Both the associative and the transactional strategies involve claiming that our political obligations are *special* moral requirements. That means, as we have seen, that political obligations (on these approaches) will be based in our special transactions, relationships or roles, and will be owed to particular others or groups. The natural duty approaches, however, understand our political obligations as general requirements, which bind us irrespective of these special features of our lives and which are owed to persons generally or to nobody at all.

Now it is, as we have also seen, common to understand our political obligations as moral requirements that bind us specially to *our own* countries (communities, governments, states, constitutions) above all others, and that are based in the special relationships or dealings we have with our own countries or fellow citizens. Political obligations, we typically suppose, are owed *to* our particular states, governments, or fellow citizens. And it seems clear that the associative and transactional strategies, by appealing to special moral requirements in their accounts, can easily explain these features of ordinary thought about political obligation in a way that natural duty strategies cannot.

This is the problem of *particularity*. Political obligations, properly understood, must bind us to one particular political community or government in a way that is special; if an obligation or duty is not "particularized" in this way, it cannot be what we ordinarily think of as a political obligation. As we have seen, political obligations are associated with bonds of obedience, allegiance, loyalty, and good citizenship. But we do not normally suppose that it is possible to fully satisfy such requirements with respect to many political communities at the same time; indeed, it may be incoherent to suppose this. If political obligations are special requirements, this particularity requirement seems to be straightforwardly satisfied. Socrates was the offspring of only one political community, was given the goods of citizenship by only one community, and only promised to "persuade or obey" one state's laws. Indeed, even if some more cosmopolitan Socrates had subsequently made promises to (or received goods from) *other* states, he could acquire obligations to second (and subsequent) states only insofar as these obligations were *consistent with* his prior obligations to Athens. And we may suppose, I think, that this means that his obligations to other states, however real, would have to be in certain ways – and perhaps in many important ways – less complete than or secondary to his obligations to Athens. Thus, (our counterfactual) Socrates' true or primary obligations would still all be specially owed to one particular state, as the particularity requirement demands.

One can, of course, consistently satisfy the legal demands of more than one state at once, as holders of multiple citizenship routinely do. One can pay required taxes to more than one state, obey the laws in more than one state, even serve in the military of more than one state, and so on. What is less clear is whether one can satisfy all of the *possible* demands of obedience and support to more than one state simultaneously, or even fulfill one's basic legal duties where these are simply more restrictive than we might like them to be. We cannot consistently be obligated to "serve (in the military, on a jury) when called" in more than one state. We cannot honestly accept an obligation to defend more than one state "against all enemies, foreign or domestic." Nor can we both obey legal commands from our government to refrain from dealings with, say, Iraq, and still satisfy political obligations we might suppose we owe to Iraq. Political obligation, as this is commonly understood, requires a kind of exclusivity in many of our dealings with political communities. It is only good fortune that allows holders of dual citizenship to satisfy all of the political obligations that we normally suppose citizens lie under. But it may well be that in the final analysis, if we really believe that all citizens owe their states political obligations, we must believe as well that the position of dual (or multiple) citizenship is simply morally untenable. And that would seem to imply that transactional and associative accounts of political obligation only *can* justify or explain obligations specially owed to one particular state, above all others, as the particularity requirement demands.

Natural duty accounts of political obligation, as I've characterized them above, portray our political obligations instead as belonging to the class of general moral duties. These duties bind those who have them not because of anything those persons have done, or because of the special positions those persons occupy, but because of the moral character of the required acts. Justice must be done and promoted because of the moral value or importance of justice, period. Happiness must be promoted because happiness is good. Murder must be refrained from because of the moral significance of murder. This means that my general moral duties will hold as strongly with respect to states that are not my own and persons who are not my fellow citizens as they do with respect to those that are. Murdering Russians is as wrong as murdering Americans. The happiness of Israelis is as valuable as the happiness of my neighbors. Just Swedish political institutions merit support as much as, and for the same reason as do, just political institutions in the United States. Because all this is true, it is difficult to see how a general moral duty, of the sort employed in natural duty accounts of political obligation, could ever bind citizens specially to their own particular countries, communities, or governments. It is easy to see why Socrates should support and promote justice, by supporting just states or laws. It is much harder to see why Socrates should specially support *his own* just state or laws over all others, if it is the value or importance of *justice* that grounds his duty in the first place.

A government's or state's being *ours*, of course, usually has consequences that might well seem to tie us specially to it. But these consequences – such as the benefits we receive from it alone, or the reliance it alone places on us – all involve transactional or associative features of the citizen–state relationship, features for which a natural duty approach cannot, it seems, independently account. Now a general duty to promote justice (or happiness) could obviously give us a moral reason to support *our own* just (or happiness-producing) state, among others, if these impartial values (of justice or happiness) would be well served by doing so. But a moral reason for supporting other states as fully as we support our own could not be a political obligation. Equally obviously, such general moral duties could even, quite contingently, give us moral reasons to support *only* our own state, if only our own state were just or if only supporting our own state would best (or satisfactorily) promote happiness. But we do not normally take our political obligations to depend on such contingent factors as whether another just state has come into or gone out of existence. The point here is only to observe that the natural duty strategy for explaining our political obligations faces an immediate and considerable hurdle that the other two strategies I've identified do not. It must explain how general duties can bind us specially and non-contingently to our own particular political communities, without overtly or covertly utilizing in its explanation associative or transactional features of our relationships with those communities. Or it must explain why non-particularized moral duties should nonetheless be thought of as "political obligations" in some recognizable sense. It is not at all clear that any natural duty account of political obligation can clear this hurdle. When combined with the further difficulties for such theories noted above, natural duty accounts must be regarded as unpromising. We shall turn, then, to the prospects for the other two strategies.

Associative Accounts

Associative accounts of political obligation and authority, as we have seen, try to justify the relevant requirements and rights by appeal to basic facts about persons' identities or facts about the social and political roles they occupy. Usually such accounts form part of a broadly communitarian approach to the central issues of political philosophy, though associative accounts have also been defended by some prominent liberals (e.g., Dworkin in Raz, 1990). In some versions of this approach, the claims made are especially strong: it is alleged to be analytic or to be a conceptual truth that citizens are subject to the de jure authority of their states and owe them political obligations. But these uses of the associative strategy are either wildly implausible or simply irrelevant. Nobody believes that just anyone who occupies the legal position of "citizen" in any kind of state is morally bound to give it support and obedience. States can be monstrously unjust and oppressive (and so illegitimate), and they can name whomever they please as their "citizens." But if we modify the argument to claim that only citizens of legitimate states are subject to de jure political authority and bound accordingly, we have claimed something true (indeed, something analytic) at the cost of claiming something utterly uninteresting; for we have said nothing at all about what it is that *grounds* political obligation or authority, which is the question our argumentative strategies are supposed to address.

More convincing associative accounts have fallen into three main camps, which we can call nonvoluntarist contract theories, identity theories, and normative independence theories (Simmons, 2001). According to nonvoluntarist contract theories, citizens of decent political societies simply come to find themselves involved in networks of expectation and commitment that jointly define a kind of nonvoluntary, but nonetheless binding, contract with one another to act as good citizens of that society (by, e.g., obeying the law and accepting the authority of the state). But while such theories may seem well equipped to address the obligations that friends and neighbors might owe one another, they appear quite incapable of explaining how members of a large-scale, pluralistic political community could be taken to owe obligations to all of their fellow citizens (or to their state generally); for the interactions of typical members, hence their opportunities for commitment and for raising expectations, are routinely quite local, not national.

Identity theories (e.g., Horton, 1992) attempt to base our obligations in the practical incoherence of denying certain aspects of our identities, such as our roles as obligated members of some political community (which roles are taken by some to be central to their sense of who they are). But it is unclear why we should think such mere identification with a social role sufficient to ground genuine moral obligations. The mere fact that, for instance, one's role as citizen of the Third Reich is central to one's practical identity surely does not show that one has a moral obligation to discharge all of the duties associated with that role (such as revealing the hiding places of Jews). Only, it seems, when our social and political roles are themselves morally defensible (and non-refusable by those unwilling to occupy them) could the duties associated with them be taken to be morally binding; but that simply returns us to the independent question of the appropriate arguments to use for demonstrating the moral authority of certain kinds of political arrangements.

The last associative approaches – normative independence theories – simply affirm what the arguments above implicitly reject: namely, the normative authority of local practices. If the source of (some of our) genuine moral obligations is simply their assignment to individuals by local social and political practices, then there is every reason to suppose that widespread political obligations might be among these genuine obligations, given the widespread local social expectations of compliance with and support for the legal and political institutions of our states of residence. But to accept this style of argument is to accept that the mere social instantiation of a practice, independent of any externally justifying point or virtues, is sufficient to allow that practice's rules to define genuine moral obligations for those subject to the rules. And accepting that, I think, is to reduce the relevant idea of a moral *justification* for obligation claims to a farce; something cannot count as a justification of X if it does not claim for X some special point or advantage. If, however, associativists allow that only externally justified practices can define genuine moral obligations, then they owe us an explanation of why we should regard the practice, rather than the values that certify it, as the source of the relevant obligations. For this reason (along with those noted above), associative accounts of political obligation and authority, though enjoying the advantage of a ready explanation for the particularity of political obligations, have failed to satisfy reasonable standards for argumentative plausibility.

Transactional Accounts

Transactional accounts of political obligation and authority have typically utilized either consent theories (as in Plato's *Crito*; Locke, 1689; and Beran, 1987) or reciprocation theories (as in Klosko, 1992). According to consent theories, our political obligations (and the political authority with which these correlate) arise from those of our deliberate acts that constitute voluntary undertakings of political obligations, such as our promises or contracts to support and obey or our consent to be so bound. Reciprocation theories portray our political obligations as required reciprocation for the receipt or acceptance of benefits provided by our states, governments, or fellow citizens. Both kinds of transactional accounts have been defended in many varieties, but all varieties face by-now-familiar obstacles.

Consent theories differ principally in the kinds of consent to which they appeal in their justifications. Locke (Locke, 1689) famously appealed to the *actual* consent of persons to justify their obligations, distinguishing between actual express consent (i.e., consent explicitly given in, e.g., an overt promise, contract, or oath) and actual tacit consent (i.e., consent given inexplicitly by kinds of acts whose conventional point is not solely that of giving consent). Both kinds of consent bind us fully, Locke thought, though express consent binds more permanently. Other philosophers, however, have appealed to kinds of non-actual consent in their accounts of political obligation. Dispositional accounts hold that we are bound not only to that conduct to which we have actually consented, but also to that to which we would have freely consented had the occasion for giving consent arisen. And hypothetical consent/contract theories derive our obligations from the consent that would be given by some idealized version of ourselves, ranging from versions of ourselves that are merely purged of obvious defects to perfectly rational (and motivationally simplified) versions of ourselves (Rawls, 1971). Dispositional accounts, however, seem straightforwardly implausible; from the fact, for instance, that I would freely have agreed to purchase your property last year had I known it was available, it surely does not follow that I now have an obligation to pay for it. And hypothetical consent theories are really better understood as a kind of natural duty account than as a kind of transactional account, despite their being clothed in the language of consent. For the point of appealing to the consent of idealized persons (rather than that of actual persons) is precisely to stress that our obligations flow not from our actual transactions with our states, but rather from the virtues or qualities of those states that would elicit the consent of ideal persons (who rightly perceive and appreciate true virtue or quality, which actual persons may not do). Actual consent theories, then, seem to be the only promising form of transactional consent theory.

But actual consent theories face some clear difficulties of their own. The most obvious are difficulties in terms of realism and voluntariness. Consent theories rely on the model of the free promise for their intuitive force, for everyone seems to accept that free promises yield genuine moral obligations. But real citizens in real political communities seldom do anything that looks much like either a promise or any other kind of freely made commitment to support and comply with their laws and political institutions. The occasions for making explicit oaths of allegiance seldom arise except in situations tainted with threats of state coercion; and even free acts such as voting in democratic elections are typically performed against a conventional background assumption that such acts are *not* to be taken to be the source of our political obligations (since those obligations are taken both to precede one's acts of voting and to be in no way limited by one's declining to vote). Similarly, it is difficult to locate any kind of act performed by most citizens in decent states that could be plausibly understood as an act of tacit consent to state authority. Mere continued residence (Locke's suggestion) or non-resistance, for instance, while widely practiced, are particularly feeble candidates. For many persons there are few viable alternatives to remaining in their states, and for most, resistance to the state is impossible (while for all of us there are no real alternative options to living in *some* state that makes statelike demands on us); and these facts raise serious doubts about the voluntariness (hence, bindingness) of the alleged consensual acts (Hume, 1742).

Transactional reciprocation theories fall into two main groups: those that appeal to the requirements of fairness and those that appeal to debts of gratitude (or simple mandatory return for benefits conferred). Fairness theories maintain that persons who benefit from the good-faith sacrifices of others, made in support of a mutually beneficial cooperative scheme, have obligations to do their own fair shares within those schemes. To take benefits in a cooperative context without doing one's part would be to unfairly ride free on the sacrifices of others. Gratitude theories maintain more simply that we are obligated to make an appropriate return for services rendered by others. Since political life in decent states seems to involve both elaborate mutually beneficial schemes and the provision of important services by the state, both styles of reciprocation theory seem prima facie promising.

But gratitude theories of political obligation and authority (such as that in Plato's *Crito*) collapse under even quite charitable analyses of moral debts of gratitude. Even if it is true that we owe others a return for unsolicited benefits they provide for us, *what* we owe others cannot be characterized in any way that makes it plausible to think of political obligation as such a debt. What is owed for a benefit received is at most some kind of fitting return; and if anything on the subject is clear, it is that our benefactors are not specially entitled to themselves specify what shall constitute a fitting return for their benefaction. I may not confer benefits upon you and simply name my reward. It is, however, crucial to the ideas of political obligation and authority that our states (our "benefactors" in this case) *are* specially entitled, at least within limits, to specify the content of our obligations, by specifying what shall be valid law within the state.

Fairness theories have in the twentieth century been the more popular option for reciprocation theorists, largely due to the influence of Hart and Rawls (in, e.g.,

Rawls in Edmundson, 1999). But even Rawls eventually rejected fairness theory (in Rawls, 1971), arguing that persons in actual political societies seldom freely accept (routinely only receiving) the benefits their societies provide and so cannot reasonably be thought to be treating others unfairly if they decline to reciprocate. Those who have attempted to avoid this objection by maintaining that even benefits we have not freely accepted obligate us, provided those benefits are substantial enough (e.g., Klosko, 1992), threaten thereby to collapse the fairness theory either into a simple (inadequate) gratitude theory or into a natural duty account, focused on the independent moral importance of providing the benefits in question (rather than on genuine issues of fairness). Finally, it seems appropriate to question whether the model of the small-scale cooperative venture, on which fairness theories rely in motivating their obligation claims, can even be realistically applied to the kinds of large-scale, pluralistic, loosely associated polities within which political obligations and authority have to be demonstrated; for in small-scale ventures, much of our sense that participants are bound to do their parts derives from their shared personal interactions and subsequent reliance on one another, features missing in large-scale groups marked by social, regional, economic, or racial divisions (Simmons, 1979).

Pluralist and Anarchist Responses

All of the accounts of political obligation and authority discussed above – natural duty, associative, and transactional – can be defended in less conservative forms than is standard in political philosophy. That is, such accounts can be defended as correct accounts of the obligations and authority actually possessed by persons and their states, but with the admission that few actual persons or states satisfy the requirements of the account. Thus, actual consent might be defended as the sole ground of political obligation and authority, but with the admission that few persons in fact give binding political consent and that few states enjoy extensive authority; or associative ties could be defended as the true ground, but with the admission that few actual political societies qualify as the kind within which genuine associative political obligations could arise. In light of the difficulties facing all of the argumentative strategies discussed above, this less conservative approach to the problem appears especially attractive. Those who acknowledge these difficulties have tended to opt for one of two responses to them. Either they have retained conservative ambitions and tried to cobble together a pluralist account of political obligation and authority (e.g., Gans, 1992), or they have abandoned those ambitions and embraced anarchist conclusions. The former response acknowledges the inability of the various accounts to separately justify sufficiently general obligations and authority, but maintains that the various accounts can collectively accomplish this end. The latter response involves accepting the apparently counterintuitive result that few (if any) citizens of existing (or possible) states have political obligations and that few (if any) existing (or possible) states have de jure or legitimate political authority.

Pluralist theorists have not yet been able to show that the traditional accounts of political obligation and authority explain the obligations of enough real persons in modern political societies that they can even collectively provide a suitably general result. Instead, pluralists seem to offer not much more than lists of some-times applicable reasons for obeying the law and supporting our political institu-tions. But this falls far short of an adequate general account of political obligation, and in fact seems to yield the field to the anarchists, who deny such general obli-gations (without ever having denied the existence of sometimes applicable reasons for complying with legal requirements).

Anarchists deny general state authority and general political obligations, but they differ on both the strength and the consequences of this denial. Some anarchists have argued on *a priori* grounds that a legitimate, authoritative state is conceptually impossible (e.g., Wolff, 1970), while others have argued (only *a posteriori*) that all existing states fail to live up to standards for legitimacy (e.g., Simmons, 1979). Anarchists are also divided between those (the "political anar-chists") who take the anarchist denial of state legitimacy to imply that all states must be opposed and if possible destroyed, and those (the "philosophical anar-chists," e.g., Wolff, 1970; Simmons, 1979) who take the anarchist denial to imply only that persons must make no presumption in favor of obedience, but instead decide on a case-by-case basis what response to the state is best. While all anar-chist theories must embrace apparently counterintuitive conclusions about politi-cal obligation, *a posteriori* philosophical anarchism seems to be less counterintuitive than its rivals in the anarchist camp; for it can acknowledge both the possibility of legitimate authority and political obligation (e.g., in an ideally free and just con-tractual democracy) and the wrongness of acting in ways that undermine the useful functioning of decent states. *A posteriori* philosophical anarchism may prove to be on balance the most defensible position on the problem of political obligation and authority.

Bibliography

Beran, H. (1987). *The Consent Theory of Political Obligation*. London: Croom Helm.

Connolly, W. (ed.) (1984). *Legitimacy and the State*. New York: New York University Press.

Edmundson, W. A. (ed.) (1999). *The Duty to Obey the Law*. Lanham, MD: Rowman & Littlefield.

Gans, C. (1992). *Philosophical Anarchism and Political Disobedience*. Cambridge: Cambridge University Press.

Green, L. (1990). *The Authority of the State*. Oxford: Clarendon Press.

Green, T. H. (1882). *Lectures on the Principles of Political Obligation*. Ann Arbor: University of Michigan Press, 1967.

Horton, J. (1992). *Political Obligation*. Atlantic Highlands, NJ: Humanities Press.

Hume, D. (1742). "Of the original contract." In D. Hume, *Essays Moral, Political and Literary*. Indianapolis: Liberty Classics, 1985.

Klosko, G. (1992). *The Principle of Fairness and Political Obligation*. Lanham, MD: Rowman & Littlefield.

Locke, J. (1689). *Second Treatise of Government*. In Locke, *Two Treatises of Government*. Cambridge: Cambridge University Press, 1980.

Pateman, C. (1979). *The Problem of Political Obligation*. Berkeley, CA: University of California Press.

Rawls, J. (1971). *A Theory of Justice*. Cambridge, MA: Harvard University Press.

Raz, J. (ed.) (1990). *Authority*. New York: New York University Press.

Simmons, A. J. (1979). *Moral Principles and Political Obligations*. Princeton, NJ: Princeton University Press.

——(2001). "Associative political obligations." In A. J. Simmons, *Justification and Legitimacy: Essays on Rights and Obligations* (pp. 65–92). New York: Cambridge University Press.

Wolff, R. P. (1970). *In Defense of Anarchism*. New York: Harper & Row.

Woozley, A. D. (1979). *Law and Obedience*. London: Duckworth.

Chapter 2

Liberty, Coercion, and the Limits of the State

Alan Wertheimer

The subject of this chapter is a distinctly modern question. Classical political philosophy, as exemplified by the works of Plato and Aristotle, was primarily concerned with the nature of a good life and a good state. It simply assumed that a primary task of any state is to get its members to live moral lives. Early modern political philosophy, such as we find in the social contract tradition of Hobbes, Locke, and Rousseau, was primarily concerned with the question of political legitimacy: Why and when is anyone entitled to exercise political power over other people? Modern political philosophy shifts the focus of concern. We assume that the state is legitimate, at least if it is democratic. And the question becomes, to put it simply: What sorts of public policies should the state adopt? This chapter considers one dimension of that question.

At the most basic level, the problem is this. We believe that the individual is the primary locus of moral value and that individual freedom is of the utmost importance. At the same time, we think that the state is justified in using its coercive powers to limit individual liberty if it does so for the right reasons. Unfortunately, we disagree as to what those reasons are. In his essay *On Liberty*, the *locus classicus* on the topic, John Stuart Mill observes that "There is, in fact, no recognized principle by which the propriety or impropriety of government interference is customarily tested" (J. S. Mill, 1859, ch. I). Mill thought that he could provide that principle. In effect, our task is to determine whether Mill has done so.

Rather than launch directly into a discussion of theoretical principles, I believe it is best to begin with examples of the sorts of public policy issues at stake. The following list is quite long because the issues are diverse and complex.

Murder.   The state makes it a crime to kill another person.

Abortion.   The state makes it a crime to perform an abortion.

Seat Belts.   The state makes it illegal to ride in a car without wearing a seat belt.

Helmets.   The state makes it illegal to ride on a motorcycle without a helmet.

Prescription.   The state allows one to purchase certain drugs only with a prescription from a physician.

Converters.   The state makes it illegal to sell or use automobiles that do not have catalytic converters.

Tax Evasion.   The state makes it a crime not to pay one's taxes.

Voting.   The state requires people to vote in elections, and fines them if they do not.

Conscription.   The state requires citizens to serve in the military when needed.

Voluntary Euthanasia.   The state makes it a crime for a physician to terminate a patient's life even with the patient's consent.

Surrogacy.   The state makes it illegal for a woman to accept payment for becoming impregnated with a man's sperm on condition that she relinquish custody rights to the child after birth.

Laetrile.   Laetrile, a substance derived from apricot pits, has been touted as a cure for cancer. The Food and Drug Administration does not permit Laetrile to be sold.

Cocaine.   The state makes it a crime to sell or buy cocaine.

Blackmail.   The state makes it a crime to demand payment in return for the withholding of embarrassing information about a person.

Extortion.   The state makes it a crime to threaten to injure another person or his or her property to achieve a financial gain.

Dwarf Tossing.   The state makes it a crime to throw helmeted dwarfs at a padded wall.

Cockfights.   The state makes it a crime to enter a rooster in a contest in which two roosters try to kill each other.

Monogamy.   The state allows one to be married to only *one* member of the opposite sex.

Deduction.   The state promotes home ownership by allowing home owners to deduct interest paid on mortgages from their taxable income. Those who pay rent are not entitled to the deduction.

Noise.   The state makes it illegal to have noisy parties after 10:00 p.m. in close proximity to another dwelling.

Lewdness.   The state makes it illegal to expose one's genitals in public.

Assault.   The state makes it a crime to inflict physical injury on another person, or to threaten to do so.

Homosexual Acts. The state makes it illegal to engage in sexual relations with a person of the same sex.

Heterosexual Marriage. The state does not permit one to marry a person of the same sex.

Christian Science. The state requires all parents to get medical care for their children even if this is forbidden by their religion.

Non-discrimination. The state requires the owner of a restaurant to serve customers regardless of race.

Voyeurism. The state makes it illegal to observe another person in his or her dwelling without that person's permission.

Ticket Scalping. The state makes it illegal to sell a ticket to an entertainment event for more than $10 over its face value.

Psychotherapy. The state makes it illegal for a psychotherapist to have sexual relations with a patient.

Minimum Wage. The state makes it illegal to hire a person for less than $7.00 per hour.

Adultery. Under a state's laws, adultery is the only grounds for divorce.

Medicaid. Persons on a low income may receive free obstetrical care, but the state will not pay for abortions.

Intoxicated Consent. The state makes it a crime to have sexual relations with someone who gives consent while severely intoxicated.

DWI. The state makes it a crime to drive a car when one's blood alcohol level is over 0.08 percent.

Habitability. The state does not permit landlords to rent apartments that do not meet minimal standards of habitability.

Bad Samaritan. The state passes a law that makes it a crime not to render aid to someone in need if one can do so with minimal inconvenience.

Witness. A witness to a crime may be required to testify in court on pain of jail for contempt of court if he or she refuses.

Public Schools. The state imposes property and income tax on all citizens to pay for public schools.

Welfare. The state uses funds derived from income taxes to provide for those in need.

Organs. The state makes it illegal to buy or sell a kidney (most people have two healthy kidneys but can do well with one).

Bath Houses. The state makes it illegal to operate a "bath house" at which people engage in anonymous sexual relations.

Custody. The state passes legislation that requires that judges not award custody of a child to a parent who is homosexual.

Gun Control. The state passes legislation that prohibits the ownership of guns.

Cigarettes. The state taxes cigarettes at the rate of $3.00 per pack.

Hate. The state passes legislation that prohibits the advocation of views that express contempt for others on grounds of race, religion, ethnicity, or sexual orientation.

Blood. The state passes legislation requiring all able-bodied citizens to give at least one pint of whole blood per year.

Art. Congress allocates funds to subsidize orchestras, museums, and aspiring artists.

Barriers. The state does not require that architectural barriers to the handicapped be removed from new or renovated structures.

Liberty and Coercion

Let us ask three questions about each of these cases: (1) Does the policy constitute an interference with liberty? (2) Does the policy involve the use of state coercion? (3) Is the policy justified? This section considers the first two questions. I then go on to consider the third.

Let us say that A coerces B to do X when A proposes to make B worse off if B does not do X. Let us also agree that A limits B's freedom of action if A coerces B to do X. The paradigmatic case of state interference with individual liberty involves the use of the criminal law to forbid us from behaving in certain ways (**Murder, Abortion, Lewdness, Ticket Scalping, Organs**) or to require us to behave in certain ways (**Seat Belts, Voting, Bad Samaritan, Blood**). We may think that some of these policies are justified and others not, but they all involve interfering with people's liberty to act as they please.

Other cases are trickier. It may be argued that **Monogamy, Adultery, Heterosexual Marriage**, and **Custody** neither coerce nor limit freedom, but simply limit the terms on which the state extends the benefits of divorce, marriage, and custody. Consider **Deductions** and **Medicaid**. As a general rule, A does not interfere with B's freedom when A use *incentives* to motivate B. A coerces B when A threatens to break B's arm if B does not mow A's lawn, but A neither coerces B nor limits B's freedom if A offers B $25 to mow A's lawn. On this view, the state does not limit the liberty of people to rent or buy their homes, although it may encourage buying over renting; and the state does not limit the liberty of people to abort (assuming abortion is legal), although it may encourage poor women not to do so. Consider **Public Schools**, **Welfare**, and **Art**. These policies do not forbid, require, discourage, or even encourage people to *do* anything. The state simply taxes one's resources and uses the funds for one purpose or another.

Do the above-mentioned policies involve interference with liberty? I believe it is a mistake to put too much weight on the distinction between coercive and non-coercive policies and between those that directly limit our liberty and those that do not. If the state does not permit one to enter into agreements (**Minimum Wage**, **Habitability**) or dissolve marriages (**Adultery**), or buy products (**Laetrile**), or limits the terms on which one can buy them (**Prescription**), the state is limiting one's freedom of action. Those limitations may be justifiable, but we should not deny that they are limitations. I do not deny that there is a difference between prohibiting one from engaging in same-sex sexual relationships (**Homosexual Acts**) and not allowing same-sex marriage (**Heterosexual Marriage**), or that there is a difference between prohibiting abortion (**Abortion**) and not subsidizing it (**Medicaid**), or that there is a difference between not allowing one to buy a product (**Laetrile**, **Cocaine**) and a policy that makes it more expensive (**Cigarettes**) or requires someone else's permission (**Prescription**). At the same time, that distinction goes only so far. After all, people want to be able to attain certain benefits, such as to have their relationship officially acknowledged by society or to have custody of children, or to get abortions, or to consume products. And a state that makes it impossible or more costly for people to gain these benefits makes it more difficult for people to live their lives as they choose. So whether or not a policy involves the use of direct coercion or an interference with liberty, we can always ask whether the state should *favor* some actions over others. For the reasons that might tell against interfering with liberty may also tell against a "favoring" policy. If **Homosexual Acts** is unjustified, in part, because the state has no business preferring heterosexual relations to homosexual relations, then **Heterosexual Marriage** may be unjustified for the same reasons. If **Laetrile** is unjustified because the state has no business telling people what they can put in their bodies, then it is arguable that the state has no business making it more costly for me to smoke than to drink soda (**Cigarettes**). Some political philosophers have argued that the state should remain neutral between views of the good life. If they are right, then a large range of public policies may be unjustifiable.

What about **Public Schools**, **Welfare**, and **Art**? It may be argued that these represent expenditure policies, but do not involve interference with freedom. After all, they do not require us to do anything. But that claim can be denied. We are inclined to think that **Blood** constitutes a deprivation of our freedom because it requires us to give a (renewable) bodily resource to the state on pain of punishment. Similarly, it can be argued that to require us to give up our (nonrenewable) money on pain of punishment is to interfere with our liberty to use our financial resources as we wish. It may turn out that **Public Schools** and **Welfare** are justified whereas **Blood** and **Art** are not, but not on the grounds that **Blood** and **Art** constitute an interference with liberty whereas **Public Schools** and **Welfare** do not. Rather, it will be because there are reasons that justify a policy of taking others' resources in some cases but not in others. So libertarians may be right to regard taxation as a limitation of liberty, although they may be wrong about the reasons that justify such limitations.

Liberty-Limiting Principles

Let us now consider the central question of this essay: For what reasons is the state justified in limiting individual liberty? In his magisterial four-volume treatise on the moral limits of the criminal law, Joel Feinberg suggests that we should start from the presumption that individuals should be free to do what they wish unless we can justify a limitation of their liberty (J. Feinberg, 1984, 1985, 1986, 1988) Given that presumption, Feinberg discusses four principles that might be thought to justify state policies that limit individual liberty: *The Harm Principle*, *The Offense Principle*, *Legal Paternalism*, and *Legal Moralism*. He proposes that we ask if such principles justify limitations of liberty. Although I come to somewhat different conclusions, I cannot think of a better way to proceed, so we shall consider these principles along with three principles that Feinberg does not discuss: *The Collective Benefits Principle*, *The Justice Principle*, and *The Need Principle*. To provide a road map, let us summarize these principles. The Harm Principle says that the state is justified in limiting A's liberty, to prevent A from harming others. The Offense Principle says that the state is justified in limiting A's liberty, to prevent A from *offending* others, even if A isn't harming them. Legal Paternalism states that the state is justified in limiting A's liberty, to prevent A from harming himself. Legal Moralism says that the state is justified in limiting A's liberty, to prevent A from engaging in behavior that is or is regarded as immoral, even if A isn't harming others without their consent. The Collective Benefits Principle states that the state is justified in limiting liberty in order to provide public benefits that cannot be provided without such limitations. The Justice Principle states that we are justified in limiting liberty on grounds of justice. The Need Principle states that we are justified in limiting A's liberty to provide for other people's needs.

Before considering the various principles, we need to make four general points about them. First, to give a list of liberty-limiting principles is not to defend them. Although Feinberg discusses four major principles, he does not claim that they actually *do* justify limitations of liberty. To the contrary. He argues that the Harm Principle and the Offense Principle are the only reasons that survive theoretical scrutiny and that justify the limitation of individual liberty. I am less sure.

Second, a valid liberty principle provides *a* justification for a liberty-limiting policy. It does not provide positive reasons for a policy because there may be moral or practical reasons that "outweigh" the reasons for such a policy. For example, if we accept Legal Paternalism, and if we believe that the consumption of cocaine is bad for people, then there is a reason in favor of **Cocaine**. At the same time, the social and economic costs of enforcing **Cocaine** may be so great that we should reject the policy, all things considered.

Third, a liberty-limiting policy may be supported by more than one liberty-limiting principle. For example, we may think that **Surrogacy** is supported by the Harm Principle, on the grounds that it is harmful to the children, and by Legal Paternalism, because it prevents women from making contracts they are likely to regret, and by Legal Moralism, on the grounds that it is wrong to commodify procreational labor. We may think that **Cocaine** is supported by both the Harm Principle, on the grounds that the drug makes people more violent, and by Legal Paternalism, on the grounds that it is bad for those who use it. We must examine whether each principle provides a good reason for a policy, but we should not think that a policy is necessarily justified by only one reason.

Fourth, and as Feinberg notes, we must distinguish the question of *constitutionality* from the question of moral justifiability. **Laetrile** may be quite constitutional, and yet it might be an unjustifiable limitation of individual liberty. **Gun Control** may be a justifiable policy and yet unconstitutional (although that is quite debatable). After all, if the Second Amendment were to be repealed, thus removing any question about its constitutionality, we would still have to resolve whether **Gun Control** is a justifiable limitation of individual liberty. For our purposes, then, we shall set constitutionality aside.

The Harm Principle

In *On Liberty*, Mill boldly argues that we

> can use one and only one "very simple principle" to determine when it is legitimate for the state to limit individual liberty. That principle is that . . . the *only* purpose for which power can be rightfully exercised over any member of a civilized community, against his will, is to prevent *harm to others*. His own good, either physical or moral, is not a sufficient warrant. . . . Over himself, over his own body and mind, the individual is sovereign. (J. S. Mill, 1859, ch. I, emphasis added)

As numerous commentators have noted, Mill's own analysis reveals that the Harm Principle is hardly simple. Moreover, it may not be the *only* defensible reason to limit the individual's liberty. After all, on some (strict) readings of that principle, we must conclude that all but a few of my examples are illegitimate, a conclusion that many (including Mill) would find implausible. Nonetheless, even if we do not accept Mill's claim that harm to others is the only good reason to limit liberty, we have to see what the Harm Principle does and does not entail.

What is harm to *others*? Precisely what sorts of beings is one not permitted to harm? If "others" refers to *persons* and if the fetus is a person, then the Harm Principle supports **Abortion**. If the fetus is not a person, then it does not. There might, of course, be a reason to allow people to harm other persons, as in self-defense. But if the fetus is a person, there is a prima facie case for thinking that **Abortion** is a justifiable limitation of liberty. By contrast, if "others" refers only to *homo sapiens*, then we cannot limit behavior on the grounds that it is harmful to animals (**Cockfights**). **Surrogacy** raises a different and difficult question about existence. Suppose that the children of commercial surrogates tend to have more psychological problems than other children (this may be untrue). Is the practice of commercial surrogacy harmful to those children? Arguably not. After all, these particular children would not exist if they had not been conceived via commercial surrogacy. If they are not worse off than they would otherwise be (that is, non-existent), it is arguable that they have not been harmed.

What is *harm* to others? Here there are several issues. First, if we set aside the paradigmatic cases of death, physical injury, and theft of or damage to another's property, what should we say about the infliction of mental distress? On one hand, we do not want to say that all aversive or unpleasant experiences constitute harms. A may offend B if he uses his cell phone during a movie, but A does not harm B. On the other hand, it would be odd to say that A does not harm B if A puts B in fear by threatening physical injury (**Assault**). If mental distress can constitute harm, as **Assault** suggests, do **Lewdness**, **Noise**, and **Hate** also involve harm? If they do not, then these policies cannot be justified under the Harm Principle and we must conclude that they are unjustified or that harm to others is not the only legitimate reason for limiting liberty. In any case, if some but not all mental distress counts as harmful, we need a theory as to what mental distress counts as harm.

If unpleasant experiences are not necessarily harmful, does harm always involve an unpleasant experience? Can one be harmed by what one doesn't know or feel? Although it may seem natural to think that one can't be harmed by what one doesn't experience, if we accept this view, then **Voyeurism** cannot be justified under the Harm Principle. After all, a peeping Tom's target may be entirely unaware of his activities. On the other hand, if we say that voyeurism is harmful because A harms B when A violates B's *rights* even if B does not experience the violation, then we cannot resolve what constitutes a harm without first determining what rights people have.

A third issue concerns the distinction between harming and not benefiting. Does the Harm Principle support **Bad Samaritan**, **Witness**, and **Barrier**? Is A harming B if A fails to throw a life ring to a drowning B, or refuses to appear as a witness or refuses to remove architectural barriers to the handicapped in his building? According to Mill:

> There are . . . many positive acts for the benefit of others which he may rightfully be compelled to perform, such as to give evidence in a court of justice . . . and to perform certain acts of individual beneficence . . . things which whenever it is obviously a man's duty to do he may rightfully be made responsible to society for not doing. (J. S. Mill, 1859, ch. I)

The problem is this. If we say that inactions never constitute harm, then we cannot say that the parent harms the child if she refuses to get medical care (**Christian Science**). If, following Mill, we say that "a person may cause evil to others not only by his actions but by his inaction," how do we determine when inaction causes harm and when it does not? Does A harm a panhandler if he refuses to give him anything? Mill says that an inaction constitutes a harm only when it is "obviously a man's duty" to act. If so, then the decision as to what counts as a harm is based on a prior view as to what duties we have. Once again, when we move beyond paradigmatic cases, it becomes clear that what constitutes harm is not self-explanatory.

Let us assume that A's action constitutes a harm to B. It does not follow that the state is justified in limiting one's liberty to harm. As Mill notes, the Harm Principle applies only to the infliction of "loss or damage not justified by [one's] own rights" (J. S. Mill, 1859, ch. IV). Consider business competition. If Borders opens a bookstore in my town (it did) and this drives a local merchant out of business (it did), its actions were harmful to the local merchant. But they have a right to open their bookstore. Similarly, A may harm B if A publishes truthful information that is damaging to B's reputation, but we think that the state should not limit A's liberty to do so. Other cases are more difficult. Consider **Blackmail**. Suppose that A has taken a picture of B with his mistress at a restaurant. A tells B that he will give this picture to B's wife unless B pays A $1,000. If A has a right to give the picture to B's wife (it's hard to see why he doesn't), and if A has the right to sell the picture to B (it's hard to see why he doesn't), then A is not proposing to do anything that he doesn't have a right to do. So unlike **Extortion**, where A threatens to do something he has no right to do, it is not clear whether the Harm Principle allows the state to prohibit blackmail.

Fourth, the Harm Principle does not justify limiting A's liberty to harm B if B consents – *volenti non fit injuria* (to one who consents, no [legally recognizable] injury is done). As Mill puts it, society has no business interfering with conduct that affects others "with their free, voluntary, and undeceived consent and participation." On this principle, it is arguable that the state exceeds its authority in **Voluntary Euthanasia**, **Surrogacy**, **Laetrile**, **Cocaine**, **Dwarf Tossing**, **Ticket Scalping**, **Psychotherapy**, **Intoxicated Consent**, **Minimum Wage**, **Habitability**, and **Organ Sales**. If B wants her physician to terminate her life, so be it. If A wants to purchase use of B's womb, or sell an ineffective drug, or sell cocaine, or toss dwarfs against a padded wall, or sell tickets for an exorbitant price, or engage in sexual relations with his patient, or hire someone for $3.00 per hour, or have sexual relations with a woman who is severely intoxicated, or rent a rat-infested unheated apartment, or buy another's kidney, the Harm Principle does not justify interference by the state so long as B consents, as well she might for one reason or another.

Of course, the consent must be "free, voluntary, and undeceived," and questions arise as to when that is so. The victim of extortion may "consent" to pay the extortioner, but he does so under duress. Other cases are more controversial.

A dying patient may not want to exhaust her family's resources (**Voluntary Euthanasia**), a patient may have become infatuated with her psychotherapist (**Psychotherapy**), a woman may not anticipate what it will be like to give up her child (**Surrogacy**), a poor person may feel she has no choice but to rent an uninhabitable apartment (**Habitability**), and so forth. Is consent voluntary in none, some, or all of these cases? We cannot say whether the Harm Principle justifies these policies without a theory as to when consent is (sufficiently) voluntary.

A fifth issue about harm is raised by **Gun Control**, **Bath House**, and **DWI**. It might be argued that the Harm Principle only justifies prohibiting behavior that actually causes harm as contrasted with behavior that (merely?) increases the risk of harm, and so it cannot justify any of these policies. On the other hand, Mill himself suggests that whenever "there is a definite damage, or *a definite risk of damage* . . . the case is taken out of the province of liberty" (J. S. Mill, 1859, ch. IV). This is a sensible approach, but it opens up a range of behaviors to the province of social control.

A sixth issue concerns the distinction between direct harm and collective or public harm. In the standard cases of harm, one individual imposes direct palpable harm (or risk of harm) on another. But **Tax Evasion** exemplifies a wide range of cases in which A's act is not (very) harmful to any other individual, but would be harmful if performed by a large number of persons. In his famous essay "The Enforcement of Morals," Lord Patrick Devlin makes the following observation:

> You may argue that if a man's sins affect only himself it cannot be the concern of society. If he chooses to get drunk every night in the privacy of his own home, is any one except himself the worse for it? But suppose a quarter or a half of the population got drunk every night, what sort of society would it be? (P. Devlin, 1968, p. 14)

Devlin is probably right about drunkenness. Widespread and continual drunkenness would have serious social and economic effects. But setting aside the particular content of Devlin's claim, the *structure* of Devlin's point is absolutely correct. If one individual does not pay his taxes, it causes little harm to anyone; if large numbers of persons do not pay their taxes, we have a serious social problem. If one person removes his catalytic converter, it does no harm; if large numbers of persons do so, it may seriously pollute the air. If we think that environmental policies such as **Converter** are justified, we must extend the Harm Principle so as to cover collective harm or supplement the Harm Principle with an additional principle. The question then arises as to whether the Collective Harm Principle might justify too much.

Consider **Homosexual Acts** and **Compulsory Voting**. If few people engage in exclusive homosexual behavior or do not vote, there may be little harm to society. But if most people eschewed heterosexual relations or did not vote, then there would be a genuine public harm. Society could not reproduce itself, and democracy would wither. Does it follow that **Homosexual Acts** and **Compulsory**

Voting are justified in order to prevent a collective harm? It does not. Unlike **Tax Evasion**, where we might have reason to think that many people will evade their taxes unless they are prohibited from doing so, we have *no* reason to think that many people will choose exclusive homosexuality or refuse to vote unless they are prohibited from doing so. So while Devlin is right to think that the phenomenon of collective harm shows that some private behavior should be amenable to social control, it is another question altogether as to when the principle actually justifies limiting liberty.

The problem of collective harm is structurally identical to what I call the Collective Benefit Principle. There are some benefits that society can provide for its members if but only if all are required to behave in some way. To exemplify, consider the use of anabolic steroids by professional football players. Assume that using steroids enhances one's strength but is harmful to one's health. If players are allowed to do as they please, each player may feel compelled to use steroids in order that other players will not gain a competitive advantage. Although each player would prefer that all players not use steroids than that all use steroids, they cannot attain this result by themselves. They need an enforceable rule that prohibits them from doing so. We can understand **Conscription** and **Minimum Wage** in these terms. All members of a society may benefit from its military capacity, but few may volunteer to serve, and so it may be necessary to require (enough) people to serve. If we allow people to work for a pittance, then (in an era of significant unemployment) many individual workers may be willing to do so and will drive the wages down. It is possible that most workers will benefit if no one is permitted to work at a sub-minimum wage.

One point should now be clear. Despite Mill's aspiration to provide a "very simple principle" by which to determine when the state can legitimately interfere with individual liberty, the Harm Principle is hardly simple. Considerable theoretical work is required just to say whether an act is harmful to others in the relevant way. The question remains as to whether the state can justifiably limit individual liberty when behavior is clearly not harmful to others. It is to that question that we now turn.

The Offense Principle

The Offense Principle claims that the state can legitimately limit A's liberty in order to prevent A from *offending* others, even if A's action does not harm others. Now even granting that some mental distress counts as a harm (**Assault**), there is an intuitive distinction between behaviors that are offensive and those that are harmful. B may be offended by A's obscene bumper sticker or body odor, but B is not harmed in these cases. I believe that normal adults are also not *harmed* by those who expose their genitals in public (**Lewdness**). Other cases are less clear. It is arguable that one is harmed and not merely bothered by one's neighbor's loud party when one is trying to go to sleep. But this depends upon our view of harm.

The interesting question is not whether there is a distinction between harm and offense, but whether the state is justified in interfering with offensive but admittedly harmless behavior. To say, "But X isn't harmful" is not an answer to that question. One can't simply assert, "I have a right to engage in offensive behavior so long as I'm not harming you," because the question at issue is precisely whether one has such a right. Somewhat surprisingly, Mill himself is sympathetic to the Offense Principle: "there are many acts which . . . if done publicly, are a violation of good manners and, coming thus within the category of offenses against others, may rightly be prohibited" (J. S. Mill, 1859, ch. V).

And why not? If offensive behavior produces unpleasant experiences, there is at least some positive value in preventing such behaviors. In addition, there is value to the community in preserving a sense of civility, a sense that public space is welcoming, a feeling that one's sensibilities are not jarred when one ventures out into the world. On the other hand, and as Mill so eloquently argued, there is also value to allowing individuals to act according to their own lights, to encouraging spontaneity and diversity, even when such behavior is offensive. If there is no absolute right to engage in offensive public behavior, how can we decide when it is legitimate for society to intervene? There is no simple formula to be had, but we can identify several criteria that society might use.

1   Avoidability.   The easier it is for people to avoid being offended, the more difficult it is to justify prohibiting offensive behavior. If one doesn't want to see nudity, then don't go to the nude beach.
2   Pervasiveness.   The more widespread the tendency to be offended, the easier it is to justify interference. We should not restrict behavior that a minority or even a bare majority find offensive.
3   Magnitude.   The more intense and durable the offense, the easier it is to justify intervention. We should not restrict behavior that gives rise to only mild or short-lived distress.
4   Legitimacy.   The more legitimate the state of being offended, the easier it is to justify intervention. Although this criterion presents its own theoretical difficulties, it seems more legitimate to be offended by the flasher than, say, by the sight of a homosexual couple embracing.
5   Social Value.   Some offensive behaviors are of a type that have greater social value than others. Mill argued that the expression of false and offensive ideas has value: "the clearer perception and livelier impression of truth produced by its collision with error." By contrast, there is little value to indecent exposure.
6   Individual Integrity.   Does prohibiting offensive behavior represent a threat to an individual's integrity? To ask someone not to expose himself or make noise does not (I think) ask A to stop being who he is. To ask someone not to express his ideas or to wear different clothing represents a greater threat to individual integrity.

Needless to say, the interpretation and application of these sorts of criteria are a difficult matter. Nonetheless, it is at least plausible to suppose that the state is sometimes justified in seeking to prevent offensive behavior. The difficult question is to determine when it is reasonable for the state to do so.

Legal Paternalism

People do many stupid things, although we may disagree as to what they are. People drink too much, ride motorcycles without helmets, ride in cars without seat belts, take useless medicines, use mind-altering drugs, have unprotected sex while drunk, sign contracts they later regret, smoke cigarettes, and climb Mount Everest. Is the state justified in protecting people from their own follies?

As we have seen, it appears that Mill rejects Legal Paternalism in the strongest possible terms: "Over himself, over his own body and mind, the individual is sovereign" (J. S. Mill, 1859, ch. I). Such seemingly absolute statements to the contrary notwithstanding, Mill's views on paternalism are actually much more subtle. No sooner does Mill make the previous statement than he says that the Harm Principle "is meant to apply only to human beings in the maturity of their faculties" (J. S. Mill, 1859, ch. I). It is one thing for a Christian Science adult to refuse medical treatment for himself, but children are another matter. Similarly, Mill might defend the New Hampshire (the "Live Free or Die" state) law that requires that children wear seat belts, but does not require this of adults.

Such exceptions aside, is the state ever justified in limiting the liberty of competent adults for their own good? If we adopt a utilitarian or consequentialist point of view, there is no serious problem in the way of justifying Legal Paternalism. Mill seemed to believe that paternalistic policies always promote less utility in the (very) long run, but, as an empirical proposition, it is hard to believe this is so. If the question is solely whether policies such as **Seat Belts** or **Helmets** promote more utility, it seems likely that they do. It is more difficult to justify Legal Paternalism if we regard individual autonomy as an independent value. Even if it would be better for people if they were required to wear seat belts or helmets, we may think that there are weighty moral reasons to respect an individual's decisions about her own life.

Suppose we take the latter perspective. Does it follow that Legal Paternalism is always unjustified? It seems not. First, we should distinguish between what is often called *hard paternalism* and *soft paternalism*. Hard paternalism involves restricting the liberty of adults when we have no reason to question their competence, freedom, information, or rationality. Soft paternalism involves restricting the liberty of adults when their decision-making capacity is compromised by cognitive or emotional deficiencies. To prohibit people from climbing Mount Everest would be a case of hard paternalism (unless we believe that one would have to be irrational to attempt the climb). Mill presents a case of soft paternalism.

> If [one] saw a person attempting to cross a bridge which had been ascertained to be unsafe, and there were no time to warn him of his danger, they might seize him . . . without any real infringement of his liberty; for liberty consists in doing what one desires, and he does not desire to fall into the river. (J. S. Mill, 1859, ch. V)

Mill's thought is that we do not really compromise a person's autonomy if we limit her liberty only when she lacks the capacity for autonomous action, as is probably true in the bridge case. The problem is to determine when this is so.

To see the problem more clearly, consider two additional versions of Mill's bridge story:

1   The person knows that the bridge is unsafe and is attempting to commit suicide because he is severely depressed.
2   The person knows that the bridge is unsafe, but has a hobby of crossing rickety bridges.

Would we be justified in interfering in either of these cases? If we believe that severe depression compromises one's rational capacities, then version 1 would represent a case of soft paternalism. Such a person is not, as Mill put it, in the "maturity of their faculties." This does not mean that it is always irrational to want to end one's life, as in some cases of voluntary euthanasia. But an attempted suicide by, say, an otherwise healthy twenty-four-year-old woman is, I believe, a very different matter, and we may be justified in preventing such actions. By contrast, version 2 seems to be a case of hard paternalism. I might think that this hobby is crazy, but unless we want to regard all dangerous activities (mountain climbing, hang gliding) as irrational, we must probably bite the bullet and respect this choice. To put the previous point slightly differently, it is easier to justify policies on paternalistic grounds when we have reason to question the actor's understanding of the *facts* than when we question her *values*. It is one thing to prevent a person from crossing the bridge because she is unaware that the bridge is unsafe, but quite another because we do not think that crossing rickety bridges is a worthwhile endeavor.

Weakness of will presents a particularly difficult problem for the soft paternalist strategy. Put roughly, let us say that A experiences weakness of will when he makes a choice that runs counter to his settled long-term or higher-order preferences. I experience weakness of will when I eat fattening foods, fail to exercise enough, or do not wear my seat belt. I do not suffer from any cognitive defect about the relationship between my behavior and my health or safety, and I do not want to die. I just find it hard to motivate myself to do what I know I should do and want to do. If we include weakness of will among the conditions that compromise the voluntariness of our choices, then we can offer a soft paternalistic justification for some liberty-limiting policies along these lines.

Given the previous discussion, what should we say about **Seat Belts, Helmets, Voluntary Euthanasia, Prescription, Laetrile, Cocaine, Surrogacy, Dwarf**

Tossing, **Psychotherapy**, **Minimum Wage**, **Intoxicated Consent**, and **Organs**? I do not think we can say anything with any assurance, in part because we need more empirical data about the effects of these decisions on the decision-makers. That said, I think that **Seat Belts** is a good case for justifiable soft paternalism, particularly if most people fail to buckle up because of weakness of will (laziness) rather than because they genuinely prefer to incur a greater risk of death or injury in exchange for feeling unencumbered. In my view, **Helmets** is a case of hard paternalism because some cyclists knowingly and intentionally prefer to incur a greater risk of injury as the price for what they take to be a more enjoyable experience.

Voluntary Euthanasia is a difficult case, in part because we can never know whether people regret their decisions. Surely many patients who choose voluntary euthanasia do suffer from cognitive and emotional impairments produced by age, disease, medication, and stress. At the same time, such decisions are not obviously irrational, and not to allow patients to make such decisions is to require them to go on living. So, given the alternatives, we may think that, on balance, we do not have sufficient paternalistic reason to interfere (although there may be other reasons to do so).

If prescriptions were not required for many drugs, it is possible that many people would use drugs in a harmful way because they were insufficiently informed or not able to understand the information. Given that **Prescription** represents a minimal (but not trivial) limitation of individual liberty, it may not be difficult to justify.

If cancer patients ask for Laetrile because their decision-making capacities are impaired, and if it deters them from choosing superior treatments, then **Laetrile** may be justifiable. If most people choose Laetrile only as a last resort, there is much less reason to intervene.

I do not think that most users of cocaine suffer from a cognitive or emotional impairment or, for that matter, that they regret their decisions, or even that using the drug does not enhance their utility. Some, certainly yes. Most? That is questionable. There may be other reasons to support **Cocaine** but it is not clear that we can do so on soft paternalistic grounds.

Many people have defended **Surrogacy** on soft paternalistic grounds. They argue that women must choose in the face of an intrinsic cognitive defect, because they are unable to anticipate the trauma of relinquishing custody of the child (A. Wertheimer, 1996, ch. 4). There is something to this claim, but we should not exaggerate the importance of exceptional cases. If most surrogate mothers do not regret their decisions, then we have little cause for interfering on paternalistic grounds. We could say similar things about **Dwarf Tossing**, **Minimum Wage**, and **Organs**. It is by no means clear that these choices are bad for the people who make them or that those who make such choices suffer from any cognitive or emotional impairment, or that they regret their decisions.

By contrast, I think **Psychotherapy** is different. There is considerable evidence that patients who consent to sexual relations with their therapists typically suffer from cognitive and emotional impairments and that such choices typically do not work out well for them, and so it seems eminently justifiable to prohibit all such relations (A. Wertheimer, 1996, ch. 6).

Few states have enacted anything like **Intoxicated Consent**, but many universities have done so. One can offer a soft paternalist argument that one who is severely intoxicated cannot give competent consent, and thus we have no difficulty supporting such a policy if B's intoxication is itself involuntary (as when A spikes B's drink). It presents a more difficult problem if B is voluntarily intoxicated, for we might think that the voluntariness of her intoxication flows through to the voluntariness of her consent.

In addition to soft paternalistic arguments, there is another way to think about the justification of Legal Paternalism. Thomas Schelling has observed that we often act as if we have "two selves." In what we might regard as *self-imposed* paternalism, our "rational" self will sometimes interfere with the liberty of our "irrational" self (T. Schelling, 1984, ch. 4). One's rational self may place the alarm clock on the other side of the room to force one's irrational self to get up in the morning, or, as in the most famous such case, Odysseus told his crew to tie him to the mast so he could hear the siren's call without endangering the ship (J. Elster, 1979). I assume that there is nothing morally problematic about self-imposed paternalism. If I want to limit my own liberty for my own good, then I should ordinarily be able to do so. Less obviously, I believe that we can understand some cases of Legal Paternalism in just this way. To the extent that we regard a democratic legislature as representing the wishes of the citizenry, then we can understand policies such as **Seat Belts** and **Prescription** as genuine cases of self-imposed paternalism. It is not that some people are limiting the liberty of others for their own good. Rather, citizens are (through their representatives) limiting their own liberty for their own good. **Helmets** is different. In **Seat Belts** and **Prescription**, a majority is coercing itself for its own good, because most people ride in cars and use prescription drugs. By contrast, in **Helmets**, a majority is coercing a minority for its good, and that is more difficult to justify. In any case, to the extent that we can legitimately understand a policy as a case of soft paternalism or self-imposed paternalism, such policies are compatible with a commitment to taking autonomy seriously.

Legal Moralism

This principle holds that the state is justified in limiting one's liberty to prevent one from engaging in immoral behavior, even if it could not justifiably limit one's behavior under the Harm Principle or the Offense Principle. The "even if" clause is crucial. Murder is immoral and harmful, and immoral because harmful. Lewd behavior may be immoral and offensive, and immoral because offensive. But we can justify **Murder** and **Lewdness** under the Harm Principle or the Offense Principle. We do not need Legal Moralism. By contrast, someone might defend

Monogamy and **Homosexual Acts** on the grounds that polygamy and homosexuality are wrong even if consensual. Someone might defend **Dwarf Tossing** and **Cockfights** on the grounds that it is wrong or degrading for people to entertain themselves in this way. Someone might defend **Surrogacy** and **Organs** on the grounds that these practices wrongfully treat a person's body as a commodity. And someone might defend **Cocaine** and **Art** on the grounds that substance-induced pleasure is not a worthy experience but that artistic experience is good for the soul.

Do such arguments work? We must first note that Legal Moralism comes in several different varieties. The classical version maintains that the state can justifiably prohibit those behaviors that are "objectively" immoral. People may disagree, of course, as to what behaviors are immoral. One person may claim that consensual homosexual relationships are immoral, whereas there is nothing wrong with selling one's kidneys, while another might claim just the opposite. But both might agree that it is legitimate for the state to prohibit an activity *if* it is immoral.

A second version of Legal Moralism appeals to a form of moral paternalism. This view consists of two claims. First, it maintains that it is bad for people to perform immoral acts. This is not a tautology, and it may well be false. One might think that it is bad to steal without believing that stealing is bad for the thief, if he does not get caught. But the version of Legal Moralism I am now considering accepts Robert George's claim that "Every immoral choice . . . [damages] that aspect of the chooser's own well-being which consists in establishing and maintaining an upright moral character" (R. George, 1993, p. 168). Second, the argument maintains that the state has a responsibility to protect the actor from corrupting himself just as it may have a responsibility to protect citizens from injuring themselves. I believe that Governor Mario Cuomo invoked a form of moral paternalism when he justified his decision to sign legislation that banned dwarf tossing in New York bars by saying that "Any activity which dehumanizes and humiliates these people is degrading to us all." Cuomo does not claim that the legislation is designed to help the dwarfs, who may be well compensated for being tossed. Rather, it is designed to save New Yorkers from degrading themselves by tossing the (consenting) dwarfs.

A third – social cohesion – version of Legal Moralism makes an empirical claim that a common morality is an important basis of social cohesion, and then a moral claim, that it is legitimate for a society to preserve itself by prohibiting those behaviors that it regards as immoral – whether or not those acts are "objectively" immoral. As Lord Patrick Devlin puts it, "What makes a society of any sort is community of ideas . . . society is not something that is kept together physically; it is held by the invisible bonds of common thought (P. Devlin, 1968, p. 9). Devlin recognizes that a society's common morality may require people not to do things that they themselves do not regard as immoral and which, for all that, may not even be immoral. But, he argues, the bondage of a common morality "is part of the price of society; and mankind, which needs society, must pay its price" (P. Devlin, 1968, p. 10). Devlin's version of Legal Moralism does *not* argue that society should prohibit every activity that it regards as immoral. Those decisions will depend on how intensely society feels about a type of action, about the value of privacy, and a variety of practical considerations, such as enforceability. But Devlin would certainly think that *if* a large proportion of society regarded homosexual activity as an abomination, then **Homosexual Acts** would be justified in *that* society, just as an Islamic society might justifiably prohibit the sale of pork.

A fourth – socialization – version of Legal Moralism is a (distant?) cousin to the Harm Principle. This argument maintains that getting people to avoid immoral but harmless behaviors is one way to inculcate norms of self-restraint and respect for others that make it less likely that people will harm others. If the consumption of pornography socializes men to regard women as sexual objects, increasing the risk that men will commit violence against women, then society could legitimately restrict pornography on the grounds that restricting it leads to less harm. Similarly, we might try to justify **Cockfighting** and **Dwarf Tossing** on the grounds that the way a society entertains itself could have effects on the way that people treat each other, although I do not know that there is evidence that would support the application of these policies.

Should we accept any of the arguments for Legal Moralism? Anyone committed to the importance of individual autonomy should be reluctant to accept most versions of Legal Moralism, although it is possible that some arguments will go through. Here are two reasons for caution. First, despite the conviction with which many moral claims are advanced, there is often very little reasoning behind them. Consider **Homosexual Acts** and **Surrogacy**. I am inclined to think that when an activity is immoral this is because it is bad for people, because it sets back people's well-being or fails to promote it. Biblical claims aside, why should anyone think that there is anything immoral about homosexual activity? After all, if morality has to do with the way we treat each other, it is arguable that questions as to what persons of what gender put what organs in what places are not a matter of great moral moment. There may be something unseemly about commercial surrogacy, but we should not let our intuitive sense of seemliness take us too far too quickly. If, for example, commercial surrogacy creates children with good lives, if it typically works out well for the surrogate mothers and the adoptive parents, we should be loath to intervene just because we have the sense that there is, after all, "something" immoral about it. Second, it is arguable that one's choices may have moral value only if they are made autonomously, and so if we want people's lives to have positive moral value, we need to provide the space for them to make choices for themselves, even bad choices. This argument does not claim that all autonomous choices are of equal moral value, that being entertained by the Chicago Symphony is no more valuable than being entertained by dwarf tossing. It is to say that a choice has moral value only if it is made autonomously. If I am right, there is an important distinction between the claim that an activity is immoral and the claim that it ought to be restricted by the state. There are good reasons, good *moral* reasons for the state not to interfere with individual choices just because those choices are, in some way, immoral.

Justice

The Justice Principle says that the state is justified in interfering with individual liberty on grounds of justice. Precisely what the Justice Principle actually justifies will, of course, depend upon what a commitment to justice requires, and people disagree about that. Without taking a position on that issue, let us consider several ways in which the Justice Principle might justify interfering with people's freedom.

First, we might think that the state is justified in interfering with people's freedom to discriminate on grounds of race, religion, ethnicity, and (most recently) sexual orientation, as in **Non-discrimination**. One might say that we can justify **Non-discrimination** via the Harm Principle, but I do not think that will work. We are and should be free to make many decisions that have adverse effects on others. An employer can refuse to hire those she thinks are unqualified or obnoxious or ugly. A landlord can refuse to rent to a smoker, or someone with pets, or to undergraduate students, because we think justice prohibits treating people differently on the basis of some criteria, but not on the basis of other criteria. In addition, we may think that people should be free to discriminate on the basis of arguably irrelevant criteria in a variety of private contexts. We are free to choose our friends and mates on the basis of race or religion, even if it is not admirable that we do so. We are free to join private associations that exclude people on the basis of, say, sex or religion. Some cases are more difficult. We may think that the Jaycees or the Rotary should not be able to exclude blacks and women, because membership in such quasi-private organizations is important to people's business opportunities. But that is precisely the point. We must decide when justice requires prohibiting discrimination and when it does not. By itself, the notion of harm cannot do that.

Second, justice may require equality of opportunity. If equality of opportunity requires that children be provided with an education, then we may support **Public Schools**. We might go further. If justice requires that all children receive roughly equal educational opportunities, then the state might be justified in prohibiting communities from spending more than other communities on their children's education, a restriction that some would experience as a serious interference with their liberty (justified or not). To push this one step further, we might think that equality of opportunity requires that no people start the race of life with grossly unequal resources and so we might think that society should abolish or severely tax inheritance (see D. W. Haslett, 1986). I shall not pursue here the question as to what equality of opportunity actually requires. It is, for example, *not* obvious that the Justice Principle supports **Public Schools**. One could argue, after all, that it is unjust for people who have children to externalize the cost of their decisions onto others. The present point is that if equality of opportunity does require that people be provided with certain resources or that the distribution of certain resources be equalized, then we may think that the state is justified in interfering with people's liberty in order to attain that goal.

Third, we might think that the Justice Principle should regulate economic trans-actions. One might defend **Minimum Wage** on the grounds that it is unjust to pay people less than a "fair wage," although that requires a theory as to what con-stitutes a fair wage. One might defend **Ticket Scalping** on the grounds that certain prices are so exorbitant as to be unjust. One might defend **Organs** on the grounds that it is wrong to exploit a person's background situation even if the exploited party gains from the transaction. I am skeptical that this line of argument will gen-erally work, precisely because it prevents the exploited person from advancing her own interests, but if it does work, then we have another justification for inter-fering with consensual transactions.

Finally, we might think that justice requires that each person does his fair share in providing some public benefit, even if the public benefit would be provided if citizens were able to "free ride" on the contributions of others. Mill himself argues that one may be rightfully compelled "to bear his fair share in the common defense or in any other joint work necessary to the interest of society" (J. S. Mill, 1859, ch. I). One might maintain that to "free ride" on the contributions of others is to harm them, but I think it more accurate to say that it is unjust. Consider **Com-pulsory Voting, Conscription**, and **Blood**. It could be argued that we all have an obligation to do our part in sustaining our electoral democracy by voting, and that non-voters are free riding on the (admittedly small) sacrifices incurred by voters, that we all benefit from defense and that those who do not serve in the military are free riding on the sacrifices made by those who volunteer, and that we benefit from living in a society in which people donate blood, and that the non-donors are free riding on the sacrifices of those who give blood. Unlike the collective harm and collective benefit cases (**Converter, Tax Evasion**), where we limit liberty to ensure that a benefit will actually be provided, here the Justice Principle is riding alone, for the benefit is provided without compulsion. Whether considerations of justice are sufficient to justify intervention is a question I cannot resolve here.

Need

The Need Principle is straightforward. The principle states that we are justified in interfering with individual liberty to provide for people's needs. It does not state that we should always do what is necessary to provide for people's needs. If B will die unless she receives A's kidney, it does not follow that we should coercively extract A's kidney. But the Need Principle states that B's needs provide *a* reason to limit A's liberty. Although libertarians reject the Need Principle, we are accus-tomed to thinking that the Need Principle justifies taxation of people's resources in order to provide for others' need for medical care, food, clothing, and educa-tion, as in **Welfare**. If this is right, I see no reason to think that the Need Princi-ple might not also justify **Blood** and **Bad Samaritan**. Suppose that we need much more blood than we can obtain through voluntary donations or for pay (say, because the quality of commercial blood may be too low), that people will die because there is insufficient blood available. If we can require people to provide money because other people need goods in order to live, I do not see why we cannot require people to provide a renewable resource such as blood. If we can require people to serve as witnesses or on juries, I do not see why we cannot require people to make easy rescues. It might be said that the Need Principle is superfluous, that its point can be put in terms of justice or harm. I do not doubt that the point of the Need Principle can often be handled in other ways, but there is reason to prefer a more straightforward approach. And if we accept the Need Principle, there are a wide range of circumstances in which the state may be justified in using coercion, to limit people's liberty, that goes beyond the intervention justified by other principles.

Conclusion

As we have seen, John Stuart Mill thought that we could resolve the question as to "the dealings of society with the individual in the way of compulsion and control" by invoking "one very simple principle," namely that society is justified in limiting individual liberty only to prevent people from harming others. If I am right, Mill was wrong. First, I have tried to show that the Harm Principle itself is not so simple. Second, I have argued that it is at least plausible to suppose that there are several principles that can be used to justify the use of state coercion or restrict people's liberty. In effect, I have argued for a pluralism of principles that requires weighing and balancing a range of considerations. Moreover, as with the Harm Principle, these principles cannot be applied mechanically. It might be objected, if we accept this sort of wide open pluralism about limiting individual liberty, that we will end up justifying too much, that there will not be enough liberty left at the end of the day. That is a reasonable fear, but I do not think there is an easy way out. In the final analysis, there is no way to avoid balancing the reasons that favor limiting people's liberty with the reasons that favor leaving people alone. If we are lucky, we will get the balance more or less right.

Finally, it is a fact of political life that whatever the best view about the reasons that justify limiting individual liberty, we will disagree about the matter. We will disagree as to what principles we should accept and we will disagree as to how they should be applied. Indeed, even if we were to accept Mill's view that the Harm Principle is the only justification for limiting individual liberty, we will disagree as to how to interepret and apply that principle. It is not enough to develop theories as to when the state is justified in limiting individual liberty. We need a theory as to how we should proceed given that we will disagree about that question. But that is the topic of other essays in this volume.

Bibliography

Devlin, P. (1968). *The Enforcement of Morals*. London: Oxford University Press.

Dworkin, G. (1972). "Paternalism." *Monist*, 56: 64–84.

——(1983). "Paternalism: Some Second Thoughts." In Rolf Sartorius (ed.), *Paternalism* (pp. 105–11). Minneapolis: University of Minnesota Press.

Elster, Jon (1979). *Ulysses and the Sirens*. Cambridge: Cambridge University Press.

Feinberg, J. (1984). *Harm to Others*. New York: Oxford University Press.

——(1985). *Offense to Others*. New York: Oxford University Press.

——(1986). *Harm to Self*. New York: Oxford University Press.

——(1988). *Harmless Wrongdoing*. New York: Oxford University Press.

George, R. (1993). *Making Men Moral*. Oxford: Clarendon Press.

Hart, H. L. A. (1963). *Law, Liberty, and Morality*. Stanford: Stanford University Press.

Haslett, D. W. (1986). "Is Inheritance Justified?" *Philosophy and Public Affairs*, 15: 122–55.

Mill, J. S. (1859). *On Liberty* (cited from Hackett edition, 1978).

Olson, Jr, M. (1965). *The Logic of Collective Action*. New York: Schocken Books.

Schelling, T. (1984). *Choice and Consequence*. Cambridge, MA: Harvard University Press.

Sher, G. (1997). *Beyond Neutrality*. Cambridge: Cambridge University Press.

Wertheimer, A. (1996). *Exploitation*. Princeton, NJ: Princeton University Press.

Chapter 3

Justice

Christopher Heath Wellman

This essay surveys some of the most prominent positions, issues, and questions within contemporary discussions of justice. It addresses many key topics, but readers should bear in mind that this review was written explicitly for this volume and thus omits much of importance which will be covered in the other essays in this book, especially those focusing on democracy, equality, feminism, liberalism, and Marxism.

Utilitarianism

One of the most powerful, systematic, and popular theories of justice is utilitarianism, the view that actions, policies, and institutions are to be judged in terms of the extent to which they maximize overall happiness or well-being. Utilitarians come in various shapes and sizes, but virtually all embrace consequentialism, impartiality, and maximization. Utilitarians are consequentialists insofar as they assess actions and policies solely in terms of the consequences they generate. So-called "backward-looking" considerations (such as what people deserve in light of their past behavior) are irrelevant on this view; all that matters is the future effects. Utilitarians are impartialists because the well-being of every person (where "person" sometimes includes not just humans but all sentient beings) matters equally. No special deference is paid to the interests of the agent or her close relations; consequences for everyone are to be counted, and no one's well-being is given more weight than the others. Finally, utilitarians are maximizers because, among all the possible options, they single out that which results in the greatest overall well-being as the uniquely correct choice. There is considerable debate among utilitarians as to what good should be maximized (happiness is only one prominent answer), but all agree that the right action is that which maximizes the good.

Even this quick sketch is enough to indicate why utilitarianism is profoundly revisionary. Indeed, Jeremy Bentham, John Stuart Mill, and its other early adherents were radical reformers who worked to overhaul nineteenth-century England. In their view, the existing laws and customs were morally atrocious because they prevented, rather than promoted, overall happiness. In defiance of the status quo, utilitarians proposed new arrangements inspired by the importance of considering equally the welfare of each individual. Among other reforms, they sought to bring down property laws which unjustifiably privileged the upper classes. This leaning toward equal distribution stems from the twin assumptions of (1) impartiality, and (2) diminishing marginal returns. Impartiality, of course, is merely the above-mentioned moral stance that no one person's well-being is of greater intrinsic value than another's, and diminishing marginal returns is the economic principle that people derive a smaller amount of satisfaction from each additional increment of wealth (or other good) they obtain. To appreciate this principle, consider how much the happiness you gain by acquiring an additional pair of pants is affected by the number of pants you already own. If you have no pants and someone gives you a pair, for instance, it makes a huge difference because you can now clothe your legs. And if someone then gives you a second pair, these pants will likely have a substantial effect on your happiness (since you can now wear one pair while you wash the other) but will not make such a huge difference as the first pair. Similarly, you might be quite happy to receive the third pair of pants (because of the additional variety it introduces into your wardrobe), but the importance of adding this third pair pales in comparison with the significance of gaining your second pair. Finally, consider the additional satisfaction you derive from acquiring a fifteenth pair of pants. You might be pleased to get this additional pair, but its acquisition will be nowhere near as important to you as the first, second, or third was.

Presumably, all of this is intuitively plausible. But now consider how these observations might lead you (and the utilitarian) to distribute pants among a community of people. Imagine, for instance, that there are ten people and twenty pairs of pants. Would you arrange things so that one person had all twenty pairs and the remaining nine had none, so that four people had five pairs each, or so that each person had two pairs of pants? If you believed that the one of the four people deserved special consideration (because they were part of a higher, morally superior class, for instance) you might recommend the first or second option. But if you believe that each person's welfare is equally important – as the utilitarians do – then you are likely to recommend the last option, wherein each person gets two pairs of pants. It is this type of reasoning which led early utilitarians to lobby for sweeping legislative changes designed to redistribute wealth more equally, and it is also this logic which inspires some contemporary utilitarians to argue that we should dedicate much more to international aid. After all, where is the justice in using money to buy fancy new pairs of pants for ourselves when our closets are already filled and there are impoverished foreigners whose legs are bare? Unless we think there is some reason why our happiness is more important than theirs, it seems difficult to justify buying luxuries which will have minimal effect on our happiness when the money spent on these amenities could have a life-altering effect on those who have so much less (Singer).

Although this story is plausible, not all utilitarians embrace its conclusion. Few doubt the logic of diminishing marginal returns, but many eschew egalitarian distributions because of the incentive structures they create. Some utilitarians acknowledge that, if we assume a given number of pants, happiness is generally maximized by distributing them equally. It is wrong to assume a fixed number of pants, however, because there are different arrangements that are more, or less, conducive to the production of pants (and other goods). In particular, the amount produced depends crucially on the incentives people have to engage in production. To see the importance of this, reconsider the community of ten people mentioned above. Given the law of diminishing marginal returns, it makes sense to distribute the twenty pairs of pants equally, giving two pairs to each person. The drawback to such egalitarian distributions, however, is that they reduce the incentives to work, by externalizing the costs of leisure. In other words, if each person knows that she will get only one-tenth of whatever she produces (since the total produced will be split into ten equal parts), then no one has much incentive to produce. Suppose, for instance, that if they worked hard, each could produce ten pairs of pants. If so, there would be 100 pairs, which, distributed equally, would give each person ten. But notice that if one person decided to play rather than work, there would be only 90 pairs of pants, or nine pairs each. Given this arrangement, we would expect this person to play rather than work. The key is that because produced goods are distributed equally, the person who elects not to work enjoys 100% of the benefits of her leisure but incurs only 10% of the costs (the other 90% is incurred – in equal parts – by the other nine with whom the fruits of production are shared). Thus, one has insufficient incentive to work; it is rational to choose leisure when one pays for only one-tenth of its cost.

The problem is that this logic does not apply to only one person; it applies to everyone under this distributive arrangement, so we should expect everyone to choose leisure over production. In other words, if all pants were distributed equally, no one would voluntarily produce pants, none would be produced, and thus there would be none to distribute (Schmidtz and Goodin). This reasoning leads some utilitarians to eschew egalitarian distributive policies. The better long-term strategy, they suggest, is to harness everyone's self-interest by arranging things so that each person is assured of keeping virtually all that she produces. The point is not that the best life involves accumulating produced goods rather than enjoying leisure. The important insight is instead that, when each person fully internalizes the costs and benefits of work and leisure, she chooses a production schedule which is best for her without displacing the costs of her leisure onto others. In this way, allowing each individual to decide which type of life best suits her, maximizes overall happiness.

As this discussion illustrates, many factors must be considered when designing a distributive arrangement which maximizes happiness, and it should come as no surprise that not all utilitarians endorse the same policies. But while there is some disagreement among utilitarians, there is much more controversy over the approach as a whole. The objections to utilitarianism are many, but perhaps the most consistent worry is that, insofar as utilitarianism concerns itself exclusively with consequences, it cannot be squared with justice. Critics contend that because justice involves giving people their due, and because someone's due depends principally upon her previous actions, an ethical outlook which looks solely to the future cannot offer an account of justice. Perhaps the most popular way to express this concern is that utilitarianism cannot accommodate moral rights. For instance, if happiness would be maximized by killing a wealthy farmer and distributing her abundant crop among the starving masses, then utilitarianism would apparently recommend that we do so. The utilitarian responses to this charge are diverse and sophisticated, but the most frequent involve either (1) denying the divergence between utilitarianism and justice, (2) biting the bullet in favor of utilitarianism, or (3) distinguishing between right action and the best motivation. Consider each of these responses.

Some utilitarians insist that, in the real world at least, there is no significant divergence between what utilitarianism recommends and our ordinary moral thinking about justice. Utilitarians protest that their critics concoct radically counterfactual thought experiments which purport to highlight the divergence between justice and utility. According to defenders of utilitarianism, this tendency toward otherworldly examples is no coincidence; it is made necessary by the great concordance between maximizing utility and common convictions which occurs in real-world circumstances. (Killing wealthy farmers and redistributing their assets among the needy would never *in reality* maximize happiness, for instance, because one could not covertly implement such a plan, and public awareness of this type of redistributive policy would threaten everyone's sense of security and undermine our incentive to work and accumulate goods.) What is more, in those extremely rare situations in which utilitarianism would clearly recommend something different than what justice putatively demands (say, when one must torture an innocent baby in order to save the entire human race), we tend to side with utilitarianism – or, at the very least, our conviction that justice must trump concerns of utility is greatly diminished.

Another response – that of biting the bullet – occurs when staunch utilitarians acknowledge the incompatibility of utilitarianism and our convictions about justice, and then openly jettison justice. Often the thinking here is that, just as we would not abandon an elegant, powerful scientific theory the first time we came across outlying empirical data, we should not discard utilitarianism merely because it conflicts with a few miscellaneous moral intuitions. Given that utilitarianism is such a simple and powerful theory which so consistently generates correct answers in a wide variety of contexts, it seems wrong-headed to discard it merely because it fails to square with a random assortment of putative intuitions (Smart and Williams).

While both of the above responses are common, the most celebrated utilitarian move is to distinguish between right action and right motivation. Here utilitarians contest that, just because utilitarianism defines the right action as that which maximizes happiness, it does not follow that a utilitarian must recommend that we consciously try to maximize happiness each time we act (Mill). Utilitarians note that we often do a better job of actually maximizing happiness when we do not explicitly aim to. Because of the errors we commonly make in calculating utility, and because it is often an inefficient use of time to stop and compute the expected consequences, it is best to act from habits or rules. Perhaps the paramount reason we ought not to consider equally the happiness of all those potentially affected before we act, though, is because we know and care the most about ourselves. And since everyone is best positioned to take care of their own happiness, utilitarians can without contradiction urge us to worry principally about our own self-regarding affairs while simultaneously denying that an agent has any reason to treat her own happiness as of any greater intrinsic importance than that of the next person. Utilizing reasoning like this, many utilitarians argue that overall happiness would in fact be maximized if each of us acted as if the moral rights falsely posited by commonsense morality were genuine. In short, sophisticated utilitarians contend that over the long haul, right actions are more often performed when we are not explicitly motivated by utilitarian concerns (Hardin; Hare).

Of course, none of these three utilitarian responses quiets all critics. Those sympathetic to moral rights object that it is not enough that utilitarianism only rarely conflicts with justice in the real world or even that it plainly diverges from justice only in radically counterfactual circumstances. Detractors insist that even one hypothetical conflict between justice and utility demonstrates that utilitarianism must be rejected. Moreover, many are not satisfied that utilitarianism can approve of our acting as if we have moral rights; they insist that no theory is adequate unless it can affirm these rights themselves. The crucial point is that we *deserve* certain types of treatment, and, at best, utilitarianism can only say that we should typically act *as if* people deserve this treatment. Utilitarians standardly argue that, when one appreciates the limits of human reasoning, one sees how happiness is maximized by nonconsequential motivations. For many, this account involves "one thought too many" (Williams, p. 18).

Rawls

For quite some time, the only alternative to utilitarianism seemed to be a miscellany of retributive intuitions. In his *Theory of Justice*, John Rawls set out to remedy this situation by devising a retributive theory of justice which could rival utilitarianism's internal coherence and systematic comprehensiveness. In particular, he sought to develop an approach that was elegant and powerful like utilitarianism but which still accommodated retributive notions like fairness. In building his account of "Justice as Fairness," he drew inspiration from a simple, paradigmatically fair distributive method. Specifically, imagine that Jill and Jack had to share a pie; what would be the fairest way to divide it? One method, to which no one could object, would be to let Jill cut it into two pieces and then let Jack choose his piece first. Their pieces might not be exactly the same size, but neither could question the fairness of the distribution since Jill had the opportunity to cut the pie into equally desirable portions, and Jack could have chosen Jill's piece if he had so desired. In Rawls's view, the key to developing an adequate theory of distributive justice is to devise an analogous method which could be applied to the much more complicated division of the costs and benefits of social cooperation. To see how he attempted this, let us return to our imaginary community of ten.

To begin, suppose that ten people need a fair way to split their pie. Clearly, the best strategy would be for one person to divide the pie into ten pieces with the understanding that she will get the last piece. Naturally, the pie-cutter will do her best to divide the pie into ten equal pieces since any inequalities will result in the biggest pieces being taken first and, ultimately, the smallest piece being left for her. The only problem with this analogy is that, as we saw in the discussion of utilitarianism, we cannot assume that the size of the pie is constant. Taking the pie as analogous to the costs and benefits of social cooperation, we need to recognize that the size of the pie depends on how society's basic institutions are organized. Moreover, we have already seen how distributing products equally can inhibit the incentive to produce, and thus we see that dividing the communal pie into ten equal slices will lead to a smaller overall pie. And finally, since the pie-cutter would insist upon equal-sized slices at the expense of the absolute size of her own slice only if she were exceptionally envious, the cutter would happily allow any inequalities which would result in the last piece of pie being bigger than it would be otherwise. After all, the person who arranges the distribution of the ten pieces chooses last, and she can reasonably expect that her nine companions will leave the smallest piece for her. Thus, once we transpose the pie-cutting model to a larger group and then add the observation that our method of distribution has an effect on the size of the pie as a whole, we end up with the following recommendation: the costs and benefits of social cooperation are to be arranged so that the worst-off person has the best possible share.

Now that we have a sense of Rawls's overarching aim, let us look at how he explicates and defends his model of justice as fairness. Rawls writes of his theory involving two principles, but his second principle is two-pronged, so his account may be understood in terms of three distinct principles: the Principle of Greatest Equal Liberty, the Principle of Fair Equality of Opportunity, and the Difference Principle. The Principle of Greatest Equal Liberty, which enjoys priority over the other two, specifies that "each person is to have an equal right to the most extensive basic liberty compatible with a similar liberty for others" (Rawls, 1971, p. 60). This principle proposes that each person is to have an equal right to such liberties as the freedom of conscience, freedom of speech, freedom of political participation, the right to private property, etc. as is compatible with everyone else equally enjoying these freedoms. The Principle of Fair Equality of Opportunity requires that offices and positions be genuinely open to all under conditions of fair equality of opportunity. The idea here is simply that each person should be able to compete on an even playing field, so that those with the same talents and motivation enjoy equal opportunities to assume positions of power and prestige. And finally, the Difference Principle asserts that social inequalities are to be arranged so that they are of the greatest benefit to the least advantaged. In other words, deviating from equality is permissible only when it is to the maximal advantage of the worst-off.

It should be apparent how these principles derive their inspiration from the pie-cutting scenario, but notice that Rawls also seeks to support his theory with the same reasons which inspire our confidence in the fairness of the pie-cutting procedure. To appreciate this, it is important to remember that Jill and Jack will not necessarily get precisely equal pieces of pie. Thus, the method of division is not justified exclusively by the size of the portions; the distribution is also justified because it is the result of a procedure to which neither could reasonably object. Put simply, Jill and Jack both rationally agree to this method of division. Similarly, Rawls seeks to defend his principles by showing that they too would be agreed to by rational bargainers in a suitable-choice situation. There has been an enormous amount written about what constitutes a rational bargainer and what type of choice situation is most appropriate, but the basic idea is to construct a thought experiment which demonstrates that – like Jill and Jack with their respective pieces of pie – no one living in a society whose basic institutions are in accord with the principles of justice as fairness could reasonably contest her lot. (As Rawls points out, in a society whose basic institutions are governed by his principles, even those worst-off cannot righteously object since things could not have been ordered so as to improve their lot without reducing others to a position below that of the currently worst-off.) Thus, the description of the rational-choice situation (which Rawls labels the "original position") is extremely important because Rawls seeks to justify his theory, not only on the grounds that it squares with our considered judgments of social justice, but also because it would be agreed to by rational bargainers in circumstances which we all agree are fair.

The first thing to notice about the rational bargainers is that we cannot use actual people who are aware of their circumstances because white, male Christians are liable to lobby for rules which favor white, male Christians, and black, female Muslims might seek rules privileging black, female Muslims and so on. Moreover, because the wealthy and powerful have greater bargaining power, the principles likely to emerge from any negotiations among actual contractors would reflect these power differentials. Such principles would not necessarily be fair, of course, since they stemmed from a morally arbitrary source. To derive principles to which no one could reasonably object, then, we must strip each contractor of any morally arbitrary advantages in bargaining power, and the best way to do this, Rawls suggests, is to put the contractors behind a "veil of ignorance" where they lack all knowledge of their personal characteristics and station in society. If each contractor has no idea whether she is black or white, rich or poor, female or male, Muslim or Christian, for instance, then she will not be concerned merely to protect people of her own description. Thus, because we have reason to value principles upon which rational contractors would agree only if these contractors were unaware of their personal characteristics, Rawls wants to show that those behind the veil of ignorance would choose the principles which comprise justice as fairness.

Rawls proposes that the bargainers would reason as follows. First and foremost, they would insist on the Principle of Greatest Equal Liberty because, above all, each would want to ensure her freedom to live according to her own conscience. If a contractor knew that one was a Muslim, for instance, she might want a state which favors Muslims, but since the contractor is ignorant of her religious convictions and of which religion is dominant, her first priority will be to secure an arrangement wherein each person is at liberty to worship (or not) as she sees fit. Similarly, each rational bargainer would hope that all public offices and other positions of authority are effectively open to all. Again, unless one knew that one was a member of the privileged caste or class, one would want to make sure that everyone has an equal shot at all awards and posts of consequence. Finally, when it comes to distributing the basic goods of society, the best way to ensure that one has sufficient means to live a rewarding life is to arrange things so that one's worst-case scenario is as good as possible. In other words, one would distribute what Rawls calls "primary goods" (goods such as rights, liberties, wealth, power and opportunities, which virtually everyone needs to pursue their goals and projects) equally unless departing from equality would improve the smallest portion. Given the rationality of this reasoning, Rawls concludes that the contractors would opt for his principles of justice. And because the rational preferences of bargainers behind the veil of ignorance lend support to whichever arrangement they endorse, Rawls sees this thought experiment as compelling support for his conception of justice as fairness.

The critical response to Rawls's groundbreaking argument has been extraordinary in both its volume and its interdisciplinarity. Here I will briefly mention just two concerns: (1) not only do many question the moral significance of Rawls's thought experiment; but also (2) some suggest that it would not generate the principles he supposes. Regarding the first objection, detractors have protested that it is hard to see how the supposed preferences of hypothetical reasoners could have any moral implications for those of us living in the real world. As Ronald Dworkin says, a hypothetical contract "is not simply a pale form of a contract, it is no contract at all" (Dworkin, 1975: 18).

Of course, Rawls insists that it is important to determine which principles would be chosen behind the veil of ignorance because, insofar as he has specifically designed the original position to be a fair-choice situation, whichever principles emerge should be considered fair. Even if one agrees with Rawls on this point, however, it may not be enough to save his preferred theory because many question whether the rational bargainers would really favor Rawls's principles. Most commentators concede the Principle of Greatest Equal Liberty, and even the Principle of Fair Equality of Opportunity has not been too controversial, but there has been enormous dissatisfaction with the Difference Principle. In particular, many wonder why Rawls thinks rationality requires the contractors to be so risk-averse that they would sacrifice potentially great gains in efficiency for increased security. Put another way, why concentrate so intently on the worst-off position to the detriment of the overall aggregate of costs and benefits? It makes sense for the pie-cutter to focus exclusively on the size of the smallest piece of pie because she knows that she will choose last, but this is not true of those behind the veil of ignorance. Rawls's rational bargainers do not know what their relative position will be, but their ignorance is very different from knowing that they will be the worst-off. Given their ignorance, it seems as though they should assume that they are as likely to be relatively wealthy as to be relatively poor. If so, the bargainers should prefer whichever distribution of goods is most efficient since that is most likely to increase the average share. In sum, many critics contend that, once the Principle of Greatest Equal Liberty and the Principle of Fair Equality of Opportunity are safely in place, it would be irrational to worry exclusively about making the worst-off position as good as possible. The more rational strategy would be to prefer whichever distributive policy would make the pie as a whole the biggest since this will improve the size of the average slice.

Rawls acknowledges that the policy of maximizing one's minimum, worst-case scenario (known as the "maximin" strategy) is not always preferable to maximizing one's expected outcome, but he insists that the bargainers behind the veil of ignorance have special reasons to weight security over efficiency. In particular, Rawls invokes the "strains of commitment" which weigh on the contractors. The argument here is that the bargainers' special concern with improving the condition of the worst-off is warranted because, in agreeing to a set of principles to govern the basic institutions of society, they are irrevocably committing themselves to the resulting distribution no matter where they may end up on the social hierarchy. What is more, the contractors would be irrational to gamble with the high stakes of such an outcome because the social conditions necessary for self-respect are on the line. Finally, Rawls emphasizes that the contractors understand that they must not only be able to endure their eventual stations in society; they must be able to embrace them as active, energetic citizens in a democratic community. Thus, Rawls concludes that the highly distinctive circumstances behind the veil of ignorance require the maximin strategy, which in turn leads to the Difference Principle. In sum, Rawls argues that his conception of justice as fairness is confirmed not only by our considered judgments about social justice but also because it would be selected by rational bargainers placed in a fair-choice situation.

Before closing our discussion of Rawls, it is worth pausing to note that he places much greater emphasis on stability and legitimacy in his more recent work. In *Political Liberalism*, Rawls takes it as an inevitable fact that a plurality of comprehensive moral, religious, and philosophical doctrines will exist unless uniformity is forcibly imposed by an oppressive regime. Assuming both that a political regime will enjoy stability only if the great majority of its constituents freely support it, and that a state cannot be legitimate if it imposes rules which its constituents can reasonably reject, the fundamental question arises as to how a state can legitimately coerce all of its citizens when they subscribe to a plurality of reasonable comprehensive views. As Rawls puts it: "How is it possible that deeply opposed though reasonable comprehensive doctrines may live together and all affirm the political conception of a constitutional regime?" (Rawls, 1993, p. xviii). The solution, Rawls believes, lies in "public reason," an overlapping consensus of fundamental political ideals which exist within the public political culture of enduring liberal democracies. Thus, a state can be legitimate and stable despite the ideological diversity of its citizens as long as it can ground its laws in this overlapping consensus of public reason, as opposed to appealing to a particular comprehensive doctrine which is not shared by all. It is important to recognize that Rawls does not seek to eliminate the plurality of reasonable comprehensive doctrines; he acknowledges that they might be relevant for various associations or institutions within a state (when deciding matters within one's church, for instance). But when it comes to political decisions concerning the basic structure of society, Rawls insists that it is illegitimate to invoke anything other than public reason. Thus, in contrast to his earlier work, Rawls now emphasizes that his principles constitute a *political* conception of justice; he argues not that his theory is true but only that it is consistent with an overlapping consensus of political views which exist among the plurality of reasonable comprehensive doctrines of any longstanding democratic regime.

Libertarianism

Many embrace libertarian policies for consequential reasons; as explained above, there is good reason to think that social systems which celebrate individual freedom and responsibility make everyone better off. The more popular libertarian stance, however, stems from a respect for the inviolability of moral rights. Such libertarians offer an account of justice very different from those of utilitarianism or Rawls, and perhaps the best way to introduce their view is to explain why they reject the two previous accounts of justice.

Rights-based libertarians (hereafter simply "libertarians") like John Locke and, more recently, Robert Nozick understand the temptation to slice pies or distribute pants so as to maximize overall happiness or improve the condition of the worst-off, but they nonetheless insist that such redistribution is typically unjust. The principal concern is that pies, pants, and other products do not merely fall from the heavens; they have to be produced and normally are the property of their producer. Reconsider our community of ten as an example. If one of the ten, Antonio, bakes a pie, then we might divide it in any number of ways, depending on what goals we seek to advance. No matter what good consequences would arise from these various divisions, however, it would be unjust from the perspective of libertarianism to take even the tiniest sliver on behalf of the hungriest person without Antonio's permission. As the rightful owner of the pie, Antonio stands in a privileged position of moral dominion over it. Of course, Antonio may share the pie with the others if he would like, but he may also eat the entire pie himself or even let it go to waste if he would prefer. Letting the pie spoil when others are hungry would admittedly be inefficient, wasteful, and perhaps even mean-spirited, but it need not be unjust. Assuming that Antonio has a property right to the pie, justice requires that he be allowed to use – or waste – it in any manner he sees fit. Efficiency, charity, and the maximization of happiness are worthwhile goals, but libertarian justice insists that none takes priority over moral rights. No matter how noble our intentions, the range of our permissible actions is always constrained by the rights of others.

Given this emphasis on rights, libertarians like Nozick insist that one cannot know whether a particular distribution is just – no matter what its pattern – unless one knows how it arose. A distribution wherein Antonio is wealthy and the other nine are relatively poor could be perfectly just as long as each of the ten is entitled to precisely what she has; and conversely, a scenario in which all ten have equal portions might be unjust if some have acquired their possessions via illegitimate means. Any distribution will be just as long as each possession was acquired either through a proper initial acquisition (as when one grows a crop on one's own land or bakes a pie with one's own ingredients) or through a just transfer (as when one either buys, trades for, or is given something from its rightful owner). It is the history of each particular initial acquisition and transfer rather than the resulting overall pattern of distribution which determines the justness of a particular distribution (Nozick). Force may permissibly be used to take something back from someone who has acquired it via illegitimate means (through fraud or theft, for instance), but it is always unjust to coerce someone to surrender something to which she is entitled. There may be loads of reasons to wish that property were distributed more equally or in conformity with some other pattern (and often these reasons will inspire people to act charitably), but as long as the existing distribution is the result of just initial acquisitions and transfers only, it would be strictly impermissible to force anyone to surrender her property.

Given this account of justice, it is not surprising that libertarians tend to follow Nozick in rejecting the welfare state in favor of (at most) a minimal, "night watcher" state. The idea here is that, just as it would be unjust for an individual to take Antonio's property, it would equally be wrong of all nine to band together and commandeer a portion of his pie. Antonio's property right is a position of moral dominion which holds against all others, whether they act as individuals or have been incorporated in the form of a state. Understood from this perspective, Nozick argues that there is a sense in which living in a welfare state is morally akin to something like slavery. Imagine, for instance, that the state "redistributes" one-tenth of Antonio's income to others; suppose it takes one of the ten pies Antonio bakes daily. In a sense, Antonio is one-tenth enslaved since he is forced to work for others for a portion of every day. Thus, while libertarians have no principled opposition to voluntary charity, they insist that coerced welfare redistribution is unjust regardless of whether it is perpetrated by an individual, by

Robin Hood and his merry men, or by a sophisticated modern state. Given this stance, libertarians typically argue for a minimal state, one which merely secures the peace, enforces contracts, and perhaps protects against aggressive foreign states. On this view, the state is needed to – and may permissibly do no more than – ensure that no one interferes with the moral rights of its citizens. Because libertarians posit only minimal rights against interference, they dislike all states which, in attempting to do more than protect these few rights, regularly trample all over them.

Libertarianism is attractive both because of the simplicity and intuitive plausibility of its emphasis on rights and because of its celebration of individual freedom and responsibility. Like all accounts, however, it has critics. Two prominent objections are that (1) there is no adequate foundation for libertarian rights, and (2) if libertarians were correct about our moral rights, we could not justify even a minimal state. Consider each of these worries in turn.

First, many concede that all forced welfare redistribution would be unjust if moral rights – especially property rights – took the form libertarians presume, but they contend that there is insufficient reason to believe in rights of this description. Most contemporary students of justice believe in moral rights, but they understand them differently than libertarians would like. According to libertarianism, there can be no "positive" rights to assistance because they are ruled out by our "negative" rights to be free from interference as long as we do not harm others. (Very roughly, negative rights protect one from being harmed, and positive rights entitle one to be benefited.) The obvious question emerges, however, as to why we must agree that our negative rights leave no space for positive rights. Negative rights would do so if they were entirely general and unfailingly absolute, but this rendering ill-fits our considered moral judgments. (To offer just one example of an exception to our right to liberty, most think there is a perfect duty to perform Samaritan rescues like saving a drowning baby from a swimming pool when such a rescue requires one only to reach down and pull the child from the water.) What is more, we should revise these substantive moral judgments only if there are compelling conceptual reasons for insisting that all rights are absolute and general. The problem for libertarians is that no one has been able to supply these reasons. (Moral rights might be perfectly general and absolute if they were derived directly from a few natural laws, for example, but most have abandoned the conception of moral rules upon which such an account depends.) In short, in the absence of a theoretical explanation of why rights must be general and absolute, we cannot conclude that our negative rights rule out the possibility of positive rights. And, given our considered belief in positive rights, it seems wrong to insist that all forced redistribution of wealth must be unjust.

A second problem emerges even if libertarians can generate a convincing explanation for why our negative rights leave no room for positive rights, because, while libertarians stress that their account of justice is incompatible with forced redistribution, it also appears to conflict with the minimal, "night watcher" state. The problem is that just as a welfare state cannot redistribute funds without first forcing citizens to relinquish some of their wealth, a minimal state could not secure peace, enforce contracts, and provide military protection unless it coerced those within its territorial boundaries to both follow a single set of rules and contribute to the institutions required to draft, promulgate and enforce these rules. Albeit to a lesser extent and for fewer purposes, a minimal state is guilty of the same crime – non-consensual coercion and invasion of property rights – with which libertarians charge the welfare state. If so, libertarians must eschew even the minimal state in favor of anarchy. Of course, anarcho-libertarians urge us to embrace just such a conclusion, but most consider anarchy an unpalatable conclusion. Faced with either endorsing anarchism or abandoning libertarianism, many would opt for the latter.

Post-Rawlsian Egalitarianism

Since the emergence of Rawls's theory of justice, a number of egalitarians have defended various interpretations of the ideal of equality. In this section I will briefly review three egalitarian approaches: (1) so-called "luck" egalitarians, (2) Michael Walzer's complex equality, and (3) Elizabeth Anderson's relational theory of equality.

Although egalitarians often disagree about how the ideal of equality should be realized, they are united in rejecting the libertarian critique of welfare redistribution. In their view, the problem with allowing individuals unlimited liberty to accumulate and transfer justly acquired property is that the cumulative result of many seemingly benign transactions can result in pernicious inequalities (Cohen). It is quite possible, for instance, that Bert's parents – through a combination of ambition, preferences, and luck – amass a fortune while Ernie's become quite poor. This disparity is morally problematic because it means that, through no fault of his own, Ernie has a much worse chance than Bert of living a rewarding life. There is nothing necessarily wrong with Bert working hard and accumulating more possessions because he values possessions more and leisure less than Ernie, but it seems unjust that Bert should enjoy both more possessions and more leisure than Ernie merely because Bert was lucky enough to have been born to wealthier parents. Just as we object to the injustice of whites having better life prospects than blacks or men having better life prospects than women, we should object to the disparity between the life prospects of Bert and Ernie when this divergence has nothing to do with differences in their character or behavior.

To avoid this form of injustice, some recommend that we should divide resources equally. The problem with this "equality of resources" approach, however, is that some people might need more resources to live an equally rewarding life (Dworkin, 1981b). Imagine, for instance, that I am paralyzed and cannot get around without a special living environment and a motorized wheelchair. If everyone were simply given an equal share of resources, my special expenses would leave me with considerably less for the usual goods of life. To correct for this problem, some embrace "Equality of Welfare," the view that resources are to be distributed in whatever fashion ensures that all are equally happy. This approach is also problematic, though, because it might be that I have unreasonably expensive tastes (Dworkin, 1981a). If I can only be pleased with champagne and caviar when most are perfectly content with chicken and dumplings, then the equality of welfare seems to require that I be given enough funds to compensate for my more expensive tastes. This conclusion is awkward, however, since it seems as though society at large should not have to pick up the tab for my peculiar cravings. A more promising approach would seem to be one which split the difference between equality of resources and equality of welfare, one which compensated people for expenses beyond their control but gave no extra resources to those with controllable, expensive tastes. In fact, however, even those who concur that we should eliminate the element of luck have found it extremely difficult to agree on just how this ideal of equality requires that the burdens and benefits of social cooperation be distributed.

Distinguishing himself from those who understand equality in terms of a single ideal, Michael Walzer develops an account he calls "complex" equality, which is dramatically pluralistic in two important senses. First, rather than search for a fundamental, universal concept of justice which can be uniformly applied in all contexts, Walzer regards justice as something which must be created by each particular community. Second, each distinct type of social good comprises its own "sphere of justice" with its own distinct criterion of distribution. The criterion which governs the distribution of political power, for example, may be different from the criterion which governs the distribution of medical care. What is more, there is no reason to assume that any particular criterion is more basic than the others or that there is some overarching principle to rank the various criteria of distribution. Rather, complex equality requires merely that no one be able to dominate over others, where domination is understood in terms of converting the advantages of one sphere of distribution into advantages in another. Thus, there is no problem with your having more political power than I as long as (1) you gained this greater power in accordance with our community's criterion for who should have political power, and (2) you are not able to use your political power to get goods in other spheres like medical care. Indeed, it is not even clear how Walzer could object to your enjoying a greater amount of every good than I, as long as each particular advantage was gained in accordance with its own criterion of distribution and not because of the dominance of, say, wealth or power. (However, given the great variety of goods and the corresponding diversity of individual criteria, it would in practice be virtually impossible to achieve such uniform advantage without violating complex equality.) Thus, Walzer need not object to any given inequality which exists with respect to a particular good because Walzerian justice can coincide with various inequalities as long as (1) no one is able to dominate the rest, and (2) the inequalities are created in accordance with our social understandings of these goods.

While Walzer's complex equality has garnered a great deal of support, critics have expressed concern about his contention that particular conceptions of justice must be created by each community. If he were merely emphasizing that there are often morally relevant details which may vary from culture to culture, few would object. But Walzer does not simply mean to point out that the rules of distributive justice should not be construed in overly general terms; he embraces a brand of cultural relativism by alleging that each sphere of justice depends upon the social understandings of the community in which it exists. Most commentators shy away from this relativism, though, because it apparently leaves us unable to criticize objectionable distributive arrangements. If a community reserves the privileged religious or political posts exclusively for men, for instance, it is unclear how forcefully someone who follows Walzer in eschewing universal concepts of justice could criticize such an arrangement. Since most of us regard an inherently sexist distributive policy as unjust irrespective of its cultural pedigree, few are entirely comfortable with all elements of Walzer's pluralism.

In reaction to the "luck" egalitarians, Elizabeth Anderson offers a "relational" theory of equality. In her view, the key to developing an accurate theory of equality is understanding the point of equality. Luck egalitarians miss the mark, she suggests, because they mistakenly believe their chief concern to be eliminating the element of luck so that each person can get precisely the goods she deserves. The real reason to value equality, Anderson contends, is because inequality facilitates socially oppressive relationships. Thus, if we want to know what equality requires, we must think about what people need to avoid being oppressed by others. Adopting this view involves broadening one's focus from merely the distribution of goods themselves to a consideration of the relationships within which these goods are distributed. Anderson is particularly concerned with the relationship among fellow-citizens, and thus she develops a theory of "democratic equality." Regarding compatriots, she writes: "Negatively, people are entitled to whatever capabilities are necessary to enable them to avoid or escape entanglement in oppressive relationships. Positively, they are entitled to the capabilities necessary for functioning as an equal citizen in a democratic state." Thus, Anderson would insist that realizing the ideal of equality requires neither that Bert have no more than Ernie nor even that Ernie could have just as much as Bert if he were as talented and as willing to work. As long as Bert's privileged position does not place Ernie in an oppressive relationship, the moral ideal of equality gives us no cause to eliminate the disparity in wealth between the two.

Of course, not everyone is prepared to join Anderson in rejecting the more traditional accounts of equality. Luck egalitarians might agree with Anderson that we should condemn oppressive relationships but argue that there is more to equality than the absence of oppression. Regarding Bert and Ernie, a luck egalitarian is liable to protest that surely it remains problematic that Ernie's prospects for a rewarding life are – through no fault of his own – so much less promising than Bert's *even if these prospects will never lead to Ernie's being oppressed*. If so, then restricting our attention solely to oppressive relationships might cause us to overlook worrisome forms of inequality. Moreover, one might question how much Anderson's focus on oppression really advances the discussion since (a) "oppression" may not be a sufficiently clear notion to resolve conflicts, and (b) to the extent that it is clear, it may be parasitic on notions like rights which more traditional egalitarians endorse.

The Bounds of Justice

Assuming that justice consists of moral requirements whereas charity is morally good but not required, it is important to know where justice ends and charity begins. Exploring this issue is not only worthwhile in its own right, it is an important basis on which to evaluate theories of justice. As I will explain below, dissatisfaction with the traditional theories' accounts of the bounds of justice might lead some to adopt other approaches. A notorious difficulty for the standard theories is their divergence from ordinary moral thinking regarding the special duties we have toward those with whom we share special relationships. In particular, it is commonly presumed that while we have, at most, minimal Samaritan duties to strangers, we have much more robust obligations to friends, family members, neighbors, colleagues, and compatriots. To appreciate why many are dissatisfied with this aspect of traditional theories, consider the special obligations thought to exist among compatriots and the difficulty Rawlsians, utilitarians, and libertarians have accounting for them.

Most people believe that, while we might have minimal duties to help foreigners during times of crisis, we have much more demanding responsibilities to assist compatriots. We may have a duty to support humanitarian relief projects when other countries are struck with natural disasters, for instance, but we do not owe foreigners the same extensive welfare redistribution and social safety net which we provide to fellow citizens. Surprisingly, neither Rawls's theory, utilitarianism, nor libertarianism appears able to explain these special duties. Although some political theorists have tried to apply Rawls's methodology to international justice, his own account seems ill-equipped to shed light on redistribution between political communities because Rawls's "strains of commitment" argument requires that the bargainers in the original position assume they are designing principles to govern a self-contained community which will exist in perpetuity. In other words, because Rawls wants to ensure that the rational bargainers will not adopt too risky a strategy, he emphasizes that they are irrevocably committing themselves to whichever principles they adopt. To make this point, he requires that the bargainers understand that there is only one unit of social cooperation (i.e., they will not be able to defect later) and that the principles adopted cannot subsequently be amended if they do not like their position in society. And, if Rawls's model requires the bargainers to presume that there will be no other political states, it thereby appears incapable of explaining what type of duties might exist between these states. This utilitarianism is at odds with extending compatriots preferential treatment because, insofar as it regards each person's interests as of equal intrinsic value, it implores us to do just as much for foreigners as for compatriots. (Indeed, because utilitarians deny even that the agent's interests are more important than those of distant strangers, they often insist that we owe more to everyone – irrespective of nationality – than we currently acknowledge is due even to special relations like compatriots.) A utilitarian might counter that her theory can accommodate these special obligations because considerations of efficiency entail that everyone would be better off if each attended principally to compatriots, but efficiency would seem to justify at most attending to fellow-citizens first; it could not justify addressing the considerably less dire needs of compatriots while foreigners remain in dramatically worse shape. Libertarianism suffers from the opposite problem because, while utilitarianism seems to exaggerate the valid claims of foreigners, libertarianism appears to underappreciate the connections among compatriots. According to libertarianism, each person is at liberty to keep her property unless she freely agrees to give, trade, or sell it to someone else. Thus, unless one has agreed to transfer funds to a foreigner, one owes nothing to noncitizens. However, because most of us have not agreed to share our wealth with our fellow-citizens (indeed, this is why libertarians object so vehemently to the welfare state), libertarians cannot account for the special responsibilities thought to be owed to compatriots.

This review of the traditional theories' capacities to explain the special obligations among compatriots has been quick, but hopefully it reveals why Rawls's approach is dismissed as inapplicable, utilitarianism stands accused of demanding too much, and libertarianism is thought to require too little. Let us now turn to "associativism" and "justice as mutual advantage," two distinctive accounts of justice which some tout as better able to explain the moral importance of special relations.

Associativists (sometimes called "particularists") urge us to recognize that relational facts have a basic moral significance; on their view, I have special obligations to my sister Lesley, and we need look no further than the fact that she is my sister to explain these extra duties. We need not tell sophisticated stories about the quasi-contractual nature of sibling relationships, for example, to explain why our connection is morally significant because any relationship wherein the parties identify with one another generates special moral obligations (Miller; Tamir). This view accords nicely with our conviction that there are special obligations among family, friends, colleagues, co-nationals and compatriots because we typically identify with these associates. In other words, we feel connected to these associates in such a way that, among other things, we root for them to flourish and feel proud when they succeed or ashamed when they fail.

Associativists can cite at least three reasons to regard relationships between those who identify with one another as morally basic. First and most obviously, this approach does a better job than the standard accounts of matching our commonsense conviction that we owe more to our special relations. Second, associativism offers a direct connection between our motivations and moral requirements: given our personal investment in those with whom we identify, we have extra motivation to sacrifice on behalf of our associates, so associativism has a built-in mechanism linking our obligations to our motivations. Finally, associativists suggest that treating relational facts as morally basic accords with our moral phenomenology because it seems as though the mere fact that Lesley is my sister is what is morally significant. That is, even if we could tell a plausible story about how overall happiness is maximized when people attend principally to their siblings or about how there is a sense in which siblings can be said to have contracted with one another for special treatment, these accounts seem beside the moral point. To most of us, it is simply the fact that Lesley is my sister, and not these elaborate stories, which matters morally (Williams).

Although associativism accords well with our sentiments regarding the bounds of justice, it has other features which are more problematic. For starters, while it is plausible that those who identify with one another will be more likely to sacrifice on each other's behalf, it is not clear why it follows from this that they are specially obligated to do so. Until someone explains why the former, *psychological* claim should lead us to accept the latter, *ethical* assertion, skepticism seems warranted. Additional problems emerge because awkward implications can be derived from the principle that the relationships with which we identify generate special moral duties. Consider two examples. First, many sports fans fervently identify with a given team (just as most citizens identify with their country and compatriots), but we would hesitate to conclude that sports fans have special duties to support their team. (We might criticize a "fair weather fan" for capriciously turning her back on "her" team as soon as it loses, but here we indict her *character* rather than charge her with disrespecting a duty of *justice*.) A second, less benign example is the racist or sexist person who identifies with other whites or with men. Given that we would be loath to say that a white supremacist has extra duties toward other whites or that a misogynist has special obligations to other men, we ought not to embrace the view that all personal identifications create duties. Thus, while associativism conveniently matches our understanding of the bounds of justice, many find it unacceptable for other reasons (Wellman).

A second approach with promise on this score is "justice as mutual advantage," the view that justice is the set of those rules we would rationally follow for our own mutual advantage. On this view, the reason that justice includes prohibitions against lying, stealing, and killing, for example, is because each of us is better off speaking truthfully, respecting others' property rights, and refraining from killing others as long as everyone else follows these same rules. The principal attraction of this approach is its apparent ability to answer the question: "Why be just?" Most theories struggle mightily to explain the rationality of acting justly, but mutual-advantage theorists cite the benefits of reciprocity as the straightforward answer (Hobbes; Gauthier). Obeying the rules of justice admittedly involves opportunity costs, but these are more than outweighed by the benefits each person receives from others respecting the same rules. In other words, while there are disadvantages to not lying, stealing, and killing, they do not compare to the great advantages of living in a community wherein others also do not lie, steal, or kill.

While many champion this approach for its ability to explain the rationality of justice, it might also be applauded for its compatibility with the special duties thought to exist among special relations. A core tenet of justice as mutual advantage is that each person's fair share of the benefits of justice depends on her contributing to the production of these benefits via her own cooperation. Given this emphasis on reciprocity, it is not difficult to see how justice as mutual advantage is well positioned to explain the extra duties we owe to our special relations. We owe more to compatriots than to foreigners, for instance, because our compatriots sacrifice reciprocally for us, and we might owe our colleagues special consideration only because they extend us the same extra concern. Indeed, justice as mutual advantage seems ideally suited to explain the extra duties among special relations because, the closer the association, the greater the consideration generally reciprocated.

Although mutual-advantage theory is in good shape regarding special relations, many object that it does not really demonstrate the rationality of being just; rather, it can show only why it is rational to *appear* just (since others are more likely to treat you justly as long as they *believe* that you are reciprocating). Moreover, justice as mutual advantage does considerably less well matching our convictions regarding other boundaries of justice. Most problematically, it appears to leave those who cannot reciprocate entirely beyond the scope of protection. Someone both unable to contribute to the social surplus and incapable of threatening others, for instance, would not be protected by justice because it is to no one's advantage to contract with her. Similar conclusions apply to nonhuman animals and persons mentally incapable of committing to rules. These implications undermine justice as mutual advantage because they go well beyond suggesting that these people deserve no special treatment; this theory implies that, because these parties cannot reciprocate, it is not possible to treat them unjustly. Thus, even if the powerful wanted to do something horrific like torture these people merely for the sake of amusement, justice as mutual advantage appears incapable of explaining the injustice of doing so.

Given that the traditional theories conflict with our common convictions about the bounds of justice and that neither associativism nor justice as mutual advantage offers a fully satisfactory alternative, it is not clear how to proceed. Some theorists suggest that we must revise our pretheoretic beliefs about the special obligations thought to exist among our associates, but most are unwilling to abandon these judgments. Those who cling to our commonsense convictions have much work to do, but perhaps Elizabeth Anderson's insights point to a fruitful strategy. Recall that Anderson develops a relational theory of equality inspired by her conviction that the chief evil of inequality is its role in creating socially oppressive relationships. If Anderson is on track, it may help explain why we owe more to those with whom we share special relationships. Specifically, given that the moral significance of an inequality will depend on the nature of the relationship between the haves and have-nots, there might be greater cause for concern about the same inequalities when they exist among compatriots rather than foreigners or if they obtain between spouses as opposed to strangers. Clearly much of this story remains to be told, but it offers hope to those inclined to defend the commonsense conviction that justice requires we do more for our associates.

I have cited the special obligations among compatriots in this section to illustrate the difficulties various theories have accommodating our ordinary moral thinking about the bounds of justice, but it is worth pausing to note that this example is also emblematic of our limited understanding of international justice in general. Political theorists are increasingly focusing their attention on this subject, but the returns to this point have been modest because so many of our theoretical models are designed explicitly to speak to justice within a given political unit. Not only has there been too little systematic thinking about the responsibilities among states, political theorists are just beginning to face up to the fact that some of our most important international obligations are to non-sovereign entities such as oppressed minorities, and even imperiled individuals who are either neglected or actively persecuted by their own states. Once one questions the sanctity of each state's sovereignty over its territory – as international lawyers are beginning to do – one recognizes that our old moral road-maps may not be reliable. Matters are further complicated by the emergence of non-governmental organizations and international alliances like NATO and the United Nations, which now compete with states for the lead roles in the international drama. Finally, when one considers the extent to which increased economic and cultural interaction has eroded the significance of political sovereignty, it becomes clear how ill-equipped the traditional political models are for negotiating contemporary international politics. Of course, these same conditions make it an exhilarating time to be a student of global justice, but it is not for those uncomfortable working outside the traditional paradigms.

Beyond Justice as Distribution

Thus far I have interpreted justice solely in terms of the distribution of social benefits and burdens. Although this interpretation is not uncommon, it is important to recognize that some contest the distributive paradigm. In this final section I will first look briefly at the controversy over minority cultural group rights and its implications for understanding justice, and will then review the work of Iris Marion Young, a prominent critic of the distributive paradigm.

In light of the increasingly emphatic demands of minority groups, political theorists have recently turned their attention to the issue of cultural group rights. Following the lead of authors like Will Kymlicka and Allen Buchanan, many now believe that the best conceptions of justice provide room for some groups to have special collective rights designed to help strengthen and preserve their cultures. The basic idea here is that, because theorists like Rawls insist that justice requires that each person have an equal opportunity to lead a life of self-respect, and because one's self-respect depends crucially upon the health of the culture with which one identifies, no adequate theory of justice can ignore the health of minority cultures. Drawing on this type of reasoning, theorists increasingly allege that various groups should be extended special collective language and property rights, for instance, which give them dominion over the official languages to be used in schools and municipal buildings or over who may own property within a specified territory. Whether or not one is sympathetic to these types of group rights, it is interesting to note that the demands being made by cultural minorities (and the special rights being proposed as solutions) do not on their face fit neatly within the distributive model. To fully appreciate this point, consider the work of Iris Young.

Young begins her analysis with the grievances of victims of injustice and then concludes that these demands cannot be adequately addressed by simply redistributing the benefits and burdens among individuals in a society. Reviewing the claims of various social-justice movements leads Young to conceive of injustice in terms of oppression and domination, where oppression is understood to have the five faces of exploitation, marginalization, powerlessness, cultural imperialism, and violence. Especially key is her contention that people are oppressed not as individuals but as members of groups. Young's analysis of violence nicely illustrates her point. She writes:

> What makes violence a face of oppression is less the particular acts themselves, though these are often utterly horrible, than the social context surrounding them, which makes them possible and even acceptable. . . . Violence is systemic because it is directed at members of a group simply because they are members of that group. Any woman, for example, has a reason to fear rape. Regardless of what a Black man has done to escape the oppression of marginality or powerlessness, he lives knowing he is subject to attack or harassment. The oppression of violence consists not only in direct victimization, but in the daily knowledge shared by all members of oppressed groups that they are liable to violation, solely on account of their group identity. Just living under such a threat of attack on oneself or family or friends deprives the oppressed of freedom and dignity, and needlessly expends their energy. (Young, pp. 61–2)

Young urges us to reform those pervasive social institutions which permit or even encourage violence against specific groups, and she emphasizes that the necessary changes would involve much more than merely redistributing goods between various individuals in society. Among other things, they would require measures such as reforming those media like television, movies and pornography which play such a prominent role in producing the stereotypes and images that shape how we understand ourselves and each other.

In the end, Young's main dissatisfaction with the distributive paradigm is twofold. First, by focusing so narrowly on material goods, the distributive paradigm neglects important matters concerning power relations within the social context, which often determine the ultimate patterns of distribution. Second, when theorists try to expand the distributive paradigm beyond material things to other crucial goods, they tend to misrepresent these nonmaterial social goods as though they were static, material things which could be distributed in a manner akin to the way we divvy up income.

Young's attack on the distributive paradigm has been influential, but critics contend that, even if portions of her critique are right on target, it does not follow that the entire distributive model must be jettisoned. For instance, two of Young's strongest points are that: (1) justice involves much more than material goods, and (2) individuals are often oppressed as members of groups. But advocates of the distributive model could seemingly accept both of these claims without abandoning their overall approach. One might argue that Young's points demonstrate only that we must be aware of the distribution of nonmaterial goods like cultural influence and political power and that we need to be vigilant as to how these and other goods are distributed among groups. Of course, Young believes that we necessarily misrepresent these nonmaterial goods when we try to distribute them like income, but defenders of the distributive paradigm object that there is nothing about their model which requires one to treat all goods as akin to income or other material goods. Thus, while many join Young in rejecting the distributive paradigm, others claim that there is ample room to incorporate Young's most important insights into more sophisticated distributive models, which attend to nonmaterial goods and their distribution among groups.

Conclusion

Readers may be disappointed that I have not touted one theory of justice as uniquely correct. As much as I would like to single out one account as fully adequate, I must confess that I find many of the standard objections compelling. All of the traditional approaches have attractive elements (indeed, they would not have garnered such broad support unless they had captured important insights), but each wrongly supposes that its kernel of truth can tell the whole story. As a staunch defender of the importance of individual self-determination and individual responsibility, I am drawn to libertarianism, but it strikes me that there is insufficient reason to conclude that our rights must trump all claims which do not also stem from the core value of liberty; conversely, while utilitarianism is surely right that the welfare of others creates moral reasons for us to act, it just seems wrong-headed to conclude that future welfare is all that matters morally. Assuming that no existing theory is beyond criticism, where do we go from here?

I suspect that there are no simple answers to this question, but, for several reasons, I think we would do well to follow the lead of Elizabeth Anderson, Michael Walzer, and Iris Young. First, just as Anderson was able to advance the discussion of equality by refocusing on why we worry about inequality, it strikes me that the best way to better understand justice is to become more clear about why we care about injustice, and the best way to do this is to come out of our academic libraries and listen carefully to what actual victims of injustice are saying. In this regard, Young's work stands as a shining example of how the best theories of justice can be crafted only if we remain sensitive to the actual frustrations of those who long for justice. Another reason to take our cue from Young's work is that, like Walzer, she does not give excessive priority to theoretical simplicity. Given that justice rears its head in many forms, it should come as no surprise that Young concludes that oppression has multiple faces. It is striking, however, that – just as Walzer eschews a simple approach in favor of his pluralistic account – Young does not assume that all the faces must belong to a single, many-headed beast. In other words, Young does not insist that one face is basic and the others are derivative, nor does she presume that all must be explained in terms of the same value. While the appeal of building elegant theories which explain all of injustice in terms of a solitary value is understandable, Young is content to stay with a messy, multi-pronged approach. As a consequence, Young's account is neither as elegant nor as clean as many would like, but it has the much more important advantage of being truer to the regrettable facts of injustice. And if so, her theory stands a better chance of showing the way toward an accurate theory of justice and, most importantly, toward the promotion of justice in the real world.

Ultimately I remain hopeful that substantial progress can be made on the question of justice, but it strikes me that we must return to the traditional approaches with a new attitude. Rather than selecting a pet value and ignoring all others, we need to appreciate the real insights which attract people to each of these standard theories and then remain open to combining these various insights into a new whole. Above all, we should resist the temptation to assemble them in an over-simplified fashion. Injustice is not only lamentably pervasive, it is theoretically messy, so perhaps our best chance of explaining justice will come only when we can be content with a similarly untidy, pluralistic account of justice. Seventy years ago, W. D. Ross wrote the following in defense of his positing multiple, non-derivative sources of prima facie duties: "Loyalty to the facts is worth more than a symmetrical architectonic or a hastily reached simplicity" (Ross, p. 23). The preceding survey of contemporary theories of justice convinces me that students of justice would do well to embrace his sentiment.

Acknowledgments

I am grateful to Brad Champion, Peter Lindsay, Tim Renick, Eric Rovie, Robert Simon, and Andrew Valls for helpful comments on an earlier draft of this essay.

References

Anderson, Elizabeth S. (1999). "What is the Point of Equality?" *Ethics*, 109: 287–338.

Bentham, Jeremy (1988). *The Principles of Morals and Legislation*. Amherst, NY: Prometheus Books.

Buchanan, Allen (1988). *Ethics, Efficiency, and the Market*. Totowa, NJ: Rowan and Littlefield.

——(1991). *Secession: The Morality of Political Divorce from Fort Sumter to Lithuania and Quebec*. Boulder: Westview Press.

Cohen, G. A. (1978). "Robert Nozick and Wilt Chamberlain: How Patterns Preserve Liberty." In *Justice and Economic Distribution*, ed. J. Arthur and W. H. Shaw. Englewood Cliffs, NJ: Prentice-Hall.

Dworkin, Ronald (c. 1975). "The Original Position." In *Reading Rawls*, ed. Norman Daniels. New York: Basic Books.

——(1981a). "What is Equality? Part 1: Equality of Welfare." *Philosophy and Public Affairs*, 10: 185–246.

——(1981b). "What is Equality? Part 2: Equality of Resources." *Philosophy and Public Affairs*, 10: 283–345.

Gauthier, David (1986). *Morals By Agreement*. Oxford. Clarendon Press.

Hardin, Russell (1988). *Morality Within the Limits of Reason*. Chicago: University of Chicago Press.

Hare, R. M. (1981). *Moral Thinking*. Oxford: Clarendon Press.

Hobbes, T. (1990). *Leviathan* (1651), ed. Richard Tuck. Cambridge: Cambridge University Press.

Kymlicka, Will (1989). *Liberalism, Community, and Culture*. Oxford: Clarendon Press.

——(1995). *Multicultural Citizenship: A Liberal Theory of Minority Rights*. Oxford: Clarendon Press.

Locke, John (1988). *Two Treatises of Government*, ed. Peter Laslett. Cambridge: Cambridge University Press.

Mill, John Stuart (1979). *Utilitarianism*, ed. George Sher. Indianapolis: Hackett.

Miller, David (1995). *On Nationality*. Oxford: Clarendon Press.

Nozick, Robert (1974). *Anarchy, State and Utopia*. New York: Basic Books.

Rawls, John (1971). *A Theory of Justice*. Cambridge, MA: Belknap Press.

——(1993). *Political Liberalism*. New York: Columbia University Press.

Ross, W. D. (1988). *The Right and the Good*. Indianapolis: Hackett.

Schmidtz, David and Robert E. Goodin (1998). *Social Welfare and Individual Responsibility*. Cambridge: Cambridge University Press.

Singer, Peter (1972). "Famine, Affluence, and Morality." *Philosophy and Public Affairs*, 1: 229–43.

Smart, J. J. C. and Bernard Williams (1963). *Utilitarianism: For and Against*. Cambridge: Cambridge University Press.

Tamir, Yael (1993). *Liberal Nationalism*. Princeton, NJ: Princeton University Press.

Walzer, Michael (1983). *Spheres of Justice: A Defense of Pluralism and Equality*. New York: Basic Books.

Wellman, Christopher Heath (2000). "Relational Facts in Liberal Political Theory: Is There Magic in the Pronoun 'My'?" *Ethics*, 110: 537–62.

Williams, Bernard (1981). *Moral Luck*. Cambridge: Cambridge University Press.

Young, Iris Marion (1990). *Justice and the Politics of Difference*. Princeton, NJ: Princeton University Press.

Chapter 4

Equality

Richard J. Arneson

The ideal of equality requires that everyone have the same, or be treated the same. The ideal takes many different forms corresponding to the different ways in which it might be thought important to treat people equally or render them equal. Any such ideal of equality expresses an underlying conception of the equal basic worth and dignity of human persons. At this level egalitarianism opposes elitist, aristocratic, racist, and other views that assert that some persons are inherently superior to others. The various ideals of equality also to some extent oppose one another, since rendering people the same or treating them the same in one respect can induce inequality in other respects.

Equality of Lockean Rights

Writing in 1690, John Locke asserts that in order to understand the conditions under which claims to political authority are justified, we should think about a prepolitical situation, the "state all men are naturally in." This prepolitical situation is a

> state also of equality, wherein all the power and jurisdiction is reciprocal, no one having more than another: there being nothing more evident than that creatures of the same species and rank, promiscuously born to all the same advantages of nature, and the use of the same faculties, should also be equal one amongst another without subordination or subjection.[1]

God might legitimately order an end to this natural moral equality, Locke acknowledges. But he adds that God does not in fact do this, so the presumption of moral equality stands.

Locke is arguing for limited government and against the claims of kings to unlimited legitimate authority over their subjects. Every individual has rights which even kings must respect. According to Locke, we are all normatively equal in that we possess the same rights, which should equally always be respected. Locke also gestures vaguely at a claim that the basis of this moral equality is that human individuals are roughly equal in their natural powers and talents. Locke was not alone in asserting that all individuals have natural moral rights, but he is one of the first exponents of this idea, which has continuing vitality in contemporary political thought.

Natural moral rights are rights one has independently of social arrangements or human conventions. To say one has a right is to say that people ought to behave in ways that respect the right. In this sense one can have a right to one's property even if the king's agents seize it and do so by authority of law, and one can have a right not to be jailed for one's religious beliefs even if public opinion and entrenched social practices unite in favor of the Inquisition (and even if the person being jailed thinks no wrong is being done to her). A moral right is a claim, pertaining to an individual, that society (other people) ought to honor.

Rights might be interpreted as waivable or nonwaivable, forfeitable or nonforfeitable, alienable or inalienable. One alienates a right by transferring it to another person. One forfeits a right by doing something morally wrong that entirely or partially nullifies a right one would otherwise have. One waives a right by permitting a person to do what the right would forbid, absent one's consent. In the Lockean tradition natural rights are thought to be forfeitable. Whether or not they are alienable or waivable tends to be controversial. (Can I legitimately consent to becoming the slave of another?)

The Lockean tradition is associated with a view that assigns a certain content to natural rights. Very roughly, one's basic natural rights are (1) to act in whatever way one chooses with whatever one legitimately owns so long as one does not thereby harm others in certain ways, and (2) not to be harmed by others in those certain ways. The Lockean view asserts as a further basic premise that each person is the rightful full owner of herself, and it is thought that one can derive strong permanent rights of private property in land and moveable goods from these basic premises. In contemporary political thought, advocates of a view of natural rights akin to Locke's are sometimes referred to as libertarians or classical liberals.[2]

An important ambiguity should be noted. The Lockean position holds that all human persons have the same basic natural moral rights, but does not thereby place a value on bringing about the condition in which everyone's rights are fulfilled to the same extent. For the Lockean, rights are viewed as constraints on the set of actions among which one is morally free to choose, and not as goals to be promoted in whatever way is most effective.[3] This means that even if I can bring it about that several people's right not to be murdered or unjustly imprisoned can be safeguarded if I murder or unjustly imprison one person, according to the Lockean, morality forbids me to violate anyone's rights, even to bring it about that the outcome is greater rights fulfillment or a more equal overall rights fulfillment on the whole.

Democratic Equality

The ideal of a democratic political order contains an ideal of equal citizenship. In a democracy, each citizen has the equal right to vote and to stand for public office in free elections. A free election is one held against a background of freedom of expression. All votes count equally and the winner gains a majority (or plurality) of votes. In a democracy, power to name public officials is controlled directly or indirectly by majority rule of the people, and laws that are enforced on the populace are chosen either directly or indirectly by a majority-rule process. In an indirectly democratic lawmaking process, citizens elect lawmakers, who then choose laws.

The ideal of equal democratic citizenship is opposed to the view that a king or aristocracy or communist elite is entitled to exercise political rule. It is also opposed to denial of full citizenship rights to any adult resident of a society in virtue of the individual's sex, skin color, supposed race, ethnicity, religious affiliation, and so on.

Equality of Opportunity

In William Shakespeare's play *King Lear*, Edmund complains,

> . . . Wherefore should I
> Stand in the plague of custom, and permit
> The curiosity of nations to deprive me,
> For that I am some twelve or fourteen moonshines
> Lag of a brother? Why bastard? Wherefore base?
> When my dimensions are as well compact,
> My mind as generous, and my shape as true,
> As honest madam's issue?
>
> (I.2.2–9)

Edmund is a villain, but he has a point. An accident of birth quite beyond the child's capacity to control determines whether he is legitimate or a bastard. Why should ascribed status of this kind prevent a person from rising in the world, or falling, according to his personal traits as they are assessed by others, and by their expression in his actions that bear good fruit or bad? The principle to which the resentful illegitimate son appeals points beyond feudal hierarchy to modern society, from status to contract to meritocracy. Shakespeare here alludes to a significant ideal of equality, though it is not one to which the playwright himself subscribes. The ideal is formal equality of opportunity, also known as careers open to talents.

Formal equality of opportunity (FEO) holds that jobs in private firms and in government service, and opportunities to borrow capital from lending institutions, should be open to all applicants, and applications should be assessed on their merits and the position or opportunity offered to the most qualified. The principle can also be applied to education: places for students in educational institutions should be open to all applicants, applications should be assessed on their merits, and the places should be offered to the most qualified (whose enrollment may be made contingent on payment of fees). The relevant qualifications for a post are traits in applicants that render it the case that their performance in that post would better promote the morally innocent goals of the firm or agency than would the performance of other applicants. For firms operating in a market economy, the normal goal to be promoted is the maximization of the firm's profits, and similarly the best applicant for a loan is the one to whom granting the loan would maximize the expected profits of the lender. The importance of requiring that loans of capital be made to the most qualified applicants is to ensure that not only employment but also the opportunity to start and operate a private business is regulated by FEO.

FEO is an antifeudal, anticaste principle. It forbids the reservation of office and positions or privilege to members of a hereditary elite group, be it an aristocracy, a superior caste, a hierarchy based on skin color, or the like. It equally forbids the reservation of office and privilege to members of a religion or cultural group that anyone is free to join, as for example in a regime that discriminates in favor of Christians and against Jews.

The spirit of the ideal of careers open to talents calls for a society in which racial, religious, ethnic, sexual, and similar forms of prejudice and bigotry do not hamper anyone's pursuit and attainment of desirable positions in the economy and government. Evidently the principle needs some tinkering if its letter is to correspond to this spirit. Imagine a society like the segregated US South of the Jim Crow era except that the pattern of segregation is maintained by cultural norms rather than by legal enactments. If consumers are bigoted, and prefer not to purchase merchandise and services unless the skilled high-paid labor embodied in these goods is done entirely by white males, even if goods produced by the skilled labor of blacks and women would be cheaper and better, then profit-maximizing firms in a competitive market setting will find that hiring white males only, for necessary skilled jobs yields higher profits. White male applicants will then be more highly qualified than other applicants for these skilled jobs, since their performance in these jobs would boost sales and profits. But the spirit of FEO or careers open to talents is evidently violated in this imagined scenario. Some refinement of the idea of being qualified for a position is evidently needed.

The principle of careers open to talents conflicts with the prerogatives of private ownership of property as usually understood. If I own something, I can do what I like with it, so long as I do not thereby harm nonconsenting others in certain ways, e.g., by assaulting them. So if I own a factory, I am free to hire my unqualified brother-in-law if I choose, or to hire only my friends, or fellow members of my religious congregation, or to hire on some whimsical basis. Allowing careers open to talents limits the right of property owners to do whatever they please with it if the property provides employment opportunities or is loaned by a bank.

The anticaste implications of careers open to talents extend just so far. FEO requires that anyone may apply for a post or opportunity and that the most qualified is chosen, but it imposes no constraints on the processes by which people become qualified. It could turn out that for no desirable job in a society can anyone become qualified except by means of expensive socialization and education and that only a small segment of society can afford the necessary socialization and education. In this state of affairs there is equal opportunity for the equally qualified, as required by careers open to talents, but opportunities to become qualified are very unequally distributed.

Notice that a public school system funded by general taxation and available to all children in a society at no cost reflects a move in the direction of ensuring that each child has some opportunity to develop her native talents and become qualified for desirable posts. State enforcement of minimally adequate standards of childrearing by parents and legal guardians also moves in this same direction.

A society might go further in the direction of equalizing the opportunity to become qualified according to one's native talent than operating public schools for all children. It might provide extra educational resources targeted toward those whose parents are either less able or less willing than the average parent to provide a nurturing and stimulating home environment for their children.

John Rawls has proposed a principle of equality of fair opportunity that in effect requires public education and state-provided educational resources targeted at the educationally deprived to be extended to the point at which they fully compensate for any deficits in parental upbringing efforts.[4] Equality of fair opportunity is satisfied in a society just in case any two adults who have the same native talent and abilities and the same ambition will have the same prospect of success in competitions for positions that confer advantages in the society. This norm requires that if a child born to impoverished parents has the same talent and ambition to be a highly paid lawyer as a child born to wealthy and socially well connected parents, each individual will face the same prospect of becoming a highly paid lawyer. In the society that satisfies this Rawlsian ideal, the advantages of wealth and class and social connections are entirely nullified, so that parents exert no net impact on their children's prospects of competitive success except via the mechanism of genetic inheritance.

Since parents and other family members are strongly inclined to use whatever superior advantages they possess to give family children greater than average access to favorable educational and socializing experiences and hence better prospects to obtain competitive success than other children, it is difficult to envisage a society in which Rawls's equality of fair opportunity is fulfilled or even closely approximated.

Equality of Condition

Some modern market economies may come tolerably close to achieving the ideal of careers open to talents, though none comes remotely close to the Rawlsian classless ideal of equality of fair opportunity. In thought one can transcend these limits, and imagine a society that perfectly fulfills both formal and Rawlsian equality of opportunity. This utopia of equal opportunity would still be regarded as objectionable from the standpoint of another range of ideals of equality. The idea of a perfect Rawlsian meritocracy by itself sets no limits on the superior advantages and privileges that accrue to those who win the fair competitions and contests and are either chosen for the positions that yield these advantages or succeed in entrepreneurial ventures. Writing about careers open to talents, R. H. Tawney raises doubts and worries that would apply even in a perfect meritocracy:

> So the doctrine which throws all its emphasis on the importance of opening avenues to individual advancement is partial and one-sided. It is right in insisting on the necessity of opening a free career to aspiring talent; it is wrong in suggesting that opportunities to rise, which can, of their very nature, be seized only by the few, are a substitute for a general diffusion of the means of civilization, which are needed by all men, whether they rise or not, and which those who cannot climb the economic ladder, and who sometimes, indeed, do not aspire to climb it, may turn to as good account as those who can.[5]

Along with advocating a radical extension of the ideal of equality of opportunity, Rawls also suggests that social justice includes a principle that regulates the general diffusion of the means of civilization.

When there is a general diffusion of the means of civilization, those who formerly had less than an average share of these means will get more of them. This does not necessarily imply movement toward equal holdings of these means. With economic growth, the poor can become richer while the rich are becoming even richer at a faster rate. With constant or declining means, their greater diffusion does imply a trend toward equality of condition.

Equality of condition admits of different interpretations. Recent discussions in the theory of justice work to clarify the varieties of equal condition and to explore which variety, if any, is morally attractive. This is the "equality of what?" issue.

The "equality of what?" issue that is the focus of this section should be distinguished from another issue, one about measurement. Suppose we have decided that people should be made equal in some particular aspect of their condition. The next question is, for any such account of the relevant aspect, how can one measure people's condition in this respect, so as to determine when a distribution is equal and when it is unequal? Even if it is assumed that the chosen equalizandum admits of cardinal interpersonal comparison, so that in principle one can say who has more and who has less and by what extent the person with more exceeds the score of the person with less, all of this still leaves open the question of how far a given distribution that is unequal departs from the ideal of equality. Suppose for simplicity that it is deemed that people should ideally be equal in bank account wealth, so that determining how much such wealth each person has poses no difficulty in principle. There are evidently different ways of measuring how far a given distribution that is unequal departs from equality. Which to choose?

The discussion to follow bypasses this issue by assuming implicitly that it is possible to determine not only whether a given distribution of goods among a given set of persons is equal or not but also the degree to which it deviates from strict equality if it is unequal. Yet it is not obvious how to measure degrees of inequality. Economists and others have proposed various ways of measuring inequality, but it is not clear that the ordinary idea of people having the same or equal shares includes a determinate notion of degrees of inequality.[6]

One might think that equality is equality, and that's that. When people have equal holdings, their holdings are the same, or identical. What is the fuss about?

But whether or not a distribution is equal is relative to a description of it. If a stock of large trousers is distributed to stout Smith and thin Jones, and they receive the same number of trousers, the distribution is equal in that respect. But Smith has received four pairs of pants that fit, and Jones got none, so in that respect the distribution is unequal. To get a clear position on the table for debate, the advocate of equality needs to specify a conception of equality.

The discussion in the remainder of this section presupposes that native talent itself is unequally distributed and that some unfortunate individuals will have very little of it. The task for justice is then to compensate the given individual for lack of talent in some way deemed appropriate. We might just mention that further thought is needed to the extent that developing medical technology brings it about that the genetic inheritance of talents and traits can itself be altered by alteration of the sperm and egg material that unites to form a new individual.[7] In this scenario one might extend the scope of justice so it specifies not only required compensation for given individuals with their native talents but also obligations concerning what sorts of individuals with what sorts of native talents may be brought into existence.

Economic equality

Consider then the proposal that other things being equal, it is morally good that people have equal amounts of money (purchasing power over tradeable goods) or equivalently that tradeable goods are divided into identical lots, one for each person, which the recipient is then free to trade. In this exercise goods are distinguished until each one is homogeneous in quality, and it is assumed each such good can be divided as finely as one chooses.

Of this sort of economic egalitarianism, Michael Walzer has observed that it is an ideal "ripe for betrayal."[8] What he has in mind is that it would not be stable over time. If equality is established on one day, individuals will choose to do various things with their resource shares, so that soon the cumulative impact of people's choices to trade and deal, consume and save, will yield economic inequality, which the ensemble of individuals' choices will have no tendency to restore. One could clamp restraints on individual choice in order to prevent inequality from emerging from initial equality, but any serious attempt to sustain equality would require a massively coercive state apparatus and would institute, according to Walzer, another and worse form of inequality. This would be inequality of political power between those who control the enforcing state that clamps restraints and the individuals on whom restraints are clamped. Robert Nozick makes a similar objection against the ideal of economic equality. He stresses that maintenance of equality (or any other distributive pattern for that matter) would require what in his view would be continuous wrongful violation of people's Lockean rights.

These objections are resistible. In the absence of a compelling argument that Lockean rights have priority over competing moral values, the conflict between equality and Lockean rights is not fatal to the claim that equality should prevail. Moreover, one might favor equality of condition among other values, and hold that on balance some economic inequality is acceptable but extreme inequality is not. The looser the requirements of equality that one favors, the less tight need be the constraints on individuals needed to sustain it. Also, social-scientific ingenuity might discover ways to avoid extreme inequality that do not involve excessively invasive interference with individual liberty. For a simple example, one might combine progressive income taxation with an estate tax that breaks up large fortunes at the death of the wealthy person. Finally, the extent to which people experience limits on their freedom as onerous depends to a considerable extent on the degree to which they see the constraints as efficiently advancing goals they support. For example, traffic laws involve extensive and continuous interference with the liberty of car drivers, but as these rules efficiently help to sustain the flow of traffic, few experience them as oppressive. If people regarded economic equality as very valuable, and saw that certain limits on liberty were needed to sustain equality, and worth their cost, they would not balk at the restrictions. If one pictures egalitarian laws as bearing down on people who care nothing for equality, of course the laws will seem tyrannical. The issue then is whether economic equality is or is not per se significantly morally desirable.

A reason for doubting that economic equality is desirable in and of itself emerges once one reflects on the way that individuals with very different traits, abilities, and susceptibilities would find themselves having very unequal real freedom in a regime of equality of income and wealth. Consider Smith and Jones, who have equal initial allotments of money. Smith is unintelligent, blind, legless, and lacks natural charm. Jones is intelligent, and has normal eyesight, sound legs, and lots of natural charm. With equal money the two individuals will face very unequal life prospects, very unequal opportunity to lead whatever sort of life they might want to lead. In light of this example, one might doubt that economic equality is important, except perhaps sometimes as a means to some further goal that does matter for its own sake. People want money and material goods for what the goods can do to help satisfy their aims and desires. These goods are generally not valued for their own sake, so why regard equality in people's holdings of these goods as inherently desirable?

Equality of functioning capabilities

Pursuing this line of thought, Amartya Sen proposes that we should care about what individuals are enabled to be and do with the resources they possess, given their other circumstances. These beings and doings Sen calls "functionings," and what matters is the freedom or capability that people have to gain functionings that are significant, that they have reason to value.[9] If we care about equality of condition, the equality that is morally attractive is equality in people's capability to function in significant ways. To take a simple example, if the functioning of concern is being adequately nourished, different amounts of resources would have to be made available to a thin man, a stout man, an individual doing daily hard physical labor, a lactating woman, and so on.

Having the capability to function in a certain way is having real as opposed to formal freedom to gain that functioning. I am formally free to go to Paris if no law prevents me from going and no one would interfere with an attempt I might make to go there. Having formal freedom so construed is compatible with my not actually being able to go to Paris, because I lack the money to pay for a plane ticket and the strength to swim the Atlantic. If I have the real freedom or capability to go to Paris, then if I choose to go there, I can get there.

The capability interpretation of equality raises several issues. One question is why the norm of equality should be deemed to be satisfied if people have the freedom to function in a certain way rather than if people reach the relevant functioning. Why focus on capability rather than functioning? Suppose that a group of people is enabled to attain a multitude of enormously valuable functionings, achieving some of which would constitute a wonderful life. However, it turns out that everyone fritters away their capabilities, or deliberately turns their back on them. In the end, though people have a high level of capability, they have a zero level of functioning. One might take the position that just as one does not generally care for resources for their own sake, but for what one can do with them, so one generally cares for freedom not for its own sake but for the good outcomes to which the exercise of freedom is expected to be instrumental. If I am given the freedom to order what I like from a varied menu, I am more likely to get a meal I enjoy than if one set of dishes is simply imposed on me. But if one cares for freedom for this reason, one's care should evaporate in cases where having freedom does not promote getting to desired outcomes. If focus on economic resources as though they were intrinsically valuable is fetishistic, perhaps focusing on real freedom as though it were intrinsically valuable is also fetishistic.

One response to this doubt about the importance of capability is to note that many people do indeed care about having wide individual freedom, many options available to choose from, for its own sake, and not merely for the goods that the exercise of freedom can bring. A second response is to hold that the theory of justice assigns limited responsibility to society – all of us regarded together – for the well-being and life outcomes that any adult member of society reaches. At most, society is responsible for placing people so that they can live a valuable and worthy life if they choose to do so and act on their choice. Given adequate real freedom or capability to function, the individual herself is responsible for the choices she makes and the quality of the life she comes to lead.

Regarding this second response, one might worry that the idea of a limited responsibility or obligation of society to provide individuals a good quality of life is not adequately captured in the capability approach, at least as stated so far. Consider an individual in an affluent and ordered society who receives along with all other members of society an equal capability to function in a variety of significant ways. Now suppose the individual negligently squanders or fritters away the resources and opportunities that provided her this equal capability. She then no longer has an equal capability. If justice or fundamental moral principles require that each person in society be sustained in equality of capability to function, then justice requires the channeling of further resources to this negligent individual, to restore her to a position of capability equal to that enjoyed by others. But we can imagine this process being repeated over and over. Surely at some point the responsibility of society gives out and it is morally acceptable to say to the person who now lacks equality of capability, "You had your chance. Society bears no further responsibility to sustain you in equality of capability on a par with those who have made sensible use of their opportunities."

Of course, one could harness an account of personal responsibility – an account of the proper division of obligation and responsibility between individual and society – to the capability approach. In such an account the obligation to sustain equal capability for all would be limited somehow by considerations of personal responsibility. But the account of personal responsibility might just as well be harnessed to an outcome-oriented account of what egalitarian justice requires, as to a capability-oriented account. The question resurfaces, why focus on capability?

As outlined by Sen, the capability approach is noncommittal as to the comparative assessment of the functioning capabilities that might be provided to a person. But for any given individual at any time, whatever her circumstances, an indefinitely large agglomeration of capabilities will be available to her. Most will be utterly trivial, or trivial variants on some nontrivial capability. Except for cases in which one set of capabilities dominates or contains another set, one will not be able to compare different individuals' capabilities and judge that one person has more capabilities overall than another unless we have some way of assessing diverse capabilities on a common scale.

Equality of resources

Several theorists of distributive equality reject the suggestion that what we owe to one another by way of justice obligations is determined by assessing the value of people's opportunities and resources on any common scale. One basis for this rejection is the thought that in a modern society with freedom of expression and diverse culture people disagree – and, moreover, disagree reasonably – about what is ultimately valuable and worth seeking in human life. A closely related thought is that each individual has a responsibility to herself to think through for herself a conception of what is worthwhile and to develop a plan of life aimed at making something worthwhile and valuable out of this life. Society, along with the government as agency of society, owes it to each individual to leave free room for all individuals to exercise their evaluative autonomy. What we owe to each other by way of justice obligations includes this duty of respect, and the duties of concern for the well-being of individuals must be understood in a way that does not violate this duty of respect. This stance of respect for each individual's evaluative autonomy requires the state to be neutral on the question of the good life, or of what is worthwhile in human life.

Ronald Dworkin advocates neutrality on the good as just described. He also advocates a version of distributive equality.[10] It might seem that neutrality on the good precludes holding that justice requires equality in the distribution of goods, for an ideal of equality requires some measure of how well off or badly off individuals are, and any such measure, it would seem, must violate neutrality.

Dworkin has an ingenious response to this puzzle embedded in a complex account of equality that welds together the ideal of equality with an ideal of personal responsibility.

According to Dworkin, the duties of equality in its various manifestations are owed by the state – by all citizens acting through the state – to its individual citizens. Equality is owed in the public sphere, not the private sphere. A private individual may permissibly favor friends or family over others. The state, acting in the name of all citizens and coercively enforcing its rules, has a special duty to treat all its citizens with equal concern and respect. The norm of distributive equality follows from this more general duty of equal concern and respect, in the story of justice as Dworkin tells it.

Dworkin divides proposed norms of distributive equality into two families: equality of welfare and equality of resources. He develops and defends a version of the latter. Equality of welfare says that resources should be distributed so that each person's welfare or well-being is the same. The fundamental flaw in equality of welfare according to Dworkin is that any implementation of it would entangle the state in determining what is good for each individual and how to live. That violates the duty of respect the state owes to all citizens. A responsible citizen assigns to herself the task of deciding what is worthwhile and how to live her life and does not acquiesce in the assumption by the state of this fundamental individual responsibility.

According to equality of resources, people should be made equal in their resource holdings so far as their holdings are the consequence of unchosen, brute luck rather than chosen, option luck. The measure of the value of anyone's holdings is the subjective evaluation of the market. The value of a resource assigned to one person is what others would be willing to pay for it in a situation in which everyone's initial brute-luck-determined purchasing power is equal. Dworkin explains the distinction between option luck and brute luck as follows: "Option luck is a matter of how deliberate and calculated gambles turn out – whether someone gains or loses through accepting an isolated risk he or she should have anticipated and might have declined."[11]

So characterized, the distinction appears a matter of degree along three dimensions.[12] Consider a lottery or gamble with various probabilities of various payoffs. As a limit case, a lottery might contain just one payoff, that will accrue with certainty to anyone who has gambled in a particular way. (1) The lottery may be more or less avoidable by the agent. (There may be more or fewer actions the individual can take, that would avoid his taking part in the lottery.) (2) The lottery may be more or less reasonably avoidable, where the more it is the case that an individual has options that it makes sense for him to adopt, that would avoid his taking part in the lottery, the more avoidable it is. (3) And the fact that the lottery looms (that he will take part in it unless he takes some action to avoid it) might be more or less foreseeable by the agent. In the case where an individual faces a risk, but he can alter the payoffs or probabilities that he faces by an action he could choose, regard the individual as substituting one lottery for another. To decide in a given case in which an individual incurs a risk of benefit and loss whether the risk should count as option luck or brute luck and to what degree, one must weigh the three factors and pool their results to yield an overall brute luck/option luck score.

A simplified picture of a regime of equality of resources will capture the flavor of the proposal. Suppose all tradeable goods are auctioned off initially to the members of society, all of whom have equal purchasing power, and from then on they live their lives interacting on a competitive market, in which all outcomes are option luck not brute luck in their character. Then equality of resources is fulfilled for these individuals. The picture is simplified in supposing that individuals in their adult lives do not face brute luck occurrences. But a greater simplification arises from the fact that an important wrinkle in Dworkin's account of equality of resources has not been mentioned so far.

Recall the worry that equality of money or (equivalently) equality of tradeable goods is inadequate insofar as it fails to address inequalities in the native traits and abilities and susceptibilities generated for each individual by the genetic lottery. (For convenience I use the term *talents* for all three of traits, abilities, and susceptibilities.) Dworkin meets this worry straightforwardly. He proposes that we consider an individual's talents to be resources that help her achieve her aims and ambitions. But these resources are not like others. One cannot transfer Smith's musical talent to Jones or Jones's wizardry at computers to Johnson. One can compensate an individual for poor talents, however. Dworkin amends the story of the hypothetical equal auction for tradeable goods to include two hypothetical insurance markets, one for marketable talent and one for handicaps or negative talent. The details need not concern us here, but the basic idea is that we determine what insurance an individual would have purchased against the possibility of having low talent if we imagine him with his present desires but not knowing either what handicaps he might incur or what the market demand for his marketable abilities would be. The insurance an individual would have purchased in this hypothetical scenario fixes what compensation he is owed so that all things considered, initial resources are equally distributed.

Dworkin's opposition to equality of welfare can now be restated in a way that registers his account of personal responsibility as it is integrated into his ideal of equality of resources. In principle, equality of welfare could dictate compensation to an individual, in the name of equality, for a taste she has that is expensive to satisfy. If tradeable goods are equally distributed to all individuals and they differ only in that one of them likes expensive champagne and the rest like cheap beer, so that with the same resources, the champagne lover has less welfare than the beer lovers, then equality of welfare dictates a resource transfer from those with a taste for beer to those with a taste for champagne. Dworkin regards the result as a sure sign that the ideal of equality of welfare is deeply morally unattractive. For Dworkin, if an individual finds himself with a craving he does not identify with and regards as just an obstacle to the satisfaction of desires and aims he does identify with, then that unwanted craving counts as a handicap that in principle could legitimately trigger compensation to the person afflicted with the craving according to the hypothetical insurance market mechanism. But if one is glad to have a preference or ambition, then it does not count as a resource, but as a part of oneself for which one must take responsibility. One cannot legitimately claim that in the name of distributive equality one should be compensated for having preferences and aims that one identifies with as constituting part of one's conception of what is good and admirable.

Rawls, who takes a similar position that the principles of justice should not render it the case that what one is owed in the name of justice varies with one's aims and ambitions, for which one must take responsibility, refers to this norm as "responsibility for our ends."[13] The individual and not society takes responsibility for that very individual's ends, provided that social justice is being implemented, which includes a provision of fair education for each individual.

Dworkinian equality of resources ties together attractive ideas about what should be thought to constitute equality of condition. Does this synthesis hold together or unravel?

There are two lines of thought concerning individual responsibility combined in Dworkin's conception of equality. It is far from clear that they are compatible. One idea is that individuals should be held responsible for option luck but not for brute luck, for chosen but not unchosen risks. The other idea is that individuals should be held responsible for their aims and ambitions, for the preferences that they are glad to have, and for the choices they make to achieve them, but not for their native talents and initial resource endowments. In this context an outcome that one is held responsible for is one that should not trigger compensation for the agent on whom the outcome falls if its quality is deficient. My responsibility in this sense for the outcomes of my action corresponds to the absence of obligation on the part of other people to compensate me for its costs that fall on me (and also to the obligation on my part to compensate other people who are harmed wrongfully by my action, but to simplify discussion this further aspect is ignored).

The problem is that among one's native talents, for which one is not to be held responsible, are value-forming, preference-forming, choice-making, and choice-executing talents. These then have a large influence on the values and preferences one comes to have and the choices and actions one makes. If Maria has top quality talents in these areas, and I have low grade talents, and as a result she makes good choices that yield her a fine quality of life and I make bad choices that yield me a grim and squalid quality of life, I do not see how it makes sense to hold me fully responsible as Dworkin's equality ethic does for my bad values and choices that flow from my low grade talents. If I should be compensated for what does not lie within my power to control, for my brute luck not my option luck, then my values and choices here are less a matter of option luck and more a matter of brute luck and should be to some degree eligible for compensation according to an equality ethic.

What then becomes of the duty of respect that the state owes all its citizens, which according to Dworkin includes the duty to respect the evaluative autonomy of each individual, and which ought to shape our understanding of distributive equality and lead us to embrace equality of resources not equality of welfare? We should perhaps examine this idea with skepticism.

Dworkin points out that one cannot sensibly in one's own voice claim that a preference that one is glad to have is an affliction and ask to be compensated for the losses it causes in one's life. But from a third-person perspective the judgment that a preference is an affliction can be made. Suppose I am a heroin addict, and for the sake of the argument just assume that heroin addiction is in itself undesirable. I may be glad to be an addict; I am a righteous dope fiend. Still, the addiction may constitute degradation. If I am not reasonably held responsible for developing the pro-heroin preference, perhaps I should be compensated. From a moral perspective that insists that people should not be held fully responsible for choices they are led to make by poor resource endowments, responsibility for ends, with its associated norm of individual autonomy, is not a moral trump card, but is sometimes itself trumped by competing values.

Welfarist equality

Notice that the position that distributive equality should measure each individual's condition in terms of the welfare or well-being that her resources in conjunction with her other circumstances enable her to gain can be adjusted to integrate a conception of personal responsibility.[14] In fact the formulation in the previous sentence gives an example of how this might be done: responsibility-catering welfarist equality of condition holds that it is morally desirable that all persons be made equal not in the level of welfare they actually get but rather in the level they are enabled to attain. In other words: equality of condition requires that people's initial resource allotments and circumstances be set so that each person can attain the same level of welfare if she behaves prudently throughout her life after the initial moment. Call this view *equal opportunity for welfare*. An alternative specification would require that individuals' opportunities are equal when each would have the same expected welfare, the same prospect of welfare, if she behaved prudently throughout her life. On these equal-opportunity conceptions, egalitarian justice requires that society provide each individual a path in life and a guarantee that if the individual takes this path she will have the same welfare that anyone else who behaves prudently can reach (or alternatively the same expectation of welfare).

The content of an "equal opportunity for welfare" view varies depending on how one interprets the idea of individual welfare or well-being. The idea we are trying to construe is the goodness or desirability of a life for the person who lives it. Welfare is what a person who is acting prudently seeks for its own sake. The most plausible and ethically attractive account of equal opportunity for welfare would be yoked to the philosophically most defensible account of welfare.

Some objections to the idea that welfare or well-being is the aspect of people's condition that is relevant to egalitarian justice appear to gain their plausibility by invoking an inadequate conception of well-being and then querying whether equality of *that* is an adequate conception of egalitarian justice. But the appropriate response to any such objection is to seek a more adequate conception of well-being, not to reject the idea that well-being matters for justice.

Skepticism about this project might take the form of asserting that, given pluralism of belief in modern society, individuals will tend reasonably to embrace many diverse and opposed views of human good, so no account of the good can be the object of rational consensus among members of society and serve as a public standard of equal justice. If this skepticism is correct, egalitarian welfarism is doomed.

Even if the welfare component of welfare-oriented conceptions of distributive equality is not mistaken, the way in which the "equal opportunity for welfare" norm integrates equality, welfare, and personal responsibility is problematic.

It is too demanding to formulate an equal-opportunity account so that the welfare level one's resources enable one to attain is counted as the welfare level one would gain if one were perfectly prudent throughout one's life. Perfect prudence may be impossible for some, given their choice-making and choice-executing talent deficits. Even if a prudent and reasonable choice can be made by two individuals, doing so may be easy for one and difficult for the other, and pleasant for the one and intensely painful for the other. One might accommodate this concern by reformulating equal opportunity for welfare by the stipulation that the opportunity for welfare a person's resources and circumstances accord her is the welfare level she would reach if she behaved from then on as prudently as it would be reasonable to expect, given the difficulty and pain required for that person to conduct herself prudently. But even as reformulated, an "equal opportunity for welfare" conception might seem too unforgiving, for an individual given equal opportunity might deviate very slightly from its soft responsibility requirement, but experience very bad luck, and suffer extreme misfortune.

Current philosophical discussions suggest a variety of ways of balancing concerns about personal responsibility in an egalitarian framework. No consensus is currently in sight. The difficulties encountered by the various strategies for catering to responsibility raise question marks about welfarist equality but also about the adequacy of any of its rivals currently on offer.

Equality Among Whom?

The ideal of equality of condition is not rendered fully determinate by settling what aspect of people's condition should be made the same for all. One needs to specify the group of people whose condition should be rendered equal in the relevant respect. In this specification several questions arise.

One might hold that the ideal of equality of condition should be applied to each separate community or political community in isolation. On this view it might be held morally undesirable if some Swedes are worse off than others, and undesirable if some Nigerians are worse off than others, but not undesirable if Nigerians on the average are worse off than Swedes on the average. If equality should obtain across community lines, one might limit its scope to the global level, or extend it across the universe.

Framing the issue for consideration as "Among which people should equality of condition obtain?" makes an assumption some egalitarians would reject. Some hold that equality of condition should hold across all sentient beings, including nonhuman animals along with humans. A rival view would hold that equality should obtain, at most, only among persons.

Just assume that the equality-of-condition ideal is to hold only for persons. The egalitarian might be opposed only to equality of condition among contemporaries or near-contemporaries (those whose lives overlap in time) or hold rather that it is morally bad if some people living at any time are worse off than other people living at that time or any other time.

When one holds that people's condition should be equal, one might mean that people's overall advantage level measured over the lifetime of each person should be the same for all persons. One might alternatively hold that at each moment of time, all people alive at that moment should have equal advantage levels – all should be equally well off at each moment. Another possible choice of unit of equality is the life stage. Divide each person's life into stages – say childhood, adulthood, and old age. Over time, the morally pertinent "equality of condition according to life stage" egalitarianism is sustained to the degree that people in the same stage are at the same advantage level. These different versions of the ideal of equality of condition would have different implications for public policy choice that differentially benefits the old and the young.

Equality of Condition: Objections and Alternatives

Is equality of condition morally desirable for its own sake? Equality in a given setting might promote community solidarity or other values. If so, equality is to that extent instrumentally valuable. But is equality morally desirable as an end?

This question is hard to answer, because it is easily confounded with others. We can imagine a situation in which a few individuals possess the great bulk of land and moveable goods and the vast majority of the population confronts a crushing poverty that imposes grim and squalid conditions of life. Responding to this example by urging that there should be a transfer of economic resources from the wealthy few to the impoverished many does not necessarily reflect endorsement of equality of condition as valuable as an end. Many moral principles would tend to justify transfer of economic resources in the direction of equal distribution in this setting.

The doctrine of utilitarianism holds that, of those available, one should always choose the act that maximizes the sum total of human utility (human good) in the long run. When egalitarian economic resource transfers would be the most effective available means to promote utility, utilitarianism implies that one ought to carry out these egalitarian transfers. But this understanding of why equality of a sort should sometimes be promoted does not support the judgment that equality of any sort is morally desirable for its own sake.

Concerning the distribution of economic resources, one might hold that it is morally important that each person should have "enough," and that what is morally objectionable about the lopsidedly unequal wealth-distribution example is not that everyone does not have the same but rather that some do not have enough.[15] On this view, the moral task is to determine the threshold level of resources at which an individual has enough to sustain a good enough quality of life, and to bring it about that each individual has this sufficient level, so far as this is feasible. Sufficientarianism is the doctrine that justice requires that as many as possible of those who shall ever live be sustained at a level of resources that provides a good enough quality of life.[16] A close relative of this view holds that justice requires that we give priority to getting benefits to those who are below the threshold of a good enough quality of life. Neither sufficientarianism nor its relative values equality for its own sake, though both favor transfers toward economic equality in certain situations.

Consider the norm that one should bring it about that the condition of the very worst off is made as advantageous as possible.[17] This maximin view (so called because it instructs us to *maximize* the advantage level of the person with the *minimum* level of advantage) is at the extreme of a continuum of norms that affirm to varying degrees that it is morally more important to achieve a benefit or avoid a loss for a person, the worse off she would be, compared with others, in the absence of this benefit or avoidance of loss. A close relative of these views is the priority view, which asserts that the moral value of achieving a gain of a given size for an individual is greater, the worse off in absolute terms the individual would be in the absence of this benefit.[18]

Principles such as maximin and the family of norms associated with the priority view will in a wide range of circumstances recommend transfers of resources from wealthy to poor in a way that can mimic what an adherent of equality for its own sake would favor. To be assured that equality of condition is morally valuable as an end, one must be assured that achieving or approximating equality of condition is valuable in circumstances in which these other views, that value equality only as a means to other values, would not favor movement toward equality.

Another moral view that will recommend moves in the direction of equality of condition without regarding equality of condition as more than instrumentally valuable is the principle that one's good fortune should be proportional to one's deservingness. When those on the short end of an inequality are no less deserving than those who are better off, proportional desert will favor movement toward equality.[19]

By itself, the norm that everyone should enjoy the same level of advantage will favor a change that renders everyone more equal but worse off. The advocate of equality might not favor such a change all things considered, if she also affirms other principles that militate against such levelling down. But the doctrine that equality of condition is intrinsically desirable must hold that even if levelling down is sometimes or even always undesirable all things considered, the situation that results from levelling down is in one respect improved, since equality of condition is thereby fulfilled to a greater extent. Against the view that equality of condition is intrinsically valuable the objection has been raised that levelling down is not desirable in any respect. But as stated, this objection just denies what the doctrine of equality of condition asserts. Nonetheless, reflection on cases of levelling down persuades some that they do not value equality of condition of any sort for its own sake. They rather value some nonegalitarian principle or principles that mimic the implications of equality in some circumstances.

What Renders All Human Persons Morally Equal?

If individuals are entitled to some form of equality – of rights, or status, or condition, or treatment – an account is needed of the basis of equality. A broad range of views insists on some form of fundamental equal moral status for all human persons. In virtue of what features of human persons is this fundamental equal status justified?

This question might seem to invite an easy and obvious answer. Being a member of the human species entitles one to a fundamental equal moral status and dignity, the same for all humans. Ideologies and creeds that deny the fundamental equality of humanity are guilty of prejudice and bigotry. They are beyond the moral pale. For example, sexist views that claim men to be superior to women, racist views that hold that some human groups defined by skin color or lineage are superior to others, and aristocratic doctrines that divide humanity into those naturally fit by quality of birth for membership in a privileged caste or class and those fit for the lower rungs of fixed hierarchies, do not merit serious consideration by reflective minds.

Racist, sexist, and aristocratic caste ideologies are indeed unfounded, but the puzzle of the moral basis of equality is not so easily solved. Mere membership in the human species does not necessarily pick out all and only those who merit fundamental equal status. Nonhuman beings in regions of the universe beyond earth might for all we know exhibit intelligence and sociability that should entitle them to the status of persons even though they are not human persons. A more troublesome worry is that not all members of the human species share the traits that are standardly cited to distinguish the moral status of humans from that of other animals. Inherited genetic anomaly, accident, and disease cause some members of the human species to lose at some phase of their lives, and others never to gain, the traits that are plausible candidates for being regarded as necessary and sufficient for personhood status.

We might say it is not merely being human but being a person that counts, where one just stipulates that a person is a being that possesses the traits, whatever they might be, that confer full moral status. But the question still remains: Why should we think there is an equal basic moral status that all normal humans possess? In general terms there is probably wide agreement that humans are distinguished from nonhuman animals on earth by their possession of greater cognitive powers. Humans have rational agency capacity which other animals lack. In virtue of this capacity to perceive the true and the good, to adopt goals and choose actions to attain them, and to regulate action by some conception of what is owed morally to others, humans are superior to other animals and are entitled to superior moral status. No doubt more needs to be done to characterize the traits that render a being a person. Aside from this, there is the further worry that the cognitive capacities that form rational-agency capacity all vary by degree. The question then arises, if I claim to have greater moral rights and moral standing than (for example) a gorilla, on the ground that I am much smarter, why does not this same argument establish that (for example) Albert Einstein, who is much smarter than I, has greater moral rights and moral standing than that to which I am entitled? Why human equality? One might say that if one possesses rational-agency capacity at or above some threshold level, one has enough to qualify for the equal status accorded to all persons, and above the threshold, inequalities in cognitive capacity do not matter. But why not? There are further questions in this region to be explored.

Notes

1 See Locke (1980), p. 8.
2 The libertarian conception of Lockean rights is elaborated and defended in Nozick (1974).
3 See Nozick (1974), ch. 3; also Sen (1982); Scheffler (1994), ch. 4.
4 Rawls (1999a), pp. 73–8.
5 Tawney (1964), pp. 109–10.
6 See Temkin (1993), esp. ch. 2; also Sen (1997).
7 See Buchanan, Brock, Daniels, and Wikler (1999).
8 Walzer (1983), p. xi.
9 Sen develops his views in several publications. For a summary, see Sen (1992).
10 See Dworkin (2000); also Rakowski (1991).
11 Dworkin (2000), p. 73.
12 On this point I am indebted to Peter Vallentyne.
13 Rawls (1999b), p. 369.
14 On this point, see Cohen (1989), Arneson (1989), and Roemer (1996).
15 For this argument, see Frankfurt (1987).
16 According to Walzer (1983), justice requires roughly that everyone should have enough to be a fully participating member of a democratic society. Anderson (1999) further develops this view. See also Nussbaum (1999).
17 Rawls's theory of justice incorporates the difference principle, which requires max-iminning of social and economic benefits. See Rawls (1999a).
18 Parfit (1997).
19 Kagan (1999) provides a subtle discussion of how judgments about deservingness might better account for judgments that on their face looked to be based on the view that equality of condition is intrinsically morally valuable.

Bibliography

Anderson, Elizabeth (1999). "What is the point of equality?" *Ethics*, 109: 287–337.
Arneson, Richard (1989). "Equality and Equal Opportunity for Welfare." *Philosophical Studies* 56: 77–93.

——(1997). "Equality and equal opportunity for welfare." In Louis P. Pojman and Robert Westmoreland (eds.), *Equality: Selected Readings* (pp. 229–41). Oxford: Oxford University Press.

Buchanan, Allen, Dan W. Brock, Norman Daniels, and Daniel Wikler (2000). *From Chance to Choice: Genetics and Justice*. Cambridge: Cambridge University Press.

Cohen, G. A. (1989). "On the currency of egalitarian justice." *Ethics*, 99: 906–44.

Dworkin, Ronald (2000). *Sovereign Virtue: The Theory and Practice of Equality*. Cambridge, MA: Harvard University Press.

Frankfurt, Harry (1987). "Equality as a moral ideal." *Ethics*, 98: 21–43.

Kagan, Shelly (1999). "Equality and desert." In Owen McLeod and Louis P. Pojman (eds.), *What Do We Deserve?* (pp. 298–314). Oxford: Oxford University Press.

Locke, John (1980). *Second Treatise of Government*. Indianapolis: Hackett (originally published 1690).

McKerlie, Dennis (1989). "Equality and Time." *Ethics*, 99: 475–91.

Nagel, Thomas (1991). *Equality and Partiality*. Oxford: Oxford University Press.

Nozick, Robert (1974). *Anarchy, State, and Utopia*. New York: Basic Books.

Nussbaum, Martha (1999). "Women and cultural universals." In Martha Nussbaum, *Sex and Justice* (pp. 29–54). Oxford: Oxford University Press.

Parfit, Derek (1997) "Equality and priority." *Ratio* (new series), 10: 202–20.

Rakowski, Eric (1991). *Equal Justice*. Oxford: Clarendon Press.

Rawls, John (1999a). *A Theory of Justice* (revised edn). Cambridge, MA: Harvard University Press.

——(1999b). "Social unity and primary goods." In Samuel Freeman (ed.), *John Rawls: Collected Papers* (pp. 359–87). Cambridge, MA: Harvard University Press.

Roemer, John (1996). *Theories of Distributive Justice*. Cambridge, MA: Harvard University Press.

Scanlon, T. M. (2000). "The diversity of objections to inequality." In Matthew Clayton and Andrew Williams (eds.), *The Ideal of Equality* (pp. 41–59). New York: St. Martin's Press.

Scheffler, Samuel (1994). *The Rejection of Consequentialism* (revised edn). Oxford: Oxford University Press.

Sen, Amartya (1982). "Rights and Agency." *Philosophy and Public Affairs* 11: 3–39.

——(1992). *Inequality Reexamined*. Cambridge, MA: Harvard University Press.

——(1997). *On Economic Inequality* (expanded edn). Oxford: Clarendon Press.

Shakespeare, William (1980). *King Lear*. In *The Complete Works of William Shakespeare* (the Cambridge Text established by John Dover Wilson) (pp. 921–54). London: Octopus Books (originally published 1605).

Tawney, R. H. (1964). *Equality*. London: Allen and Unwin. (First published 1931.)

Temkin, Larry (1993). *Inequality*. Oxford: Oxford University Press.

Walzer, Michael (1983). *Spheres of Justice: A Defense of Pluralism and Equality*. New York: Basic Books.

Chapter 5

Preference, Rationality, and Democratic Theory

Ann E. Cudd

Introduction

This essay will address the question: What ought to be the role of individuals' preferences in a democracy? By "preference" I am referring to the concept of an ordering of a person's best judgments about which states of affairs the individual desires. Preferences normally result in actions that individuals think will bring about the most preferred state within the individual's power to enact. In the case of voting, then, one normally votes for that candidate or option that one most prefers. At first blush, it seems that the answer to the question should be obvious: individuals' preferences should collectively determine social decisions in a democracy – that is, after all, definitive of democracy. But as is often the case with first blushes, this one pales under the light of scrutiny. First, votes or expressions of preference, not preferences themselves, determine outcomes, at best, and it is not clear that individuals' preferences determine their votes. Second, to say that individual preferences determine social decisions is just not to say enough about how the aggregation of individual preferences is to be accomplished. For the analogy between individual and social decision-making breaks down precisely when one considers how social preferences are to be determined when the individual preferences conflict. Third, it is not clear that every individual should have a vote on every issue in a democracy. Preferences may be perverted, misinformed, or misdirected in many ways – as this essay will discuss – and so may be rationally or morally unacceptable as the determinants of collective decisions.

Democracy is a social decision-making procedure for making "coercively enforceable collective decisions."[1] Literally "democracy" means rule of the people by the people. But over what matters may they make coercively enforceable decisions, and how are the many voices of the people to be combined to make a single, coherent sound? If we are going to answer the question of what role individual preference *should* play in a democracy, and at the same time defend democracy as the best form of government, it will be important to look first to the justification of democratic rule. There are three sources of justification of a decision-making procedure: a rule may be justified by showing that it is rationally or that it is morally required, or by showing that it leads to the best (in some sense of best) outcomes.[2] This latter standard, the consequentialist or perfectionist standard, either coincides with the rationality standard or it is not a form of democracy – rule *by* the people – at all. If it does not coincide with the rationality justification, then it must argue that democracy somehow brings about the best outcome directly, but not as a result of the voters' deliberations on which they base their votes. In a democracy it is not enough that people get what they want; they must intend their collective action, which they expect will bring about their collective intention. Thus, I shall not consider the consequentialist standard further in this essay.

To say that a decision-making procedure is rational is possibly to say a number of different things. First, one might mean instrumental rationality, as assumed in rational-choice arguments. To say that a decision procedure is instrumentally rational is to say that it maximizes the satisfaction of an individual's self-interest, where self-interest is determined by the individual and may be selfish or altruistic, so long as it is non-tuistic.[3] On this view of justification, a social-decision procedure would be justified if it were instrumentally rational for the individuals in the society, and individuals might be self-interested in, among other things, a stable polity, opportunities for cooperation with their fellows, and avoiding predation by untrustworthies. Second, one might mean by "rational" the achievement of (Kantian) autonomy. To say that a social-decision rule is rational in this sense would be to say that it supports or promotes the autonomy, or self-governing abilities, of the individuals in the society. Rational decision-making in this sense means adherence to norms for behavior that are universalizeable among some group of persons with whom one identifies.[4] While these senses of rationality may be in conflict, they may also happily come together in the political choice of a stable, relatively responsive government.

The other standard of justification has to do with moral ideals or conceptions of how a society ideally is to be organized. Democracy may be justified by some appeals to moral ideals such as equality – that each person is to count for one – and the preservation of human dignity – that no one is to be subjected to a rule which she had no part in choosing. An additional moral demand that has been more recently recognized is that diversity be not only tolerated but valued.[5] By "diversity" I mean to refer not only to the differences of opinion that arise from what Rawls (1993) termed "the burdens of judgment," but also to the wide differences in cultural practices that are exemplified by the populations of contemporary multicultural democracies.

Ideally, then, democracy promotes rationality, autonomy, equality, dignity, and diversity, and is justified to the extent that it is the best means to do so. These can be competing criteria; indeed, some might argue that in the context of democracy the competition among these criteria is inevitable. Persons may see their interests best furthered by the denial to others of autonomy or equality. Some may reject claims that others make that their way of life is valuable diversity, and instead find it a threat to dignity or rational self-interest. To some extent, the form or procedures of a particular democratic regime can address these issues, but to defend democracy as a viable means to govern ourselves, we will have to argue that human nature can tolerate some reasonable compromise among the justificatory ideals.

I begin with the assumption that democracy, as the rule of the people, where each citizen[6] counts for one, means that each gets a single, equally-weighted, vote on every issue, and the option with the most votes is enacted by the group. I take this to be the decision procedure of simple majority rule. Each of the standards of justification provides a critical standpoint from which to refine our conception of democracy. In this essay I will survey a number of criticisms that have been raised in the literatures on preference, rational choice, and democracy, from the perspectives of both rationality and morality, to this conception of democracy. We shall see that this simple conception cannot work for many reasons. Some reasons have to do with the structural instability of the decision procedure of majority rule, and some with the perversities of individual preference. In taking account of these criticisms of simple majority rule, we shall have to alter the social-decision procedure, and yet do so in a way that arguably retains the essence of democratic rule. Next I will examine the claims of some theorists that individual preference is irrelevant to democratic rule, that individuals in fact ought not vote their preferences. Finally I will suggest an outline for liberal democracy that takes individual preference to be an important but not always determinative element of social decision-making, avoids the surveyed criticisms, and can be justified morally and rationally.

Structural Problems with Democracy as Mechanism of Social Choice

Majority rule has for a long time been known to have certain structural problems associated with it. By "structural problems" I refer to paradoxes, internal inconsistencies, and conflicts with the justificatory criteria that are independent of the particular contents of the issues voted on or the preferences expressed in the votes. Some of these arise with majority rule in particular, others with any voting mechanism, where a voting mechanism is a social-decision procedure that takes votes as the only inputs to social decisions. In this section I survey four such structural problems.

1   Voting paradoxes

The original voting paradox afflicting majority rule is the Condorcet paradox, which refers to the problem that with at least three voters and three choices, it is always possible to find a set of possible preference orderings that yield a cyclical or intransitive social preference. For example, suppose that the possible choices are x, y, and z. Suppose A prefers x to y and y to z, B prefers y to z and z to x, C prefers z to x and x to y. Now if we ask whether there is a social preference between x and y, we see that x beats y, similarly, with x and z, z beats x, and with y and z, y beats z. But that means that socially, x is preferred to y, y to z and z to x, which is intransitive. The probability of a Condorcet paradox only gets worse with greater numbers of outcomes and greater numbers of voters, and thus it seems to be a general problem with majority rule. Although any given occasion of voting may result in a winner, it will be the arbitrary (or worse, manipulated) result of the order in which the issues were voted on. What this means is that we cannot always derive a non-arbitrary, truly representative social-preference function from majority rule. As Peter Ordeshook puts it, "we cannot underestimate the importance of [the Condorcet paradox] because it undermines fundamentally any approach that treats institutions and collectivities as though they are people."[7] However, it is also important to note that the generality of the paradox rests on the assumption that all possible preference orderings are equally likely. In a community in which much is agreed upon and many of the possible orderings are ruled out by each of the voters, the likelihood of an intransitivity arising falls considerably. Thus, if majority rule is to be a rational, non-arbitrary way of making social decisions, it will have to be confined to issues over which there is already a certain amount of community agreement.

2   Arrow's Impossibility Theorem

Even more than the Condorcet paradox, Arrow's Impossibility Theorem threatens the very coherence of collective decision-making by means of individual preferences. According to the theorem, there is no way generally to construct a complete and transitive collective-preference ordering that is determined by the preference orderings of the members of the collective, that meets four seemingly simple rational and/or democratic criteria. These four are as follows: (1) any individual preference orderings (that are complete and transitive) are allowable (Unrestricted Domain); (2) if everyone prefers one option to another, then the social ordering ranks the two options that way (Pareto Principle); (3) the collective preference between x and y depends only on how all the individuals in the collective rank order x and y (Independence of Irrelevant Alternatives); and (4) no one person is decisive for every pair of options (Non-dictatorship). The proof proceeds by showing that when all of the other conditions are met, the only way to guarantee a transitive ordering is to have a dictator. The upshot is that we cannot guarantee that majority rule will be democratic and rational for every possible set of preference orderings that the citizens may have.

Kurt Baier (1967) argued that Arrow's Theorem does not profoundly affect the argument for democracy. There are many reasons for democratic and liberal law-makers to override individual preferences, he claims, such as the problems with preferences that I will explore in the next section. Therefore, Arrow's theorem makes a much less significant critique than it would if individual preference could be counted on to be settled, rational, moral and liberal. But we must not accept this evasion of Arrow too quickly.[8] If we decide that we will rely on any aggregation of individual preferences, it will be important to see whether the restrictions placed on individual preferences rule out dictatorship[9] and allow a transitive social ordering when they are to be relied on. That is, just because the conditions – the antecedents of the conditional – are violated does not guarantee that the outcome – the consequent – will always be avoided. Even if Arrow's Theorem does not strictly apply, the specter of intransitivity and dictatorship will haunt decisions made on the basis of aggregated individual preferences. Furthermore, we should note that Baier's defense amounts to saying that, since a democracy will have some undemocratic features, Arrow's Theorem will have less bite. But this can hardly be comforting to the strict adherent to majority rule.

3   Irrational voting; rational ignorance

Another structural problem with voting is that in elections with large numbers of voters, where each voter is unlikely to be the one to cast the deciding vote, it is not instrumentally rational to vote because the expected benefit of voting is lower than the cost of voting. Yet, we see that in the real world people vote, even when they are not legally compelled to do so. Clearly they are getting some extra value from voting over and above their effect on the outcome of the vote, perhaps from the fact that they are participating in a community endeavor that is greater than the instrumental value of their votes. If there are large numbers of citizens who do not vote, then the social-decision scheme that results from majority rule violates the moral criteria of equality and dignity. Yet, it hardly seems appropriate to respect these moral criteria by coercing people to vote. This problem with voting suggests that a justifiable form of democracy will have to provide additional incentives to convince people voluntarily to vote.

Associated with the problem of the instrumental irrationality of voting is what is known as the problem of "rational ignorance." If it is irrational for individuals to vote, then it is rational for each voter to invest only small amounts of effort, if any, into understanding the issues. But the consequence of this may be an ignorant citizenry, hardly the ideal of autonomy, equality or dignity that democrats would like to suppose. Like the problem with the irrationality of voting, though, we can see that many people find an additional value, beyond the instrumental expected value of their well-informed vote, to becoming well-informed about political issues. How else could one account for the popularity of the C-SPAN network which presents political speeches and conferences? Still, this problem suggests that a democratic society must find ways to encourage people to become informed about political issues.

Should we be content to say just this, that democracy should encourage informed voting, or are these paradoxes somewhat deeper, suggesting that people would be simply deluding themselves that their votes make a difference if they inform themselves and vote? My response to the irrationality-of-voting problem, which generates the rational-ignorance problem, is to distinguish between voting in individual instances and having a policy of voting, and to point out that voting is a public act with consequences for each person's reputation. Now the irrationality-of-voting problem has something like a "prisoner's dilemma" structure:[10] each is better off not voting if the others vote, but all are worse off if none vote than they would be if all of them voted. For if people were to simply abdicate their power en masse, as the rationality arguments suggest, then the chance that a dictator or demagogue would move the society from democracy to totalitarianism is likely. Since it is clear that a totalitarian state meets none of the criteria of justification, this outcome is unacceptable. I want to suggest that the policy of voting can be defended as a rational strategy for avoiding tyranny, if individuals are made to suffer some bad reputation effect by not voting. The procedure that a state puts in place for voting makes it more or less a public act. One's neighbors and fellow citizens can see when one does or does not go to the polls. It can be made more or less a matter of public discussion. A policy of voting is a rule for action that concerns not just each single act of voting in an election, but rather voting in elections as a general rule. If it is advantageous for one to have the reputation of being a voter, then the benefit to having a policy of voting can be enough to change the payoff structure of voting from a prisoner's dilemma into an assurance game, where each does best by voting so long as the others vote too. In contrast to the prisoner's dilemma, in an assurance game one equilibrium for such a game would be where the citizens all have the policy of voting. If the reputation effect were enough to completely overwhelm the cost of voting, then the game would be one with a unique equilibrium where everyone votes.[11] Hence, it is instrumentally rational to vote after all, provided that others do as well. My point here is that it is possible to make voting both socially and individually rational, and the specter of the totalitarian menace provides justification for democracies to put policies in place to do so.

4   Manipulability

The voting paradoxes showed that it is not generally possible to generate a definitive social preference from the individual preferences alone. But there may be a more sinister problem here than arbitrariness. Allan Gibbard (1973) showed with his General Manipulability Theorem that a savvy voter can, conceivably, bias an outcome in her direction. A "voting scheme" is any scheme which makes a community's choice depend entirely on individuals' professed preferences, and an individual "manipulates" a voting scheme if she secures an outcome she prefers by misrepresenting her preferences. Suppose, for example, there are three candidates, A, B, and C, for a position, and the one with the majority of first-place votes will win the position. Suppose that on a straightforward, honest representation of preferences, A would have 6 first-place votes, B would have 7 first-place votes, and C would have 2. If the voters who prefer C know that their candidate has no chance, and if they both prefer A to B, then by voting for their second favorite candidate, they can manipulate the vote so that A comes out the winner. Gibbard's theorem proves that "any non-dictatorial voting scheme with at least three possible outcomes is subject to individual manipulation."[12] Now this initially sounds like a more serious problem than it actually is. Gibbard admits that just because it is possible to manipulate a voting scheme this does not mean that anyone in the actual world would be in a position to do so. However, the reasons that one would not be in a position to do so are ignorance, stupidity, or integrity. Still, the "ignorance" and "stupidity" required here are just the ordinary conditions of human existence. The information that would be required successfully to manipulate the vote is knowledge of the others' votes.[13] At most we can conclude with Gibbard that "no straightforward appeal to informed self-interest can make the outcome a non-trivial function of preferences regardless of what those preferences are."[14] The matter is much more complicated, and one's best bet for achieving the social outcome one desires may not recommend voting one's true preferences, but the conditions under which one can know how to precisely manipulate an election are extremely rare in a society of many individuals.

To summarize this section, then, I have argued that the voting paradoxes and Arrow's Theorem are troubling, but not decisive, objections to majority rule, if there are limiting conditions on when individual preferences can be determinative of social decisions. Where there is a great deal of community agreement already it is unlikely that there will be intransitive cycles. Arrow's Theorem will not directly apply in many instances because the scope of individual preference is circumscribed. However, it will be important for a democracy to consider whether there is an intransitivity in its collective preferences, and where there is, a dictator will have to be named to decide non-arbitrarily what the collective action ought to be. I will offer suggestions in the conclusion for how this can be justifiably accomplished. I have argued that it is possible and justifiable for a democracy to pursue methods to encourage informed voter participation. Finally, it seems that although manipulability is a theoretical possibility in a democracy, practically speaking the information requirements are too high for it to pose a serious threat. Now we will move on to other objections to individual preferences.

Reasons to Override Individual Preferences

In addition to the structural problems with majority rule as a social-choice mechanism, there are many reasons for objecting to the particular contents of individual preference, and thus overriding individual preference in social decision-making. Recall that the goal is to promote rationality, autonomy, equality, dignity, and diversity, and we said that democracy is justified to the extent that it is the best means to do so. Now we have to ask whether democracy is best served by allowing voters unlimited rights to decide how they as individuals will vote. Many reasons can be given for restraining persons from voting their "mere" preferences in a democratic society. Here is a list of them.

1 Some preferences are irrational or uninformed

In the rational-choice literature, preferences can only be an input to a rational decision if they are consistent (one does not prefer x to y and y to x) and if they do not form an intransitive cycle. Otherwise, it would be incoherent to claim that the person has a goal that she wishes to pursue in an effective way. Likewise, unsettled preferences, or preferences that shift rapidly over time, make pursuit of a goal impossible, as the goal shifts from one moment to the next. In this category, I would argue, we can also treat incontinent preferences, or first-order preferences that conflict with longer-standing second-order desires. The real problem with these first-order preferences is either that they shift back and forth (I want the cigarette; I don't want the cigarette), or that they simply cause an inconsistency when combined with the second-order ones (I want the cigarette; I don't want to want cigarettes; this is a case of wanting cigarettes; therefore I don't want what I want). Hence, they violate instrumental rationality in the same way as inconsistent preferences.

Uninformed preferences, i.e., preferences based on false beliefs or on incomplete information about options, risk violating both the instrumental-rationality and autonomy criteria. However, the matter is not simple here, since having false beliefs and incomplete information is an inevitable part of the human epistemic condition. To say that these preferences are unacceptable for rational or autonomous decisions, they have to be false or uninformed in spite of readily (relative to the agent) available information. Otherwise the bar is too high for rationality and autonomy. The solution to the problem of uninformed preferences is clearly to make information about matters on which votes will be taken readily available, and then to give incentives, as I discussed above, to citizens to inform themselves.

2   *Some preferences are non-autonomously formed*

This is the problem, raised by several preference theorists and further refined by several feminist theorists, known as adaptive preference formation or deformed preferences.[15] Jon Elster (1983) defines an adaptive preference as a preference that has been formed without one's control or awareness, by a causal mechanism that isn't of one's own choosing. Adaptive preferences have a typical "fox and grapes" structure, that is, if the grapes are out of the agent's reach, the agent's preferences, if they are like the fox's, will turn against the grapes, the agent declaring them sour anyway. The "sour grapes" phenomenon is familiar to us all: after I found out that eating scallops would make me violently ill, I found that I had no taste for them; following my discovery that there was no organized football league that admitted members of my gender (not to mention short, small, and slow persons), I desired to watch the game less. Not all adaptive preferences are bad for the agent herself, since some may allow the agent to get more welfare from her feasible set of options. There are less innocent examples of this phenomenon, though. Those adaptations that are forced on persons by social deprivation and injustice ought not to be automatically respected by a democracy. If one's preferences adapt to the circumstances in this way, then the preferences of agents under conditions of deprivation will turn away from goods and even needs that, absent those conditions, they would want.[16] Oppressed persons will come to see their conditions of oppression as the limits within which they *want* to live. A social-decision procedure that takes such preferences as the fixed inputs violates the justificatory criteria of autonomy, equality, and dignity.

A closely related form of adaptive preference formation is the habituation of preference.[17] Not only do persons tend to become content with whatever they see as their lot in life, they also become accustomed to great privilege and are greatly affected for the worse should they be deprived of this privilege, however unfair it might be.[18] In an oppressive situation in which some suffer great deprivation and others enjoy great privilege, states of affairs in which things are more fairly distributed will not be preferred by the oppressed and will be greatly dispreferred by the privileged. Girls and women are encouraged by multiple sources to think of the kind of work that oppresses them as the work that they ought, by nature, by sentiment, and even by God, to do. All of these sources have powerful effects on emotions, making it likely that women's preferences will favor their oppressive condition. It's not that they will prefer oppression to justice, or subordination to equality, rather they will prefer the kinds of social roles that tend to subordinate them, make them less able to choose, or give them fewer choices to make. These sources also suggest to women, and to men, that it is not social oppression at work, but rather nature (or the supernatural) that puts women in their place. As John Stuart Mill noted in *The Subjection of Women*, the oppression of women is the one kind of oppression that is maintained in part by the affections of the oppressed for the privileged class. Many religions, at least the past and current interpretations of them, insist that women's place is in the domestic sphere, and most prohibit them from becoming religious leaders.[19] Religion also powerfully engages the emotions, and so affects preferences. But social decisions made from such habituated preferences will compromise autonomy, equality, dignity, and diversity. Thus, as democrats, we should be wary of individual preferences that reinforce the oppression of women.[20]

Other non-autonomous preference-formation processes should also give the democrat some reason to pause, at least. Peer-pressure, addictions, and the effect of (possibly unjust, immoral, or irrational) social norms on persons can cause them to prefer, or to express themselves as if they prefer, options that absent those constraints they would not prefer. Again, if the social decision-making procedure reflects these preferences, autonomy will be compromised.

Another feminist criticism of the notion of preference was raised by Eva Feder Kittay (1999). There she notes that the notion of preference assumes an independence of persons that is not compatible with the interdependence of seriously dependent persons and their caretakers, whom Kittay terms "dependency workers." On the standard account, preferences are taken to belong to a single person, and to be, if not self-regarding, at least non-tuistic. Each person is to be considered a "self-originating source of claims." But seriously dependent persons (infants and small children, the severely disabled, the very ill, the frail elderly) often cannot make claims for themselves; they may be unable to express their needs and desires, or even to frame the concept of needs and desires adequately. Thus, dependency workers are forced to make claims on behalf of their charges, and so their preferences must to some degree reflect the preferences of two persons. The sense in which they are "forced" to do so is, of course, not an outright denial of their autonomy, for they are forced by the demands of morality, and perhaps love or commitment, to care for their charge. However, caretaking is a social need, and someone has to do it. Those who do not fulfill the social need are free-riding on those who do. A social-choice rule that does not have a mechanism for registering both persons' preferences, then, will violate the equality criterion.

3   Some preferences are self-defeating

Mill argued that for a liberal state to respect the preference of an individual to sell himself or herself into slavery would be self-defeating, in that it precludes the possibility of future choice-making for that individual. A democracy must be similarly concerned with such preferences, since self-defeating preferences violate the ideals of equality, autonomy, and dignity. Although I endorse this general prohibition on truly self-defeating preferences, deciding which preferences are self-defeating is a more difficult matter. There are employment contracts that approximate slavery, either by temporarily taking away autonomy from the worker or by compensating workers so poorly as to coerce them into working much longer and harder than would be considered reasonable, for example. Should persons be allowed to make such contracts on the grounds that they prefer such work to their other feasible alternatives? One might similarly question whether an individual's choice of voluntary euthanasia is self-defeating.[21] In both cases I am inclined to say no, that these are not self-defeating preferences. But my inclinations here aside, these questions show that democracy must be concerned about self-defeating preferences and must make the general issue of what constitutes a self-defeating preference a matter of public decision-making. While this will not guarantee that all and only self-defeating preferences will be questioned, by making the general issue of what constitutes a self-defeating preference (rather than particular preferences as they arise) a matter of deliberation, a reasonable judgment about the matter is more likely to come about.

4 Some preferences are immoral

Some people have preferences for discrimination and domination. They prefer that their social group be regarded as better than others, that their social group have unfair advantages in the competition for social resources. They might argue that their social group is worthy or deserving of advantages. Because they are so clearly self-interested, such claims must be considered seriously biased. The Rawlsian difference principle, which allows inequalities only when they are to the advantage of the least well off, may be the appropriate test for such claims. In general, though, respecting preferences for discrimination and domination violates the criteria of equality, dignity, and diversity.

5 Some preferences are illiberal

Finally there are preferences that ought not to be respected because they interfere unnecessarily or unjustly with other persons' liberty. Illiberal or meddling preferences, which are preferences about someone else's tastes and lifestyle, derive either from an aesthetic or ethical disagreement, or from differing metaphysical or religious conceptions of the good. Meddling preferences deny others the right to live their lives as they see fit, as far as those matters that affect primarily themselves are concerned. When forced upon persons who disagree, such preferences violate the criteria of rationality, equality, and diversity. Even more serious are those preferences that are formed on the basis of some metaphysical or religious belief that is not commonly shared in the society. For example, consider an individual's preference that no one have access to abortion because he believes that the fetus is a person from the moment of conception. In order to receive support, such a belief has to be based on either a metaphysical or a religious view of personhood that is either shared commonly or derivable from commonly shared premises. Rawls argues that only preferences based on public reasons, by which he means reasons that "each could reasonably expect that others might endorse as consistent with their freedom and equality,"[22] ought to be used for voting in a liberal democracy. Ultimately the reason for so limiting the appeal to preference or to "the whole truth," as the adherents of the comprehensive doctrines see it, is that not doing so will violate the ideals of autonomy and equality from which democracy derives its legitimacy.[23] A social decision-making procedure that takes these preferences as inputs violates the criteria of equality, autonomy, dignity, and diversity.

Can we have a democratic decision procedure that takes as its inputs individuals' preferences, but screens out the problematic preferences to the degree necessary to uphold what I have been calling the justificatory criteria of democracy? Before I try to answer this question, we should examine arguments that attempt to pre-empt this question, suggesting that democracy does not or ought not use individual preferences as the determinants of social decisions, at all.

Should Individual Preference Determine Social Decisions?

David Estlund (1990) claims that democratic voting is not properly conceived as an expression of (self-)interest but rather as an expression of common interest. Since I am going to argue that individual preference does indeed play a crucial role in determining democratic decisions, it is important to critically evaluate this argument. His argument proceeds as follows. He sets out three conditions on democratic voting: aggregability – democratic social choices must be determined by the cumulative impact of multiple impacts;[24] advocacy – democratic inputs must be for or against certain choices, as distinct from being just opinions that something is the case;[25] activity – democratic inputs must be acts.[26] He then argues that preference, whether understood as the expression of desires, interest, or dispositions to act, cannot meet all three conditions. First, preferences must be reports of preferences in order to be acts. But if they are reports of "my interests (desires/dispositions)" then they are not aggregable because of what he calls the "indexical problem." In reporting my desire ("I prefer x to y" = A prefers x to y) I am reporting on something different from what you are reporting on when you vote ("I prefer y to x" = B prefers y to x). But, Estlund argues, each vote is about something different, and in particular not about what society prefers. This point is either obtuse or question-begging, however. If we take "society" as majority rule does, to be the sum of the individuals, then majority rule says take the sum of the votes over the individuals by taking each individual's preference as a component of that preference. So in a society of three members, A, B, and C, we might have: A prefers x to y and B prefers y to x and C prefers x to y means (by the rule of majority rule) A and B and C prefer x to y (by a vote of 2 to 1). That is to say, majority rule just is the aggregation rule for turning individual votes into social preferences. The fact that each individual is reporting on a different fact is just what is required on this conception of majority rule.

Estlund next argues that understanding voting as an expression of common interest meets all three conditions. This claim is insufficient to show that voting ought to be for the common interest when that conflicts with individual preference. By "statements of common interest" Estlund means a statement that something is or is not in the interest of the group that includes the speaker. Now we can understand majority rule either as constitutive of common interest, or as the method by which the common interest is discovered. The former interpretation seems particularly ill-suited to Estlund's project, and better suited to my interpretation of majority rule as aggregation rule. The latter interpretation is either irrational or incoherent, I suggest, if individuals are not voting for their preferences. There seem to be two alternatives for generalizing the character of the common interest that they are expressing: either the aggregation of individual preferences (which Estlund has rejected for formal reasons that I eschewed above), or some opinion of the common interest that is different from "mere" individual preference. Suppose that they are voting for what they think others want, then they are voting others' preferences. But there is no reason in general for them to think that others' preferences are rationally or morally more relevant than their own, so it is irrational. Suppose then that they are voting for what they think others will think is the common interest, then if they are not voting others' interests and are not supposing that others are voting others' interests, then they are voting for what they think will arise when everyone votes for what? There seems no general description of the content that they are voting for, if not their own or others' preferences. So, if Estlund is to make out his argument in favor of voting as an expression of common interest, he will have to offer a general characterization of common interest.

Let me discuss two possible ways of generating a general account of common interest that are not immediately equivalent to the aggregation of individual preferences. The common interest might come from a commitment to a shared goal among members of a social group, or from beliefs about what society ought to do, relative to some objective account of what ought to be done. Amartya Sen (1977) argued against what he took to be the blind use of the concept of preference by economists. He claims that individual preference neglects other important motivations to action that cannot be reduced to mere preference. For example, moral, political, religious, or personal commitments might motivate someone to act against her interest, and hence her preferences, with the result that her individual welfare will not be furthered by her action. A mother might prefer to see her son acquitted of murder charges, but feel compelled by her commitment to justice to testify against him. Sen writes: "commitment does involve, in a very real sense, counterpreferential choice,"[27] and he goes on, "it drives a wedge between personal choice and personal welfare."[28] Sen argues simply that one might choose to act contrary to one's preferences, because of some commitment one has to something or someone else. Elizabeth Anderson (forthcoming) uses Sen's conception of commitment to derive a notion of rationality based on commitment to a shared goal. On this conception, persons find themselves sharing goals (whether for a short-term or a long-term project) with others, and come to see themselves as jointly committed to acting together. Acting together as a single agent requires them to pursue a joint strategy aimed at reaching that goal. The adoption of a joint strategy then allows them to maximize the overall well-being of the group. However, Anderson argues that persons need not set out with a shared goal in mind. Rather, she argues that it is part of the logic of personal identity formation to identify with a group, and that identifying with a group means committing ourselves to acting on a joint strategy. To be a person, on this view, is to seek out group membership and thereby find oneself with commitments to shared goals. In formulating their joint strategy, Anderson supposes that group members will ask themselves, "What reasons do *we* have to act?" and the outcome will be a policy that is universalizeable, at least in the universe of the group.

On this view voting is rational because it is part of being a member of a democracy to vote, that is, part of the joint strategy of the demos. The content of individuals' votes will be determined by their shared commitments with the groups by which they identify themselves. There is no general way of predicting what groups will form or what goals the groups will develop. Nor is there a general way of predicting which group membership will govern an individual's vote. Since some groups with which individuals identify are anti-democratic or morally or socially suspect, the rationality of the joint strategy itself does not testify in its favor.

I find this view of rationality attractive, but it is open to criticism as an alternative to the aggregated-individual-preference theory of democracy. It relies on a claim about human psychology: that persons not only seek out group membership, but put aside self-interest once they identify with a group. Although the claim does not ring entirely false, it is clearly often false. Even if they derive value from their group membership, such persons open themselves to being taken advantage of, and thus it is not instrumentally rational to wholly identify with the group. Anderson might respond that persons do not and should not entirely lose themselves in the group for just this reason. But keeping the group at arm's length by not wholly identifying with it suggests that when it is in the person's self-interest to defect from the group, she can and will do so. In that case, the whole argument takes on an instrumental-rationality cast. Then it can be argued that in fact it is a matter of self-interested preference that leads one to identify with the group and play one's part in the joint strategy. Common interest, on this account, would turn out to be grounded in individual preference after all.

The second possibility for filling out the account of common interest is Susan Hurley's (1989) "cognitive theory" of democracy, in which citizens vote according to their beliefs about what should be done all things considered, rather than their preferences. The cognitive theory denies both that citizens vote for their preferences rather than their beliefs about what should be done all things considered, and the views of political liberalism that political decisions ought to be independent of particular conceptions of the good. Instead, Hurley claims that the goal of government is to deliberate to find the truth about what should be done, not merely to satisfy the preferences of the majority. The cognitive theory thus demands that those in authority should be divided in a way that will prevent them from relying on "debunked" beliefs, i.e., beliefs that are formed through some non-rational process such as self-deception or bribery. Furthermore, the cognitive theory demands that the procedures and institutions foster the capacity for deliberation and formation of undebunked beliefs so that the truth is more likely to be plain to the voters.

Relying on voters to vote according to their beliefs about what ought to be done rather than what they want to be done runs into the problem of incentive compatibility, the problem that individuals' self-interest will conflict with what they ought to do, at least according to this theory. What would motivate the voters to vote this way, and what prevents some from cheating? Hurley defers this problem to the design of institutions and agenda-setting. The idea is that the social institutions, including the voting procedure itself, are to be so designed that there is a positive motivation to vote according to one's beliefs, coming from the desire to participate in the collective action of social self-determination. However, the question of whether it is rational to vote according to one's beliefs about what the state ought to do rather than what one prefers the state to do is not easily separated from the question of the form that these institutions will ultimately take. For if it were irrational to vote according to one's beliefs, then it may well be irrational to agree to the institutions that motivate one to vote according to one's beliefs. Why might it be irrational to agree to such institutions? Precisely because they would recommend to people to vote in ways that violate one's interests. And to agree to that one would have to think that others' interests are morally or rationally more relevant than one's own. But why should one assent to that in a democracy where everyone, not just some recognizable experts, is going to have a say? For the same reasons that I rejected Estlund's appeal to common interest, I would reject this appeal to beliefs about what ought to be done, insofar as that is construed as something different from one's preferences.

One final argument against the appeal to individual preference that I will consider is Joshua Cohen's (1989) argument that the point of democracy is to make a decision through the deliberation of members, not just a decision via individual preferences. What makes democracy stable and morally justifiable, he argues, is not its appeal to individual preferences but rather that it promotes the ideal of rational, informed deliberation among its members. The deliberative-democracy interpretation has become quite influential, and among its adherents I would include Rawls (especially the Rawls of *Political Liberalism*), Habermas, Carol Pateman, Martha Nussbaum, Cass Sunstein, and Philip Pettit, among others. Elster (1997) distinguishes usefully between two types of deliberative democracy. One is the "Habermasian" (equally, the Rawlsian) theory, where the goal of politics is rational agreement, rather than political compromise, and the decisive political act is engaging in public debate with the goal of consensus. The other is what Elster calls "participatory democracy," where the goal is transformation and education of participants, and he associates it with Mill and Pateman (and I would add Nussbaum). These three theorists are feminists, one of whose main concerns is to protect individuals against the influence of their own and others' sexist adaptive preferences. Elster argues against this theory on the grounds that it is inherently self-defeating, however. His point is that the apparent goal of participation in a democracy is to pursue one's interests through deliberation and decision. If that is merely apparent, and the point actually is to transform the participants, then if they become informed of that goal they may no longer have an *ex ante* incentive to participate. Many people would find it patronizing,[29] after all, to learn that they are included in a process *so that* they will be changed. That leaves the Habermasian (Rawlsian) theory as the main competitor to liberal democracy, where liberal democracy has as its main aim to pursue the will of the people through their expressions of individual preference, taking those preferences as given. My main concern with this political liberal version of democracy is that in demanding consensus, it demands too much from a diverse population. When there are irreconcilable differences, that come from deeply held moral principles, such as is the case in the abortion question, consensus cannot be had. To demand it will inevitably be to forge a fraudulent and unstable simulation of consensus. Better, in my view, to search for what Rawls terms a *"modus operandi,"* where each side is respected for its right to a position, but no one is pressured to give in to the demand for consensus on pain of complete political breakdown. In the final section of this essay I will present a version of the liberal theory that I think will not fall prey to the dangers we have discussed in the two previous sections, but will also allow greater flexibility and individual liberty in the face of irreconcilable diversity.

Conclusion

Recall the questions I asked before the preceding section: Can we have a democratic decision procedure that takes as its inputs individuals' preferences, but screens out the problematic preferences to the degree necessary to uphold what I have been calling the justificatory criteria of democracy? In the tradition of American democracy, I will argue that there is a largely procedural solution, though it will have to be enhanced by some substantial constraints on the influence of individual preference.

Consider the argument of James Madison in his famous *Federalist Paper* #10, in which he addresses the problem of factions in democracies. Madison states the problem in his pejorative definition of "faction": "a number of citizens whether amounting to a majority or minority of the whole who are united and actuated by some common impulse or passion, or of interest, adverse to the rights of other citizens, or to the permanent and aggregate interest of the community."[30] The problem is that citizens can form coalitions, or sub-groups, that have common interests that they can, by working together, further at the expense of interests of some of the rest of the people or of the whole community. For example, drug manufacturers can, using their immense market power due to the inelastic demand for drugs, further their own narrow economic interests at the expense of the health and well-being of the whole community. According to Madison, there are two possible ways to solve the problems of factions. First, we could try to remove the causes of factions. But there are only two ways to do this, and both are unacceptable. Either by disallowing the freedom of association necessary to form coalitions, a possibility he discards immediately as abolishing the "liberty which is essential to political life,"[31] or by making sure everyone has the same opinion, but this is impossible – it is in the "nature of man" for people to have different opinions. The only other possibility is to control the effects of factions. This is the purpose of the government constructed by the Constitution: to create a democracy that is as immune as possible to the damages of factions.

Analogously, there are two possibilities for solving the problems of individual preferences. We could try to remove the causes of the problems of individual preferences, or we could control their effects. In this case, we need to employ both strategies in a limited way. We need to try to remove the problems of individual preferences, when that can be done without violating the liberty essential to political life, and to control their effects, when they are problematic but cannot be legitimately avoided. Let me briefly address the means by which these things can be accomplished within a liberal democratic framework.

Some of Madison's solutions to the problem of factions apply here as well. The democracy should be limited in two ways. First, it should be a representative government, where the people elect the representatives, who then make legislative and executive decisions. This form of government will help to respond both to the problems of voting paradoxes and Arrow's Theorem, and to the problem of uninformed preferences. Second, there should be a system of liberal rights to protect against non-autonomous, self-defeating, immoral (discriminatory and dominating), and illiberal preferences. Of course, such protection will not be complete, but will only extend to those matters of most intimate concern to the individual. But a balance must be struck between democracy and liberty, between the ability of the people to rule themselves (and so not be ruled by others), and the tyranny of the majority over minorities. Where that balance is struck depends on how much individual liberty is to be protected by the system of rights.[32]

The most pervasive and trenchant problem with the contents of individual preferences is the problem of adaptive and habituated preferences, specifically that they tend to reinforce oppression. Liberal rights, then, should be fashioned with an eye to limiting the oppressive effects of adaptive and habituated preferences on others. The proper principle for fashioning liberal rights might be something like this Mill-inspired principle: The only justification the state has for directly coercing individuals to act contrary to their preferences is to prevent oppression.

Rights can only protect persons so far, however. In a liberal democracy where citizens vote their preferences, there are bound to be additional effects from oppressive preferences. For example, if individuals vote on the basis of adaptive preferences for encouraging women to maintain traditional roles, women's oppression will be further reinforced, even if their rights are not violated. But this problem seems to me not to be unique to *liberal* democracy, but to be common to all forms of democracy. It is the Madisonian problem of factions, with the particular twist that the factions are formed by persons with similar oppressive, adaptive preferences. In addition to liberal rights, then, there will need to be mechanisms to encourage citizens to envision life beyond the oppressive social structures in which their preferences have been molded. Education, freedom of conscience, public support for mind-expanding experiences such as art, music, and leisure activities, and public deliberation among a diverse and active citizenry are the only hope for democracy to avoid tyranny. And the alternative to democracy is almost certain tyranny.

Notes

1 Coleman (1989), p. 194.
2 Compare with Jules Coleman's (1989) strategy for justification.
3 I am using this term "non-tuism" in the sense that Gauthier (1986, p. 87) used it, that is, to say that a preference ordering is non-tuistic is to say that it does not take an interest in the interests of those with whom one is engaged in exchange. So, except for where one is in direct competition with another, one can take others' interests to be part of one's own.
4 Anderson (forthcoming).
5 Ferejohn (1993); Rawls (1993); Nussbaum (2000)
6 I will ignore for the purposes of this essay the question of who counts as a citizen, though, as Dahl (1979) points out, the question of inclusion is closely tied to the justification of a democratic decision procedure.
7 Ordeshook (1986), p. 56.
8 Others, such as Hurley (1989), have relied on similar evasions of Arrow to which my caveat also will apply.
9 Of course, over some decisions, a liberal would argue, dictatorship is just what is morally required; namely, over the private decisions that a system of liberal rights is designed to guarantee.
10 I say "something like" because, first, there are more than two players involved here, although we might represent them as one vs. all the others, and so, as if there are two players. But this will not precisely capture the character of the situation, as Jean Hampton (1987) argued, because of the "step good" structure of voting, as I characterize it. That is, there is some greater benefit to all from half the people voting rather than none, but greater still from all the people voting rather than just half – it is neither continuously dependent on the number of voters, nor what Hampton calls a pure step good, where either all or none of the benefit of voting is reaped with any given number of voters.
11 I am imagining here the following three payoff matrices. First the matrix for the prisoner's-dilemma-like situation that arises when only the individual's costs and benefits from deciding the issue with her vote are considered:

	Others	
	vote	don't
vote	2,2	4,1
me		
don't	1,4	3,3

Second, the assurance-game payoff matrix when reputation effects are introduced, but do not completely overwhelm the individual's costs and benefits from deciding the issue with her vote:

	Others	
	vote	don't
vote	1,1	3,2
me		
don't	2,3	2,2

Third, the payoff matrix when the reputation effects override:

	Others	
	vote	don't
vote	1,1	2,3
me		
don't	3,2	2,2

12 Gibbard (1973), p. 358.
13 Knowing the preferences of the others would not be enough, for that would leave open the possibility that others who are also trying to manipulate the vote, or who are simply making a mistake in the voting booth, could cause the effort to manipulate the vote to fail.
14 Gibbard (1973), p. 366.
15 Elster (1983); Sen (1995); Agarwal (1997).
16 I argued in Cudd (1994) that women often face incentives through the social structure to choose ways of life that will further their oppression. The example that I used to illustrate this was a couple deciding on how to allocate unpaid and paid labor between them, and I argued that the gender wage gap (or any of a number of other structural incentives) would make it rational, from a total household perspective at least, for the wife to do the unpaid domestic labor and the husband to do the paid market labor. But, given the exit options that this choice would give each of the spouses, the woman's power to control resources and outcomes in the marriage and in bargaining over goods would be seriously reduced. Hence, the oppressive conditions that give rise to the choices would then tend to be reinforced by those choices. Yet, to make an opposite choice might require a degree of power in the marriage that was already precluded by the relative bargaining positions of men and women. Women prefer housework against this background of oppression.
17 Sen (1995); Sunstein (1993).
18 Branscombe (1998).
19 I do not mean to suggest here that democracy requires religious intolerance whenever a religion discriminates invidiously against women (or ethnic minorities). At this point,

I am simply illustrating the kinds of undemocratic preference deformations that can occur under the influence of religion. In the end I think that the only way to have a justifiable democratic system is to guarantee a set of personal rights that will some-times conflict with democratic outcomes. Although freedom of religion will be an important right to protect, a democratic society ought to exclude religion from the public sphere. This will be a delicate balance. The details of the balancing process will depend on many local and historical conditions, and are beyond the scope of this essay.

20   Weberman (1997).
21   I am grateful to Robert Simon for this example, and for forcing me to examine Mill's prohibition on self-defeating preferences.
22   Rawls (1993), p. 218.
23   Similar arguments for the virtues of civility and public participation are given by Pettit (1998).
24   Estlund (1990), p. 395.
25   Ibid., p. 396.
26   Ibid., p. 397.
27   Sen (1977), p. 96.
28   Ibid., p. 97.
29   Persons from dominated social groups might find it even worse than patronizing, but rather colonizing, and coercive to be included in such a process.
30   Madison (1961), p. 78.
31   Ibid., p. 78.
32   The question of where such a balance should be struck is, of course, an enormous issue that I cannot take up here.

Bibliography

Agarwal, Bina (1997). "'Bargaining' and gender relations: Within and beyond the house-hold." *Feminist Economics*, 3: 1–51.

Anderson, Elizabeth (forthcoming). "Unstrapping the straitjacket of 'preference': Comment on Amartya Sen's contributions to Philosophy and Economics." *Economics and Philosophy*.

Aranson, Peter (1989). "The democratic order and public choice." In Geoffrey Brennan and Loren E. Lomasky (eds.), *Politics and Process* (pp. 97–148). New York: Cambridge University Press.

Baier, Kurt (1967). "Welfare and preference." In Sidney Hook (ed.), *Human Values and Economic Policy* (pp. 120–35). New York: New York University Press.

Branscombe, Nyla (1998). "Thinking about one's gender group's privileges or disadvan-tages: Consequences for well-being in women and men." *British Journal of Social Psy-chology*, 37: 167–84.

Broome, John (1989). "Should social preferences be consistent?" *Economics and Philoso-phy*, 5: 7–17.

Christiano, Thomas (1993). "Social choice and democracy." In David Copp, Jean Hampton, and John E. Roemer (eds.), *The Idea of Democracy* (pp. 173–95). New York: Cambridge University Press.

——(1996). *The Rule of the Many*. Boulder: Westview Press.

Cohen, Joshua (1989). "Deliberation and democratic legitimacy." In Alan Hamlin and Philip Pettit (eds.), *The Good Polity* (pp. 17–34). Oxford: Blackwell Publishers.

Coleman, Jules (1989). "Rationality and the justification of democracy." In Geoffrey Brennan and Loren E. Lomasky (eds.), *Politics and Process* (pp. 194–220). New York: Cambridge University Press.

Cudd, Ann E. (1994). "Oppression by Choice." *Journal of Social Philosophy*, 25: 22–4.

——(1998). "Psychological explanations of oppression." In Cynthia Willett (ed.), *Theorizing Multiculturalism* (pp. 187–215). Malden, MA: Blackwell Publishers.

Dahl, Robert A. (1979). "Procedural democracy." In P. Laslett and J. S. Fishkin (eds.), *Philosophy, Politics and Society*, 5th Series (pp. 79–133). Oxford: Blackwell Publishers.

——(1956). A *Preface to Democratic Theory*. Chicago: University of Chicago Press.

Elster, Jon (1997). "The market and the forum: Three varieties of political theory." In Robert E. Goodin and Philip Pettit (eds.), *Contemporary Political Philosophy* (pp. 128–42). Oxford: Blackwell Publishers.

——(1983). *Sour Grapes: Studies in the Subversion of Rationality*. Cambridge: Cambridge University Press.

Estlund, David (1990). "Democracy without preference." *Philosophical Review*, 99: 397–423.

Ferejohn, John (1993). "Must preferences be respected in a democracy?" In David Copp, Jean Hampton, and John E. Roemer (eds.), *The Idea of Democracy* (pp. 231–41). New York: Cambridge University Press.

Gauthier, David (1986). *Morals By Agreement*. New York: Oxford University Press.

Gibbard, Allan (1973). "Manipulation of voting schemes: A general result." *Econometrica*, 41: 587–94.

Goodin, Robert E. (1993). "Democracy, preferences, and paternalism." *Policy Sciences*, 26: 229–47.

Hampton, Jean (1987). "Free rider problems in the production of collective goods." *Economics and Philosophy*, 3: 245–73.

Hardin, Russell (1990). "Public choice versus democracy." In John Chapman and Alan Wertheimer (eds.), *Minorities and Majorities: Nomos XXXII* (pp. 184–203). New York: New York University Press.

Held, David (1996). *Models of Democracy*, 2nd edn. Palo Alto: Stanford University Press.

Hurley, Susan (1989). *Natural Reasons*. Oxford: Oxford University Press.

Kittay, Eva Feder (1999). *Love's Labor*. New York: Routledge.

Madison, James (1961). *The Federalist Papers*. New York: NAL Penguin Inc.

Nussbaum, Martha (2000). *Women and Human Development*. New York: Cambridge University Press.

Ordeshook, Peter C. (1986). *Game Theory and Political Theory*. New York: Cambridge University Press.

Pettit, Philip (1998). "Reworking Sandel's republicanism." *Journal of Philosophy*, 95: 73–96.

Rae, Douglas W. (1969). "Decision-rules and individual values in constitutional choice." *American Political Science Review*, 63: 40–56.

Rawls, John (1993). *Political Liberalism*. New York: Columbia University Press.

Sen, Amartya K. (1995). "Gender inequality and theories of justice." In M. Nussbaum and Jonathan Glover (eds.), *Women, Culture, and Development* (pp. 259–73). New York: Oxford University Press.

——(1982). "The impossibility of a paretian liberal." In *Choice, Welfare and Measurement* (pp. 285–90). Oxford: Basil Blackwell.

——(1977). "Rational fools: A critique of the behavioural foundations of economic theory." *Philosophy and Public Affairs*, 6: 317–44.

Sunstein, Cass R. (1991). "Preferences and politics." *Philosophy and Public Affairs*, 20: 3–34.

——(1993). *The Partial Constitution*. Cambridge, MA: Harvard University Press.

Weberman, David (1997). "Liberal democracy, autonomy, and ideology critique." *Social Theory and Practice*, 23: 205–33.

Wollheim, Richard (1962). "A paradox in the theory of democracy." In P. Laslett and W. G. Runciman (eds.), *Philosophy, Politics, and Society*, 2nd Series (pp. 383–92). Oxford: Basil Blackwell.

Part II

Liberalism, Its Critics, and Alternative Approaches

Chapter 6

Marx's Legacy

Richard W. Miller

At the climax of Volume One of *Capital*, Marx concludes hundreds of pages of theory and narrative by describing "the historical tendency of capitalist accumulation": "the mass of misery, oppression, slavery, degradation and exploitation grows; but with this there also grows the revolt of the working class, a class constantly increasing in numbers, and trained, united, and organized by the very mechanism of the capitalist process of production. . . . The knell of capitalist private property sounds. The expropriators are expropriated" ([1867], p. 929). Few people now believe that modern social development has this trajectory. And yet, Marx's descriptions of mechanisms of domination and resistance in capitalist societies, from which he derived this apocalyptic vision, remain of enduring interest to many who reject the vision itself. For what is still plausible in Marx's account of capitalism casts a distinctive light on the nature of wage-labor, freedom, democracy, political legitimacy and community, and even on the authority of the moral point of view. This essay will describe currently promising uses of Marx's legacy to challenge or expand mainstream social and political philosophy, and will sketch some of the leading controversies among those engaged in this project of retrieval.

Marx's Capitalism

Since this project attempts to extract pieces of current wisdom from Marx's whole theory of capitalist society, it is helpful to begin with a sketch of this source. In Marx's view, societies are most fundamentally distinguished by dominant social relations of control in the production of material goods. The dominant form of production in capitalist societies is wage-labor in which those – the proletariat – who control no significant means of production sell the use of their labor power to those – the bourgeoisie – who control the means of production that they work and the proceeds from the sale of what they produce.[1]

For reasons that partly derive from Adam Smith's discussion of wage-determination, Marx believes that proletarians in every capitalist society bargain at a severe disadvantage when they "sell their lives piecemeal" in the labor market. Typically, when a proletarian seeks employment from a capitalist firm, the firm has substantial funds in reserve while the applicant has no substantial savings, and the firm has less of an interest in hiring this particular applicant than the job-seeker has in landing a job now. So the firm is under less pressure to make a deal. Because firms in a typical local labor market are both under less pressure and vastly less numerous than their potential employees, they are in a better position to collaborate (usually tacitly) in resisting increased wages than proletarians are in resisting decreases. Because of the different relationships of employment change and investment change to personal life, "If you don't like it here, try to get a job elsewhere" threatens in a way that "If you don't like our terms for working, invest elsewhere" does not. The bourgeoisie can respond to low unemployment with labor-saving devices, while proletarians cannot use technology to reduce their need for employment. For these and other reasons, if people advance themselves solely through capitalist economic transactions, Marx thinks that the typical outcome of the labor market would be a wage no higher than what *capitalists* require – a wage that keeps workers alive, covers costs of training, and makes it possible for workers to raise children to serve as future grist for the capitalist mill.

According to one caricature of Marx, he thought an iron law of reduction to this physical minimum was irresistible, over the long run, unless capitalism was overthrown. In fact, at least in his post-1848 writings, Marx states that workers can often resist this "tendency of *things*" ([1865], p. 228) and maintain the value of their labor-power through nonrevolutionary collective action transcending market activity, for example, by resorting to trades-union militancy and engaging in political activity leading to economic reforms. According to Marx's labor theory of value, the value of the labor-power used in a working day is the labor time, using currently typical techniques, needed to produce the commodities bought with a day's wage that sustains the current proletarian standard of living. So constancy in value and increasing productivity entail an increase in the commodities that proletarians standardly consume.

Nonetheless, workers' wages will not, over the long run, exceed workers' needs, because needs grow as people perceive growth in what their society can provide. "[L]et a palace arise beside the little house, and it shrinks from a little house to a hut" ([1847], p. 84). Because of the enduring advantages of the bourgeoisie, Marx does not think that proletarians will be able to reduce the economy-wide ratio of surplus-value, i.e., the labor value of capitalists' consumption-goods and means of economic expansion, to the value of labor-power. At best, they will maintain their proportionate share of technological improvements, barely keeping pace with the growth of their needs, determined by "comparison with the state of development of society in general" (ibid., p. 85).

In Marx's view, the conflict between the bourgeoisie and the proletariat shapes political and cultural institutions, as well as the economy: the most socially important features of respectable political and cultural institutions are due to their role in advancing the interests of the bourgeoisie, despite the frequent conflict of those interests with those of the vast majority. In this sense, the bourgeoisie is "the ruling class" politically and in the realm of ideas. Yet Marx evades other caricatures by avoiding speculations about vast conspiracies in favor of appeals to such banal sources of bourgeois influence as governments' need to finance the national debt. One aspect of the project of retrieval, then, is to show how Marx's sober specific descriptions of the mechanisms of bourgeois influence could support the flamboyant general metaphors of class rule.

If, under capitalism, nonrevolutionary activity can preserve the value of labor-power, while the state and ideological institutions are instruments of class rule, won't capitalism last forever? Marx, of course, thinks not: the processes constituting any capitalist society inevitably give rise to its destruction, through the increasing misery and increasing unity described in the apocalyptic passage from *Capital*. Capitalist firms plan production on an ever larger scale, mobilize increasingly capital-intensive technology, and find less and less pre-capitalist territory to exploit, coping with consequent obstacles to successful expansion in the absence of a central plan and in the face of an increasingly knowledgeable and coordinated workers' movement. As a result, workers are victimized by increasing and increasingly violent instability – deepening industrial depressions, wars of mounting severity, and the abandonment of parliamentary democracy for unconstrained and brutal repression. Meanwhile, the advances in education and communication that capitalist production requires, and collective resistance that the burdens of capitalist labor promote, create a proletariat that is aware of common class interests, prepared by a growing history of reciprocal aid to make the individual sacrifices required for successful revolution, and capable of efficient democratic control of a modern economy. In one or another crisis, capitalism is replaced by workers' control of production: at first, through a workers' state, mobilizing individual economic incentives, then, when the psychological residues of capitalist life have dwindled and "all the springs of cooperative wealth flow more abundantly" ([1875], p. 325), through a noncoercive coordinative apparatus implementing a general willingness to work according to ability and provide according to need.

In justifying this vision, Marx often shows awareness of capitalist realities to which most of his learned contemporaries were blind. But the evidence yielded by the twentieth century made this a highly implausible conception of the trajectory of modern society. Should Marx, then, be treated as a shrewd observer of his time, with some attitudes and observations that are still of interest – a nineteenth-century social observer of the limited stature of Ruskin and Carlyle, who disastrously succeeded, where they fortunately failed, in inspiring successful revolutions? Or is he a social theorist whose falsehoods are mixed with general insights of enduring systematic importance – all the more important now, because they shed light on what capitalist triumphalism obscures?

Exploitation

One source of hope that Marx's legacy might have this larger importance is his insistence that capitalist wage-labor is a burden for reasons that are independent of the suffering described in his grimmest indictments. For example, in his last major work, a critique of the 1875 Gotha Program inaugurating the Socialist Workers' Party of Germany, Marx condemns as "truly outrageous" its appeal to an iron law that wages under capitalism tend to decline to the minimum compatible with physical survival: "the system of wage labor is a system of slavery . . . whether the worker receives better or worse payment" ([1875], p. 329).

Because we are still in an era of production by wage-labor, though not in an era of mounting proletarian misery, such passages have excited much interest. "Exploitation," a word that Marx applies to capitalist wage-labor as such, has become the standard term for posing the central question in this project of retrieval, "What is it about capitalist wage-labor that makes it a form of exploitation?" After examining responses that do not appeal to Marx's other celebrated indictment of capitalist wage-labor, as alienated, I will consider the virtues of integrating these two parts of Marx's legacy.

At a certain abstract yet superficial level, it is clear enough why Marx took capitalist wage-labor to be exploitive. He thought that capitalists took advantage of the inferior bargaining power of proletarians in a way that is objectionable. But a *useful* legacy of Marx's discussion will consist of a specific and plausible description of the nature of the objection. Even though Marx thinks that capitalist wage-labor sometimes, initially, has a "historical justification" by reason of its expansion of productive powers, cooperative tendencies and individual prerogatives, he thinks that other reasons for objecting to the capitalist wage-labor system, justifying the label "exploitation," are always part of the system. What could these inherent reasons be?

Such terms as "subjugation," "force," and "slavery" pervade Marx's descriptions of the wage-labor system, and everyone agrees that they indicate a necessary element in its indictment as exploitive. If someone who is delighted to play basketball twice a week for nothing decides to expand his purchases of luxuries by accepting a local promoter's offer to play for so much per game, the transaction hardly seems exploitive. It is too unforced. But Marx's proletarians are not literally slaves. Nothing forces them to work for one capitalist rather than another, and no person forces them to work at all. Why is their engagement in wage-labor forced?

In his discussions of the forced character of the system of freely contracted labor, Marx says that a proletarian is forced to work for the capitalist class, i.e., for one capitalist or other, though not for any particular capitalist. She is forced to do so by her circumstances in the capitalist labor market, even though no person or group forces her to engage in wage-labor. Admittedly, if the constraining circumstances entirely derived from unlucky dealings with nature, they might generate no objection to the social order. But the absence of control over means of production on the part of the vast majority was created and is sustained by coercive acts. In blazing narratives, Marx describes the role of violent dispossession, imperial conquest and repression in the historical process which ultimately made such circumstances the typical worker's fate. More importantly, he also insists that non-violent capitalist competition, starting with a situation of equal possession, would produce analogous circumstances over time, through the class-differentiation of winners and losers and their descendants. The forced character of capitalist wage-labor essentially depends on the current, politically enforced rules of self-advancement and the limited alternatives to wage-labor that they yield.

If proletarians' only alternative to wage-labor were starvation, few would deny that proletarians are forced by their circumstances to sell the use of their labor-power. But this circumstance is not essential to capitalist exploitation. Despite his flamboyant resort to "work or starve" scenarios, Marx must have been aware that the rural folk flocking to the new factories of the Prussian Rhineland, in his youth, were often escaping a physically tenable but utterly dreary existence as poor peasants.

On the other hand, it would hardly do to characterize the choice of wage-labor as forced just because it is rationally preferable to the alternatives (cf. the basket ball player). The other alternatives, in a forced choice of wage-labor, must be, not just rationally dispreferred, but sufficiently bad, posing a choice that one would prefer not to contemplate, even though one might have to, in order to avoid a fate that is even worse. Unlike the basketball player, typical proletarians, in Marx's view, have no real choice because of the badness of the alternatives to wage-labor. Like the prospect of slogging through deep mud that forces a hiker to take the other fork in the road, this badness can fall far short of physical extinction.

Once force is associated with the unacceptability of alternatives to wage-labor, those who seek a currently productive legacy in Marx need to ask whether the alternatives really are so circumscribed. For example, proud owners of thriving small businesses sometimes started out as proletarians, getting where they are by working long hours for little initial reward in the face of large risks of failure. Are workers forced into wage-labor if this escape is available? Cohen (1983) argues that even if each individual proletarian is free for this reason, proletarians as a class are unfree: no large proportion could actually escape by this route, since the consequent undermining of capitalist production would undermine small proprietors, who depend on its flourishing.

Others have insisted that the risks and burdens of the escape routes available to any individual proletarian whose situation is at all typical make them fit for a menu of alternatives constituting forced choice. Also, some (for example, Reiman, 1987) take the time required for exit to be compatible with an ascription of forced choice in the meantime.

Any of these specifications of the forced nature of wage-labor could, in principle, be part of a celebration of wage-labor, illuminating its virtues by contrast with the bad alternatives. So other ingredients of the "exploitation" charge must be characterizations of what proletarians actually choose. Of course, it is important that capitalists benefit from the circumstances forcing proletarians to sell them the use of their labor-power. Exploitation involves deriving a benefit from someone on account of a weakness (as Wood, 1995, emphasizes). But another ingredient seems to be required. After all, dentists benefit from others' being forced by toothaches to seek their aid. Yet we do not take them, on this ground, to exploit their patients or their patients' suffering (cf. ibid., p. 136). The nature of this missing ingredient, the objectionable feature of the way in which bargaining weakness forces proletarians to work on terms that benefit capitalists, is the central controversy over Marxian exploitation (a controversy much invigorated by Roemer's thesis (e.g., in Roemer, 1985) that exploitation does not in fact merit normative interest from Marxists).

"Unpaid" labor

According to some, the needed ingredient, in addition to capitalist benefit from workers' bargaining weakness, is provided by Marx's characterization of the benefit itself. A capitalist firm will not last for long unless the wage paid for a working day is worth less than what a worker adds to output in a working day. Marx often characterizes the working day remaining after the worker produces the equivalent of her wage as "unpaid" (though he also often concedes that this usage is not literally correct). Perhaps Marx thought that capitalism was exploitive because "its social structure is organized so that unpaid labor is systematically forced out of one class and put into the disposal of another" (Reiman, 1987, p. 3; see also Holmstrom, 1977).

But is this surplus-extraction sufficient, by itself, to make a social process exploitive? At the start of the *Communist Manifesto*, without a trace of irony, Marx celebrates a heroic era in which capitalism overcomes technological stagnation, geographic isolation, stultifying conformity to tradition, and abject feudal deference. These benefits depend on the extraction of "unpaid" labor, which provides incentives and resources for capitalist improvement of productive powers. In principle, if not in Marx's view of actual history, the benefits could make capitalism the best feasible system, on balance, for workers in a certain phase of a certain society. Marx's quip about well-paid slaves implies that capitalist wage-labor would still count as exploitation. But unless more is said about the process of surplus-extraction, the charge of exploitation seems farfetched.

Granted, if a capitalist and a proletarian employee are typical occupants of their social roles, their incomes will be quite out of proportion to the time that they invest in economic activity. But, as Arneson (1981, pp. 206f) and others have noted, such disproportion need not be a basis for condemning a relationship as exploitive. If healthy workers are taxed to help those who are physically unable to work, the frail will benefit out of proportion to their labor, but this does not seem to constitute exploitation. Indeed, such transfers are characteristic of the post-capitalist societies that Marx regards as overcoming exploitation (see [1875], pp. 322f, 325).

Unfairness

If the proletarian disadvantage from which capitalists benefit is an unfair circumstance, then the charge of exploitation is apt. And some, for example, Arneson (1981), have taken the charge that the underlying differences in control of means of production are unfair to be implicit in Marx's critique of capitalist wage-labor. They are well aware that Marx strenuously avoids talk of unfairness in his indictments, even mocks praise of the superior fairness of socialist distribution in the Gotha Program as "ideological nonsense" ([1875], p. 325), but they take these features of his writings to reflect limited, tactical aims, or to represent a false and dispensable part of his legacy.

Even so, Marx's avoidance of fairness-talk in his indictments would be significant for the project of retrieval. He thought he could describe what makes wage-labor exploitive without applying the label "unfair." Those who think that unfairness is part of a valid charge should concede that this more specific description would be his central achievement. For them, it is a description of what makes the capitalist labor market unfair.

Inequality

The disadvantages of proletarians are due to unequal control over means of production. Is this what makes wage-labor exploitive, perhaps because it makes the capitalist labor market unfair? Mere unequal control does not seem sufficient. If a rule that the first to farm a plot gets to own it were to benefit all, because of the incentives it provides for irrigation and fertilization, the resulting advantages, due to unequal control, of first-farmers over newcomers need not be exploitive. Suppose, then, that exploitation is restricted to situations of unequal control in which some would be better off in a situation of equality. Then we lack an account of why progressive capitalism can constitute exploitation even if equal control would be so inefficient that everyone loses.

Alienated labor

These difficulties may dictate a more thorough appropriation of Marx's legacy, including the discussions of alienation which occur throughout his life, even though they are most prominent early on.

Marx takes the domination of economic life by capitalism to alienate people from one another and from themselves. People are alienated from one another above all because the other's neediness, which could be an object of positive concern in a valued relationship, is instead used as a source of tactical advantage ("the *means* whereby I acquire power over you," [1844a], p. 275) or confronted as a source of resistance to one's own aspirations. The prime example of this estrangement is the capitalist labor market, in which capitalists, if they are to stay in business, must do what they can to take advantage of needs driving people to seek employment (the word "exploit" comes very naturally, here), and to find the response to workers' demands that most enhances their own profits. Because the other's needs are not themselves a source of concern yet express her aspirations to human dignity, Marx characterizes relationships that are wholly determined by the imperatives of the market in a Kantian way, as relationships in which one person "makes use of the other . . . as his means" ([1857–8], p. 243), and the capitalist treats "the real producer as a means of production, material wealth as an end in itself" ([1866], p. 1037).

It is natural to characterize someone as exploiting another's needs when she benefits from them *and* is only sensitive to them as useful information in her promotion of her independent interests. A dentist who charges as much as he can from those driven by pain to seek his services and who avoids preventive advice that will make a patient less lucrative does exploit his patients' suffering. But something more, something more encompassing, is going on in the capitalist–proletarian relationship, which constitutes exploitation of the proletarian, not just exploitation of his neediness. The outcome is the alienation of the worker from himself. Even if the outcome of the proletarian's bargaining weakness is not a life scarcely better than death by starvation, Marx thinks it is (always or almost always) a work-life that is endured as a sacrifice, "not the satisfaction of a need, but a mere *means* to satisfy needs outside itself" ([1844], p. 326). Such an existence is an option that the worker, if self-respecting, could not embrace as an expression of who he is, as "an activation of *his own* nature" ([1844], p. 326). Rather, he must be disposed to resist it as not "worthy and appropriate for . . . [his] human nature" ([1894], p. 959).

In part, Marx regards this need not to identify with one's work-life as the worker's alienation from herself, because work-life under capitalism takes up so many of a proletarian's waking hours. But the thesis of self-alienation also reflects an assessment of the value of production. (If Marx thought that only leisure was worthy of enjoyment, he would have regarded all work as alienated.) Like Aristotle (see Miller, 1981), Marx thinks that the molding of one's environment according to one's imaginatively formulated plans, guided by one's aspirations, is fundamental to a worthwhile human life. Circumstances that make someone's productive activity unworthy of her enjoyment make it impossible for her life as a whole to be an adequate expression of her humanity.

This verdict does not depend on the proletarian's enduring the mind-numbing drudgery described in the most heartrending reportage in *Capital*. But it does depend on the features of work-life under capitalism that Marx sometimes calls the "real subsumption of labor under capital" ([1866], pp. 1034f), which inevitably results from its "formal subsumption," the control of the labor-process by the bourgeoisie. In pursuit of discipline, coordination and efficient use of technology, capitalist firms will so structure proletarian work that proletarians are ordered around in activities that do not merit much interest, permit much initiative or mobilize a broad range of human capacities.

Suppose that in capitalist production those with significant control over the means of production benefit from bargaining disadvantages that others are forced to endure, to which they are responsive as tactical advantages to be used or sources of discontent whose cost is to be minimized. That a relationship is characterized by this alienated response to others' imposed weakness does seem a reason (which is not to say a conclusive reason) to object to it, and does seem a basis for regarding the relationship as exploitive. Suppose, in addition, that the outcome for the weaker party is forced acceptance of certain terms for living that are not fully worthy of a human being, and that the stronger party benefits from the imposition of these terms. Then one might naturally say that the stronger party exploits the weaker party. So perhaps Marx's theory of exploitation and his theory of alienation are continuous. Capitalist wage-labor is a form of exploitation because capitalists benefit, in an alienated way, from socially imposed weaknesses in others, benefiting from the capacity to impose work lives on them that alienate those others from themselves.[2]

Many, probably most wage-earners in any modern capitalist economy could see themselves as the exploitees in this portrait. But the vast majority of them think that further gains from this form of production, including gains derived from added efficiency, make some form of capitalism better for working people than any non-capitalist alternative. Suppose that they are right. Does the view that capitalist wage-labor exploits workers still have a bearing on modern political choice? It does if one takes seriously the forced and alienated character of capitalist exploitation.

According to one familiar perspective on political choice, government interference with individuals' efforts to retain the full benefits of capitalist self-advancement is a troubling interference with freedom, justifiable, if at all, by the need to take account of other values, such as economic equality. But if a complaint of exploitation is a complaint of being forced to have a work-life with which one cannot self-respectfully identify because it does not enjoyably exercise a reasonably wide range of valuable human capacities, then it is a complaint of unfreedom. If taxation or restrictions of freedom of contract are feasible ways of mitigating or compensating in response to exploitation, then these measures will often express a proper valuing of freedom. To adapt an example of Raz's (1986, p. 374): a woman who must spend eight hours a day devoting her energies to evading a tiger is significantly unfree. If the Island Council can help her by requiring someone to cage his pet, they need not be troubled by the thought that freedom has been reduced to promote another good.

In addition to its challenge to restricted understandings of freedom characteristic of libertarian political philosophy, the Marxist theory of exploitation also casts doubt on forms of liberal egalitarianism in which the ultimate perspective of equality avoids reliance on a ranking of ways of life. Liberals count equal freedom as a specially important aspect of equality, and, for reasons just noted, this seems to make complaints of exploitation serious, the more serious the greater the degree of exploitation. These degrees correspond to differences in alienation due to the "real subsumption of labor" and differences in the difficulty of escape routes on the menu of alternatives, as well as to differences in the ratio of "unpaid" to "paid" labor. Yet mitigation of the distinctive burdens of those whose exploitation is relatively intense may produce a reduction in their net income, the "all purpose resource" favored by liberal neutralists in their judgments of economic justice. For example, this trade-off is posed by costly restrictions on prerogatives to fire employees and by public funding of access to cultural resources that facilitate the enjoyment of a broad range of capacities but do not add to income. At such junctures, it is hard to see how neutrality among ways of life can be observed if complaints of exploitation are given appropriate weight. But it is also hard to see how the dismissal of these complaints in the name of neutrality could be reconciled with the liberal valuation of freedom.

Finally, if the Marxist critique of exploitation is valid, the emphasis on equality of life-chances in current liberal politics as well as liberal–egalitarian political philosophy is one-sided. The fundamental project of economic justice is often envisaged as the elimination of unjustified disadvantages in "starting places" at birth (Rawls, 1971, p. 7). Certainly, those who are sympathetic to Marx will share the concern with the lower prospects of economic success of those whose parents or communities have not fared well in capitalist competition. But sensitivity to harms of exploitation can support strong criticism of the structure of economic success and failure, which is independent of inequality in life-chances. Suppose (probably *per impossibile*) that a reasonably efficient capitalist society could so arrange education and initial economic resources that everyone has an equal initial chance of winding up on top. If, nonetheless, some, inevitably, spend significant parts of their lives being severely exploited, those sympathetic to Marx will discern an objectionable form of inequality. As usual, they extend routine democratic attitudes toward politics into the economic realm: an enduring regime of tyranny is not much improved if a lottery system gives everyone an equal initial chance to be a tyrant.

The State and Capitalism

Those who have lost hope in Marx's vision of post-capitalist society while sympathizing with his accounts of harms generated by capitalism will look to government action to reduce those harms. So they need to assess Marx's further view that the bourgeoisie is the political ruling class under capitalism.

"[T]he bourgeoisie has . . . conquered for itself, in the modern representative State, exclusive political sway. The executive of the modern state is but a committee for managing the common affairs of the bourgeoisie" ([1848], p. 37). "[T]he State power which nascent middle-class society had commenced to elaborate as a means of their own emancipation from feudalism . . . full-grown bourgeois society had finally transformed into a means for the enslavement of labour by capital" ([1871], p. 290). What can Marx have meant by these claims? They seem to announce far-flung conspiracies uniting the leaders of politics and commerce, yet Marx engages in no such speculation, and, indeed, makes the second claim right after noting the blithe disengagement of businesspeople from political activity under Louis-Napoleon.

Three general claims are jointly summed up in the blazing metaphors of class rule:

1   *Government actions serve the long-term interests of the bourgeoisie as a whole, even if those interests conflict with those of the rest of society.*   This is *not* to deny that shifts in government policy may satisfy or forestall proletarian demands whose existence is not in the interest of the bourgeoisie. Since the bourgeoisie have an important (though not an all-important) interest in acquiescence and stability, such accommodation may be essential to their long-term interests as a whole. Still, at least in a mature capitalist society, Marx thinks that all shifts in policy that, taken in isolation, impose significant costs on the bourgeoisie function as prudent tactical retreats from disruption or the threat of disruption – prudent, that is, from the standpoint of the bourgeoisie.

2   *This bias in interests served is sustained by mechanisms that are part of the social context of political choice, sufficient mechanisms which will exist, in one form or other, so long as capitalism endures.*   In particular, in describing ties between government action and bourgeois interests in stable parliamentary democracies, Marx ascribes the pattern of choice on the part of successful elected officials to underlying relations of economic power rather than bribery or conspiracy. The approval of bourgeois-controlled media is a centrally important resource for electoral success. Elected officials rely on the bourgeoisie to finance the national debt. Those at the top of political hierarchies are isolated from the lives and problems of most people, and drawn into the cultural milieu and interpersonal networks of those at the top of economic hierarchies. (For this reason, Marx celebrates the Paris Commune's restriction of officials' salaries to no more than a skilled worker's wage as part of what made it "the political form at last discovered under which to work out the economic emancipation of labour" ([1871], p. 294).) Many people outside of the bourgeoisie falsely identify their own interests because of bourgeois control of media and other "means of intellectual production" or because their social situation spontaneously gives rise to false hopes and distorted beliefs, such as the hopes leading small farmers to align themselves with business interests that will ultimately destroy them, or the retreat of the oppressed into faith in heavenly redemption.

3   If a social movement threatens to end the bias toward bourgeois interests, the old connection between class and government will be defended through violence which mobilizes residual bourgeois political resources, violence which can only be defeated by organized counter-violence, rooted, in part, in non-electoral activity.   Even within the bounds of apt metaphor, the state would not be a means for the enslavement of labor if bourgeois dominance of society could be ended by legally protected electoral activity. Marx thought that a bourgeoisie confronted with this prospect would either successfully promote a regime of direct and violent repression, such as Louis-Napoleon's, or, at a minimum, support a "pro-slavery rebellion" against an elected working-class government (see Engels' Preface to the English edition of *Capital*, volume 1 (Marx, [1867], p. 113)). If the latter regime could be defended, this would be because of resistance led by proletarians, taking advantage of extensive experience of non-electoral conflicts in which workers had confronted capitalist firms and prior, pro-capitalist regimes.[3]

It is, to put it mildly, hard to tell whether reforms benefiting workers at direct cost to capitalists are best explained as the result of social mechanisms making government action sensitive to long-term bourgeois interests including interests in acquiescence, or as the result of the independent power of the exercise of democratic rights, a process that is capable of producing departures from the long-term interests of the bourgeoisie. In the absence of a compelling argument that the bourgeoisie (alias big business) is more than an exceptionally influential interest group, what could be the value of this part of Marx's legacy?

One currently quite plausible feature of Marx's theory of the capitalist state is his view that the existence of mechanisms insuring that state action will be importantly biased toward the interests of the bourgeoisie is an inevitable feature of capitalism. Suppose that private campaign contributions are illegal and everyone has the means to form political opinions through intelligent, sufficiently leisured reading of the most informative nonspecialized media. Still, managers and professionals at the top of the capitalist economic division of labor, who tend, for obvious reasons, to over-identify the interests of the bourgeoisie with the interests of society as a whole, will have knowledge, skills and networks of acquaintance that make them especially likely to be recruited to positions of political power or to offer influential advice. Resource allocation will still be dominated by a stock market driven by the lust for returns of self-interested investors, so that political leaders must take care to avoid creating anxiety among investors about their returns. Marx and his critics agree that such underlying sources of bias toward the bourgeoisie could not be eliminated without destroying requirements of reasonable efficiency in capitalist production. Moreover, capitalist ownership of media gives rise to disproportionate influence over public opinion, which (even apart from the dangers of stultifying domination) pervasive state ownership would hardly remove, given bourgeois influence on the state.

A common and plausible view of capitalism, which I will sometimes call "the post-Marxist synthesis," combines this core of Marx's theory of the capitalist state with two other elements. First, even if the conflict between the interests of the bourgeoisie and the interests of most working people is not as severe as Marx supposed, there are often serious conflicts between the interests of the bourgeoisie and measures reducing burdens of life under capitalism in desirable ways, through feasible reductions in the degree of exploitation, unemployment, inferiority in economic opportunity, and inequalities that push minorities to the margins of civic life. Because such measures add to costs of production, make work discipline harder to achieve, or make it harder for those in or allied with the bourgeoisie to maintain their personal wealth and status and pass them on to their children, the structural political power of the bourgeoisie will seriously limit responsiveness to disadvantage. The other element in the post-Marxist synthesis is the quite non-Marxist view that some form of capitalism is better, for all, than any form of non-capitalism.

This mixture has an important bearing on views of legitimacy and loyalty in the mainstream of political thought. Like the positions that Marx criticized from his more radical perspective, these views (if the post-Marxist synthesis is right) exaggerate the importance of purely political processes through neglect of inequalities of economic power. Ironically, these criticisms are more powerful because of the concession that some form of capitalism is best.

To begin with, the post-Marxist synthesis is a challenge to political liberalism, the most important explicit affirmation, in current political philosophy, of the primacy of the purely political (see Rawls, 1993). According to political liberalism, citizens of a democracy should strive to resolve questions of basic justice, including basic economic justice, through principled, mutually attentive deliberations establishing a broad consensus concerning the proper interpretation of purely political liberal values, such as civil liberty and equal citizenship. This restriction to consensus based on liberal political values assessed in the forum of public reason is not arbitrary, political liberals say, because it is required to reconcile the inevitable coerciveness of political choice with the mutual respect that citizens owe to one another.

However, if the post-Marxist synthesis is right, political choice constrained by political liberalism will, in important cases, be incompatible with respect for fellow-citizens. Suppose that those who are exploited have a serious complaint against the laws and policies that make exploitation such as theirs inevitable, the more serious the higher the degree of exploitation. (Virtually all political liberals accept this, as they should, given the implications of their attitude toward coercion.) One can combine respect for the exploited with insistence that a political response to their complaints take place through certain channels, only if this political process is not biased against them. But, according to the residue of Marx's ruling-class thesis, the process of consensus formation through principled discussion is biased against the exploited in any capitalist society. If, in response, the political liberal protests that the intended forum of public reason excludes such systematic distortion, then the thesis of the superiority of some form of capitalism comes into play: the constraint restricted to unbiased processes applies to no society which ought to be promoted.

Those who reject political liberalism on these grounds can still insist that coercion of those who protest out of conscientious adherence to principles is always a serious cost, especially if the protest is grounded on an interpretation of liberal values. But they will take such costs to be justifiable in systematically important cases. Because of their view of the dynamics of social change, they will be especially concerned to allow that non-officials in a constitutional democracy may sometimes advance their political programs by coercive means even as reasonable discourse continues. The sitdown strikers of the 1930s in the United States, Canada, Sweden and elsewhere did not wait for a consensus on the meaning of equal citizenship and civil and political liberties to develop and to sustain their aspirations by appropriate legislation. If they had waited, this consensus might never have emerged.

Political liberalism is one special way of further developing an assumption about political legitimacy that is much more widely shared: any morally responsible citizen should help to achieve a polity whose legislation ought to be upheld, by each citizen, even if she regards it as unwise or unjust, because of the political process that produced it and the overall division of benefits and burdens that this process sustains; this support for each outcome of the whole process may, of course, include efforts to change the law, but each citizen should have grounds for regarding it as everyone's duty to help implement the law until it is changed. Whether or not they are political liberals, many political theorists regard this as a feasible goal, so that it is at least an open question whether current societies have attained it. Even if they take the answer to be "no," many are inclined to suppose that current democracies have come close enough that the disobedient should, at the very least, honor the political process as a whole by disobeying symbolically and publicly, and willingly submitting to punishment. But the ideal is utopian from the standpoint of the post-Marxist synthesis.

The actual consent of all will not be forthcoming as a basis for the general duty of political commitment. In any case, consent can be irrelevant because of the pressures that create it. For these and other reasons, the most likely basis for the duty of political commitment is a condition which, apart from consent, makes it wrong for someone not to uphold the outcomes of a collective process. Plausible descriptions of such circumstances incorporate requirements of fair treatment, as in the claim that it is wrong to disobey rules governing a collective process if one has benefited from general conformity and if the benefits and burdens of the process are fairly shared. But at least if the collective process dominates one's whole life, as the process of government does, it is essential that this fair sharing involve adequate equality in responsiveness to one's needs, interests and desires as compared to others'. Given the threat of destructive chaos, Ivan the Terrible's autocracy may have been by far the best feasible regime from the standpoint of the serfs, but they had no duty to obey all the mandates resulting from a process in which they counted for so much less than others. Similarly for some citizens of any modern state, according to the post-Marxist synthesis: any feasible and desirable political arrangement is too systematically biased in favor of others' interests for these citizens to have a comprehensive, overriding duty to uphold its outcomes because of the kind of polity it is. They might still conform on humanitarian grounds, because of harmful consequences of nonconformity, but not because the nature of the political process makes disobedience wrong.

In addition to these doubts about political legitimacy, Marx's legacy yields a cosmopolitan reassessment of patriotic loyalties. Marx himself scornfully rejects such loyalties. "The workingmen have no country. We cannot take from them what they have not got" ([1848], p. 51). In its full extent, this radical cosmopolitanism depends on views of the destructiveness of rule by the local bourgeoisie and of the international proletarian interest in world revolution that now seem outmoded. The post-Marxist synthesis does leave some room for duties of special concern for compatriots that bind proletarians. In a modern democracy – most post-Marxists would accept – everyone benefits from the general preference for principled persuasion and support for democratic rights and civil liberties. A proper valuing of this civic respect can require special loyalty to its source, one's fellow-citizens, analogous to the special loyalties of friendship. Also, ongoing active political participation in capitalist democracy is a duty, in the post-Marxist synthesis, and there is a special obligation to mitigate burdens of disadvantage created by a process of political coercion in which one actively participates.

Still, Marx's legacy adds considerable weight to cosmopolitan considerations, extending them far beyond ordinary humanitarian concerns, on account of current international economic relations. The critique of exploitation cannot stop at the borders: because people in countries with high per-capita income benefit from the especially intense international exploitation of people in poor countries, they have a special obligation to help them. A proper valuing of nonalienated relationships, in which others' needs are a source of positive concern, entails a commitment to change a world economy in which the needs of those in poor countries are exploited (and, sometimes, created) as sources of tactical advantage in a process that is facilitated by international institutions. Finally, if (as post-Marxists think) inequalities of bargaining power based on the mobility of capital and the capacity of capitalist firms to shift productive tasks elsewhere still dominate workers' lives, the growth of international ties among workers and their allies is a central means of reducing exploitation.

Morality and Social Interests

In addition to many discussions of capitalism that have normative implications, Marx occasionally directly confronts general moral perspectives. His arguments against these particular perspectives may also shed light on brief, shocking, unargued gibes in which Marx seems to criticize morality as such.

Equal rights

Marx's criticisms of large normative perspectives are typically arguments that this or that consideration of equality is not decisive. Certainly, he has only scorn or pity for those who would make mere equality of well-being the overriding social standard, so that leveling downward would be an advance. What is more surprising is the ferocious attack on appeals to equal rights that he launches in response to the Gotha Program's call for "a fair distribution of the proceeds of labour," ending in his condemnation of this passage for perverting the realistic outlook which German socialist workers had gained with "ideological nonsense about rights and other trash so common among the democrats and French socialists" ([1875], p. 325). For Marx's own strategic goals are naturally characterized in terms of rights. For example, in his critique of the Gotha Program, he proposes that the first stage of socialism would implement an equal right of all able-bodied adults to gainful employment and to reward in proportion to labor time and skill. At a higher stage, in communist society, each has a right to be provided for according to his or her need, from the social output to which all have a duty to contribute according to ability.

Still, Marx insists that every right *"is a right of inequality"* (ibid., p. 324). He seems to have in mind that every right definite enough to regulate social cooperation will favor some people's interests or goals over others' in ways that violate a rival principle of right that also merits consideration; no super-principle of equal right is broad and powerful enough to provide a satisfactory rights-based adjudication of all such conflicts among social rights. His prime example is the neglect of the needs of relatively frail workers or those with many dependants at the first stage of socialism, in comparison with the later standard of provision according to need. But analogous comparisons of capitalist rights with socialist rights are also apt (if out of tune with a socialist manifesto such as the Gotha Program). The first stage of socialism that Marx describes prevents self-denying entrepreneurial strivers from establishing capitalist enterprises, and this violation of the right to peaceful self-advancement through voluntary agreement merits a non-question-begging justification – one which (Marx implies) cannot rest on an appeal to rights.[4]

Utilitarian impartiality

In denying that all politically important conflicts among rights can be adequately adjudicated by appeal to a further, deeper right, Marx agrees with utilitarianism.[5] Yet Marx's discussions of utilitarianism drip with contempt for what he sees as crass neglect of the diversity of human experiences and relationships. Jeremy Bentham is mocked as "a genius in the way of bourgeois stupidity," who takes what is useful to the modern English shopkeeper to be absolutely useful ([1867], p. 759). Reflecting the subordination of all relationships to "the one abstract monetary–commercial system" in modern bourgeois society, utilitarianism is said to commit the manifest "stupidity of merging all the manifold relationships of people in the *one* relationship of usefulness" ([1845–6], p. 409).

In these acid discussions (especially ibid., pp. 409–19), Marx seems to criticize utilitarianism for a failure to cope with the diversity of competing forms of happiness, which parallels the failure of rights-based morality to cope with conflicts among standards of equal right. If utilitarianism measures overall well-being solely by the extent and intensity of pleasurable feelings, then, despite its claim to impartiality, it is arbitrarily biased against most people's life-goals, which are not crudely hedonistic, and is fated to rate relationships solely by their pleasurable payoffs, so that, for example, a relationship grounded on successful mutual shameless flattery is worth no less than a relationship of mutual respect and concern. On the other hand, a Millian proposal to employ the rankings of kinds of experiences to which all would agree if they had the relevant experiences must confront relationships between forms of enjoyment and social situations that Marx repeatedly emphasizes. Different social experiences give rise to different rankings of competing forms of enjoyment, such as the zest of competition versus the warmth of mutual support, pleasures of material consumption versus pleasures of materially modest leisure, enjoyment of the pursuit of enormous income, with some prospect of success, versus enjoyment of the security of a guaranteed modest minimum without the possibility of enormous income. In a class-divided society, the differences in dispositions to enjoy are sufficiently rigid that further experience of alternative ways of life would not produce a unanimous ranking, uniting, for example, industrial workers, maids, investment bankers, commodity brokers, farmers and shopkeepers.

Admittedly, if Marx were right about the consequences of modern capitalism and the socialist alternative, the joint verdicts on kinds of enjoyment would be determinate enough to dictate the choice of socialism on utilitarian grounds, since capitalism would expose many more people to forms of suffering and premature death which are dire fates in any ranking. Still, a class-neutral standard would be an inadequate guide to evaluations which might be crucial at other junctures, such as policy-choice in the first stage of socialism, and which would sometimes be crucial in a post-Marxist view of current social facts.

Forms and limits of morality

In the *Manifesto*, responding to an imagined protest that "Communism abolishes . . . all morality, instead of constituting [it] . . . on a new basis," Marx blithely notes that "it is no wonder" that such a radical revolution "involves the most radical rupture with traditional ideas" ([1848], p. 52). In *The German Ideology*, his criticisms of utilitarianism end with the broadly anti-moral declaration that communism "has shattered the basis of all morality, whether the morality of asceticism or of enjoyment" ([1845–6], p. 419). To what extent did Marx really intend to reject reliance on morality? There may be no way to resolve this much-discussed exegetic question. For example, what seem to be broad attacks on morality could be hyperbolic indictments of all specific, respectable conceptions of fairness, justice and morality in his time, which he took to be obstacles to the workers' movement. Still, as the brief, tantalizing bits of apparent anti-moralism indicate, Marx's explicit discussions of the failures of rights-based morality and utilitarianism to cope with social conflict suggest more general limits to reliance on morality.

Whether Marx provides a basis for criticizing reliance on morality in social choice will, of course, depend on how "morality" is understood. On one construal, someone is committed to a morality if he thinks that choices of his and others that adhere to certain norms are rational in light of their circumstances, even when they involve sacrifices of the chooser's personal interests and the interests of beloved intimates, and he takes such choices to be worthy of praise while taking insufficiently mitigated failure so to choose to be worthy of condemnation. On this construal, Marx was a stern and eloquent partisan of morality. He takes adherence to the goals and strategies of revolutionary socialism to be rational in light of burdens that capitalism engenders and opportunities for removing them under socialism. At the same time, he thinks that such commitment will, at crucial junctures, require considerable self-sacrifice, which he eventually epitomized and celebrated in his moving eulogy commemorating the "heroic self-sacrifice" of the Paris Communards, at the end of *The Civil War in France*.

Marx's emphasis on the essential role of class interest does entail that sufficiently strong and pervasive motivation for socialist revolution depends on the motivational power of the thought that success will benefit those in one's proletarian situation (including oneself if one survives), ending the social domination from which one has suffered. But Marx's theory of the state makes engagement in revolutionary activity risky business, while the success of the workers' movement would be a public good, available to proletarians who took no such risks. So class loyalty, based on self-respect, not the mere maximization of expected personal benefit, is essential to Marx's revolutionary hopes, which endorse a demanding morality on the first construal.[6]

Still, even if Marx was committed to a practice of reasoned self-sacrifice in pursuit of large social goals, he could have rejected morality in another sense as an inadequate basis for political choice. The moral point of view is often understood as an *impartial* standpoint for choice, the authoritative perspective in which one chooses with equal concern or respect for all. Thus, each of the specific moral standpoints that Marx criticizes is typically offered as a favored interpretation of the demands of moral impartiality. Perhaps the anti-moral remarks reject ultimate reliance on an impartial perspective.

Certainly, Marx regarded impartial concern and respect as insufficient to motivate the successful pursuit of the social goals he advocated. However sincere their professions of impartial concern or respect, the interests of the bourgeoisie and their allies would lead them to reconcile these moral commitments with the defense of the status quo, and proletarian loyalty based on class solidarity would be necessary to motivate its overthrow. In addition, Marx may have thought that there were important limits to the capacity of morality, in the second, impartialist sense, to *justify* political choices that reflect the reasoned commitments constituting his morality in the first, broad sense. These doubts might have been based on extrapolation from inadequacies he discerned in all of the impartial moralities of his time. However, they may also indicate a further legacy to be derived from Marx's social theories, a concern for the epistemic consequences of social division.

The deep problems of utilitarianism (of which Marx's objections are only a sample) suggest that the standpoint of impartial morality is, most fundamentally, a standpoint of equal respect for persons. But notoriously, people in any modern society are divided in their conscientious interpretations of the demands of equal respect. How can political choices expressing the dictates of equal respect lead some to force institutions on others, which these others regard as incompatible with equal respect? When important life-long interests are at stake, an appeal to majority rule is not sufficient – otherwise it could be too easy to justify, say, the imposition of a state church on a religious minority. But (as political liberals emphasize in our time), the dogmatic stipulation of a particular interpretation of equal respect for persons is not sufficient either. For example, someone could accept that extensive interference with market-generated inequalities is required by the standards that he would choose behind Rawls's "veil of ignorance," while protesting that the Rawlsian interpretation of respect for fellow-members of one's society leads to disrespectful taking of people's benefits gained from their uses of their actual talents and assets in honest, peaceful self-advancement. If one simply dismisses his construal of respect for persons and forces him to conform, one can hardly claim to act as respect for persons requires.

Because of the plurality of competing interpretations, the project of basing political choice on the dictates of equal respect for all requires an appropriately impartial basis for interpreting these dictates. When I am aware that others are drawn to different interpretations, I am, nonetheless, justified in relying on my construal of the dictates of equal respect if I am justified in believing that the others would share it if we all rationally reflected on relevant facts and put to one side our special interests and other morally irrelevant biases. So politics can be based on impartial morality if partisans can be warranted in taking their choices to be relevantly untainted.

Marx's insistence on the robust connection between people's social positions and their evaluative stances suggests that this interpretive project may be epistemically utopian. There may be important areas of social choice in which the pursuit of untainted interpretations is neither feasible nor desirable.

It is not easy to be sure that one's favored controversial specification of an abstract moral principle does not essentially depend on one's own special interests, the special interests of a social group with which one identifies or some cast of temperament that lacks moral authority. In some cases, actual agreement among people of diverse interests, backgrounds and temperaments or the actual trend of increasing agreement in response to shared information offer adequate assurance

that partiality does not intrude. But there is often no such evidence of the innocence of one's response to a controversial principle of social choice. If one's distinctive moral inclinations correspond to the interests of those in one's social
situation (a tendency from which intellectuals are hardly exempt), there may be
no adequate assurance that those inclinations do not essentially depend on those
partial interests. Even when inclinations depart from social background, as in
Marx's case, they may simply reflect the forces that give a temperament its distinctive cast (in Marx's case, a cast of defiance).

It might seem that equal respect would still require striving to free oneself from
partial interests, even though one's best effort may very well be inadequate. But
Marx's theory of ideology suggests that this effort is not a means of moving closer
to a determinate perspective of equal respect, for most people when they reflect
on fundamental questions of social choice. What *does* determine choice if one has
broken the hold of one's special interests and inclinations? Presumably, the moral
milieu in which one has grown up. But where social choice is concerned (Marx
argues), this milieu reflects a process of reconciling social stability with the dominance of an economic elite. If this is true to a significant extent, then detachment
from their special interests by those outside of the elite will not be a route to equal
respect, even though attachment to those interests poses its own threats of cal-
lousness, intolerance and envy.[7]

Given Marx's empirical beliefs, this indeterminacy might not affect the choice
of socialism over capitalism, because of the differences between these alternatives
on all dimensions of concern to those who are striving, however diversely, to show
equal respect for all. Still, given the dangers, uncertain prospects and speculative
goals of any particular socialist revolutionary initiative, orthodox Marxists won-
dering whether to call workers to the barricades may well have found it impossible to resolve the question on the basis of impartialist morality. In any case,
nowadays, in the absence of old empirical convictions, the diversity of specifications of respect, justice and well-being may make the sphere of indeterminacy quite
extensive in the choice of whether and how to intervene to change market-based
economic fates.

Suppose that there are spheres of political choice, too fundamental to be
grounded on the rule: "Whatever the majority favors is, by that token, the right
choice," in which no partisan is in a position to claim that her choice is a dictate
of equal respect for all. Does it follow that partisans must give up the project of
reconciling their activity with equal respect for all, regarding it as a constraint only
appropriate to a future, more harmonious society? No, for what impartial morality does not require, impartial morality may (or may not) permit. When I do not
have a warrant for regarding my construal of equal respect as uniquely compelling,
I may still be warranted in supposing that my reasons for seeking to impose my
alternative are sufficiently serious to make my political activity respectful of everyone's interests, in light of the costs imposed by others' alternatives. The reduction of exploitation, poverty and marginalization could be sufficiently serious
reasons. So an heir of Marx's legacy in moral epistemology can be concerned to

reconcile her political commitments with impartial morality, even if she does not regard all these commitments as *dictates* of impartial morality. Morality in the first, broad sense fills the gaps left by morality in the second, impartialist sense.[8]

Of course, what counts as a sufficiently serious justification depends on empirical scrutiny of likely gains and losses. And here, the post-Marxist social democrat often faces a peaceful analogue of the Marxist revolutionary's quandary. In many cases, she lacks reasons for confidence that a costly initiative in helping the poor or exploited or marginalized will be effective. Given those costs (as well as possible harms to the intended beneficiaries), it would be self-indulgent to appeal to her fine goals. But perhaps oldtime Marxism has something to contribute. Marxists who chose militance or revolution in the name of socialism were aware that harm was certain and success was not on the current occasion. But they also thought that their ultimate goal of human liberation could not be attained unless people in circumstances of uncertain success took initiatives that impartial morality did not require. Similarly, a post-Marxist who is uncertain whether a particular attempt to reduce burdens of capitalism would succeed may have adequate reason to believe that the long-term project of reducing these burdens is doomed in the absence of a political movement that produces such attempts and learns from their failures as well as their successes. Despite its now all-too-evident dangers, perhaps the old talk of historical mission still has a use in justifying engagement in political movements that impose risks and costs and do not merely implement requirements of impartial morality.

Notes

1 Marx also uses less pretentious terms for the key groups, such as "the workers" for the proletariat, when the reference is clear, and so will I. Further specification of this general conception of capitalist relations of production would clarify the crucial ascriptions of control, distinguish different sources of power or vulnerability within the two classes, and characterize other classes in capitalist societies. Wright (1997) presents an influential effort to develop specifications that provide a framework for explaining current social phenomena.

2 Earlier forms of surplus-extraction, such as slavery and serfdom, also have these features, and are forms of exploitation – though, here, the direct coercion through which the stronger force the weaker to work for them is probably enough to justify the label.

3 Avineri (1970), Moore (1975) and others either have denied that organized political violence was ever essential to the establishment of socialism in Marx's view or have taken him to have departed from this judgment after the failure of the revolutions of 1848. This is hard to reconcile with his enduring emphasis on the actively pro-capitalist role of the state under capitalism and with such late texts as *The Civil War in France*.

4 Brenkert (1983) argues that Marx relied on a morality of freedom, but such a morality similarly confronts conflicts among different people's freedoms and different kinds of freedom.

5 Indeed, Allen (1973) and others have argued that Marx implicitly relied on some form of utilitarianism. However, Marx's explicit criticisms of utilitarianism turn out to cut deep.

6 Olson (1965), who first noted the public-goods problem, took it to undermine Marx's account of revolutionary motivation. Buchanan (1979) argues that Olson's challenge has not yet been answered. My sketch of an answer is along the lines of Holmstrom (1983) and of Miller (1984); which also further develops the Marxist critiques of moralities and morality in this essay and the analysis of Marx's theory of the state).

7 Brudney (1998) discusses Marx's concern with social barriers to moral justification, in the 1840s.

8 Arguably, specific kinds of moral judgments, such as judgments of justice, might, nonetheless, be excluded, where impartiality is unavailable, because they intrinsically appeal to dictates of moral impartiality. The case of justice has been specially significant in controversies over Marx and morality because of the stimulus of Wood's argument (1972) that Marx regarded justice as a non-normative property, involving conformity to stabilizing social rules.

Bibliography

Allen, D. (1973). "The Utilitarianism of Marx and Engels." *The American Philosophical Quarterly* 10: 189–99.

Arneson, R. (1981). "What's wrong with exploitation?" *Ethics*, 91: 202–27.

Avineri, S. (1970). *The Social and Political Thought of Karl Marx*. Cambridge: Cambridge University Press.

Brenkert, G. (1983). *Marx's Ethics of Freedom*. London: Routledge and Kegan Paul.

Brudney, D. (1998). *Marx's Attempt to Leave Philosophy*. Cambridge, MA: Harvard University Press.

Buchanan, A. (1979). "Revolutionary motivation and morality." *Philosophy and Public Affairs*, 9: 59–82. (Also in Cohen, Nagel and Scanlon (1980).)

——(1982). *Marxism and Justice: The Radical Critique of Liberalism*. Totowa, NJ: Rowman & Littlefield.

Chapman, J. and J. Pennock (eds.) (1983). *Nomos XXVI, Marxism*. New York: New York University Press.

Cohen, G. A. (1978). *Karl Marx's Theory of History: A Defense*. Princeton: Princeton University Press.

——(1983). "The structure of proletarian unfreedom." *Philosophy and Public Affairs*, 12: 3–34. (Also in Cohen (1988), Cohen, Nagel and Scanlon (1980), Nielsen and Ware (1997).)

——(1988). *History, Labour and Freedom: Themes from Marx*. Oxford: Oxford University Press.

Cohen, M., T. Nagel, and T. Scanlon (eds.) (1980). *Marx, Justice and History*. Princeton: Princeton University Press.

Elster, J. (1985). *Making Sense of Marx*. Cambridge: Cambridge University Press.

Gilbert, A. (1981). *Marx's Politics*. New Brunswick, NJ: Rutgers University Press.

Holmstrom, N. (1977). "Exploitation." *Canadian Journal of Philosophy*, 7: 353–69. (Also in Nielsen and Ware (1997).)

——(1983). "Rationality and revolution." *Canadian Journal of Philosophy*, 13: 305–25.

Marx, K. (1844). *Economic and Philosophical Manuscripts*. (Cited from K. Marx (1975).)

——(1844a). *Excerpts from James Mill's "Elements of Political Economy"*. (Cited from K. Marx (1975).)

——([1845–6] 1976). *The German Ideology*, written with F. Engels. In K. Marx and F. Engels, *Collected Works* (vol. 5), pp. 15–539.

——(1847). *Wage Labour and Capital*. (Cited from K. Marx and F. Engels (1968).)

——(1848). *Manifesto of the Communist Party*, written with F. Engels. (Cited from K. Marx and F. Engels (1968).)

——([1857–8] 1973). *Grundrisse* (trans. M. Nicolaus). New York: Vintage Books.

——(1865). *Wages, Price and Profit*. (Cited from K. Marx and F. Engels (1968).)

——(1866). *Results of the Immediate Process of Production*. In K. Marx ([1867] 1976).

——([1867] 1976). *Capital* (vol. 1) (trans. B. Fowkes). New York: Penguin.

——(1871). *The Civil War in France*. (Cited from K. Marx and F. Engels (1968).)

——(1875). *Critique of the Gotha Programme*. (Cited from K. Marx and F. Engels (1968).)

——([1894] 1981). *Capital* (vol. 3 [posthumous edn. by F. Engels]) (trans. D. Fernbach). New York: Penguin.

——(1975). *Early Writings* (trans. R. Livingstone and G. Benton). New York: Penguin.

——and F. Engels (1968). *Selected Works in One Volume*. New York: International Publishers.

Miller, R. W. (1981). "Marx and Aristotle." In K. Nielsen and S. Patten (eds.), *Canadian Journal of Philosophy*, suppl. vol. 7. *Marx and Morality*.

——(1984). *Analyzing Marx: Morality, Power and History*. Princeton: Princeton University Press.

Moore, S. (1975). "Marx and Lenin as Historical Materialists." *Philosophy and Public Affairs*, 4: 171–94. (Also in Cohen, Nagel and Scanlon (1980).)

Nielsen, K. and S. Patten (eds.) (1981). *Canadian Journal of Philosophy*, suppl. vol. 7: *Marx and Morality*.

Nielsen, K. and R. Ware (eds.) (1997). *Exploitation*. Highland Park, NJ: Humanities Press.

Olson, M. (1965). *The Logic of Collective Action*. Cambridge, MA: Harvard University Press.

Rawls, J. (1971). *A Theory of Justice*. Cambridge, MA: Harvard University Press.

——(1993). *Political Liberalism*. New York: Columbia University Press.

Raz, J. (1986). *The Morality of Freedom*. Oxford: Oxford University Press.

Reiman, J. (1987). "Exploitation, force and the moral assessment of capitalism: Thoughts on Roemer and Cohen." *Philosophy and Public Affairs*, 16: 3–41. (Also in Nielsen and Ware (1997).)

Roemer, J. (1985). "Should Marxists be interested in exploitation?" *Philosophy and Public Affairs*, 14: 30–65.

Wood, A. (1972). "The Marxian critique of justice." *Philosophy and Public Affairs*, 1: 244–82.

——(1981). *Karl Marx*. London: Routledge & Kegan Paul.

——(1995). "Exploitation." *Social Philosophy and Policy*, 12: 136–58. (Also in Nielsen and Ware (1997).)

Wright, E. O. (1997). *Class Counts*. Cambridge: Cambridge University Press.

Chapter 7

Feminism and Political Theory

Virginia Held

Feminism is committed to the equality of women. This is first of all a normative commitment to the equal worth of women and women's experiences. It is also a political commitment to strive to change the practices and beliefs that have subordinated women and treated them as less than equal.

Feminists deplore that in virtually all societies throughout history women have been considered inferior to men. Feminists deny that the subordination of women is inevitable. Social and cultural arrangements modify and shape biological or evolutionary tendencies that can be found in human beings, and could counter male inclinations to be aggressive or to dominate, if these exist.

The task for feminist political theory is to understand how equality for women might be achieved. This is usually seen as much more than a merely political matter, since it involves culture and society and economic and personal life at many levels and not just the political system or the realms of law and politics. It also involves uncovering the deep biases that exist in political theory as previously developed, reconceptualizing its leading concepts and contesting which concepts should be central to it, inventing new theory for societies and institutions that might achieve the equality of women, and recommending political and social action to overcome women's oppression (Clarke and Lange, 1979; Held, 1993; Jaggar, 1983; Okin, 1979; Shanley and Narayan, 1997). Within the broad goals of feminism, there is much diversity of view and debates are ongoing (Jaggar, 1994).

Feminism and Liberal Individualism

Some feminist political theorists have adopted a traditional liberal political framework and applied it to issues of interest to women and neglected by nonfeminists. They show, for instance, how justice requires a more equitable division of labor in the household, equal pay for comparable work, security of the persons of women against violence, rights for women to control their own reproduction, and a fair share for women around the world of the available food and educational opportunities in a family and in society (Nussbaum, 1999; Okin, 1989; Rhode, 1989). Feminism is even seen by some as equivalent to demanding equal rights for women. This approach has the advantage of speaking to liberals on their own ground, appealing to principles of justice, equality, and equal rights to which liberals are already committed, and with arguments with which many people initially inhospitable to feminism may find it hard to disagree.

The liberal response then sometimes becomes one of disputing that these positions are distinctively feminist, since any liberal can agree with them. What feminists note is that prior to the feminist challenge, these issues were not addressed by liberal theory or practice. At the global level, agreement on even very basic equal rights for women is a long way from being achieved. Women are often not yet recognized as individuals with rights. Partly for this reason, a liberal feminist philosopher such as Martha Nussbaum can say that the problem is not too much liberal individualism but too little (Nussbaum, 1999, p. 65).

Many other feminist political theorists, on the other hand, present a critique of liberal individualism as a major theme (Benhabib, 1992; Fraser, 1989; Frazer and Laccy, 1993; Young, 1990). They fault liberal individualism for neglecting the social structures within which persons develop and the relations between persons that are so much of what an actual person is. For instance, family ties, membership in groups, and social connections are part of what constitutes a person as who she is. To see only abstract liberal agents as the units of political thought, as in social contract theory or rational choice theory, is seen as deficient, a denial of the interdependence that characterizes human life and a denial of history.

Understanding the embeddedness of persons in social and historical contexts helps us to see that we should not merely supplement the traditional concept of an abstract, rational, liberal individual, historically thought of as male, with a concept of an abstract essential woman, as some feminists at first tended to do. We are never simply women-as-such, but also always white or black or Latina, privileged or poor, heterosexual or lesbian, and so on. The perspectives of feminists of color and of nonWestern feminists have contributed greatly to reconceptualizations of identity, personhood, the self, and thus of politics and society (Collins, 1990; Hoagland, 1989; Spelman, 1988; Williams, 1991).

Much feminist thought also differs from liberal individualism in attending especially to particular others and relations between particular persons rather than only to either individuals or universal moral norms (Benhabib, 1992; Held, 1993). The moral theory built on liberal individualism recognizes the individual self or ego on the one hand, and the universal all or everyone on the other. The individual's pursuit of his interests are to be restrained by the universal norms to which all other human beings could agree, for instance. But between the individual self and the universal all others, traditional liberal moral theory is virtually silent. It has little to say about the moral issues of such intermediate regions as family relations, friendship, or group identity. Feminists, in contrast, pay particular attention to the moral claims of particular others enmeshed with the self in particular relations, and to selves moved by empathy, attachments, and human concern (Jaggar, 1994).

Traditional Marxists and communitarians have also seen the person as social rather than as the abstract individual of the liberal tradition. Like their liberal confreres, they sometimes dispute that there is anything distinctive in the feminist critique. But feminists respond that although they may have been influenced by Marxist or communitarian arguments, their critique of liberal individualism is often different from non-feminist ones (Ferguson, 1989; Jaggar, 1983; Mackenzie and Stoljar, 2000; Sargent, 1981). It centers on an appreciation of women's experiences in relations between actual persons. It sees the gender structure as central to these relations, and sees persons as relational in a different way than as the outcome of the relations of economic production emphasized by Marx or of the communal relations, traditionally patriarchal, emphasized by communitarians. And many feminists believe their view of the person as relational is not likely to be lost. Jean Keller writes that "the insight that the moral agent is an 'encumbered self,' who is always embedded in relations with flesh and blood others and is partly constituted by these relations, is here to stay" (Keller, 1997, p. 152).

Women's experiences have been neglected by non-feminist theorists, from liberals to Marxists to communitarians. Feminist thought, in contrast, takes women's experience as worthy of trust and central to its project. Many feminists believe that what women do and feel and think in contexts of responsibility for and interdependence with others, such as in dealing with the moral issues involved in caring for children and others who are not independent and self-sufficient, is especially relevant for moral and political thought (Held, 1993; Kittay, 1999; Ruddick, 1989; Tronto, 1993). They reject as biased ideology the longstanding and dominant traditional view that the experience of women in the household is of little relevance to morality because it is determined by "nature" or biology while the life of man in the *polis* transcends these.

Brian Barry has characterized liberalism as "the vision of society as made up of independent, autonomous units who co-operate only when the terms of co-operation are such as to make it further the ends of each of the parties" (Barry, 1973, p. 166). This model was put forward most starkly by Hobbes, but it has continued in modified form through the present. Another form of liberalism is more Kantian and less egoistic, but no less individualistic. It sees us cooperating on the basis of rational principles to which we could agree as free and equal but mutually disinterested individuals. Society, in the various forms of the liberal view, should rest on a social contract, and appropriate moral relations between persons are contractual.

From the perspective of many women's experiences, this model of persons and societies is unsatisfactory, normatively as well as descriptively. It imagines an independent rational agent who only interacts with others to further his own interests or on the basis of a voluntary choice to do so, yet persons are embedded in social relations that are often involuntary throughout their lives. None of us can choose our parents, for instance. And we recognize many sources of moral responsibility other than our own interests, voluntarily pursued, or than abstract rational principles. Society is deeply noncontractual. We need views of the political that reflect these understandings, which this model, deeply entrenched in liberal political thought, does not do.

On the basis of a feminist understanding of human experience, liberal political thought is implicated by this model because of its artificiality and implausibility for all but a very narrow range of choices, such as those of a consumer in the marketplace with adequate funds to spend, or an abstract rational legislator devising an ideal constitution. As Marxists have argued, the "choice" of most workers to sell their labor to one oppressive employer rather than another, can hardly be best understood as a free choice. And as feminists have emphasized, a woman denied access to any other means of economic support than being dependent on a man is hardly making a free choice in deciding to marry a domineering husband to escape a domineering father. Yet all these situations are political in the sense that structures of power keep them in place. And moral questions of responsibility for and identification with those with whom we have social ties, often unchosen and between unequals, are continually present.

The economic system that political power allows or supports is a political and moral issue. And as feminists have made clear, the gender structure of every society that renders women subordinate in such a wide range of ways is fundamentally a political and moral issue. For understanding such issues, the model of the liberal individual, with its assumptions of independence and free choice to enter into social relations or not, is inadequate.

Some defenders of liberal individualism, including feminist defenders, criticize the feminist critique as resting on the empirical claim that, for instance, workers and women are not in fact self-sufficient, whereas the liberal argument is normative (Hampton, 1993). They interpret the social-contract tradition of political theory as asking: if we would be free and equal and independent, what political arrangements would we freely agree to? The liberal argument is that its principles would be justified because they would be based on a normatively persuasive procedure for arriving at them. But this argument against the feminist critique misses what is at least as important to it as its claims that the liberal model is distortingly unrealistic. The feminist critique is also a normative critique of individualism as a moral ideal. Many feminists do not think of relations with others as mere encumbrances to be free from in order to arrive at what has normative value, nor as mere preferences to be pursued or not as the liberal individual wishes. These feminists value interdependence as well as recognize how limited independence is. They value autonomy, but as relational (Clement, 1996; Mackenzie and Stoljar, 2000). They hold that relations between people – relations of caring, trust, friendship, and the like – have value, and can be evaluated morally, not just described empirically (Held, 1993). Like communitarians, they may argue that until there is a certain kind of attachment between persons, there will not be a society within which to bring about the respect for rights which both liberals and feminists value.

Moreover, feminists may argue that making the assumptions inherent to liberal individualism tends to undermine interdependence and to promote as an empirical reality the very assumption that is asserted as being merely procedural and normative. "Liberal morality," Annette Baier writes, "may unfit people to be anything other than what its justifying theories suppose them to be, ones who have no interest in each others' interests" (Baier, 1994, p. 29).

Interesting empirical support is being found for this claim. A number of studies show that studying economics, with its "repeated and intensive exposure to a model whose unequivocal prediction" is that people will make their decisions on the basis of self-interest, causes economics students to be less cooperative and more inclined to free-ride than others (Frank et al., 1998, p. 61).

It is plausible to suppose, then, as feminists often do, that a society guided by liberal individualism, with its assumptions that individuals only do, or should, engage with others when it is in their interest to do so, or on a contractual basis, will itself promote a society of atomistic individuals who take no interest in each others' well-being for these others' sakes. As long as the pains or deprivations of these others pose no threat to the individual in question, or present no need for contractual agreements, the liberal individual has no motive – of empathy or caring – to concern himself with these others. Such a society will be a disintegrating society, lacking the trust needed for a society to flourish. It will lose the solidarity that holds a society together, and it will certainly fail to develop adequate appreciations of how best to bring up its children, deal with its social problems, or safeguard its environment or the globe for the sake of future generations.

The Public and the Private

Defenders of liberal individualism and of the rational choice theory that generalizes and deploys its assumptions argue that it is a theory for relations between strangers, not for the personal relations between lovers or spouses or parents and children, where emotion is dominant. But this leads to questions that have been fundamental to feminist theorizing: what is political and how should the distinction between the public and political on the one hand, and the private and personal on the other, be drawn? (Elshtain, 1981; Landes, 1998).

An early slogan of the women's movement that began in the US in the late 1960s was "the personal is political." It expressed the insight that the greater power of men – politically, economically, and socially – affected the ways in which women suffered domination in what had been imagined to be the personal and private and non-political domain of the household, and the ways in turn that this effect of men's power on women's personal lives limited women's capacities and undermined their development in the workplace and in the public domain.

Feminists have been re-examining and rethinking the public/private distinction ever since. There is widespread agreement that the traditional conception is unsatisfactory. At the very least, women and children need public protection from domestic violence. The traditional view that the home was a man's castle into which the law should not intrude left women and children vulnerable to "private" tyranny. In many parts of the world, women are still subject to domestic violence on a massive scale because the public realm of law fails to protect them.

On the other hand, law often interferes with women's private decisions concerning reproduction, and with the private sexual behavior of both women and men, and law orders marriage and the family in all sorts of ways (Callahan, 1995; Petchesky, 1985). But even when the public sphere of law is consistent in leaving the household alone, the greater public power of men renders women unequal at home. Hence, public principles of justice requiring an equal distribution of benefits and burdens or a persuasive justification for a departure from this, should be applied to the family as well as to governmental decisions. The tasks of household maintenance and childrearing should be equitably shared, or departures should be freely and mutually agreed upon (Held, 1984; Okin, 1989).

Women have traditionally had very little privacy, even at home. Feminists seek reconceptualizations of privacy, not, as sometimes charged, the abolition of the private (Anita Allen, 1988). Women do not want to sacrifice the ideals of affiliation and caring to self-centered demands to be left alone, but the subordinate and caretaking roles imposed on them have largely deprived them of the experience of privacy. To be confined to the "private sphere" is not to enjoy privacy, and the many women now in the labor force are still burdened by household responsibilities that leave them unfairly limited opportunities to take advantage of privacy (ibid.).

A number of feminist theorists who can be characterized as radical feminists believe that sexuality and the way it is socially constructed is the deepest cause of women's secondary status. Male sexuality, on this view, has been developed in such a way that the domination of women is inherent to it, and violence, often against women, has been sexualized. To many radical feminists, the pornography that feeds this construction and the violence against women that indicates it are strong contributors to male domination and female disempowerment. According to these feminists, the sexuality that is often thought of as most private is actually the most important factor in the gender structure that pervades all societies and gives men the power to dominate women in most areas of life, public as well as private. As Catharine MacKinnon puts it, "Women and men are divided by gender, made into the sexes as we know them, by the requirements of its dominant form, heterosexuality, which institutionalizes male sexual dominance and female sexual submission. If this is true, sexuality is the linchpin of gender inequality" (MacKinnon, 1989, p. 179).

Many feminists do far more than criticize the way the traditional lines between public and private have been drawn. This is connected with the feminist revaluation of the moral values of the personal realm, and the rethinking of moral theory involved. Then, with a transformed view of moral theory, and of persons, values, and social relations, the view of "the political" is transformed.

Liberalism and Rights

The feminist critique of liberal political theory should not be understood as a rejection of what has been achieved by the liberal tradition of individual rights and democratic government. Compared with the conservatism – whether libertarian or communitarian – that seeks to keep patriarchy in place, it is of course progress. There is appreciation of the progressive aspects of liberalism and even those feminists most critical of liberal individualism usually seek, at the level of institutions and policies, to improve on liberalism not destroy it.

The way these issues have developed can perhaps best be seen in feminist discussions of rights. Historically, feminists have focused their demands on equal rights for women. In the eighteenth century, Mary Wollstonecraft argued, against Rousseau, that the same rights and freedoms based on rational principles that were being sought for men should be accorded to women also (Wollstonecraft, 1967). John Stuart Mill and Harriet Taylor called in the nineteenth century, in opposition to prevailing views at the time, for an extension to women of equal rights and opportunities and for an end to the subjection of women. They argued that women should have the same rights as men to receive education, to own property, to vote, and to enter any profession (Mill and Mill, 1970). Women's movements in the twentieth century often concentrated their efforts on winning for women the right to vote; this was achieved in the United States in 1920, in France in 1946, in Switzerland not until 1971. The second wave of the women's movement that gathered strength in the United States in the 1970s, after a lapse of almost four decades, placed great importance on adding an Equal Rights Amendment to the US Constitution. Though the amendment failed to be ratified by the required number of states, efforts to end discrimination against women in all its forms continued (Rhode, 1989). These were attempts to have the rights of women to equal protection by the laws recognized. Many also argued, on liberal as well as other grounds, for welfare rights. These are especially important for women: persons cannot enjoy equal rights if they have no assurance of the means to stay alive and feed their children. Either employment and affordable child care must be available, or persons must have access by right to the basic necessities of life for themselves and their children. The negative freedom from interference of the liberal tradition is insufficient; persons must also have positive enablements to be free and equal agents (Gould, 1998; Held, 1984; Sterba, 1989).

We should think of rights as either legal or moral, or both. Many of the legal rights recognized in and protected by an actual legal system are based on moral rights seen as justifiable moral claims (Held, 1984). Examples are such rights as to not be murdered or raped or assaulted. But some of the legal rights that actual political and legal systems have protected, such as the rights of husbands to do to their wives what would otherwise be rape, are not morally justifiable and ought not to be legal rights.

Arguments for the equal rights of women are especially prominent for feminists when women are denied such fundamental rights as to own property or to vote, when they are subject to widespread legally permitted domestic violence, and when they suffer blatant discrimination in education and employment. These are still the conditions of many women around the world (French, 1992). But feminism has also moved far beyond demands that rights articulated for men, such as the right to vote, be extended equally to women. For instance, for women to have genuinely equal opportunities in employment, they may need rights to pregnancy leave, and child care for their children. Feminism has also contributed by now fundamental critiques of the language and concepts of rights. Overcoming the pervasive patriarchy of traditional and existing societies is thought by some to require a shift of focus away from rights, as well as reconceptualizations of what equal rights for women really require.

Some of the critique of rights is based on developing thought in the area of ethics, and moral theory and practice. Some feminists are deeply critical of the tendency in traditional ethics to interpret all or almost all moral problems in terms of rights and justice. An ethic of care, in contrast, values connections between persons and the trust and caring that can characterize human relationships, rather than focusing on the assertion of individual rights against others. Feminists developing an ethic of care argue for the importance for morality of empathy, sensitivity, and attention to the particular aspects of persons and their needs, in contrast to the focus of rights on the rational recognition of how all persons are the same, and interchangeable.

Some advocates of care ethics see the morality of rights and justice as inherently masculine and hostile to the understanding of moral problems as women tend to interpret them. Carol Gilligan points out that "a morality of rights and noninterference may appear frightening . . . in its potential justification of indifference and unconcern" (Gilligan, 1982, p. 22). Nel Noddings notes that in contexts of caring for others, we should be wary of rules and principles, and thus the rights that reflect them, because they often play a "destructive role." She suggests that although relying on rules can be useful at times when we cannot respond to each particular situation as would be best, if we "come to rely almost completely on external rules [we] become detached from the very heart of morality: 'the sensibility that calls forth caring'" (Noddings, 1986, p. 47).

Other feminists point to the suspect history of the development of rights as central to moral and political theory (Pateman, 1988). Annette Baier writes that "the moral tradition which developed the concept of rights, autonomy, and justice is the same tradition that provided 'justifications' of the oppression of those whom the primary rights-holders depended on to do the sort of work they themselves preferred not to do. The domestic work was left to women and slaves," and the official morality ignored their contribution. In Baier's view, "rights have usually been for the privileged," and the "justice perspective" and the legal sense that goes with it "are shadowed by their patriarchal past" (Baier, 1994, pp. 25–6). Eva Feder Kittay argues that the liberal tradition of individual rights constructed an equality for heads of households and counted that head as an independent and self-sufficient individual (Kittay, 1999). With others, she argues that this image fosters a harmful illusion. It suggests that dependencies do not exist, and that society need not deal with them because it is composed of independent, free and equal individuals who meet their own needs and come together voluntarily to form associations. In fact, what independence some persons have rests on social cooperation as a prior condition. As children we are all dependent, most of us are sometimes ill or frail, and even men who imagine themselves most independent must rely on a vast network of social bonds providing the conditions within which they enjoy the "fruits of their labor." Moreover, the meanings of "dependency" and "citizenship" and of how they are connected need to be reconceptualized so that all who participate in a society's life can attain dignity (Shanley and Narayan, 1997).

Feminist theorists who focus primarily on law are also critical of the conceptions of rights so central to traditional legal, political, and moral theory. Feminist analyses have shown how the law is a patriarchal institution and how its scheme of rights supports the subordination of women. Carol Smart sees law and masculine culture as congruent; she examines how law "disqualifies women's experience" and women's knowledge and she urges feminists to resist focusing on rights (Smart, 1989, p. 2). Catharine MacKinnon argues that "In the liberal state, the rule of law – neutral, abstract, elevated, pervasive – both institutionalizes the power of men over women and institutionalizes power in its male form. . . . Male forms of power over women are affirmatively embodied as individual rights in law. . . . Abstract rights authorize the male experience of the world" (MacKinnon, 1989, pp. 238–48). Further, even where the written law appears gender-neutral, the mechanisms of law – police, prosecutors, and judges – often apply it in biased ways. The state has permitted much domestic violence and has been reluctant to challenge patriarchal power in the family (Smith, 1993). It has been especially deficient in protecting the rights of women of color (Crenshaw, 1993). And legal theory as distinct from the law itself has been no less supportive of male dominance. Robin West sees the whole of modern legal theory as "essentially and irretrievably masculine" in its acceptance of the thesis "that we are individuals 'first,' and . . . that what separates us is epistemologically and morally prior to what connects us" (West, 1988, p. 2).

To some feminists, then, rights are seen as inherently abstract and biased toward a male point of view. Some argue that using the discourse of rights leads social movements to unduly tailor their aims to what can be claimed as rights within existing legal systems, and that this weakens such movements (Schneider, 1986). Many feminists influenced by postmodernism and the critical legal studies approach are deeply skeptical of any claims to the truth or objectivity of any assertions about rights; they see law as an expression of power rather than of morality (Schneider, 1986; Smart, 1989; Smith, 1993).

Even these very fundamental critiques, however, do not amount to a rejection of rights by most feminists. They lead instead to demands for reformulations of existing schemes of rights, to suggested reconstructions of the concept of rights, and to recommendations for limiting the reach of law to an appropriate sphere rather than thinking of rights as the model for all moral and political thinking. Feminist jurisprudence has contributed many detailed analyses of what equal rights for women would require (Bartlett and Kennedy, 1991; Cornell, 1998). It is examining when differences between men and women, and differences between some women and others, need to be taken into account. And it is questioning the practice of taking male characteristics as the norm according to which women's characteristics, such as the capacity to become pregnant, are seen as different and hence present a problem. Men, it is noted, are as different from women as women are from men.

Christine Littleton argues that what is often required by the equal-protection clause of the US Constitution is not sameness of treatment but equality of disadvantage brought about by the treatment. Thus, if a pension scheme that excludes part-time workers and appears to be gender-neutral actually affects women much more adversely than men, it is discriminatory. Littleton's argument is that difference should not lead to disadvantage but should instead be costless (Littleton, 1987). A similar argument can be used with respect to racial disadvantages. Achieving equality may well require positive action, including governmental action, rather than merely ignoring differences. Arguments for pregnancy leave, child care provision, and affirmative action programs all combine a recognition of equality and difference, and deny that we must choose between these.

Legal rights often help bring about aspects of the social change needed. The area of sexual harassment shows well the potential of legal rights to improve the lives of women. The injuries that women had long experienced were turned by feminist jurisprudence into a form of discrimination from which legal protection could be sought. Catharine MacKinnon herself writes that the law against sexual harassment is a test of the "possibilities for social change for women through law." Women subject to harmful and demeaning sexual pressure in the workplace "have been given a forum, legitimacy to speak, authority to make claims, and an avenue of possible relief. . . . The legal claim for sexual harassment made the events of sexual harassment illegitimate socially, as well as legally for the first time" (MacKinnon, 1987, pp. 103–4).

There are many examples of the uses of rights to reduce the subordination of women, but there are often disadvantages in these uses. Acknowledging differences between women and men, for instance in protecting girls through statutory rape laws, often stigmatizes women and perpetuates sexist stereotypes (Olsen, 1984). The backlash against affirmative action has made it more difficult politically to argue for positive efforts to overcome gender and racial disadvantages. But there is a strong determination on the part of feminists to maintain the rights achieved. It is generally argued that reproductive rights are a precondition for most other rights for women, yet they are continually threatened. To Patricia Smith, "it is inconceivable that any issue that comparably affected the basic individual freedom of any man would not be under his control in a free society" (Smith, 1993, p. 14).

Various strong voices have also reminded feminists of the centrality of rights arguments to movements for social justice. Taking issue with the critical legal-studies critique of rights, Patricia Williams writes that "although rights may not be ends in themselves, rights rhetoric has been and continues to be an effective form of discourse for blacks" (Williams, 1991, p. 149). Subordinate groups can describe their needs at length, but doing so has often not been politically effective, as it has not been for African Americans. Williams asserts that what must be found is "a political mechanism that can confront the denial of need," and rights have the capacity to do this (p. 152). Uma Narayan also warns against a weakening of feminist commitments to rights. She describes the colonialist project of denying rights to the colonized on grounds of a paternalistic concern for their welfare. Resisting this, the use of rights discourse by the colonized to assert their own claims contributed significantly to their emancipation. And then in turn, asserting their rights was important for women in opposing the traditional patriarchal views often prevalent among the previously colonized (Narayan, 1995).

It is widely understood among feminist critics of rights that rights are not time-less or fixed, but contested and developing. Rights reflect social reality and have the capacity to decrease actual oppression. Achieving respect for basic rights is often a goal around which political struggles can be organized, and many of the most substantial gains made by disadvantaged groups are based on a striving for justice and equal rights. Feminists do not suggest that these gains and goals be abandoned. On the other hand, rights arguments may not serve well for the full range of moral and political concerns that feminists have, and the legal framework of rights and justice should perhaps not be the central discourse of morality and politics. Rights are one concern among others, not the key to overcoming the sub-ordination of women. From the perspective of many feminists, the person seen as a holder of individual rights in the tradition of liberal political theory is an artificial and misleading abstraction. Accepting this abstraction for some legal and political purposes may be useful (Frazer and Lacey, 1993). But we should not suppose that it is adequate for morality or political theory in general (Held, 1993).

Some legal theorists have argued that rights need to be fundamentally reconceptualized. Martha Minow criticizes rights rhetoric for ignoring relationships, and argues that we should never lose sight of the social relations of power and privilege within which individual rights are constructed. She advocates a conception of "rights in relationships" that can be used against oppressive forms of both public and private power. We need, she writes, "a shift in the paradigm we use to conceive of difference, a shift from a focus on the distinctions between people to a focus on the relationships within which we notice and draw distinctions" (Minow, 1990, p. 15). She wants, however, to "rescue" rights, not abandon them, seeing that there is something "too valuable in the aspiration of rights" for us to dispense with the discourse of rights (p. 307).

Much of the criticism of rights can perhaps best be seen as resistance to the idea that the approaches and concepts of law and rights should be generalized to the whole of morality and political thinking. It is not so much an attempt to dispense with rights in the domain of law as to limit legalistic interpretations to the domain of law rather than see them extended to all moral and political issues. Once we think of the framework of law and rights as one to be limited to a somewhat narrow range of human concerns rather than as the appropriate one within which to interpret all moral and political problems, other moral approaches can become salient and social and political organization can be based on other goals and concerns as well as on those of rights.

The Ethics of Care

If morality should not be dominated by the model of the liberal individual with his rights and economic interests and legal protections, what are the implications for political theory? The ethics of care was initially developed with an emphasis on the experience of women in activities such as caring for children, or taking care of the ill or the elderly, or cultivating ties of friendship and personal affection. It was realized that moral issues abound in these domains, about which standard moral theory had almost nothing to say (Gilligan, 1982; Noddings, 1984; Ruddick, 1989). Care ethics has by now developed far beyond its original formulations, and there is an extensive and diverse literature on this alternative moral approach (Card, 1991, 1999; Held, 1995; Tong, 1993).

Dominant moral theories such as Kantian ethics and utilitarianism are universalistic and rationalistic. Although much has been written about the differences between them, from a feminist perspective their similarities are more pronounced than what divides them. Both rely on a single, ultimate universal principle – the Categorical Imperative or the Principle of Utility. Both are rationalistic in their moral epistemologies and both employ a conception of the person as a rational, independent, liberal individual.

In Margaret Walker's estimation, these are "theoretical-juridical" accounts of morality which repeatedly invoke the image of "a fraternity of independent peers invoking laws to deliver verdicts with authority" (Walker, 1998, p. 1). In Fiona Robinson's evaluation, dominant moral theories give primacy to values such as autonomy, independence, non-interference, self-determination, fairness, and rights, and involve a "systematic devaluing of notions of interdependence, relatedness, and positive involvement" in the lives of others (Robinson, 1999, p. 10).

These dominant moral theories that have both supported and reflected liberal political theory have either ignored altogether the experiences of women in caring activities or they have dismissed them as irrelevant. Caring for children has been seen as "natural" or instinctive behavior not "governed" by morality, or family life has been thought of as a personal preference individuals may choose to pursue or not. Walker shows how the theoretical-juridical accounts of morality are put forward as appropriate for "the" moral agent, or as recommendations for how "we" ought to act. But these canonical forms of moral judgment are the judgments of someone resembling "a judge, manager, bureaucrat, or gamesman" (Walker, 1998, p. 21). They represent in abstract and idealized forms the judgments of dominant persons in an established social order, not the moral experiences of women caring for children or aged parents, of ill-paid minority service-workers in a hospital, or of the members of colonized groups relying on communal ties for their survival.

To feminists, the experience of women is of the utmost relevance, to morality and political theory as well as to other endeavors. Women's experience does not count merely when women enter the "public" realms symbolically if not now exclusively designated as male. And the experience of marginalized and subordinate groups is as relevant as is that of those who occupy positions of privilege. Perhaps it is more relevant, since privilege can so easily distort one's views of society and morality. Women's experiences of caretaking and of cultivating social ties are being taken by feminist theorists as highly important for understanding the morality not only of family life, but of public life as well. The ethics of care gives expression to women's experience of empathy, of mutual trust, and of the emotions helpful to morality. This experience is part of and can be more of men's experience also, but it has not been reflected in dominant moral theories.

The ethics of care appreciates the ties we have with particular others and the actual relationships that partly constitute our identity. Although we often seek to reshape these ties, to distance ourselves from some persons and groups and to develop new ties with others, the autonomy we seek is a capacity to reshape our relationships, not to be the unencumbered abstract individual self of liberal political and moral theory (Clement, 1996; Mackenzie and Stoljar, 2000; Meyers, 1997). Those who sincerely care for others act for particular others and for the actual relationship between them, not for their own individual interests and not out of duty to a universal law for all rational beings, or for the greatest benefit of the greatest number.

Universal rules of impartiality often seem inapplicable or inappropriate in contexts of family and friendship (Friedman, 1993). Certainly, however, we need moral theory to evaluate relations between persons and the actions of relational persons in what have been thought of as personal contexts. Virtue theory has often been thought to offer more promising approaches for these contexts; Aristotle and Hume are frequently invoked. But virtue theory, like liberal morality, may be tainted by its patriarchal and individualistic past. The Man of Virtue concerned for his dispositions, like The Man of Reason dissected by feminist critiques (Lloyd, 1984), may still bear little resemblance to the woman or service-worker engaged in affectionate care. The ethics of care that does speak for persons in relations should then not be thought of as valuing a mere preference or extra that impartial rules can permit while retaining priority, but as a challenge to universalistic morality itself.

The dominant moral theories claim to offer moral guidance for all moral problems; if their rules do not apply to certain kinds of issues, these are overlooked or seen as not moral issues. However, as Susan Mendus writes, to apply moral rules to love and friendship is to use a "deformed model" for these contexts (Mendus, 1996). We should not, though, conclude that these contexts are "beyond" or "outside" morality. We should find morality that illuminates and gives guidance for them, as the ethics of care tries to do. In contrast to the rationalist epistemologies of dominant moral theories, the ethics of care values the emotions, not only in carrying out the dictates of reason but in helping us understand what we ought to do. Empathy, sensitivity, and openness to narrative nuance may be better guides to what morality requires in specific actual circumstances than are rational principles or calculations.

The ethics of care is needed most clearly in such contexts as those of family and friendship. But it should not be thought of as limited to these. Some feminists would like to see it displace entirely the dominant ethics of justice and rights, or universal rules. Most others seek an appropriate integration of justice and care, liberal rights and empathetic concern. No advocate of the ethics of care seems willing to see it as a moral outlook less valuable than the dominant ones (Clement, 1996). To imagine the concerns of care ethicists as ones that can merely be added on to the dominant theories is unsatisfactory. To confine the ethics of care to the private sphere while holding it unsuitable for public life is no less to be rejected. But how the ethics of care and liberal political theory are to be meshed remains to be seen.

Most who defend the ethics of care recognize that care alone cannot adequately handle many questions of justice and rights. For instance, members of a privileged group may feel compassion towards and even care for members of a group they consider unfortunate, but fail to recognize that the latter deserve respect for their rights – including rights to such basic necessities as food, shelter, and health care – not paternalistic charity. Yet care may be the wider framework within which we should develop civil society and schemes of rights. Without some degree of caring, persons will be indifferent to the fates of others, including to violations of their rights. And in the process of respecting persons' rights, such as to basic necessities, policies that express the caring of the community for all its members will be superior to those that grudgingly issue an allotment to the unfit.

Many feminists argue for the relevance of care for the political domain (Held, 1993, 1995; Kittay, 1999; Ruddick, 1989; Tronto, 1993, 1996). Elevating care to a concern as important as the traditional concerns of liberal individuals might require a deep restructuring of society. Arrangements for the upbringing and health, education and development of children would move to the center of public attention, not be left to the vagaries of the market or the inadequacies of arbitrary local or charitable support. Caring for the elderly would be seen as a public concern, not a burden for individual adult children, usually women (Harrington, 1999). Considerations of how culture could enlighten and enrich human life would replace the current abandonment of culture to the dictates of economic gain that now determine how culture is produced and distributed (Schiller, 1989). Economic activity would be socially supported to serve human well-being rather than merely the increased economic power of the economically powerful.

Joan Tronto argues that we should think of care as a political concept, and she attributes the failure to do so to gendered assumptions that underlie standard political views. Caring activities, largely left to women and ill-paid minority workers, have been seen as either "below" politics, too narrow and natural to be of concern to politics, or they have been seen as charity and thus "above" politics. She argues that such views ignore "that care is a complex process that ultimately reflects structures of power, economic order . . . and our notions of autonomy and equality." The activities that constitute care are "crucial for human life," and seeing care as a political concept would enable us to realize that "a society flourishes when its citizens are well cared for" (Tronto, 1996, pp. 142–4). Recognizing care as political gives us recommendations for employment policies, school expenditures, access to health care, and overcoming discrimination.

Care is not only relevant to politics, but also to international affairs. Fiona Robinson develops a "critical ethic of care" capable of moving beyond the personal not only to the public life of a given society, but to dealing with issues of global conflict, poverty, and development (Robinson, 1999). She cites, for instance, many examples showing that in mitigating global poverty, it is vital to build strong relationships between local communities in the South and organizations in the North, and to develop abilities to be attentive to others. Care should not be thought of as sentimental or paternalistic; it can be effective and responsible. Many feminists have been concerned with the adverse effects of globalization and development on women, and seek feminist approaches to dealing with these trends.

The ethics of care builds trust and mutual responsiveness to need on both the personal and wider social level. Within social relations in which we care enough about each other to respect each other's rights, we may agree for limited purposes to imagine each other as liberal individuals, and to adopt liberal policies to maximize individual benefits. But we should not lose sight of the restricted and artificial aspects of such conceptions. The ethics of care offers a view of both the more immediate and the more distant human relations on which a satisfactory politics can be built. And with the new moral insights made available by the ethics of care, we can begin to see how political life will need to be transformed.

Postmodernism and Feminism

Many feminist political theorists have been influenced by postmodernism (Benhabib and Cornell, 1987; Nicholson, 1990). Critiques, by such writers as Foucault, Derrida, Richard Rorty, and Lyotard, of Enlightenment claims to rational and universal truths have helped many feminists dismantle gendered concepts and assumptions taken as certainties. In place of biased claims to universal and timeless rational understanding, postmodernism and many feminists offer social criticism, from many different cultural and racial perspectives, that is fractured, contextual, pluralistic, and ad hoc. Glimpses, images, and collages of observations are often thought to provide more insight than misleading totalizing abstractions.

In the project of reconstruction, however, many feminists have found a postmodern stance less helpful. Attempts to delineate a social order more hospitable to women and other disadvantaged groups fall prey to the same weapons of irony and deconstruction used on the order they aim to displace. To a number of feminists, postmodern approaches are seen as hostile to the political goals of feminism. These theorists fear that postmodern celebrations of disunity undermine political efforts to resist the hegemony of corporate capitalism and to achieve progress.

What feminists need, Nancy Hartsock argues, is not a wholesale and one-sided rejection of modernity, but a transformation of power relations, and for this "we need to engage in the historical, political, and theoretical process of constituting ourselves as subjects" engaged in making a different world. She acknowledges that some will dismiss her view as "calling for the construction of another totalizing and falsely universal discourse," but she rejects the view that Enlightenment thought and postmodern disassemblings are the only alternatives. Members of marginalized and oppressed groups are not "likely to mistake themselves for the universal 'man'," but they can still name and describe their experiences and work to transform the political process (Hartsock, 1996, p. 42). Many other feminists appreciate postmodern contributions but are similarly aware of their political weaknesses.

Feminism and Power

We must not lose sight of power as the very real capacity to oppose what morality, even if persuasive, recommends, nor of the power of the structures that keep oppression in place. This brings some feminists back to political theory in the more traditional sense, seeing politics as inherently about power and focusing on it. As Christine Di Stefano says, "power, along with its associated concept, the political, is the subject matter of feminist political philosophy" (Di Stefano, 2000, p. 96). But power is itself one of the concepts undergoing feminist reconceptualizations. In an early treatment, Nancy Hartsock analyzed what she took to be a feminist alternative to the standard conception of power as the capacity to dominate, of power over others. She found a number of women theorists writing of power as energy and competence, or "power to" rather than "power over," and she developed this alternative idea (Hartsock, 1983). Feminists have also explored the power, for instance of mothers, to empower others.

More recently, Amy Allen examines three conceptions of power that feminists have been working with. They recognize power as resource, power as domination, and power as empowerment. She finds the first inadequate because it suggests that power can be "possessed, distributed, and redistributed, and the second and third are unsatisfactory because each of these conceptions emphasizes only one aspect of the multifaceted power relations that feminists are trying to understand" (Amy Allen, 1999, p. 3). She discusses the work of Foucault, Judith Butler, and Hannah Arendt, and develops her own conception that construes power as "a relation rather than as a possession," but avoids the tendency "to mistake one aspect of power," such as domination or empowerment, for the whole of it (p. 3).

Feminist critics of the project of bringing the values of care and concern, trust and relatedness to public and political life worry that doing so may lead us to lose sight of the power, especially in the sense of power to dominate, that may be arrayed against progress (Di Stefano, 2000). There is no doubt that a backlash against women's advances has occurred in many forms along with the gains women have made in recent decades. But advocating that political life ought to be guided much more than at present by the values of care and trust in no way entails soft-headedness about the obstacles feminists must expect in transforming society.

There are many conflicts of an economic, religious, and ethnic kind wracking the globe, that non-feminist and some feminist critics see a politics of care as unsuitable for addressing. But an ethic of care is quite capable of examining the social structures of power within which the activities of caring take place (Tronto, 1993). And there is nothing soft-headed about care. As Sara Ruddick emphasizes, family life and bringing up children are rife with conflict. Sometimes rules must be established and enforced, and punishments meted out. But those adept in the skills of mothering, of defusing conflicts before they become violent, of settling disputes among those who cannot just leave but must learn to get along with one another, have much to teach peacemakers and peacekeepers in other domains (Ruddick, 1989). As international mechanisms evolve for dealing with conflict and for persuading the uninvolved to contribute the funds and personnel needed to control violence and build tolerance, they will depend heavily on citizens caring about potential victims, wanting to prevent their suffering, and understanding what needs to be done (Robinson, 1999). And this factor of relatedness to other human beings may be more important than a mere rational recognition of abstract liberal rights, though progress in understanding and respecting human rights is surely important also.

Furthermore, in countering the corporate power that threatens to overwhelm politics as well as all other aspects of global life with its ideology of Social Darwinism, liberal individualism offers weak defenses (Kuttner, 1996; Schiller, 1989). Corporate power is often exercised through enticement rather than coercion. It can increase its reach and the influence of its values in many ways without violating liberal rights. What is needed to restrain its imperialistic expansion is an assertion of alternative values, such as care and trust and human solidarity.

Feminism and Political Change

Feminism seeks to overturn the gender hierarchy that has in various forms maintained its power and permeated almost all aspects of every known society throughout human history, and to replace it with equality between men and women. This will require the transformation of what is thought of as knowledge, of the ways people think and behave at almost all levels, of almost all institutions, of culture, of society. Doing this is certainly revolutionary and cannot be imagined to be a historical change to be accomplished rapidly. Feminists do not seek to simply replace men with a comparable number of women in the existing positions of power determining how society will develop, they seek to change the way these positions are thought about and structured.

Most feminists who reject postmodern warnings about positing any alternatives to the failed ones of modernism suggest such imaginable though distant goals as an end of domination, exploitation, and hierarchy as inherent features of society. They seek an ordering of society along cooperative lines that foster mutual trust and caring. As an ideal, a democratic political system may seek to treat citizens equally, but it may presume conflicting interests between them, and may allow an economic system that promotes conflict and self-interest far more than cooperation. As the economic system dominates more and more of the society, as in capitalist societies at present, cooperation is more and more marginalized. The feminist ideal of democracy is often different.

The dominant way of thinking about democracy since the seventeenth century has seen it as what Jane Mansbridge calls "adversary democracy," in which conflicting interests compete, limited only by contractual restraints, and the strongest win (Mansbridge, 1983). She notes that in practice, citizens in actual democratic systems have often sought to persuade rather than merely overpower their opponents. But the leading views of the past several decades continue to see democracy as adversarial, and political practices seem increasingly to accord with such views.

Mansbridge would like to see this kind of democracy replaced by one "where mutual persuasion helps realize shared goals and interests" (Mansbridge, 1996, p. 123). She thinks that feminist understandings of maternal and other forms of connectedness can help us bring about the more consultative and participatory processes that many theorists advocate (Cunningham, 1987; Gould, 1988) and that she sees as "unitary democracy." Many leading theorists of democracy think of deliberation as limited to what is "reasoned" and impartial, but feminists examine how activating feelings of empathy and responsibility is also needed to reach shared objectives. Of course, some emotions are dangerous, but others ought to be included in our understanding of what democracy requires and should be welcomed into democratic discourse (Phillips, 1995; Taylor, 1995; Young, 1990). Mansbridge notes that concern for ongoing relationships, listening, empathy, even common interests, have been coded as female and therefore devalued by political theorists eager to be seen as tough-minded. Feminist theorists are showing, in contrast, how these considerations are essential for acceptable uses of power, including democratic power. They understand at the same time that power is pervasive in human life and cannot be ignored. But it can be developed and used in morally appropriate ways (Jones, 1993).

The extent to which the world is still wracked by ethnic and racial divisions that have not yielded to liberal universalism must be acknowledged. The feminist understanding of how both equality and difference can be respected can be useful in showing how politics can deal with group conflict. As we have come to see concerning women, members of groups can be both equal to, but different from, dominant groups. To be respected as an equal should not mean being reduced to sameness, which purported sameness has historically reflected the characteristics of the dominant group (Mendus, 1992; Young, 1990).

In a society increasingly influenced by feminism and the values of care and concern, the need for law and coercion would not disappear, but their use might become progressively more limited as society would learn to bring up its children so that fewer and fewer would sink to violence or insist on pursuing their own individual interests at the expense of others or without reasonable restraints. Even in the most cooperative societies, politics would still be needed to make appropriate decisions and to determine suitable policies. But the terms of the contests might be political in the sense that the best arguments would be persuasive. They would not need to be political in the sense of the power to coerce, through political position or legal sanction or economic power or sheer numbers of votes, determining the outcome. Economic power would be limited so that it would not control political and cultural discourse. And we could foresee that much more public debate would be conducted in the domain of a culture freed from economic domination (Held, 1993). Such a culture could approach the free discourse on which democratic decisions ought to be based, along with the protections of basic rights. The outcomes might then much more nearly approach consensus than political coercion. While using political power to coerce is progress over using violence or military force to do so, freely given accord is better still. And the discourse influenced by feminist values would not be limited to the rational principles of traditional public and political philosophy. Images and narratives appealing to the moral emotions of empathy and caring would also contribute (Held, 1993; Landes, 1998). Feminist ethical views would be on a par with traditional ones as persons would defuse conflict with conversation and seek cooperatively to provide for children and care for their global environment.

References

Allen, Amy (1999). *The Power of Feminist Theory: Domination, Resistance, Solidarity.* Boulder, CO: Westview Press.

Allen, Anita (1988). *Uneasy Access: Privacy for Women in a Free Society.* Totowa, NJ: Rowman and Littlefield.

Baier, Annette C. (1994). *Moral Prejudices: Essays on Ethics.* Cambridge, MA: Harvard University Press.

Barry, Brian (1973). *The Liberal Theory of Justice.* London: Oxford University Press.

Bartlett, Katherine T. and Rosanne Kennedy (eds.) (1991). *Feminist Legal Theory: Readings in Law and Gender.* Boulder, CO: Westview Press.

Benhabib, Seyla (1992). *Situating the Self: Gender, Community, and Postmodernism in Contemporary Ethics.* New York: Routledge.

——and Drucilla Cornell (eds.) (1987). *Feminism as Critique: On the Politics of Gender.* Minneapolis: University of Minnesota Press.

Callahan, Joan (ed.) (1995). *Reproduction, Ethics, and the Law: Feminist Perspectives.* Bloomington: Indiana University Press.

Card, Claudia (ed.) (1991). *Feminist Ethics.* Lawrence: University Press of Kansas.

——(ed.) (1999). *On Feminist Ethics and Politics.* Lawrence: University Press of Kansas.

Clarke, Lorenne and Lynda Lange (eds.) (1979). *The Sexism of Social and Political Thought.* Toronto: University of Toronto Press.

Clement, Grace (1996). *Care, Autonomy, and Justice.* Boulder, CO: Westview Press.

Collins, Patricia Hill (1990). *Black Feminist Thought: Knowledge, Consciousness, and the Politics of Empowerment.* Boston: Unwin Hyman.

Cornell, Drucilla (1998). *At the Heart of Freedom: Feminism, Sex, and Equality.* Princeton, NJ: Princeton University Press.

Crenshaw, Kimberle (1993). "Mapping the Margins: Intersectionality, Identity Politics and Violence Against Women of Color." *Stanford Law Review*, 43: 6.

Cunningham, Frank (1987). *Democratic Theory and Socialism.* Cambridge: Cambridge University Press.

Di Stefano, Christine (1991). *Configurations of Masculinity: A Feminist Perspective on Modern Political Theory.* Ithaca, NY: Cornell University Press.

——(2000). "Feminist Political Philosophy." In *APA Newsletter on Feminism and Philosophy*, Spring: 196–200.

Elshtain, Jean Bethke (1981). *Public Man, Private Woman.* Princeton, NJ: Princeton University Press.

Ferguson, Ann (1989). *Blood at the Root: Motherhood, Sexuality and Male Domination.* London: Pandora.

Frank, Robert A., Thomas Gilovich, and Dennis T. Regan (1998). "Does Studying Economics Inhibit Cooperation?" In Charles K. Wilber (ed.), *Economics, Ethics, and Public Policy.* Lanham, MD: Rowman and Littlefield.

Fraser, Nancy (1989). *Unruly Practices: Power, Discourse, and Gender in Contemporary Social Theory.* Minneapolis: University of Minnesota Press.

Frazer, Elizabeth and Nicola Lacey (1993). *The Politics of Community: A Feminist Critique of the Liberal–Communitarian Debate.* Toronto: University of Toronto Press.

French, Marilyn (1992). *The War Against Women.* New York: Simon and Schuster.

Friedman, Marilyn (1993). *What Are Friends For? Feminist Perspectives on Personal Relationships and Moral Theory.* Ithaca, NY: Cornell University Press.

Gilligan, Carol (1982). *In a Different Voice: Psychological Theory and Women's Development.* Cambridge, MA: Harvard University Press.

Gould, Carol C. (1998). *Rethinking Democracy: Freedom and Cooperation in Politics, Economy, and Society*. Cambridge: Cambridge University Press.

Hampton, Jean (1993). "Feminist Contractarianism." In Louise M. Antony and Charlotte Witt (eds.), *A Mind of One's Own: Feminist Essays on Reason and Objectivity*. Boulder, CO: Westview Press.

Harrington, Mona (1999). *Care and Equality: Inventing a New Family Politics*. New York: Knopf.

Hartsock, Nancy C. M. (1983). *Money, Sex, and Power: Toward a Feminist Historical Materialism*. New York: Longman.

——(1996). "Community/ Sexuality/ Gender: Rethinking Power." In Nancy J. Hirschmann and Christine Di Stefano (eds.), *Revisioning the Political: Feminist Reconstructions of Traditional Concepts in Western Political Theory*. Boulder, CO: Westview Press.

Held, Virginia (1993). *Feminist Morality: Transforming Culture, Society, and Politics*. Chicago: University of Chicago Press.

——(1984). *Rights and Goods: Justifying Social Action*. New York: Free Press.

——(ed.) (1995). *Justice and Care: Essential Readings in Feminist Ethics*. Boulder, CO: Westview Press.

Hoagland, Sarah Lucia (1989). *Lesbian Ethics: Toward New Value*. Palo Alto, CA: Institute of Lesbian Studies.

Jaggar, Alison (1983). *Feminist Politics and Human Nature*. Totowa, NJ: Rowman and Allanheld.

——(ed.) (1994). *Living with Contradictions: Controversies in Feminist Social Ethics*. Boulder, CO: Westview Press.

Jones, Kathleen B. (1993). *Compassionate Authority: Democracy and the Representation of Women*. New York: Routledge.

Keller, Jean (1997). "Autonomy, Relationality, and Feminist Ethics." *Hypatia*, 12, 2: 152–65.

Kittay, Eva Feder (1999). *Love's Labor: Essays on Women, Equality, and Dependency*. New York: Routledge.

Kuttner, Robert (1996). *Everything For Sale: The Virtues and Limits of Markets*. New York: Knopf.

Landes, Joan B. (ed.) (1998). *Feminism, the Public and the Private*. New York: Oxford University Press.

Littleton, Christine (1987). "Reconstructing Sexual Equality." *California Law Review*, 75, 4: 1279–337.

Lloyd, Genevieve (1984). *The Man of Reason: "Male" and "Female" in Western Philosophy*. Minneapolis: University of Minnesota Press.

Mackenzie, Catriona and Natalie Stoljar (eds.) (2000). *Relational Autonomy: Feminist Perspectives on Autonomy, Agency, and the Social Self*. New York: Oxford University Press.

MacKinnon, Catharine A. (1987). *Feminism Unmodified: Discourses on Life and Law*. Cambridge, MA: Harvard University Press.

——(1989). *Toward a Feminist Theory of the State*. Cambridge, MA: Harvard University Press.

Mansbridge, Jane (1983). *Beyond Adversary Democracy*. Chicago: Chicago University Press.

——(1996). "Reconstructing Democracy." In Nancy J. Hirschmann and Christine Di Stefano (eds.), *Revisioning the Political: Feminist Reconstructions of Traditional Concepts in Western Political Theory*. Boulder, CO: Westview Press.

Mendus, Susan (1992). "Losing the Faith: Feminism and Democracy." In J. Dunn (ed.), *Democracy: The Unfinished Journey*. Oxford: Oxford University Press.

——(1996). "Some Mistakes about Impartiality." *Political Studies*, 44: 319–27.

Meyers, Diana Tietjens (1989). *Self, Society, and Personal Choice*. New York: Columbia University Press.

——(ed.) (1997). *Feminists Rethink the Self*. Boulder, CO: Westview Press.

Mill, John Stuart and Harriet Taylor Mill (1970). *Essays on Sex Equality* (ed.) Alice S. Rossi. Chicago: University of Chicago Press.

Minow, Martha (1990). *Making All the Difference: Inclusion, Exclusion, and American Law*. Ithaca, NY: Cornell University Press.

Narayan, Uma (1995). "Colonialism and Its Others: Considerations on Rights and Care Discourses." *Hypatia* 10, 2: 133–40.

Nicholson, Linda (ed.) (1990). *Feminism/Postmodernism*. New York: Routledge.

Noddings, Nel (1986). *Caring: A Feminine Approach to Ethics and Moral Education*. Berkeley: University of California Press.

Nussbaum, Martha C. (1999) *Sex and Social Justice*. New York: Oxford University Press.

Okin, Susan Moller (1989). *Justice, Gender, and the Family*. New York: Basic Books.

——(1979). *Women in Western Political Thought*. Princeton: Princeton University Press.

Olsen, Frances (1984). "Statutory Rape: A Feminist Critique of Rights Analysis." *Texas Law Review*, 63: 387–432.

Pateman, Carole (1988). *The Sexual Contract*. Stanford, CA: Stanford University Press.

Petchesky, Rosalind P. (1985). *Abortion and Women's Choice: The State, Sexuality, and Reproductive Freedom*. Boston: Northeastern University Press.

Phillips, Anne (1995). *The Politics of Presence*. Oxford: Oxford University Press.

Rhode, Deborah L. (1989). *Justice and Gender: Sex Discrimination and the Law*. Cambridge, MA: Harvard University Press.

Robinson, Fiona (1999). *Globalizing Care: Ethics, Feminist Theory, and International Affairs*. Boulder, CO: Westview Press.

Ruddick, Sara (1989). *Maternal Thinking: Towards a Politics of Peace*. Boston: Beacon Press.

Sargent, Lydia (ed.) (1981). *Feminism and Revolution: A Discussion of the Unhappy Marriage of Marxism and Feminism*. Boston: South End Press.

Schiller, Herbert I. (1989). *Culture Inc.: The Corporate Takeover of Public Expression*. New York: Oxford University Press.

Schneider, Elizabeth M. (1986). "The Dialectic of Rights and Politics: Perspectives from the Women's Movement," *New York University Law Review*, 61: 593–652.

Shanley, Mary Lyndon and Uma Narayan (eds.) (1997). *Reconstructing Political Theory: Feminist Perspectives*. University Park: Pennsylvania State University Press.

Smart, Carol (1989). *Feminism and the Power of Law*. London: Routledge.

Smith, Patricia (ed.) (1993). *Feminist Jurisprudence*. New York: Oxford University Press.

Spelman, Elizabeth V. (1988). *Inessential Woman: Problems of Exclusion in Feminist Thought*. Boston: Beacon Press.

Sterba, James (1989). *How To Make People Just*. Lanham, MD: Rowman and Littlefield.

Taylor, Charles (1995). *Philosophical Arguments*. Cambridge, MA: Harvard University Press.

Tong, Rosemarie (1993). *Feminine and Feminist Ethics*. Belmont, CA: Wadsworth.

Tronto, Joan C. (1996). "Care as a Political Concept." In Nancy J. Hirschmann and Christine Di Stefano (eds.), *Revisioning the Political: Feminist Reconstructions of Traditional Concepts in Western Political Theory*. Boulder, CO: Westview Press.

——(1993). *Moral Boundaries: A Political Argument for an Ethic of Care*. New York: Routledge.

Walker, Margaret Urban (1998). *Moral Understandings: A Feminist Study in Ethics*. New York: Routledge.

Weiss, Penny (1998). *Conversations with Feminism: Political Theory and Practice*. Lanham, MD: Rowman and Littlefield.

West, Robin (1988). "Jurisprudence and Gender." *University of Chicago Law Review*, 55: 1–72.

Williams, Patricia J. (1991). *The Alchemy of Race and Rights*. Cambridge, MA: Harvard University Press.

Wollstonecraft, Mary (1967). *A Vindication of the Rights of Woman* [1792]. New York: Norton.

Young, Iris Marion (1990). *Justice and the Politics of Difference*. Princeton: Princeton University Press.

Chapter 8

Liberalism and the Challenge of Communitarianism

James P. Sterba

In his Inaugural Lecture for the McMahon/Hank Chair of Philosophy at the University of Notre Dame, entitled "The Privatization of the Good," Alasdair MacIntyre argues that virtually all forms of liberalism attempt to separate rules defining right action from conceptions of the human good.[1] On this account, MacIntyre contends, these forms of liberalism not only fail but have to fail because the rules defining right action cannot be adequately grounded apart from a conception of the good. This is the initial form of the communitarian challenge to liberalism.

Responding to this challenge, some liberals have openly conceded that their view is not grounded independently of some conception of the good.[2] John Rawls, for example, has made it very clear that the form of liberalism he defends requires a conception of the political good, although not a comprehensive conception of the good.[3] Unfortunately, this defense of liberalism, although helpful, is still inadequate in the light of an even more serious challenge that can be brought against the view. This challenge is that defenders of liberalism can give no non-question-begging defense of the particular conception of the good they do endorse. Moreover, this challenge applies to both defenders and critics of liberalism alike because neither has provided a non-question-begging defense of the particular conception of the good they happen to endorse.

In this essay, I will try to sketch a defense of liberalism against this more fundamental challenge. As I see it, there are four necessary elements to an adequate defense of liberalism. First, liberals need to provide a non-question-begging argument for a moral rather than a self-interested conception of the good.[4] Unfortunately, most liberals have not even attempted this task,[5] and it is just where critics of liberalism, like MacIntyre, have pressed their attack.[6] Second, since most liberals do not limit themselves to simply endorsing negative rights of noninterference but also endorse positive rights (such as a right to welfare and a right to equal opportunity), these liberals need to provide a non-question-begging argument for a conception of the good that includes positive rights as well as negative rights. More specifically, these liberals need to provide a non-question-begging defense of positive rights against libertarians who claim that only negative rights are required. Unfortunately, although many liberals have attempted to defend their view in this regard, most have simply begged the question against the libertarian view.[7] Third, liberals need to provide a non-question-begging argument specifying the economic structure of the society required by the rights they endorse. Specifically, would it be capitalist or socialist and what sort of equality would prevail? Now while liberals have had much to say on this topic, rarely have they based their considerations on premises that are acceptable to defenders of both opposing perspectives.[8] Fourth, liberals need to provide a non-question-begging argument for enforcing a partial rather than a complete conception of the good. Here, in contrast to the other required elements of an adequate defense of liberalism, liberals have presented an essentially successful non-question-begging defense of their views, but the confusing terminology they have employed has made it difficult for others to appreciate the force of their defense.[9] Accordingly, here I propose to simply eliminate the confusing terminology and recast the underlying defense.

Of course, the defense of liberalism that I propose to provide, like any defense, is embedded in a tradition with its presuppositions.[10] Nevertheless, the basic presupposition of this defense, namely, that views that can be supported with non-question-begging arguments are rationally preferable, is hardly open to challenge.

I   A Moral Conception of the Good

There is little doubt that providing liberals with a non-question-begging defense of their commitment to a moral rather than a self-interested conception of the good is the most difficult part of defending liberalism. But to see how such a defense is possible, let us begin by imagining that we are, as members of a society, deliberating over what sort of principles governing action we ought to accept. Let us assume that each of us is capable of entertaining and acting upon both self-interested and moral reasons and that the question we are seeking to answer is what sort of principles governing action it would be rational for us to accept.[11] This question is not about what sort of principles we should publicly affirm since people will sometimes publicly affirm principles that are quite different from those they are prepared to act upon, but rather it is a question of what principles it would be rational for us to accept at the deepest level – in our heart of hearts.

There are people who are incapable of acting upon moral reasons, of course. For such people, there is no question about their being required to act morally or altruistically. Yet the interesting philosophical question is not about such people but about people, like ourselves, who are capable of acting morally as well as self-interestedly and are seeking a rational justification for following a particular course of action.

In trying to determine how we should act, let us assume that we would like to be able to construct a *good* argument favoring morality over egoism, and given that good arguments are non-question-begging, we accordingly would like to construct an argument that, as far as possible, does not beg the question. The question at issue here is what reasons each of us should take as supreme, and this question would be begged against egoism if we proposed to answer it simply by assuming from the start that moral reasons are the reasons that each of us should take as supreme. But the question would be begged against morality as well if we proposed to answer the question simply by assuming from the start that self-interested reasons are the reasons that each of us should take as supreme. This means, of course, that we cannot answer the question of what reasons we should take as supreme simply by assuming the general principle of egoism:

Each person ought to do what best serves his or her overall self-interest.

We can no more argue for egoism simply by denying the relevance of moral reasons to rational choice than we can argue for pure altruism simply by denying the relevance of self-interested reasons to rational choice and assuming the following general principle of pure altruism:

Each person ought to do what best serves the overall interest of others.[12]

Consequently, in order not to beg the question, we have no other alternative but to grant the prima facie relevance of both self-interested and moral reasons to rational choice and then try to determine which reasons we would be rationally required to act upon, all things considered. Notice that in order not to beg the question, it is necessary to back off from both the general principle of egoism and the general principle of pure altruism, thus granting the prima facie relevance of both self-interested and moral reasons to rational choice. From this standpoint, it is still an open question, whether either egoism or pure altruism will be rationally preferable, all things considered.

In this regard, there are two kinds of cases that must be considered: cases in which there is a conflict between the relevant self-interested and moral reasons, and cases in which there is no such conflict.

It seems obvious that where there is no conflict and both reasons are conclusive reasons of their kind, both reasons should be acted upon. In such contexts, we should do what is favored both by morality and by self-interest. Of course, defenders of egoism cannot but be disconcerted with this result since it shows that actions in accord with egoism are contrary to reason at least when there are two equally good ways of pursuing one's self-interest, only one of which does not conflict with the basic requirements of morality. Notice also that in cases where there are two equally good ways of fulfilling the basic requirements of morality, only one of which does not conflict with what is in a person's overall self-interest, it is not at all disconcerting for defenders of morality to admit that we are rationally required to choose the way that does not conflict with what is in our overall self-interest. Nevertheless, exposing this defect in egoism for cases where moral reasons and self-interested reasons do not conflict would be but a small victory for defenders of morality if it were not also possible to show that in cases where such reasons do conflict, moral reasons would have priority over self-interested reasons.

Now when we rationally assess the relevant reasons in conflict cases, it is best to cast the conflict not as a conflict between self-interested reasons and moral reasons but instead as a conflict between self-interested reasons and altruistic reasons.[13] Viewed in this way, three solutions are possible. First, we could say that self-interested reasons always have priority over conflicting altruistic reasons. Second, we could say just the opposite, that altruistic reasons always have priority over conflicting self-interested reasons. Third, we could say that some kind of compromise is rationally required. In this compromise, sometimes self-interested reasons would have priority over altruistic reasons, and sometimes altruistic reasons would have priority over self-interested reasons.

Once the conflict is described in this manner, the third solution can be seen to be the one that is rationally required. This is because the first and second solutions give exclusive priority to one class of relevant reasons over the other, and only a completely question-begging justification can be given for such an exclusive priority. Only by employing the third solution, and sometimes giving priority to self-interested reasons, and sometimes giving priority to altruistic reasons, can we avoid a completely question-begging resolution.

Notice also that this standard of rationality will not support just any compromise between the relevant self-interested and altruistic reasons. The compromise must be a nonarbitrary one, for otherwise it would beg the question with respect to the opposing egoistic and altruistic perspectives.[14] Such a compromise would have to respect the rankings of self-interested and altruistic reasons imposed by the egoistic and altruistic perspectives, respectively. Since for each individual there is a separate ranking of that individual's relevant self-interested and altruistic reasons (which will vary, of course, depending on the individual's capabilities and circumstances), we can represent these rankings from the most important reasons to the least important reasons as follows:

Individual A Self-Interested Reasons	Altruistic Reasons	Individual B Self-Interested Reasons	Altruistic Reasons
1	1	1	1
2	2	2	2
3	3	3	3
.	.	.	.
.	.	.	.
.	.	.	.
N	N	N	N

Accordingly, any nonarbitrary compromise among such reasons in seeking not to beg the question against either egoism or pure altruism will have to give priority to those reasons that rank highest in each category. Failure to give priority to the highest-ranking altruistic or self-interested reasons would, other things being equal, be contrary to reason.

Of course, there will be cases in which the only way to avoid being required to do what is contrary to your highest-ranking reasons is by requiring someone else to do what is contrary to her highest-ranking reasons. Some of these cases will be "lifeboat cases," as, for example, where you and two others are stranded on a lifeboat that has only enough resources for two of you to survive before you will be rescued. But although such cases are surely difficult to resolve (maybe only a chance mechanism, like flipping a coin, can offer a reasonable resolution), they surely do not reflect the typical conflict between the relevant self-interested and altruistic reasons that we are or were able to acquire. Typically, one or the other of the conflicting reasons will rank significantly higher on its respective scale, thus permitting a clear resolution.

Now we can see how morality can be viewed as just such a nonarbitrary compromise between self-interested and altruistic reasons. First, a certain amount of self-regard is morally required or at least morally acceptable. Where this is the case, high-ranking self-interested reasons have priority over low-ranking altruistic reasons. Second, morality obviously places limits on the extent to which people should pursue their own self-interest. Where this is the case, high-ranking altruistic reasons have priority over low-ranking self-interested reasons. In this way, morality can be seen to be a nonarbitrary compromise between self-interested and altruistic reasons, and the "moral reasons" that constitute that compromise can be seen as having an absolute priority over the self-interested or altruistic reasons that conflict with them.[15]

It is also important to see how this compromise view has been supported by a two-step argument that is not question-begging at all. In the first step, our goal was to determine what sort of reasons for action it would be rational for us to accept on the basis of a good argument, and this required a non-question-begging starting point. Noting that both egoism, which favored exclusively self-interested reasons, and pure altruism, which favored exclusively altruistic reasons, offered only question-begging starting points, we took as our non-question-begging starting point the prima facie relevance of both self-interested and altruistic reasons to rational choice. The logical inference here is analogous to the inference of equal probability sanctioned in decision theory when we have no evidence that one alternative is more likely than another.[16] Here we had no non-question-begging justification for excluding either self-interested or altruistic reasons as relevant to rational choice, so we accepted both kinds of reasons as prima facie relevant to rational choice. The conclusion of this first step of the argument for the compromise view does not beg the question against egoism or pure altruism because if defenders of either view had any hope of providing a good, and hence, non-question-begging argument for their views, they too would have to grant this very conclusion as necessary for a non-question-begging defense of either egoism, pure altruism, or the compromise view. In accepting it, therefore, the compromise view does not beg the question against a possible non-question-begging defense of these other two perspectives, and that is all that should concern us.

Now once both self-interested and altruistic reasons are recognized as prima facie relevant to rational choice, the second step of the argument for the compromise view offers a nonarbitrary ordering of those reasons on the basis of rankings of self-interested and altruistic reasons imposed by the egoistic and altruistic perspectives respectively. According to that ordering, high-ranking self-interested reasons have priority over low-ranking altruistic reasons and high-ranking altruistic reasons have priority over low-ranking self-interested reasons. There is no other plausible nonarbitrary ordering of these reasons. Hence, it certainly does not beg the question against either the egoistic or altruistic perspective, once we imagine those perspectives (or their defenders) to be suitably reformed so that they too are committed to a standard of non-question-beggingness. In the end, if one is committed to a standard of non-question-beggingness, one has to be concerned only with how one's claims and arguments stake up against those of others who are also committed to such a standard. If you yourself are committed to the standard of non-question-beggingness, you don't beg the question by simply coming into conflict with the requirements of other perspectives, unless those other perspectives (or their defenders) are also committed to the same standard of non-question-beggingness. In arguing for one's view, when one comes into conflict with bigots, one does not beg the question against them unless one is a bigot oneself.

Now it might be objected that even if morality is required by a standard of non-question-beggingness, that does not provide us with the right kind of reason to be moral. It might be argued that avoiding non-question-beggingness is too formal a reason to be moral and that we need a more substantive reason.[17] Happily, the need for a substantive reason to be moral can be met because in this case the formal reason to be moral – namely, avoiding non-question-beggingness – itself entails a substantive reason to be moral – namely, to give high-ranking altruistic reasons priority over conflicting lower-ranking self-interested reasons and high-ranking self-interested reasons priority over conflicting lower-ranking altruistic reasons, or, to put the reason more substantively still, to avoid inflicting basic harm for the sake of nonbasic benefit. So, as it turns out, morality as compromise can be shown to provide both formal and substantive reasons to be moral. In this way, therefore, liberals can provide a non-question-begging defense of their commitment to a moral rather than a self-interested conception of the good.

II   A Conception of the Good with Positive Rights

Assuming then that we have a non-question-begging defense for endorsing a moral rather than a self-interested conception of the good, the next step in the defense of liberalism is to provide a non-question-begging defense of a moral conception of the good that incorporates positive as well as negative rights. Specifically, we need to address the view of libertarians who contend that only a conception of the good that incorporates negative rights is required. To counter the libertarian view, we need to focus on a typical conflict situation between the rich and the poor. In this conflict situation, the rich have more than enough resources to satisfy their basic needs. By contrast, the poor lack the resources to meet their most basic needs even though they have tried all the means available to them that libertarians regard as legitimate for acquiring such resources. Under circumstances like these, libertarians usually maintain that the rich should have the liberty to use their resources to satisfy their luxury needs if they so wish. Libertarians recognize that this liberty might well be enjoyed at the expense of the satisfaction of the most basic needs of the poor; they just think that liberty always has priority over other political ideals, and since they assume that the liberty of the poor is not at stake in such conflict situations, it is easy for them to conclude that the rich should not be required to sacrifice their liberty so that the basic needs of the poor may be met.

Of course, libertarians would allow that it would be nice of the rich to share their surplus resources with the poor. Nevertheless, according to libertarians, such acts of charity are not required because the liberty of the poor is not thought to be at stake in such conflict situations.

In fact, however, the liberty of the poor is at stake in such conflict situations. What is at stake is the liberty of the poor to take from the surplus possessions of the rich what is necessary to satisfy their basic needs. When libertarians are brought to see that this is the case, they are genuinely surprised, one might even say rudely awakened, for they had not previously seen the conflict between the rich and the poor as a conflict of liberties.

Now when the conflict between the rich and the poor is viewed as a conflict of liberties, either we can say that the rich should have the liberty to use their surplus resources for luxury purposes, or we can say that the poor should have the liberty to take from the rich what they require to meet their basic needs. If we choose one liberty, we must reject the other. What needs to be determined, therefore, is which liberty is morally preferable: the liberty of the rich or the liberty of the poor.

I submit that the liberty of the poor, which is the liberty to take from the surplus resources of others what is required to meet one's basic needs, is morally preferable to the liberty of the rich, which is the liberty to use one's surplus resources for luxury purposes. To see that this is the case, we need only appeal to one of the most fundamental principles of morality, one that is common to all moral conceptions of the good, namely, the "ought" implies "can" principle. According to this principle, people are not morally required to do what they lack the power to do or what would involve so great a sacrifice that it would be unreasonable to ask them to perform such an action, and/or in the case of severe conflicts of interest, unreasonable to require them to perform such an action.[18]

For example, suppose I have promised to attend a departmental meeting on Friday, but on Thursday I am involved in a serious car accident which puts me into a coma. Surely it is no longer the case that I ought to attend the meeting now that I lack the power to do so. Or suppose instead that on Thursday I develop a severe case of pneumonia for which I am hospitalized. Surely I could legitimately claim that I no longer ought to attend the meeting on the grounds that the risk to my health involved in attending is a sacrifice that it would be unreasonable to ask me to bear. Or suppose the risk to my health from having pneumonia is not so serious that it would be unreasonable to ask me to attend the meeting (a supererogatory request), it might still be serious enough to be unreasonable to *require* my attendance at the meeting (a demand that is backed up by blame or coercion).

What is distinctive about the formulation of the "ought" implies "can" principle is that it claims that the requirements of morality cannot, all things considered, be unreasonable to ask, and/or in cases of severe conflict of interest, unreasonable to require people to abide by. The principle claims that reason and morality must be linked in an appropriate way, especially if we are going to be able to justifiably use blame or coercion to get people to abide by the requirements of morality. It should be noted, however, that while major figures in the history of philosophy, and most philosophers today, including virtually all libertarian philosophers, accept this linkage between reason and morality, this linkage is not usually conceived to be part of the "ought" implies "can" principle. Nevertheless, I claim that there are good reasons for associating this linkage between reason and morality with the "ought" implies "can" principle, namely, our use of the word "can" (I can't come to the meeting) as in the examples just given, and the natural progression from logical, physical and psychological possibility found in the traditional "ought" implies "can" principle to the notion of moral possibility found in this formulation of the "ought" implies "can" principle. In any case, the acceptability of this formulation of the "ought" implies "can" principle is determined by the virtually universal acceptance of its components and not by the manner in which I have proposed to join those components together.

Now applying the "ought" implies "can" principle to the case at hand, it seems clear that the poor have it within their power willingly to relinquish such an important liberty as the liberty to take from the rich what they require to meet their basic needs. Nevertheless, it would be unreasonable to ask or require them to make so great a sacrifice. In the extreme case, it would involve asking or requiring the poor to sit back and starve to death. Of course, the poor may have no real alternative to relinquishing this liberty. To do anything else may involve worse consequences for themselves and their loved ones and may invite a painful death. Accordingly, we may expect that the poor would acquiesce, albeit unwillingly, to a political system that denied them the right to welfare supported by such a liberty, at the same time that we recognize that such a system imposes an unreasonable sacrifice upon the poor – a sacrifice that we could not morally blame the poor for trying to evade. Analogously, we might expect that a woman whose life was threatened would submit to a rapist's demands, at the same time that we recognize the utter unreasonableness of those demands.

By contrast, it would not be unreasonable to ask and require the rich to sacrifice the liberty to meet some of their luxury needs so that the poor can have the liberty to meet their basic needs.[19] Naturally, we might expect that the rich, for reasons of self-interest and past contribution, might be disinclined to make such a sacrifice. We might even suppose that the past contribution of the rich provides a good reason for not sacrificing their liberty to use their surplus for luxury purposes. Yet, unlike the poor, the rich could not claim that relinquishing such a liberty involved so great a sacrifice that it would be unreasonable to ask and require them to make it; unlike the poor, the rich could be morally blameworthy for failing to make such a sacrifice.

Consequently, if we assume that, however else we specify a moral conception of the good, it cannot violate the "ought" implies "can" principle, it follows that, despite what libertarians claim, the right to liberty endorsed by them actually favors the liberty of the poor over the liberty of the rich.

Yet couldn't libertarians object to this conclusion, claiming that it would be unreasonable to require the rich to sacrifice the liberty to meet some of their luxury needs so that the poor could have the liberty to meet their basic needs? As I have pointed out, libertarians don't usually see the situation as a conflict of liberties, but suppose they did. How plausible would such an objection be? Not very plausible at all, I think.

For consider: what are libertarians going to say about the poor? Isn't it clearly unreasonable to require the poor to sacrifice the liberty to meet their basic needs so that the rich can have the liberty to meet their luxury needs? Isn't it clearly unreasonable to require the poor to sit back and starve to death? If it is, then, there is no resolution of this conflict that it would be reasonable to require both the rich and the poor to accept. But that would mean that the libertarian ideal of liberty cannot be a moral conception of the good, for a moral conception of the good resolves conflicts of interest in ways that it would be reasonable to require everyone affected to accept. Therefore, as long as libertarians think of themselves as putting forth a moral conception of the good, they cannot allow that it would be unreasonable *both* to require the rich to sacrifice the liberty to meet some of their luxury needs in order to benefit the poor and to require the poor to sacrifice the liberty to meet their basic needs in order to benefit the rich. But I submit that if one of these requirements is to be judged reasonable, then, by any neutral assessment, it must be the requirement that the rich sacrifice the liberty to meet some of their luxury needs so that the poor can have the liberty to meet their basic needs; there is no other plausible resolution, if libertarians intend to be putting forth a moral conception of the good.

Now it might be objected that the rights that this argument establishes against the libertarian are not the same as the rights endorsed by most liberals. This is correct. We could mark this difference by referring to the rights that this argument establishes against the libertarian as "negative welfare rights" and by referring to the rights endorsed by most liberals as "positive welfare rights." The significance of this difference is that a person's negative welfare rights can be violated only when other people through acts of commission interfere with the exercise of those rights, whereas a person's positive welfare rights can be violated by such acts of commission as well as by acts of omission. Nonetheless, this difference will have little practical import, for once libertarians come to recognize the legitimacy of the negative welfare rights I've defended, then in order not to be subject to the discretion of rightholders in choosing when and how to exercise these rights, libertarians will tend to favor the only morally legitimate way of preventing the exercise of such rights: they will institute adequate positive welfare rights that will then take precedence over the exercise of negative welfare rights. Accordingly, if libertarians adopt this morally legitimate way of preventing the exercise of such rights, they will end up endorsing the same sort of welfare institutions favored by most liberals.

In brief, I have argued that a libertarian conception of the good can be seen to support a right to welfare through an application of the "ought" implies "can" principle to conflicts between the rich and the poor. In the interpretation that I have used, the "ought" implies "can" principle supports such rights by favoring the liberty of the poor over the liberty of the rich. In another interpretation (developed elsewhere), the principle supports such rights by favoring a conditional right to property over an unconditional right to property.[20] In either interpretation, what is crucial to the derivation of these rights is the claim that it would be unreasonable to require the poor to deny their basic needs and accept anything less than these rights as the condition for their willing cooperation.

III A Conception of the Good Requiring Socialist Equality

Assuming then that we have a non-question-begging defense of a moral conception of the good that incorporates positive as well as negative rights, the next step in the defense of liberalism is to provide a non-question-begging argument specifying the economic institutions required by this conception. In particular, would the conception allow the inequality that is characteristic of capitalism or require the equality that is characteristic of socialism? What I propose to show is that it is the equality that is characteristic of socialism that is required. To keep my argument non-question-begging, I will continue to argue from premises that are acceptable to libertarians.

In view of the argument of the previous section, libertarians would have to accept a right to welfare but they would still want to deny that this would lead to anything like the equality of a socialist state. At most, libertarians would concede that the argument of the previous section shows that a non-question-begging moral conception of the good supports a welfare state but not a socialist state. They would claim that this is because, at least in an affluent society, a right to welfare could be fully secured while inequalities of wealth and privilege incompatible with the socialist ideal of equality remain.

I now hope to show why this is not the case. To begin with, it should be clear that, as libertarians see it, the fundamental rights recognized by them are universal rights, that is they are rights that are possessed by all people, not just those who live in certain places or at certain times. To claim that these rights are universal rights does not mean that they are universally recognized. Obviously, the fundamental rights that flow from a libertarian conception of the good have not been universally recognized. Rather, to claim that they are universal rights, despite their spotty recognition, implies only that they ought to be recognized because people at all times and places have or could have had good reasons to recognize these rights, not that they actually did or do so.

Nor need these universal rights be unconditional. This is particularly true in the case of the right to welfare, which, I argued in Section II, flows from a libertarian conception of the good. For this right is conditional upon people doing all that they legitimately can do to provide for themselves and conditional upon there being sufficient resources available so that everyone's welfare needs can be met. Where people do not do all that they can to provide for themselves or where there are not sufficient resources available, people simply do not have a right to welfare.

Yet even though libertarians have claimed that the rights they defend are universal rights in the manner I have just explained, it may be that they are simply mistaken in this regard. Even when universal rights are stripped of any claim to being universally recognized or unconditional, still it might be argued that there are no such rights, that is, that there are no rights that all people ought to recognize.

But how would one argue for such a view? One couldn't argue from the failure of people to recognize such rights because we have already said that such recognition is not necessary. Nor could one argue that not everyone ought to recognize such rights because some lack the capacity or opportunity to do so. This is because "ought" implies "can" here, so that the obligation to recognize certain rights only applies to those who actually have or have had at some point the capacity and opportunity to do so. Thus, the existence of universal rights is not ruled out by the existence of individuals who have never had the capacity and opportunity to recognize such rights. However, it would be ruled out by the existence of individuals who could recognize these rights but for whom it would be correct to say that they ought, all things considered, not to do so. But we have just seen that even a minimal libertarian conception of the good supports a universal right to welfare. And, as I have argued in Section I, when "ought" is understood self-interestedly rather than morally a non-question-begging conception of rationality favors a moral conception of the good over a self-interested conception. So for those capable of recognizing universal rights, it simply is not possible to argue that they, all things considered, ought not to do so.

Still, it might be granted that there are universal rights, even a right to welfare, that can be supported by a libertarian conception of the good, but still denied that such rights lead to a socialist rather than a welfare state. But to see why this is not the case, consider what would be required to recognize a universal right to welfare.

At present there is probably a sufficient worldwide supply of goods and resources to meet the normal costs of satisfying the basic nutritional needs of all existing persons. According to the former US Secretary of Agriculture, Bob Bergland:

> For the past 20 years, if the available world food supply had been evenly divided and distributed, each person would have received more than the minimum of calories.[21]

Other authorities have made similar assessments of the available world food supply.

Needless to say, the adoption of a policy of supporting a right to welfare for all existing persons would necessitate significant changes, especially in developed countries. For example, the large percentage of the US population whose food consumption clearly exceeds even an adequately adjusted poverty index might have to alter their eating habits substantially. In particular, they might have to reduce their consumption of beef and pork in order to make more grain available for direct human consumption. (Currently, 37% of worldwide production of grain and 70% of US production is fed to animals.[22]) Thus, the satisfaction of at least some of the nonbasic needs of the more advantaged in developed countries will have to be forgone if the basic nutritional needs of all those in developing and under-developed countries are to be met. Of course, meeting the long-term basic nutritional needs of these societies will require other kinds of aid, including appropriate technology and training and the removal of trade barriers favoring developed societies.[23] In addition, raising the standard of living in developing and under-developed countries will require a substantial increase in the consumption of energy and other resources. But such an increase will have to be matched by a substantial decrease in the consumption of these goods in developed countries; otherwise, global ecological disaster will result from increased global warming, ozone depletion, and acid rain, lowering virtually everyone's standard of living.[24] For example, some type of mutually beneficial arrangement needs to be negotiated with China, which, with 50% of the world's coal resources, plans to double its use of coal within the next two decades yet is currently burning 85% of its coal without any pollution controls whatsoever.[25] Furthermore, once the basic nutritional needs of future generations are also taken into account, the satisfaction of the nonbasic needs of the more advantaged in developed countries would have to be further restricted in order to preserve the fertility of cropland and other food-related natural resources for the use of future generations. Obviously, the only assured way to guarantee the energy and resources necessary for the satisfaction of the basic needs of future generations is to set aside resources that would otherwise be used to satisfy the nonbasic needs of existing generations.

When basic needs other than nutritional ones are taken into account as well, still further restrictions will be required. For example, it has been estimated that presently a North American uses about fifty times more goods and resources than a person living in India. This means that in terms of resource consumption the North American continent's population alone consumes as much as 12.5 billion people living in India would consume.[26] So, unless we assume that basic goods and resources, such as arable land, iron, coal, oil, and so forth are in unlimited supply, this unequal consumption would have to be radically altered in order for the basic needs of distant peoples and future generations to be met.[27] In effect, recognizing a universal right to welfare applicable both to distant peoples and to future generations would lead to an equal sharing of resources over place and time. In short, socialist equality is the consequence of recognizing a universal libertarian right to welfare.[28]

It might be objected that this argument falls victim to its own success. If a universal right to welfare requires an equal sharing of resources, wouldn't talented people simply lack the incentive to produce according to their ability when such a right is enforced? But what sort of incentive is needed? Surely there would be moral incentive for the talented to make the necessary sacrifices if even a libertarian conception of the good requires a right to welfare.[29] Yet, except for those who closely identify with such moral incentives, there would not be sufficient self-interested incentive to accept the equality of resources required by a universal right to welfare. Even so, in light of the argument of Section I that a moral conception of the good has priority over a self-interested conception, there is no question of what ought to be done.

IV A Partial Rather than a Complete Conception of the Good

Assuming then that we have a non-question-begging defense of a moral conception of the good that incorporates positive rights and the equality of resources that is characteristic of a socialist state, the next step in the defense of liberalism is to provide a non-question-begging argument for enforcing a partial rather than a complete conception of the good. Now it is important to note that this is not how the contrast between liberals and their communitarian critics is usually formulated. Instead, liberals are usually said to defend the view that society should be neutral with respect to conceptions of the good, while communitarians are usually said to defend the view that society should enforce a particular conception of the good. For example, according to Ronald Dworkin:

[L]iberalism takes, as its constitutive political morality, that theory of equality [which holds that] political decisions must be, so far as possible, independent of any particular conception of the good life, or of what gives value to life.[30]

By contrast, MacIntyre contends that:

Any political society . . . which possesses a shared stock of adequately determinate and rationally defensible moral rules, publicly recognized to be the rules to which characteristically and generally unproblematic appeals may be made, will therefore, implicitly or explicitly, be committed to an adequately determinate and rationally justifiable conception of the human good.[31]

But this way of putting the contrast – liberals favoring neutrality with respect to conceptions of the good, and communitarians favoring commitment to a particular conception of the good – has bred only confusion. What it suggests is that liberals are attempting to be value-neutral when they clearly are not. Liberals, like their communitarian critics, are committed to a substantive conception of the good. For example, the political conception of the good that Rawls endorses rules out any complete or comprehensive conception of the good that conflicts with it.[32] It also rules out, without much argument, a libertarian conception of the good.[33] So clearly, in this respect, Rawls makes no claim to being neutral with respect to conceptions of the good.

Rawls further contends that his political conception of the good marks the limits of enforceability. To enforce anything more, Rawls claims, would require "the oppressive use of state power."[34] So for Rawls, as for liberals generally, only a partial conception of the good can be justifiably enforced. This still would permit the adoption of any complete or comprehensive conception of the good which is compatible with the substantive, yet partial, conception of the good liberals want to enforce.[35] And it is only in this limited respect that liberals can be said to be neutral with respect to conceptions of the good, that is, they are neutral in the sense that they are not committed to enforcing any complete or comprehensive conception of the good, but only to enforcing a partial conception of the good. Accordingly, it seems far better to avoid the terminology of neutrality altogether and simply describe the liberal view as requiring the enforcement of a partial rather than a complete conception of the good.[36]

But is there any non-question-begging defense of this liberal commitment to enforcing a partial rather than a complete conception of the good? I think that there is once we recognize that the conception of the good we are looking for should be able to provide sufficient reasons, accessible to all those to whom it applies, for abiding by its requirements. So it must be a conception of the good that is capable of justifying the use of power to enforce its basic requirements. To do that, it must be possible to justifiably morally blame those who are coerced for failing to abide by its requirements. If that were not the case, people could justifiably resist such uses of power on the ground that they would lack moral legitimacy.[37] People cannot be morally required to do something if they cannot come to know, and so come to justifiably believe, that they are required to do so. So if a conception of the good is to be able to justify the use of power to enforce its basic requirements, there must be sufficient reasons accessible to all those to whom it applies for abiding by those requirements. What this means is that the conception of the good we are seeking must be partial rather than complete because no complete conception of the good would be accessible to all those to whom it applies. In addition, the partial conception we are seeking must be secular rather than religious in character because only a secular conception would be accessible to everyone; religious conceptions are primarily accessible only to the members of the particular religious groups who hold them, and as such they cannot provide the justification that is needed to support the use of power to enforce the basic requirements of morality.

Now it might be objected that at least some religious conceptions are accessible to virtually everyone who has been exposed to them. Of course, many people today have not even been exposed to the teachings of the four dominant religions, Christianity, Islam, Buddhism and Hinduism, and even for those who have, mere exposure, by itself, is not enough to guarantee the kind of accessibility that would justify the use of power against those who fail to abide by their teachings. For that to be the case, exposure must necessarily lead to the idea that it would be unreasonable to reject those teachings as such. In the case of Christian moral teachings, this would mean that it would be unreasonable to reject these teachings as part of a unique Christian salvation history, which has as key events an Incarnation, a Redemptive Death, and a Resurrection.

Of course, this is not to deny that some religious teachings can be given a justification that is independent of their religious origin (e.g., the story of the Good Samaritan[38]) – a justification that is accessible to virtually everyone exposed to these teachings on the grounds that virtually everyone so exposed would understand that it would be unreasonable to reject them so justified. But the objection we are considering does not address the possibility of justifying religious moral teachings in this way. Rather, it claims that religious moral teachings are justified because *as such* they are accessible to virtually everyone exposed to them, with the consequence that it would be unreasonable for virtually anyone so exposed to reject them.

But is this the case? Surely many Christian moral teachings, for example, are understandable to both Christians and non-Christians alike, but the sense of "accessible" we have been using implies more than this. It implies that persons can be morally blamed for failing to abide by accessible requirements because they can come to understand that these requirements apply to them and that it would be unreasonable for them to fail to abide by them. So understood, it would seem that, for example, Christian moral teachings *as such* are not accessible to everyone exposed to them. Too many non-Christians, who seem otherwise moral, do not recognize the authority of Christian moral teachings as such, even though they may grant that some of these teachings have an independent justification.

Accordingly, we need to restrict ourselves to a conception of the good that is partial and secular in character and thus one that can provide sufficient reasons accessible to all those to whom it applies for abiding by its requirements. Only such a conception would be capable of justifying the use of power to enforce its basic requirements.

Nor is there anything in the above argument that begs the question against the communitarian view because there is no reason why communitarians should be committed to enforcing a complete conception of the good. In fact, I have just been arguing that no one, communitarians included, is justified in enforcing a complete conception of the good.

Yet even if one accepts the view that society should enforce a partial rather than a complete conception of the good, this still leaves open the question of what sort of partial conception should be enforced, and here obviously liberals and communitarians might still disagree. Nevertheless, if the arguments of sections I, II and III of this essay are correct, and liberalism can be provided with a non-question-begging defense of a moral rather than a self-interested conception of the good, a conception that incorporates positive rights and the equality of resources that is characteristic of a socialist state, then the domain over which reasonable debate can still take place is considerably narrower in scope than most philosophers today have yet to realize.

Acknowledgment

I wish to thank Alasdair MacIntyre for his comments on an earlier version of this essay.

Notes

1   *Review of Politics* (Summer, 1990).
2   See Carlos Nino, "The Communitarian Challenge to Liberal Rights," *Law and Philosophy* (1989): 37–52; Allan Buchanan, "Assessing the Communitarian Critique of Liberalism," *Ethics* (1989): 852–83; Gerald Doppelt, "Is Rawls's Kantian Liberalism Coherent and Defensible?" *Ethics* (1989): 815–51; and my own work *How To Make People Just* (Totowa: Rowman & Littlefield, 1988), especially pp. 58–9; "Recent Work in Liberal Justice," *Philosophy and Law Newsletter* (1984): 3–11.
3   John Rawls, *Political Liberalism* (New York: Columbia University Press, 1993), Lecture V.
4   Of course, there are (Aristotelian) ways to understand self-interest so that it includes the moral. In such views, the contrast I am referring to reappears as a contrast between the priorities given different (possible) interests of the self.
5   Rawls, for example, simply assumes egoism away. See John Rawls, *A Theory of Justice* (1971), pp. 132–6. Other liberals like Kurt Baier, Alan Gewirth and Stephen Darwall have attempted a defense of this sort, but there are weaknesses in their defenses that

need to be overcome. For a survey of such attempts, see my "Justifying Morality: The Right and the Wrong Ways," in James P. Sterba, *Contemporary Ethics* (1989), pp. 138–54.

6   Alasdair MacIntyre, "The Privatization of the Good," *Review of Politics*, vol. 52 (1990), pp. 344–61; and *After Virtue* (1981), especially chs. 2, 4–5, 17, and the Post-script to the second edition of *After Virtue* (1984).

7   As I did in "Neo-Libertarianism," *American Philosophical Quarterly* (1978), but see its expanded version in my *Justice: Alternative Political Perspectives* (Wadsworth Pub-lishing Co., 1979). For a similar mistake, see Allan Buchanan, "Deriving Welfare Rights from Libertarian Rights," in *Income Support: Conceptual and Policy Issues*, edited by Peter Brown, Conrad Johnson and Paul Venier (Rowman and Littlefield, 1981).

8   See, for example, Ronald Dworkin, "Liberalism," in *Public and Private Morality*, edited by Stuart Hampshire (1978), pp. 113–43.

9   John Rawls, *Political Liberalism* (New York: Columbia University Press, 1993), Lecture IV; and Ronald Dworkin, "Liberalism". The classical defense of liberalism on this point is John Stuart Mill, *On Liberty* (1859).

10 I take this to be one of the central points of MacIntyre's *Whose Justice, Which Ratio-nality?* (1988), but what MacIntyre has not yet acknowledged in this book or else-where, and I hope to establish, is that there exists sufficient "common ground" among the presuppositions of various traditions to provide a defense of liberalism.

11 "Ought" presupposes "can" here. Unless the members of the society have the capac-ity to entertain and follow both self-interested and moral reasons for acting, it does not make any sense asking whether they ought or ought not to do so.

12 I understand the pure altruist to be the mirror image of the pure egoist. Whereas the pure egoist thinks that the interests of others count for them but not for herself except instrumentally, the pure altruist thinks that her own interests count for others but not for herself except instrumentally.

13 This is because, as I shall argue, morality itself already represents a compromise between egoism and altruism. So to ask that moral reasons be weighed against self-interested reasons is, in effect, to count self-interested reasons twice – once in the com-promise between egoism and altruism and then again when moral reasons are weighed against self-interested reasons. But to count self-interested reasons twice is clearly objectionable.

14 Notice that by "egoistic perspective" here I mean the view that grants the prima facie relevance of both egoistic and altruistic reasons to rational choice and then tries to argue for the superiority of egoistic reasons. Similarly by "altruistic perspective" I mean the view that grants the prima facie relevance of both egoistic and altruistic reasons to rational choice and then tries to argue for the superiority of altruistic reasons.

15 For further discussion, see my *Justice for Here and Now* (New York: Cambridge University Press, 1998), ch. 2.

16 See R. Duncan Luce and Howard Raiffa, *Games and Decisions* (New York: John Wiley & Sons, 1967), ch. 13.

17 Thomas Scanlon discusses this problem in *What We Owe to Others* (Cambridge, MA: Harvard University Press, 1998), ch. 3.

18 I first appealed to this interpretation of the "ought" implies "can" principle to bring libertarians around to the practical requirements of welfare liberalism, in an expanded

version of an article entitled "Neo-Libertarianism," which appeared in the fall of 1979. In 1982, T. M. Scanlon in "Contractualism and Utilitarianism" appealed to much the same standard to arbitrate the debate between contractarians and utilitarians. In my judgment, however, this standard embedded in the "ought" implies "can" principle can be more effectively used in the debate with libertarians than in the debate with utilitarians, because sacrifices libertarians standardly seek to impose on the less advantaged are more outrageous and, hence, more easily shown to be contrary to reason.

19   By the liberty of the rich to meet their luxury needs I continue to mean the liberty of the rich not to be interfered with when using their surplus possessions for luxury purposes. Similarly, by the liberty of the poor to meet their basic needs I continue to mean the liberty of the poor not to be interfered with when taking what they require to meet their basic needs from the surplus possessions of the rich.

20   See *Justice for Here and Now*, ch. 3.

21   Bob Bergland, "Attacking the Problem of World Hunger," *The National Forum*, vol. 69, no. 2 (1979), p. 4.

22   Lester Brown, Christopher Flavin, and Hal Kane, *Vital Signs 1996* (New York: W. W. Norton, 1996), pp. 34–5; Jeremy Rifkin, *Beyond Beef* (New York: Penguin, 1992), p. 1.

23   Henry Shue, *Basic Rights* (Princeton, NJ: Princeton University Press, 1980), ch. 7.

24   For a discussion of these causal connections, see Cheryl Silver. *One Earth, One Future* (Washington, DC: National Academy Press, 1990); Bill McKibben, *The End of Nature* (New York: Anchor Books, 1989); Jeremy Leggett (ed.), *Global Warming* (New York: Oxford University Press, 1990); and Lester Brown (ed.), *The World Watch Reader* (New York: Nelson, 1991).

25   Charles Park, Jr (ed.), *Earth Resources* (Washington, DC: Voice of America, 1980), ch. 13; Lester Brown. *State of the World 1995* (New York: Norton, 1992), ch. 7; Lester Brown (ed.), *The World Watch Reader*, p. 268. China currently uses more coal than the US. See Lester Brown, *State of the World* (New York, 1997), p. 9.

26   G. Tyler Miller, Jr, *Living with the Environment* (Belmont: Wadsworth Publishing Co., 1990), p. 20. See also Janet Besecker and Phil Elder, "Lifeboat Ethics: A Reply to Hardin," in *Readings in Ecology, Energy and Human Society*, edited by William Burch (New York: Harper and Row, 1977), p. 229. For higher and lower estimates of the impact of North Americans, see Holmes Rolston III, "Feeding People versus Saving Nature?" in *World Hunger and Morality*, 2nd edn (Englewood Cliffs: Prentice-Hall, 1996), pp. 259–60; Paul Ehrlich, Anne Ehrlich, and Gretchen Daily, *The Stork and the Plow* (New York: Grosset/Putnam, 1995), p. 26.

27   Successes in meeting the most basic needs of the poor in particular regions of developing countries (e.g., the Indian state of Kerala) should not blind us to the growing numbers of people living in conditions of absolute poverty (1.2 billion by a recent estimate) and how difficult it will be to meet the basic needs of all these people in a sustainable way that will allow future generations to have their basic needs met as well, especially when we reflect on the fact that the way we in the developed world are living is not sustainable at all!

28   Of course, a society characterized by socialist equality may not have all the legal trappings of a socialist state. For example, it may not have full communal ownership of the basic means of production. However, in order to guarantee socialist equality, the private ownership of the basic means of production would be so severely restricted by

democratic controls that there would be little practical difference between a society with socialist equality and a society with full communal ownership of the basic means of production.

29   One might think that the objection from incentive is that it would prove impossible to motivate people to work for others. But people work for others once they support any kind of a welfare system, and at least in developed societies, the existence of welfare systems are nowhere threatened. Nor, it seems to me, do the recent events in Eastern Europe and the Soviet Union signal a rejection of welfare or even socialist equality. Five months of traveling and lecturing in the Soviet Union and Eastern Europe in 1989 and visits to the Soviet Union in 1990 and 1991 have convinced me that what has been rejected in Eastern Europe and is being rejected in the Soviet Union is widespread corruption and authoritarian control over *everything* by local bureaucrats and ultimately by Moscow.

30   Dworkin, "Liberalism," p. 127.

31   MacIntyre, "The Privatization of the Good."

32   John Rawls, "The Priority of Right and Ideas of the Good," *Philosophy and Public Affairs* 17 (1988), pp. 251–76.

33   There is some argument for the rejection of libertarianism in John Rawls, "The Basic Structure as Subject," in *Values and Morals*, edited by A. Goldman and J. Kim (1978), pp. 47–71, but what the argument ignores is that on the libertarian view *fairness* cannot be interpreted as choice from behind an imaginary view of ignorance.

34   John Rawls, "The Idea of an Overlapping Consensus," p 4, *Oxford Journal of Legal Studies*, vol. 7 (1987), pp. 1–25.

35   The difference between a complete or comprehensive conception of the good and a partial conception of the good is that the former encompasses all of morality while the latter only certain basic requirements of morality.

36   Nor do I think that the most defensible form of liberalism is appropriately characterized as a view in which "the right is prior to the good" because when this claim is correctly unpacked, it only asserts that a certain partial conception of the good has priority over any complete conception of the good that conflicts with it. However, what the claim incorrectly suggests is that the right has primacy and independence over both partial and complete conceptions of the good. On this point, see also Will Kymlicka, *Liberalism, Community, and Culture* (1989), ch. 3.

37   The will of the majority if it is to be morally legitimate must be backed up with more than power. The minority must have a moral duty to accept the imposition of the majority, but that could only be the case if the minority would be morally blameworthy for failing to accept that imposition.

38   *Gospel According to St. Luke*, 10:25–37.

Bibliography

Barry, Brian (1995). *Justice as Impartiality*. Oxford: Oxford University Press.

Bell, Daniel (1993). *Communitarianism and Its Critics*. Oxford: Oxford University Press.

Daly, Markate (1994). *Communitarianism*. Belmont: Wadsworth.

Horton, John and Susan Mendus (eds.) (1994). *After MacIntyre*. Notre Dame, IN: University of Notre Dame Press.

Kekes, John (1997). *Against Liberalism*. Ithaca: Cornell University Press.

Kymlicka, W. (1989). *Liberalism, Community and Culture*. Oxford: Oxford University Press.

MacIntyre, Alasdair (1981). *After Virtue*. Notre Dame: University of Notre Dame Press.

Mulhall, Stephen and Adam Swift (1992). *Liberals and Communitarians*. Oxford: Blackwell.

Rawls, John (1971). *A Theory of Justice*. Cambridge, MA: Harvard University Press.

——(1993). *Political Liberalism*. New York: Columbia University Press.

Raz, J. (1986). *The Morality of Freedom*. Oxford: Oxford University Press.

Sandel, Michael (1996). *Democracy's Discontent*. Cambridge, MA: Harvard University Press.

Sterba, James P. (1998). *Justice for Here and Now*. New York: Cambridge University Press.

Chapter 9

Liberal Theories and their Critics

William Nelson

I speak of "liberal theories," instead of "liberalism," partly because it is a matter of dispute what liberalism "really" is. Some liberals characterize it in terms of a specific methodology, others in terms of its historical role. Some believe in natural rights, some are contractualists, and some consequentialists. As a rough generalization, liberals are concerned to protect individual freedom against the power of the state and the power of other individuals or institutions. They advocate toleration of different beliefs and values. They value legal and political equality, seek to ensure opportunities and to protect individuals' economic welfare and independence. Still, liberals differ as to just what this list should contain, how key components should be understood, and which items should be regarded as fundamental, which derivative. There are many liberal theories, and liberals are themselves often the liveliest critics of other liberals. Many of the critics I discuss will be liberals criticizing the theories of other liberals.

Liberal theories are normative theories. Any such fully realized theory ought to include a reasonably precise statement of its substantive principles, a rationale for these principles, and an account of the institutions by means of which the principles can be realized. Beyond that, it ought to include a demonstration of the capacity of such institutions to function as intended and to sustain themselves. The characteristics of liberal theories listed above comprise mainly substantive aims. Theories that include (roughly) the same substantive principles will often differ in their rationales for these principles. And different rationales will often lead to different specific interpretations of the principles. Different rationales will also expose theories to different objections – and an objection directed at one rationale may fail to apply at all to a theory based on another.

Consider an example: John Kekes, in *Against Liberalism* (1997), criticizes liberalism for its inability to deal adequately with the problem posed by "the prevalence of evil (23f)." This is a problem because "the true core of liberalism," Kekes says, is a commitment to autonomy (15). "[I]t is the fostering of the autonomous functioning of all citizens that is the ultimate purpose and justification of liberalism (21)." However, Kekes goes on, more often than we might like, men and women freely choose to do evil. Thus, a society that leaves people free and even encourages this freedom is bound to encourage evil in the process. Liberalism can deal with this problem only by retreating from its most fundamental commitment.

There are many possible replies to this objection, and I will mention it later in a different context. One reply is to reject Kekes's claim that he has correctly identified *the* fundamental commitment of liberal theory. But what are the alternatives? To illustrate the possibilities, I will sketch a (somewhat selective) history of liberal thought since the middle of the twentieth century. I begin, in Section I, with John Rawls's early work, some of the responses to it, and alternatives proposed by various theorists through the 1980s. I then turn, in Section II, to "political liberalism" as it has developed since the late 1980s. I will offer an interpretation of some of its more controversial ideas, and, in light of this interpretation, I will defend it against some recent criticisms. Throughout, I mean to focus mainly on liberals' justifications for their principles and, more generally, on their ideas about what constitutes an adequate justification.

I   Theories of Justice

Rawls's theory of justice

John Rawls's publication of *A Theory of Justice*, in 1971, is surely a key moment in twentieth-century political thought generally, and in liberal thought in particular. By the time of the book's publication, though, Rawls's ideas were already well known and influential. The book culminated a project that began with Rawls's paper "Justice as Fairness" (1958). Beginning with this paper, Rawls set out to establish what he calls principles of justice for the evaluation of the "basic structure of society" – its major social, political, legal and economic institutions. The idea is that institutions are to be assessed holistically, for Rawls assumes that principles are concerned with the interests and prospects of individuals and that institutions work together to determine these prospects. Rawls's particular principles require that institutions establish the greatest possible system of equal basic liberties, a system of fair equality of opportunity, and an economic system in which typical members of the worst off economic class are economically as well-off as possible. Economic inequalities are permissible, but only subject to the condition that the economic advantages of those better off do not come at the expense of those worst off. This is what Rawls calls the "difference principle."

I state these principles informally. Their detailed exposition is a difficult task, made more difficult by the fact that Rawls does not always state them consistently even within the scope of his book. Still, the theory described falls clearly within the rough characterization of liberalism offered earlier: it gives a high priority to individual liberty and opportunity, and it also insists on securing a decent minimum income. It is perhaps worth noting, though, that Rawls does not speak of liberty, per se, and does not view every exercise of coercive state power as even a prima facie violation of the "equal liberties" principle. Instead, what he seems to have in mind is a system of specific rights, immunities, and powers of the kind found in the Bill of Rights of the US Constitution. He means them to include freedom of expression, freedom of religion, rights to acquire personal property and to its secure possession, protections against arbitrary arrest, and rights to take part in democratic self-governance. Indeed, we can generalize here. The idea of freedom, as it functions in liberal thought, is highly ambiguous. While writers, especially those associated with the "libertarian" tradition, sometimes object to *any* coercion or restraint, it is perhaps more common to emphasize particular rights (e.g., property rights or rights to free speech). If freedom in a more general sense is thought important, that is because it is thought to underlie or explain the importance of the specific rights.[1]

Rawls, however, does not take freedom or autonomy as his starting point. He thinks he can offer a unified account of the seemingly disparate elements in his theory, and he begins not with liberty but with an abstract conception of the social contract. He argues that persons in what he calls "the original position" would choose the principles I have sketched – equal liberties, fair equality of opportunity and the difference principle. These persons are presumed to know certain general facts of social theory, but they are otherwise behind a veil of ignorance. They do not know salient facts about themselves (their race, religion, sex, social status, or position in the natural lottery of talents). Nor do they know their distinctive aims and values. They choose principles only on the basis of an interest in primary goods – liberties, opportunities, income and wealth. They assume they want more of these rather than less, within the range that their society can produce for everyone, but they also assume that, at some level, their interest in more tends to diminish (Rawls, 1971, secs. 24, 26).

It should not be surprising, given these assumptions, that Rawls's principles would be chosen. The assumptions about the original position are designed to produce this choice. The idea, I believe, is to bring out clearly a set of assumptions that are sufficient to give us his results. This gives us a *proof* of the principles. Whether it is also a *justification* is another matter. Justification, Rawls says, proceeds between persons. It succeeds when it is possible to show that the conclusion can be supported not just by some assumptions, but by assumptions that the other person accepts (ibid., sec. 87).

As I read Rawls, he has, from early on, been interested in justification as well as proof. He has specifically aimed to find principles and arguments for them that can be acceptable *to* those who must live under them and to justify this aspiration itself as well. Thus, he has aimed for institutions that would generate their own support and support for the principles on which they are based; he has been concerned to solve the problem of stability, understood as involving an enduring commitment to principles. He has aimed at establishing a stable, well-ordered society: a society in which persons accept the same principles, institutions meet the requirements set by those principles, and in which it is common knowledge that these conditions are met. In such a society, clearly, the institutions could be justified to each in terms of principles each accepts. In short, Rawls assumes something like an ideal of *consent of the governed*, an ideal that figures in some other liberal theories, including some of the work of Jeremy Waldron.[2] If Rawls is right, principles derived as his are can achieve consent.

Responses to Rawls's theory

Rawls's main aim, of course, was to show that his principles are the right ones for evaluating institutions. A more specific aim was to provide an alternative to utilitarianism and thereby undermine its position as the only normative perspective for evaluating institutions. As we have later come to appreciate (Scheffler, 1994), utilitarianism embodies two distinct, controversial doctrines. The first, which Rawls targets directly, is the idea that outcomes are to be evaluated in terms of aggregate well-being, independent of distribution. The second is the idea that no type of action is morally ruled out independent of its consequences – that there are no "deontological constraints."

In *Anarchy, State and Utopia* (1974), Robert Nozick argued that the reasons for rejecting the aggregative standard for evaluating consequences (its alleged refusal to recognize "the separateness of persons") should lead us also to accept individual rights (constraints) against the state. But, once we do this, he claimed, we will then see that the liberal state in general, and Rawls's version in particular, must be rejected. Nozick adopted what he saw as a Lockean conception of individual rights – especially rights to property, but other individual rights as well; and he claimed that any state action encroaching on these rights is unjust. He holds this whether the aim is to promote aggregate utility *or* to achieve economic justice as conceived by Rawls, and by many other liberal theorists.

To the objection that this means condoning injustice, Nozick replies that Rawlsian liberals have a mistaken conception of justice. A just state of affairs, a just society, he holds, is not to be characterized by a *patterned* principle, like equality or the difference principle. Instead, a state of affairs is just if and only if it results from the free exercise of individual rights consistent with respect for the rights of others. Nozick's theory is a historical, entitlement theory.

Now, insofar as Nozick's theory embodies a strong suspicion of state action and a concern for individual rights and liberty, it coincides with a major part of liberalism as understood here. However, though he believes that protecting individual economic rights tends to benefit everyone, Nozick does not make this claim a precondition of accepting his theory. Thus, he rejects another foundational commitment of much twentieth-century liberalism, namely, the commitment to promoting individual welfare and opportunity. In this, he joined – from within philosophy – a tradition of criticism heretofore found mainly within economics. Economists like Hayek (1960), and later James Buchanan (1975), were profoundly suspicious of state intervention to redistribute income or wealth. They thought intervention to be inefficient and also to require a state apparatus that endangered liberty.

Though Nozick's suspicion of the state and his doubts about aggregative reasoning found a sympathetic hearing among many in the broadly liberal tradition, his specific list of rights did not. One of the earliest replies to Nozick's book was Thomas Nagel's "Libertarianism without Foundations" (1975). Nagel complained specifically about Nozick's failure to give an adequate argument for his system of personal and property rights. And, indeed, though Nozick offers an ingenious and often fascinating account of what states and citizens would be committed to *if* they accepted a theory of rights like the one he adopts, he agrees that his arguments in support of those rights are less than conclusive.

In retrospect, I think Nozick's book can actually make one more sympathetic to Rawls's project. Two points are worth mentioning. First, insofar as Rawls's theory addresses the question of the justice of particular holdings of particular persons, his theory is actually similar to Nozick's. Both hold that there ought to be rules of property and contract, that these ought to be respected, and that any particular person's entitlements are determined by the free operation of that system.[3] The question is just which rules, which system of rights, we ought to adhere to. But here, secondly, Rawls offers a general answer, while Nozick does not. For Rawls, a system of rights is correct only if it is part of the basic structure of a society where that structure, in turn, satisfies general principles of justice which would be chosen in the original position.

Rawls's theory purports to offer a way to achieve critical distance from particular institutions, systems of rights, and beliefs about liberty, opportunity, and the distribution of wealth. It specifies an abstract procedure for adjudicating among these different beliefs or systems and determining which can be justified. And, if Rawls is right, it is possible to produce a coherent liberal theory specifying the appropriate relations between liberty, equality and welfare. In this, Rawls's theory – but not only his – is consonant with one of the historically central ideas of modern political theory: the idea, central to enlightenment thought, that social, political and legal arrangements are to be seen not as fixed but as properly subject to alteration in light of human purposes (cf. Waldron, 1993, pp. 43–5).

While much liberal thought – and, as we will see below, not just that of Rawls – seeks to justify its policies by adopting an abstract, critical perspective on particular institutions, both feminist and communitarian critics have criticized liberalism for exactly this abstraction. Feminists, in particular, argue that the abstract conception of citizens found in Rawlsian or utilitarian thought blinds us to the particular needs and interests of particular groups, including women and racial or cultural minorities.[4]

Alternative liberal theories

Rawls's contractualist theory is not the only one that offers this kind of critical perspective on first-order liberal beliefs. Since the eighteenth century, utilitarianism has sought to do the same. For Bentham, and later for Mill and Sidgwick, the idea of the greatest happiness offered a rational standard for the critical assessment of choices of all kinds, from personal decisions to decisions about constitutional design. Bentham thought many of the laws and institutions of his own day irrational by this standard. A number of utilitarian theorists in the second half of the twentieth century, partly in response to the Rawlsian challenge, have developed sophisticated arguments to show that the utilitarian standard actually requires many of the typical institutions of the contemporary liberal state (Bailey, 1997; Hardin, 1986; Hardin, 1988; Sartorius, 1975). The arguments turn on considerations of several kinds.

One example: Utilitarianism, it might seem, should insist that each person, in each situation ought to try to maximize utility. But it does not follow that, if one were designing a constitution, one ought to create positions of authority whose occupants are authorized to pursue the project of utility maximization without restriction. It does not follow, in particular, that government officials should have the authority to censor acts of expression simply on the ground that utility requires it. Nor does it follow that the police should always have the authority to conduct searches or to engage in forms of surveillance, even if they think the consequences will be good.

Utilitarians can defend limits on authority, even on the authority to act on utilitarian considerations, by arguing that the authority itself, once granted, may so often be misused as to have bad consequences. One reason is that government offices, once created, may not be occupied by conscientious utilitarians. A more interesting reason is that even good utilitarians, like everyone else, seldom have anything like the kind of full information they would need to calculate consequences accurately. A variety of writers, including Russell Hardin, and Friedrich Hayek (1948), have emphasized this point. Not only does it provide a good defense of the limits on official authority found in works like Mill's *On Liberty* (restrictions on censorship and paternalism, for example), it also provides an argument for individual rights of property and contract: we may have limited knowledge of what is good for others, or for society at large, but we are more likely to know what we ourselves need (and, as Hayek emphasizes, how to conduct our own businesses).

Of course, liberalism usually involves more than just a commitment to limited government, specific freedoms like freedom of speech, and a belief in individual rights. Many liberals favor some restrictions on freedom of contract, such as the restrictions implicit in minimum-wage laws or closed-shop labor contracts. Many also favor limits to property rights if these are needed to secure public goods like clean air and water. But utilitarian arguments, supplemented by an understanding of the strategic features of interactions, can support these conclusions too.

Though Rawls's early work on justice aimed especially to provide an alternative to utilitarianism, later work by utilitarians showed that their theory can in fact support many of the same conclusions Rawls defends. Moreover, just as Rawls's contractualism promises to offer a critical perspective on the natural rights postulated by libertarians like Nozick, so also does utilitarianism. However, while both offer arguments in support of individual rights to property and contract, neither supports *unqualified* rights of these kinds. Both theoretical approaches, indeed, can make use of some of the same concerns about the strategic nature of interaction to support qualifications on libertarian rights.

Contractualism and utilitarianism are not the only theories offering a critical perspective on *particular* accounts of individual rights and authority. Another is Joseph Raz's. Raz says he aims to "rehabilitate" the "traditionalist affirmation of the value of freedom," and to defend a "doctrine of political authority" based on a "perfectionist political defense and promotion of liberty and autonomy." Autonomy, indeed, is his central concept, and he thinks the value of personal autonomy is what underlies the defense of political freedom (Raz, 1986, pp. 17, 19, 400f).

The argument is long and complex, with many different strands. It is broadly consequentialist, but the aim is to promote autonomy, not utility. Raz is especially concerned to show that, starting with the idea of autonomy, we end up in a different place from that of many other theorists in the broadly liberal tradition. He rejects, for one thing, the attempt to reduce the idea of liberty or autonomy to the idea of any particular system of rights. He specifically denies that autonomy is best realized in a system protecting only individual rights of the kind Nozick advocates. Instead, Raz argues that the value of autonomy can be achieved only in contexts in which society protects collective benefits, especially "social forms" constituting valuable ways of life. For autonomous choosers must choose for reasons, and that means choosing among available, valuable, alternatives. Since protecting social forms may require state action, the liberal state should not be equated with the minimal state. And since protecting autonomy itself, as well as protecting particular social forms and practices, requires legislating on the basis of values, Raz's liberal state is also not required to refrain from promoting ideals.

It is perhaps worth recalling here Kekes's critique of liberalism, mentioned at the outset, for Kekes objected to the alleged liberal preoccupation with autonomy. Neither Rawls, as I read him, nor utilitarians, actually base their theories on an ideal of autonomy, but Raz does. And Kekes objected that, when we guarantee people autonomy, we also make it likely that they will misuse their autonomy by choosing evil over good. Does this objection apply to Raz?

While it is true that Raz champions autonomy, this has to be understood in the context of his claim that his is a " 'moralistic' doctrine of political freedom" (1986,

p. 367). The ideal of personal autonomy, he says, is the ideal of persons "con-trolling . . . their own destiny . . . throughout their lives" (369). However, while Raz thinks good lives must be autonomous in this way, he does not think that any autonomous life is good. Autonomy is, as it were, a necessary, not a sufficient con-dition. Good lives are lives autonomously chosen for good reasons. "[T]he non-availability of morally repugnant options" is not a bad thing, on this view. "Autonomy is valuable only if exercised in pursuit of the good" (381). Conse-quently, for Raz, the promotion of valuable, autonomous lives is perfectly com-patible with governmental action to make valuable options available and to discourage or eliminate options that are bad. Respect for (worthwhile) autonomy does not mean we should turn people loose to choose evil or repugnant ways of life. As a result, Raz's theory is not subject to Kekes's criticism.

In this brief survey of liberal thought through the 1980s, I have focused especially on different ideas about how liberal institutions and principles can be justified, and on what kind of justification is appropriate. The theorists I emphasize all argue for basic political freedoms, toleration, equal opportunity, and the economic and social conditions that make possible the pursuit of good and meaningful lives. All of them reject extant institutions and beliefs that stand in the way of our realizing these conditions. Liberal institutions, these theorists argue, can be given a firm and convincing justification, while opposing ideas and institutions cannot. But, the fact is, even liberals disagree among themselves as to which justifications are adequate; and non-liberals do not accept the arguments offered by any liberals. Acknowledging these disagreements, some liberals have come to think about the issue of justifying liberalism in a new way. They seek a way of thinking about liberal ideas that could make liberalism more widely – even uniquely – justifiable.

II Political Liberalism and its Critics

Political liberalism

In this section, I attempt an explication and (partial) defense of the ideas its defenders refer to as "political liberalism." Despite the considerable ingenuity devoted to developing and refining the various theories described above, each remains controversial. Indeed, in both academic and nonacademic circles, oppos-ing ideas have reasserted themselves with great vigor. While the strongest acade-mic critics of liberalism in the 1960s were from the Marxist left, the next wave of academic criticism came from the libertarian right, and many subsequent critics were partisans of traditional and religious communities. It became easy to see the justificatory ideas in liberal thought as just various arbitrary starting points.

Anyone who might have hoped that careful attention to foundational beliefs and to the construction of well-grounded theories would lead to a convergence of ideas, a shared conception of the truth, would have been disappointed. Some liberal theorists in the last two decades, therefore, have come to focus even more self-consciously on the prospects and limits of justification. Calling their view "political liberalism," John Rawls, in his later work (1993), and Charles Larmore (1987, 1996) seek to strengthen the case for liberalism and to broaden its appeal partly by limiting the scope of liberal principles (they apply only to certain political questions) and partly by trying to show that liberalism, as they construe it, is the uniquely best answer to those questions, given a practical problem they think unavoidable in all modern, democratic societies. The problem arises from what they see as the *inevitable* diversity of moral, philosophical and religious ideas, even among "reasonable" persons. That political liberalism can solve this problem, they claim, justifies it (for anyone who sees it as a problem). And that other political views do not solve it, or even exacerbate it, shows that (at least in this respect) they cannot be similarly justified. Taking this approach, however, leads Rawls and Larmore to positions that put them at odds not only with various non-liberal theorists but also with utilitarian liberals and "perfectionist" liberals like Raz.

Rawls and Larmore are not alone in seeing disagreement and diversity as a problem.[5] But why it should be a *special* problem requires comment. That people disagree about right and wrong, good and bad, after all, is hardly news. It is especially not news to moral philosophers; and they have responded in various ways. One is some form of skepticism, the denial that we can know the truth in these matters or, even, that there is any truth to be had. Others, I suspect the majority among contemporary philosophers, take the fact of disagreement simply to show that some people must be wrong and that the task of philosophy is to discover what the right view is.

Rawls seems to say, in the introduction to his *Political Liberalism* (1993), that he originally saw the project of *A Theory of Justice* as an attempt to do just this: It aimed to show that the hypothetical contract was the correct starting point for moral philosophy, and so, that the principles derived there were the morally correct principles for assessing social and political arrangements. He construed political philosophy, at that time, as the application of a correct, comprehensive moral view to the particular case of political choice (1993, p. xv).

Rawls now conceives his project differently. But the reason he no longer seeks to find the uniquely correct moral theory to supplant the alternatives is that he *retains* one of the original, motivating ideas behind his theory, namely, the idea that institutions, to be legitimate, must be justifiable *to* each (reasonable) person subject to them. Yet, he also thinks it inevitable that there will never, in a democratic society, be agreement on foundational, moral and philosophical ideas. There will never be agreement on what he calls "comprehensive doctrines." That leaves us with "the problem of political liberalism": "How is it possible that there may exist over time a stable and just society of free and equal citizens, profoundly divided by reasonable though incompatible religious, philosophical and moral doctrines?" (1993, p. xviii, cf. xix, 4; see also Larmore, 1996, pp. 121–2). This is essentially the problem of creating a well-ordered society – a society whose stability rests on a principled consensus, where everyone accepts the same standards as "a reasonable public basis of justification on fundamental political questions" (1993, p. xix). What is new in the way Rawls now sees this problem is his acceptance that whatever agreement we may reach will be limited in crucial ways. It will be an agreement on certain principles for certain purposes against a background of *disagreement* on many other matters, including, perhaps, the ultimate reasons why we should seek such an agreement. How is a well-ordered society possible at all, given the fact of pluralism?

Rawls's answer – or conjecture – is that philosophical and religious doctrines, often radically different in their foundational beliefs and in many of their consequent judgments, can still coincide in endorsing the ideal of the reasonable. Partisans of otherwise different views can all be reasonable in the sense that (1) they are prepared to seek and to offer, in good faith, mutually acceptable terms of cooperation with others (and to comply with these when in force), and (2) they are prepared to accept the burdens of judgment – to accept that deeper agreement on fundamental matters simply cannot be achieved, on a widespread basis, under conditions of freedom and democracy (1993, pp. 48–58). Reasonable persons, as defined, share the aim of finding mutually acceptable principles for the assessment of shared institutions. And, to the extent that persons are reasonable in this sense, there is a basis for seeking agreement among them – despite other differences.

To the extent that persons are reasonable in the sense defined – and to the extent that the aim of political theory is construed not as justification to *everyone*, but as justification to the reasonable – it looks as if the problem of justification might be tractable. And it is, of course, not a particularly surprising idea that principles guaranteeing religious liberty, free expression, and some degree of personal privacy, would form part of a consensus among reasonable persons who otherwise disagree sharply with one another. In short, it is far from implausible that central liberal ideas can, in fact, solve the practical problem of political liberalism under conditions of reasonable pluralism.

Defenders of political liberalism sometimes go on to say it is a consequence of their approach that the state must in general be *neutral* among the reasonable comprehensive doctrines of the sort that can be expected to persist in modern democracies.[6] Or, as Thomas Nagel puts it in his rather different idiom, we must find principles representing a "highest order of impartiality": "highest order" because, as Nagel notes, the conflicting moral views prevalent in society already represent to their adherents an achievement of impartiality. They are *moral* views. Any system that can expect consent must achieve impartiality among these otherwise already impartial perspectives. And so also, to put the point negatively, the fact that particular moral views represent an achievement of impartiality is not enough to justify imposing them (Nagel, 1987).

Now, the substantive principles Rawls seeks to defend – and he is the one who offers substantive principles – have not significantly changed since *A Theory of Justice*, though he is less inclined to treat them as uniquely correct. But I do not intend to focus here on these substantive principles. Instead, I want to look at the ideas in political liberalism about the constraints on justification – the ideas about morality, truth, neutrality and impartiality to which Rawls and other defenders of political liberalism take themselves to be committed. These have themselves become matters of controversy in the recent literature. How do they come into play?

Given the fact of reasonable pluralism, Rawls and Larmore both claim, a system of principles will be able to serve as "a public basis of justification on fundamental political questions" only if it constitutes, in Rawls's phrase, an "overlapping consensus" among the diverse, reasonable doctrines in society. This does not assume that these principles are already found, in a developed form, in each doctrine. It assumes merely that they can be developed out of minimal shared assumptions in such a way that all "can reasonably be expected," at least in the long run, to endorse them (Rawls, 1993, p. 137). But they cannot be based on certain controversial, fundamental ideas. For example, they cannot be based on the *moral* idea of pluralism – the idea that the different conceptions of the value and meaning of life prevalent in society are all viable and good ways of life (Larmore, 1999, p. 122). This is just what many reject. Similarly, Larmore and Rawls join in denying that we should begin, as does Raz, by affirming the value of autonomy. The value of autonomy is a matter of controversy.

To summarize, Rawls and Larmore both claim that political principles must be acceptable to the diverse persons and groups in society; and both claim that this requires *neutrality* among different conceptions of the good life, among different comprehensive moral, religious and philosophical ideas. Moreover, Rawls even claims that liberalism must refrain from asserting the *truth* of its ideas and principles.

Critics object strongly to both ideas. Not only some conservatives, but also perfectionist liberals like Raz and Sher claim it is the state's job to promote what is genuinely good. Political philosophy should discover truths about what is good and argue for public policies based on those truths. They consequently criticize the commitment to both neutrality and "epistemic abstinence."

There is some irony in this turn of events. Thomas Nagel (1973) and Adina Schwartz (1973), among the very early critics of *A Theory of Justice*, criticized Rawls's principles for *failing* to be neutral among competing conceptions of the good: While it is true that political liberties, economic opportunities and adequate income and wealth are useful in the pursuit of many goals, they are especially useful in the pursuit of the more individualistic goals widely favored in modern, market-oriented societies. Thus the emphasis on these goods may actually encourage people in the development of individualistic goals. It may make it less likely that those with more communitarian values will be able to realize those values and live the kind of life they find best.[7]

Rawls replied, in "Fairness to Goodness" (1975), that no political theory can be genuinely neutral *in its effects*. Any set of institutional arrangements will, in fact, make some ways of living more eligible than others. Moreover, in cases where the ways of life made difficult or impossible are unjust (because they rest on racist ideologies, for example) we should not regret their passing. But even some otherwise acceptable ways of life are bound, in any system, to be more difficult to pursue than they might be otherwise; and, in that case, all we need do is assure ourselves that whatever the obstacles, they are compatible with justice and cannot be removed without causing greater injustice.

What Rawls asserted at that time was that principles and institutions were not required to be neutral *in their effects*. And, along with Larmore, Dworkin and Waldron, he still accepts that view. But while both Rawls and Larmore now express some dissatisfaction with the terminology, they also insist, as I have said, on some version of neutrality of intention or purpose.

There are then two controversial ideas associated with political liberalism: that liberalism must refrain from asserting the truth of its ideas and principles, and that the state must remain neutral among various other moral and philosophical views. I will say more about each in turn.

The moral truth

It is Rawls, primarily, who seems to advocate that liberalism abstain from claiming the truth of its principles. What does this claim amount to, and does he have a good reason to adhere to it? To answer, we need to say a little about the theory. Like any political theory, liberal theory will include directives concerning matters of constitutional design, especially specifications of the scope and limits of legal and political authority, but also matters of basic economic and social policy. It will also embody a justification for these directives. In Rawls's theory, this justification rests on various ideas – ideas about citizens, and their capacities, together with the idea of choice behind a veil of ignorance – where these ideas and resulting principles are supposed to form a stable "overlapping consensus" among persons with diverse but reasonable comprehensive doctrines. The principles, Rawls assumes, will not be found already extant in the various prevailing doctrines. Rather, they will have to be *constructed* so as to be suitable for their purpose. The procedure of construction is choice in the original position. This procedure, and the various conditions which define it, is proposed as an interpretation of the values of consent and of social cooperation for mutual advantage. These values, in turn, include a partial specification of the shared ideas of the reasonable and the rational (Rawls, 1993, pp. 90–6). The argument for the whole system is, ultimately, that it *works*. More exactly, the argument is that reasonable adherents of different comprehensive doctrines could come, in time, to share these ideas as the ideas that *should* govern their common political affairs. They will be seen as reasons. When citizens respect limits on authority and modify their own demands on the basis of these principles, they treat others in a way that can be justified to those others. And, when others make excessive demands, it will be possible to explain to them, in terms they can accept, why they are excessive.

That his political liberalism works, that it can be accepted in this way, Rawls thinks, does not mean that it is true (1993, pp. xx, 125f, 216f). More, the assertion of its truth can be no part of the argument for its acceptance. Why? It is Joseph Raz, especially, who has recently pressed this question. In "Facing Diversity: The Case of Epistemic Abstinence" (1990), he objects to several of Rawls's strategies for trying to avoid reliance on controversial theories or ideas. He observes, correctly, that Rawls now views his task as that of solving a kind of practical problem. But, he objects, even if this is his task, that is no reason to deny that his theory is *true* (15–16). If it solves the problem, then it is *true* that it solves the problem. Suppose we had an engineering problem, and we concluded that its solution required the use of a certain type of valve. In that case, it is *true* (given the context) that we should use that type of valve. How can we assert that we should use this valve and not assert that it is *true* that we should? That we should is a truism about truth. By analogy, if our problem is to find a constitution that can meet certain practical constraints, and if that requires a guarantee of religious liberty, then it is simply *true* (given the context) that we should guarantee religious liberty.

When Rawls initially denies that his principles are true, he says that to claim their truth would be to assess them "from the point of view of our comprehensive doctrine" (1993, p. 126). Now, this claim can be understood in more than one way.[8] But either way, it denies that there can be truth relative to a less than comprehensive aim or concern. I do not see why we should accept this limitation on the use of the term "true". Hence, I do not see why Rawls must refuse to say that the principles of justice, supposing they do the job they are supposed to do, are true. I also do not think this would be a serious concession on his part.

Granted, if an argument for political liberalism is to succeed, it must not contradict essential features of reasonable, comprehensive moral or religious doctrines. If it did that, then it could not be justified to reasonable adherents of any of the doctrines it contradicts. But, as long as asserting the truth of principles does not involve denying any essential feature of such doctrines, doing so does not compromise the project. If their truth consists merely of their being part of a solution to a practical problem, then there is no reason not to assert their truth. Should we go on to say that the principles represent (part of) the moral truth?

Rawls insists that political liberalism is a "freestanding" political conception (1993, p. 12). Its principles are not presented as theorems of some particular comprehensive view, but, rather, as principles for regulating political life, justifiable in terms of the idea of the reasonable. Charles Larmore has recently argued, though, that to say this is not necessarily to deny that they make true *moral* claims on us (1999). Rather, they presuppose a certain moral ideal (cf. Raz, 1990, p. 14). Should Rawls agree with this?

Rawls claims that liberal principles are reasonable. They meet the need reasonable persons have for principles that they and other reasonable persons can all accept. Reasonableness, Rawls thinks, will by itself be enough to lead persons to accept liberal principles. (If he is right, it will lead persons to accept *his* principles.) But the aim of being reasonable, Larmore claims, is itself a moral aim. It amounts to one conception of the moral ideal of respect for persons. And so, he argues, we should not shy away from asserting that reasonable principles represent moral truths.

I believe Rawls has good reason to refrain from asserting this as any part of the justification for liberal principles. To claim they are moral truths is to make an assertion that adherents of some reasonable, comprehensive views must reject. It is certainly true that the term "moral" can be, and has been, used both broadly and narrowly. We might sometimes want to reserve it for a rather narrow range of particular duties corresponding roughly to Rawls's requirements of reasonable behavior, but, on other occasions, we might take it to include ideals and conceptions of excellence that go far beyond the minimal duties we owe to one another.[9] Thus, someone *can* speak of a requirement as a moral one, in the former (narrow) sense, without taking a stand on its relation to a variety of further ideals – much less on whether it derives from the same source as those ideals. I take this to be what Larmore proposes. However, among those who are prepared to affirm the duties of the reasonable, there may be some who reject the "pluralistic" conception of the meaning of "moral." For *them*, to commit oneself to a moral claim is to commit oneself to an elaborate metaphysical idea, and they may reject that idea. For example, they may hold that morality consists of God's laws and yet reject theism. While they may be committed to reasonable principles, they have reason to deny that these are moral principles. To insist that they *are* true moral principles is gratuitously to reject assumptions they may hold dear.

I conclude that Rawls is wrong to withhold the term "true" from his principles, but justified in refusing to say that they are *moral* truths. More exactly, while he, or Larmore, may themselves be prepared to believe that these are moral truths, he is justified in insisting that liberal principles *be capable of being justified by reference merely to the idea of the reasonable*, and without a further claim that this constitutes a moral requirement.[10]

Neutrality

A more difficult issue about political liberalism is whether, or to what extent, it is committed to an ideal of state neutrality among competing views – and if it is committed to neutrality, whether this is not an objectionable commitment. I will focus particularly on neutrality in political liberalism. This is important because various liberal (and libertarian) conceptions have advocated an ideal of neutrality for various reasons. And so, different critics of neutrality focus on undermining different arguments offered to support it.

I will argue that the fundamental commitment of political liberalism is not to neutrality per se, but to the idea of justification to all reasonable persons. This requires, at most, that basic principles be neutral just with respect to comprehensive doctrines on which there is disagreement. Moreover, while principles may sometimes deny political authority to promote certain ends or values, more commonly it will simply regulate the way in which they can be promoted, perhaps by requiring that certain legislative procedures be followed. This can still allow that legislation itself may not be neutral. And I will also argue that there is good reason why some such legislation should be allowed.

Still, starting with the idea that basic principles must be justifiable to each, Larmore and Rawls conclude that this requires principles to be neutral among competing, reasonable comprehensive views.[11] On the other hand, both emphasize that this requirement applies only to basic constitutional questions, and Rawls goes on to say that citizens should be free to vote according to their comprehensive views "when constitutional essentials and basic justice are not at stake" (1993, p. 235).

Given their underlying aim, one can see the appeal of neutrality. Among persons who have very different ideas about what makes life good for a person, about what kinds of life or activity are to be admired, and about what might make such ideas right in the first place, one way to achieve agreement is simply to refrain from pronouncing on such things – to remain neutral. As against all this, however, there is a very different idea about the proper aims of the state. In *Beyond Neutrality* (1997), Sher sets out to defend the view that the state "may legitimately promote the good." (1) He rejects the view that the state "oversteps its bounds" if it "tries to make citizens more virtuous, to raise their level of culture or civility, or to prevent them from living degrading lives." (2) While political liberalism denies that the state can base at least its fundamental principles on the aim of promoting the good, Sher insists that "no reasons are inadmissible in politics" (4, cf. 248). He defends the "traditional" view that "knowledge, excellence and virtue make people's lives better" and that "political agents often have ample reason to promote such lives" (245). To do so is part of the proper function of the state.

Perfectionists like Sher or Raz will differ from defenders of political liberalism in the kind of argument they will accept for laws and institutions. In matters of substantive policy, however, it is hard to say how much perfectionists would differ from Rawls or Larmore. For one thing, different perfectionists will have different ideas as to which lives are best. Moreover, although, at the level of constitutional design, perfectionist liberals will be less concerned to find rules acceptable to all, and more concerned to create a state that will promote the good, they may, for their own reasons, endorse things like freedom of expression and freedom of religion. (Even if one thinks it justifiable to restrict offensive expression, say, one may fear authorizing the state to do so on the ground that others will likely misuse the power.) Still, perfectionists tend to prefer a narrower construction of First Amendment rights and to favor some restrictions on artistic expression when it might encourage degrading ways of life. They will certainly favor state-sponsored cultural or artistic activity when it encourages people to develop, or enables them to exercise, their talents. And they often favor relatively strict academic standards, along with moral education, in school curricula.[12]

Political liberalism would respond by reasserting that disagreement on fundamental issues of value, religion and philosophy is inevitable in modern democracies. At the least, were we to adopt, as the very foundation of our political relations with others, the idea of promoting some particular, ideal way of life, we would be unable to justify our social and political arrangements to others who reject that ideal. We would fail to solve the problem of political legitimacy as political liberalism understands it. If the aim of our association were to promote an ideal incompatible with the basic aims of some reasonable citizens, how could we justify our institutions to them?

It is not irrelevant to this reply that Sher begins his book by acknowledging an "ambivalence" toward contemporary liberalism, asserting "a confidence in the power of reason to resolve our disagreements" (ix). This is surely one of the roots of his disagreement with the liberalism of Rawls and Larmore. Even if we accept the demands of the reasonable, Sher might say, we have no need to be neutral among conflicting groups if we can win the agreement of all by reasoning. If he is right, of course, that certainly undermines the case for neutrality. But is he right?

This is not a simple question, for answering it requires sorting out two different issues. First, there is the question whether actual, smart, educated persons will continue to disagree in fact about philosophical, religious and moral issues. The answer, surely, is yes. But, second, there is the question of what sort of agreement we need. Should we be satisfied if we are convinced, on the basis of sober, reasoned investigation, that our institutions are supportable by principles that everyone else *ought* to agree to – if only they used their heads? Or must we seek something closer to actual assent of all or most persons? We have to admit that we will not *get* actual, universal, assent to anything. But I suspect the theorists of political liberalism might be interpreted as accepting an intermediate requirement: principles are adequate only if they should be accepted by all reasonable persons on the basis of beliefs and values they *already hold*.

Perhaps political liberals think they discern, in the modern history of democratic societies, a trend toward *disagreement* on matters of religion and philosophy, conjoined with a trend toward *agreement* on political ideals like toleration. I do not know. But I do suspect that, as Rawls understands the idea of the reasonable, it requires that we seek something closer to actual agreement than Sher would require – perhaps something along the lines just suggested. And this in turn suggests that the disagreement between him and Sher is a normative disagreement as to how we should behave toward others with whom we disagree. If this is right, it is not surprising that Sher, following Raz, questions Rawls's consistency by observing that Rawls's own theory is "based on a controversial moral . . . doctrine," namely, the "value of uncoerced stability" (85, 92).

Now, I believe it is right that one difference between political liberalism and Sher's perfectionism is that the former is committed to an ideal of political stability grounded on principles that are acceptable to all reasonable persons, despite enduring philosophical and religious differences. And this idea may commit liberals to something like neutrality on matters in dispute among reasonable persons.

But I do not see any inconsistency here. Political liberalism, like any view, is not without premises. There is nothing wrong with adopting a particular normative perspective and then, if that perspective requires neutrality *elsewhere*, pursuing it there. And certainly the idea of justification to all is not controversial among the reasonable. However, I do not believe that Rawls's theory (and he is the one who offers the more substantive principles) achieves a thoroughgoing neutrality. Instead, the impatience he expressed with the idea of neutrality, at the time of "Fairness to Goodness," is more in line with his current theory; and that may help to explain the discomfort with the term "neutral" that both he and Larmore now express (Rawls, 1993, p. 194; Larmore, 1996, pp. 125–6).

I suppose one idea of what neutrality might involve is the idea of a minimal state – a state that does almost nothing beyond enforcing an uncontroversial goal of order and individual security. Perhaps this is one way of arriving at something like Nozick's position. But Rawls and Larmore hope to find a rationale for a more robust, activist liberalism, and they seek ideas and principles that can serve as the "public charter" in terms of which citizens can understand and discuss their shared institutions, principles to which they can appeal in resolving, or at least clarifying, their disagreements.

To achieve the aims of political liberalism, these ideas will have to be acceptable to diverse persons who otherwise disagree sharply. Rawls's language (e.g., the idea of an "overlapping consensus") sometimes suggests that he will achieve this by drawing his principles from the shared stock of ideas already present in democratic culture, and both Sher and Raz take note of this point. Sher also portrays Rawls as taking "conceptions of the good" "out of play" with the device of the veil of ignorance (79). But I think neither idea really captures what Rawls does. The first ignores the extent to which, as noted above, Rawls's theory represents a *construction* out of a variety of ideas that are mere *specifications* of shared values; and the second ignores the fact that Rawls's argument from the original position begins with a list of goods everyone is said to want: liberties, opportunities, income and wealth.[13]

Now, to start with these ideas is not to adopt a stance of neutrality among all ideas of the good. Nor can it be said that the list of goods is completely uncontroversial.[14] But the real aim of political liberalism is not neutrality per se. It is rather to formulate a political conception that can be justified to reasonable persons holding a variety of incompatible, comprehensive doctrines. The question is whether constitutional principles guaranteeing Rawlsian primary goods can be so justified.

It is certainly plausible that principles guaranteeing equal liberties, especially freedom of religion and freedom of expression, might figure in a reasonable accommodation among those who hold conflicting doctrines. While leaving supporters of different ideas free to advocate their views, they specifically refrain from siding with any one in particular. Understood as they are in the US Bill of Rights, they remove from the political agenda the question of *which* religion or *which* moral or philosophical doctrines ought to be officially certified as true. The other

Rawlsian guarantees – the difference principle and the requirement of fair opportunity – however, may be less easy to justify. I think the requirement of fair opportunity especially problematic. Rawls says remarkably little, in his various writings, about just how this requirement is to be understood. Is it primarily concerned, for example, with the competition for economically advantageous positions, or for positions of power or prestige? Or is it instead concerned with opportunities to flourish and live well more generally?

The latter might seem more easily justifiable (especially if there is serious disagreement as to the value of economic success itself).[15] But even then it looks as if the justification will not be as straightforward as the justification for some of the other liberties mentioned. While freedom of religion, for example, removes certain issues from the agenda, fair opportunity merely postpones them. If it were understood, say, as the opportunity to acquire and exercise certain purely secular capacities and habits of skeptical inquiry, or alternatively as the opportunity to become a model socialist citizen, then there are many to whom it could not be justifiable as a requirement of basic justice at all. The same would be true if it were understood merely as the opportunity to lead an exemplary religious life and pursue a religious vocation. On the other hand, if the idea of a good life is left largely open, the requirement could be justified as a basic requirement, but only because it postpones controversy over particular attempts to implement it. Controversy over school curricula and textbooks is an obvious example.

Securing opportunity will require legislation, and a legislature empowered to enforce requirements. Disputes about these requirements will inescapably take the form of disputes about what is actually good for people, what is actually true, and so on. They will require decisions about how to promote what is good both for individuals and for society. Even the decision *not* to require certain things of everyone, given the assumption that we must provide fair opportunity, is a decision about what a person needs in order to flourish. So, voters and officials will be unable, in the formulation of actual policy, to act neutrally. If I am not mistaken, then, Rawls should actually end up with the kind of "quasi" perfectionist view Sher proposes: a view "that does not seek to *ground* the state in any particular conception of the good, but nevertheless holds that a government may legitimately *promote* the good" (1).[16] And this view is also consistent with what Rawls himself says, when he suggests that neutrality is required in dealing with constitutional questions and questions of basic justice, but that people are free to vote according to their comprehensive views in legislative matters. Indeed, both Larmore and Nagel say very much the same thing.

It helps make sense of this to see – as Rawls makes explicit – that political liberalism is concerned with more than *merely* finding agreement. This is one constraint on a more general political project, another aim of which is to constitute a "fair system of cooperation," where this idea, in turn, requires "an idea of each participant's rational advantage" (1993, pp. 15–16). Political society aims to make possible and to facilitate our gaining these advantages. The problem is to achieve this purpose in a legitimate way, where legitimacy requires, to use Waldron's term, some analogue of *consent*.

Promoting the achievement of individual good is in some tension with the legitimacy constraint – given the background of reasonable pluralism. Reasonableness (in Rawls's sense) makes some agreement possible. And it is arguable that this agreement can include the kind of substantive requirements, supplemented by a relatively unconstrained, democratic political process, which Rawls proposes. But this does not achieve the kind of thoroughgoing neutrality against which Sher argues. Legislative debates will invoke substantive values, and legislation itself will incorporate some of these values. For those, including some feminist writers, who object to what they see as excessive abstractness and who endorse a robust, democratic politics, this should be welcome (Young, 1990, ch. 5; Benhabib, 1987).

Political liberalism offers an account – an explanation – of a wide range of liberal ideas. Raz's theory, like sophisticated forms of utilitarianism, can also make sense of many of these ideas. The latter two, however, arguably fail to meet the legitimacy constraint – the requirement that at least the basic principles of a theory must be justifiable to all reasonable persons. Does that mean they are not justified, while a theory like Rawls's is? That depends on whether one accepts this requirement, and just how one interprets it. Whether we should accept it, I think, depends on whether it can be interpreted in such a way that, on the one hand, it can be met, but on the other hand, the fact that a theory meets it is morally significant.[17] The idea of focusing on reasonable persons and on what can be justified to them, is an attempt to do this. In any case, I think acceptance or rejection of this requirement marks a fundamental divide in political philosophy – and perhaps in moral philosophy as well.[18]

Notes

1 J. S. Mill's *On Liberty* (1978), a more sweeping defense of liberty, even against democratic encroachments, is a classic of liberal thought. Isaiah Berlin, in "Two Concepts of Liberty" (1969), defends a Millian "negative" liberty against "positive" liberty.

2 See Waldron (1993), pp. 50f, and 58 where he emphasizes justification *to* subjects. Note that this ideal itself may be questioned.

3 In Rawls's terms, this is a matter of "pure procedural justice," whatever results from a just system is just. For discussion, see Nelson (1980).

4 Young (1990), Benhabib (1987), but, see also Okin (1989). For further discussion, see articles in this volume by Held and Sterba.

5 Nagel (1987), Berlin (1969), Hampshire (1989).

6 On neutrality, see also Dworkin (1985), pp. 191f; Waldron (1993), ch. 7.

7 See discussion in Waldron (1993), "Legislation and Moral Neutrality," esp. pp. 165f. See also Dworkin (1985).

8 It might imply a relativistic view, that there are different truths, but each presupposes one or another comprehensive view; or it might be the view that a judgment is true

only when based on the correct comprehensive doctrine – though we disagree as to which this is.

9   This phrase is from Scanlon (1998). He insists on the plurality of conceptions of the moral and replies to some criticisms of his account of our duties to one another that they stem from moral ideals in a broader use of the term.

10 This is an argument in support of Rawls's refusal to accept his theory as a moral truth. But an analogy of this argument could also be used to defend his refusal even to say that it is true; for some may even refuse to accept the "relativized" conception of truth which I refer to as a truism. I thank Dave Phillips for this observation.

11 Larmore (1987), pp. 50f, 67f (1996), pp. 125–6; Rawls (1993), p. 194.

12 While some defenders of neutrality (perhaps, e.g., Dworkin) will reject such policies, political liberals, as I argue below, can at least permit some of them. They reject, as a basis for political association, any specific conception of the good, but they recognize the need, in practice, to provide conditions in which good lives of various kinds can flourish. They also have to face up to the hard choices that arise when the conditions for one good kind of life are incompatible with the conditions for another.

13 It has been argued by Scanlon (1975), and noted by Nagel (1987), that we need at least some theory of the good if we are to make judgments about distributive justice – for these will require judgments as to who is better or worse off.

14 Though it is relatively so – as, by the way, elements of the conception of value Sher defends in his book are relatively uncontroversial. I think a lot of what Sher says, much of it inspired by Aristotelian ideas, could be accepted by theorists like Rawls. Among those who might find Rawls's list controversial are feminists like Young and Benhabib, each of whom suggests that abstract generalizations about what persons need risk leaving out the needs of under-represented persons or groups.

15 Nelson (1984), and Sen (1992).

16 At the end of his book, Sher seems to go further, arguing that it is actually legitimate to ground a state on a conception of the good. But then he does not seem to accept the political liberal's constraint on legitimacy.

17 Raz, in the last paragraph of "Facing Diversity . . ." (1990), doubts that both conditions can be met. This essay was written before Rawls's *Political Liberalism*. Whether the ideas there – in particular, the conception of the reasonable – help, seems to me an interesting question.

18 My thanks to Greg Brown, Dave Phillips and George Sher for discussing these ideas with me and for comments on an earlier draft.

Bibliography

Bailey, J. W. (1997). *Utilitarianism, Institutions and Justice*. New York: Oxford University Press.

Benhabib, S. (1987). "The generalized and the concrete other." In S. Benhabib and D. Cornell (eds.), *Feminism as Critique* (pp. 77–95). Cambridge, Eng.: Polity Press.

Berlin, I. (1969). *Four Essays on Liberty*. New York: Oxford University Press.

Buchanan, J. M. (1975). *The Limits of Liberty*. Chicago: University of Chicago Press.

Dworkin, R. (1985). "Liberalism." In *A Matter of Principle*. Cambridge, MA: Harvard University Press.

Hampshire, S. (1989). *Innocence and Experience*. Cambridge, MA: Harvard University Press.

Hardin, G. (1988). *Morality within the Limits of Reason*. Chicago: University of Chicago Press.

Hardin, R. (1986). "The utilitarian logic of liberalism." *Ethics*, 97: 47–74.

Hayek, F. (1948). "The use of knowledge in society." In *Individualism and the Economic Order*. London: Routledge.

——(1960). *The Constitution of Liberty*. Chicago: University of Chicago Press.

Kekes, J. (1997). *Against Liberalism*. Ithaca: Cornell University Press.

Larmore, C. (1999). "The moral basis of political liberalism." *Journal of Philosophy*, XCVI: 599–625.

——(1996). *The Morals of Modernity*. New York: Cambridge University Press.

——(1987). *Patterns of Moral Complexity*. New York: Cambridge University Press.

Mill, J. S. (1978). *On Liberty*. Indianapolis: Hackett.

Nagel, T. (1973). "Rawls on justice." *Philosophical Review*, LXXXII: 220–34.

——(1975). "Libertarianism without foundations." *Yale Law Journal*, 85: 136–49.

——(1987). "Moral conflict and political legitimacy." *Philosophy and Public Affairs*, 16: 215–40.

Nelson, W. (1984). "Equal opportunity." *Social Theory and Practice*, 10: 157–84.

——(1980). "The very idea of pure procedural justice." *Ethics*, 90: 502–11.

Nozick, R. (1974). *Anarchy, State and Utopia*. New York: Basic Books.

Okin, S. M. (1989). *Justice, Gender and the Family*. New York: Basic Books.

Rawls, J. (1958). "Justice as fairness." *The Philosophical Review*, LXVII: 164–94.

——(1971). *A Theory of Justice*. Cambridge, MA: Harvard University Press.

——(1975). "Fairness to Goodness." *The Philosophical Review*, 89: 536–54.

——(1993). *Political Liberalism*. New York: Columbia University Press.

Raz, J. (1986). *The Morality of Freedom*. New York: Oxford University Press.

——(1990). "Facing diversity: The case of epistemic abstinence." *Philosophy and Public Affairs*, 19: 3–46.

Sartorius, R. E. (1975). *Individual Conduct and Social Norms*. Encino and Belmont, CA: Dickenson.

Scanlon, T. (1975). "Preference and urgency." *Journal of Philosophy*, LXXII: 655–68.

Scanlon, T. M. (1998). *What We Owe to Each Other*. Cambridge, MA: Harvard University Press.

Scheffler, S. (1994). *The Rejection of Consequentialism* (Revised edn). New York: Oxford University Press.

Schwartz, A. (1973). "Moral neutrality and primary goods." *Ethics*, 83: 294–307.

Sen, A. K. (1992). *Inequality Reexamined*. Cambridge, MA: Harvard University Press.

Sher, G. (1997). *Beyond Neutrality*. New York: Cambridge University Press.

Waldron, J. (1993). *Liberal Rights, Collected Papers, 1981–1991*. New York: Cambridge University Press.

Young, I. M. (1990). *Justice and the Politics of Difference*. Princeton: Princeton University Press.

Part III

Pluralism, Diversity, and Deliberation

Chapter 10

Deliberative Democracy

James S. Fishkin

"Deliberative democracy" refers to efforts, in both theory and practice, to reconcile the value of deliberation with other core democratic principles, such as political equality and the avoidance of "tyranny of the majority." These efforts engage normative concerns about whether deliberation is worth achieving, and at what cost, in terms of other, apparently conflicting values. Deliberative democracy also engages empirical issues about whether more deliberation would make much difference and about the kinds of institutions that might better realize deliberative democracy.

The modern debate about deliberative democracy can be thought of as an exploration into the compatibility of three principles – deliberation, political equality and non-tyranny (or the effort to avoid tyranny of the majority). Each of these principles has been connected to a distinct image of the democratic process: the filter (for deliberation), the mirror (for political equality) and the mob (for what the principle of non-tyranny attempts to avoid). These three images, bequeathed to us by longstanding debates about democracy, are difficult to reconcile in a coherent picture; more importantly, the principles they bring to mind seem to clash in ways that bedevil efforts at democratic reform. There are longstanding arguments, in other words, for believing that these principles form an incompatible triad. However, we will see that there are also ways of combining them that render them compatible. Institutions that embody deliberation, political equality and non-tyranny (the avoidance of tyranny of the majority) are, in fact, possible under some realistic conditions. Before turning to the modern debate, however, it is worth noting that these issues go back to the earliest known democratic efforts.

The Athenian Solution

One can go back to the beginnings of democracy in ancient Athens and find institutions embodying a form of deliberative democracy. The Athenians employed deliberative microcosms of the citizenry chosen by lot for many key functions. The Council of 500 chosen in that way set the agenda for the Assembly. The "graphe paranomon" was a kind of court procedure before a jury of 500 or more chosen by lot that would hear appeals about any proposal in the Assembly that was alleged to be illegal. And by fourth-century Athens, legislative commissions chosen by lot were making the final decisions about legislation. These institutions allowed for a microcosm of the citizenry on a manageable scale (500 or so) that could make deliberation possible. But since the members were chosen by lot, there was a recognizable form of political equality (at least among citizens) realized as well. Every citizen had, in theory, an equal chance of being chosen to be part of the process.

This kind of institution, the deliberative microcosm of the citizenry chosen by lot, provided a solution to a basic problem that has long bedeviled attempts to realize deliberative democracy in political systems of any significant size. At a minimum, deliberative democracy might be thought to require both a deliberative and a democratic element. The deliberative element consists, at the very least, in a balanced discussion of competing arguments and, hopefully, reasonably accurate information in support of those arguments. In the Athenian solution, the democratic element was embodied by a form of political equality – the equal chance offered by lot to every citizen to participate and then cast a vote.

A key aspect of the Athenian solution is that it maintained a claim to political equality regardless of the number of citizens in the society. Commentators long treated ancient Athens and the other Greek city-states as places where the entire citizenry could gather together and practice direct democracy. In fact, modern research shows that the Pnyx, the hill where the Assembly met in Athens, could only hold about 6,000 citizens while there were about 60,000 citizens in fifth-century Athens. The Athenians faced the same fundamental problem as more modern democratic efforts: they could not gather all relevant citizens together in the same place. Their solution was to rely increasingly on deliberative microcosms chosen by lot so as to keep the participants to a manageable number while also realizing a form of equality.[1]

When the American founders debated how to realize some form of popular control in a nation-state, the conventional wisdom was that democracy was reserved for small city-states, where everyone could gather together. James Madison even avoided the term "democracy," reserving it for direct democratic governance, and termed the founders' plan a "republic." Madison prized deliberative democracy, emphasizing the deliberative portion while, at the same time, modulating the democratic elements. The modern debate about deliberative democracy was effectively launched by the debate over the American founding, focused on competing conceptions of democracy, emphasized by Federalists (proponents of the proposed constitution) and Anti-Federalists. The competition between those competing visions of democracy continues to this day.

The Filter

As Madison reported on his own position in his notes on the Constitutional Convention, he was "an advocate for the policy of refining the popular appointments by successive filtrations."[2] Famously, he argued in *Federalist*, no. 10, that the effect of representation was "to refine and enlarge the public views by passing them through the medium of a chosen body of citizens . . . under such a regulation it may well happen that the public voice, pronounced by the representatives of the people, will be more consonant to the public good than if pronounced by the people themselves, if convened for the purpose." Running throughout Madison's thinking is the distinction between "refined" public opinion, the considered judgments that can result from the deliberations of a small representative body, on the one hand, and the "temporary errors and delusions" of public opinion that may be found outside this deliberative process, on the other. It is only through the deliberations of a small face-to-face representative body that one can arrive at "the cool and deliberate sense of the community" (*Federalist*, no. 63). This was a principal motivation for the Senate, which was intended to resist the passions and interests that might divert the public into majority tyranny.

The Founders were sensitive to the social conditions that would make deliberation possible. For example, large meetings of citizens were thought to be dangerous because they were too large to be deliberative, no matter how thoughtful or virtuous the citizenry might be. As Madison said in *Federalist*, no. 55, "had every Athenian citizen been a Socrates, every Athenian assembly would still have been a mob." A key desideratum in the Founders' project of constitutional design was the creation of conditions where the formulation and expression of deliberative public opinion would be possible.

The filter can be thought of as the process of deliberation through which representatives, in face-to-face discussion, may come to considered judgments about public issues. For our purposes, we can specify a working (and minimal) notion of deliberation: face-to-face discussion by which participants conscientiously raise and respond to competing arguments so as to arrive at considered judgments about the solutions to public problems. The danger is that if the social context involves too many people, or if the motivations of the participants are distracted by the kinds of passions or interests that would motivate factions, then deliberative democracy will not be possible. It is clear that from the Founders' perspective, the social conditions we are familiar with in modern mass democracy would be far from appropriate for deliberation.

The Mirror

While the Federalists emphasized deliberation through some kind of "filtering" process for the public's views, the opponents of the Constitution emphasized a different picture of the function of representatives – the mirror. A representative assembly should be a portrait or picture in miniature of the people.[3] In the hands of the Anti-Federalists, this notion became a basis for objecting to the apparent elitism of the filtering metaphor (only the educated upper classes were expected to do the refining, in small elite assemblies). The mirror notion of representation was an expression of fairness and equality. As one of the key Anti-Federalists, the "Federal Farmer," put it: "A fair and equal representation is that in which the interests, feelings, opinions and views of the people are collected, in such manner as they would be were the people all assembled."[4] In line with the mirror theory of representation, Anti-Federalists sought frequent elections, term limits, and any measures that would increase the closeness of resemblance between representatives and those they represented. The mirror image suggests an approximation to what the people all assembled would decide if they could somehow all gather together and have their votes counted equally. The difficulty, from the standpoint of deliberative democracy, is that the people in a nation-state cannot all gather together, at least for purposes of deliberation. While they can all vote, or have their votes counted equally, as in a referendum, it is far more difficult for large numbers to achieve meaningful face-to-face discussion.

"The people all assembled" is exactly the kind of gathering the Federalists believed would give only an inferior rendering of the public good. Recall Madison's claim that a small representative group would give a better account of the public good than would the "people themselves if convened for the purpose" (*Federalist*, no. 10). The mirror is a picture of public opinion as it is; the deliberative filter provides a counterfactual picture of public opinion as it would be, were it "refined and enlarged."

The "Mob"

There is a third image, and indeed a third principle, to introduce into this discussion. In this case, it is an image to be feared, rather than one to be prized. The Founders were clearly haunted by the possibility that factions aroused by passions or interests adverse to the rights of others, could do very bad things. The image they feared seems to be some combination of the Athenian mob and Shays's rebellion. Part of the case for deliberative public opinion is that the "cool and deliberate sense of the community" (*Federalist*, no. 63) would be insulated from the passions and interests that might motivate factions. The Founders believed that public opinion, when filtered by deliberative processes, would more likely serve the public good and avoid mob-like behavior of the kind that threatens tyranny of the majority. Hence the Founders' emphasis on deliberation was partly motivated by the effort to avoid tyranny of the majority. But their strategy for achieving deliberation came at a cost in political equality. They feared direct consultation of the people. The deliberative bodies they emphasized were representative bodies, sometimes chosen in turn by representative bodies – Madison's strategy of "successive filtrations." Recall that the initial plan for the Senate was that it was chosen by the State legislatures (a system that remained in place until the passage of the 17th Amendment in 1913). Similarly, the initial notion of the Electoral College was that it was to constitute a deliberative body, meeting on a state-by-state basis. Instead of the people voting directly for president, State legislatures selected electors who deliberated, in turn, to select the most qualified candidate for president. As time went on, the Electoral College became a crude device for aggregating votes and those electors who deliberated risked being branded "faithless" if they ever departed from the voting expressed earlier by the public. The resulting changes can be viewed as an improvement in political equality among citizens, but as the effective elimination of yet one more institution that was intended to embody deliberation.

The Apparent Conundrum

There is strong normative appeal to any vision of democracy that would somehow achieve all three principles – deliberation, political equality and non-tyranny. First, there are obvious reasons for preferring that citizens have deliberative rather than non-deliberative preferences. Democracy is more meaningful if citizens are better informed and more attentive to the issues they are voting on. Second, there are obvious reasons for preferring that all votes be counted equally. If the votes of some citizens are not counted, or if others are counted more, then the picture of the public voice that results has been distorted. Third, there are obvious reasons for preferring to avoid tyranny of the majority. If democracy produces grave injustices to some minority, then its normative claim is undermined. This condition can be viewed as a requirement of democratic theory itself or, alternatively, as a requirement for conditions of justice that need to be satisfied, if democratic theory is to have a compelling normative claim.

However, much of the debate since the American founding illustrates just how easy it is for conflicts among these three principles to arise. On the one hand, political equality seems to systematically undermine deliberation and on the other hand, political equality seems to place non-tyranny at risk (in that the pursuit of political equality may bring about tyranny of the majority). If these patterns of incompatibility cannot be avoided, then aspirations for a theory of deliberative democracy realizing all three are doomed.

Modern mass democracy attempts to realize political equality through mass participation – through direct consultation of the entire public (or, via public opinion polls, through a mirroring, in miniature, of the entire public). This strategy, unlike the Athenian solution mentioned earlier, leaves mass opinion unaffected. People have little reason to pay attention or to become informed. Equally, this strategy contrasts with the small deliberative bodies idealized by Madison in his vision of the Senate, or the Constitutional Conventions or the Electoral College. Madison's claim was that small deliberative bodies, such as the US Senate or a Constitutional Convention, allow representatives to come to a better determination of the public good than one would get just by bringing the people together and asking them. There is a difference, in other words, between the deliberative or thoughtful public opinion one can find in representative institutions, at least at their best, and the uninformed and unreflective preferences commonly found in the mass public.

A central problem in democratic theory is how to reconcile the aspiration for thoughtful and informed preferences – an aspiration expressed by the value of deliberation – with principles like political equality that support mass public consultation. Deliberative bodies may represent highly informed and competent preferences, but those preferences are often shared only by an elite. Direct consultation of mass preferences will typically involve counting uninformed preferences, those simply reflecting the public's impressions of headlines or, in a modern context, sound bites. Hence the hard choice between politically equal but unreflective mass preferences and politically unequal but relatively more reflective elite views.

Before we search for ways out of this conundrum, let us pause to get at least a working definition of *political equality*: a practice satisfies political equality when it gives equal consideration to everyone's views. For the moment, we need not concern ourselves with who is included in the term "everyone." Obviously, there have been enormous changes in suffrage, or in the definition of the relevant demos, during the period covered by this discussion.[5] There are also various ways to provide for "equal consideration." For our purposes here we can specify a root notion – an equal chance of being the decisive voter (assuming that we know nothing about the preferences of the other voters). This notion is the intuition behind indices for equal voting power such as the Banzhaf index.[6]

It is also worth noting that political equality can be applied to formal political processes such as voting in elections or primaries or referenda. It can equally be applied to unofficial processes such as public opinion polls, and to many other informal processes where it is far less successfully realized: straw polls, town meetings and other informal gatherings where opinion is loosely assessed.[7] One key issue that I have also left intentionally underspecified in this definition is the question of what "views" are to be considered equally. Political equality can be applied to give equal consideration to informed views, as in a deliberative microcosm, or equal consideration to the uninformed views commonly found in the mass public when it has little reason to pay attention to the details of public policy.

We have already seen how instituting political equality through direct consultation can undermine deliberation. The Founders presented a plausible case that the appropriate venue for deliberation was a small representative body that could carefully and conscientiously consider the competing arguments about any given proposal. They had in mind the Constitutional Conventions, the Senate, the Electoral College. They felt that even the Athenian Assembly must have been too large for real deliberation. Appeals to mass democracy were dangerous as the public was likely to be inattentive and ill informed and was likely to be aroused only by passions or interests that might be dangerous.

When the Founders talked of "tyranny of the majority," it was only loosely specified. They were clearly fearful of substantial and avoidable deprivations committed against life, liberty or property. While these notions are suggestive, we need a working definition here of those government decisions that would be so unacceptable that there would be overriding normative claims against them even when they were otherwise supported by democratic principles.

For our purposes, we can say that *tyranny* (whether of the majority or minority) is the choice of a policy that imposes severe deprivations of essential interests when an alternative policy could have been chosen that would not have imposed comparable severe deprivations on anyone. By non-tyranny I simply mean the avoidance of "tyranny" in this sense. There are, of course, interesting questions about the definition of "essential interests" and the sense in which policies are alternatives, one to another.[8] However, the basic notion does not turn on any specific account of these notions. For our purposes here, the basic idea will serve: that it is objectionable when people choose to do very bad things to some of their number, when such a choice could have been avoided entirely.[9]

Referendum Democracy versus Deliberation

The problem is that pursuit of political equality would seem to undermine both deliberation and non-tyranny. From the standpoint of the Founders, the problem was soon dramatized by the Rhode Island referendum, the only effort to consult the people directly about the ratification of the Constitution. Rhode Island was a hotbed of paper money and, from the Federalist standpoint, irresponsible government and fiscal mismanagement. An Anti-Federalist stronghold, it lived up to the Founders' image of a place where the passions of the public might undermine both deliberation and non-tyranny. It is worth pausing for a moment to consider the debate over the Rhode Island referendum, since the conflict over competing conceptions of democracy that was clearly articulated then has resonated in similar ways ever since.

The Anti-Federalists sparked a thoroughgoing debate over the proper method of consulting the people. Referendum advocates held that "submitting it to every Individual Freeholder of the state was the only Mode in which the *true* Sentiments of the people could be collected" (emphasis in original).[10] However, the Federalists objected that a referendum would not provide a discussion of the issues in which the arguments could be joined. By holding the referendum in town meetings scattered throughout the state, different arguments would be offered in each place, and the arguments offered would not get answered. "The sea-port towns cannot hear and examine the arguments of their brethren in the country on this subject, nor can they in return be possessed of our views thereof . . . each separate interest will act under an impression of private and local motives only, uninformed of those reasons and arguments which might lead to measures of common utility and public good."[11] Federalists held that only in a Convention could representatives of the entire state meet together, voice their concerns and have them answered by those with different views so as to arrive at some collective solution for the common good. The very idea of the convention as a basis for ratification was an important innovation motivated by the need for deliberation.[12] Direct consultation of the mass public, realizing political equality, would sacrifice deliberative discussion.

Federalists also noted another defect – lack of information: "every individual Freeman ought to investigate these great questions to some good degree in order to decide on this Constitution: the time therefore to be spent in this business would prove a great tax on the freemen to be assembled in Town-meetings, which must be kept open not only three days but three months or more, in preparation as the people at large have more or less information." While representatives chosen for a convention might acquire the appropriate information in a reasonable time, it would take an extraordinary amount of time to similarly prepare the "people at large."

Of course, what happened in the end, is that the referendum was held; it was boycotted by the Federalists; and the Constitution was voted down. Rhode Island, under threat of embargo and even of dismemberment (Connecticut threatening to invade from one side and Massachusetts from the other), capitulated and held the required state convention to eventually approve the Constitution.

The effort to realize political equality by directly consulting every voter undermined deliberation and, given the passions involved in the referendum campaign, posed risks of violating non-tyranny as well. This incident was an early American salvo in a long war of competing conceptions of democracy. In the long run, the Federalist emphasis on deliberation and discussion may well have lost out to a form of democracy, embodied in referend, and in other forms of more direct consultation that achieve political equality – regardless of whether or not it is also accompanied by deliberation.

In the more than two centuries since the founding, many changes, both formal and informal, in the American political system have served to further realize political equality through more direct public consultation, but at the cost of deliberation. Consider what has happened to the Electoral College, the election of Senators, the presidential selection system, the development and transformation of the national party conventions, the rise of referenda (particularly in the Western states), and the development of public opinion polling. People vote directly and their votes are counted equally (except, of course, in voting for the Senate, if we compare across states with different populations). Many aspects of Madisonian "filtration" have disappeared in a system that has taken on increasing elements of what might be called "plebiscitary" democracy (embodied in referenda, primaries and the influence of polls).

Primaries and referenda bring to the people decisions that were previously made by political elites – party leaders in the case of nominations, and legislators in the case of laws. Public opinion polls bring substantive issues directly to the public (in representative samples) without any effective opportunity for "filtering" or deliberation.

This movement to more direct consultation has come at a cost – a loss in the institutional structures that might provide incentives for deliberation. Much social science has established that ordinary citizens have a low level of political knowledge. In terms made famous by Anthony Downs, they can be thought of as suffering from "rational ignorance."[13] Each individual voter or citizen can see that his or her individual vote or opinion will not make much difference to policy outcomes, so there is little reason to make the effort to become more informed. The result is a consistently low level of knowledge in the mass public about politics and policy (a problem the American electorate shares with comparable electorates around the world).[14] The claim, to be sure, is not that the public lacks capacity, only that under most conditions, it lacks interest or effective incentive to become informed. Later we will turn to evidence that when effectively motivated, the public is certainly capable of deliberating about complex policy questions. But without an effective motivation, the pursuit of political equality through increasingly direct methods of public consultation has brought the locus of many important decisions to a mass public whose members, ordinarily, have little reason to pay attention. The result has been a loss in informed choice and deliberation.

The apparent trilemma has two essential claims: pursuit of political equality undermines deliberation and pursuit of political equality undermines non-tyranny. The Federalist claim that deliberation could only take place in small representative bodies, such as ratifying conventions or the proposed Senate, and not through direct consultation such as the Rhode Island referendum, shows how the pursuit of political equality through more direct consultation would, on their view, undermine deliberation. From a more modern perspective, the mass incentives for "rational ignorance," for citizens in the large-scale nation-state acquiring information, or even paying attention beyond a sound bite, render the prospects for deliberative democracy on a consistent and continuing basis among the mass public rather dubious.[15]

The second claim that forms the basis for the apparent trilemma is that the pursuit of political equality through more direct consultation undermines non-tyranny. As we have already seen, this was clearly a main worry of the Founders. Madison, for example, believed that without the filter of a Senate, the direct democracy of the ancients had no barriers to passions or interests that might motivate factions adverse to the rights of some minority. While a great deal of the American experience with injustice and majority tyranny cannot be pinned on the spread of political equality (indeed, it is arguable that the spread of the franchise has, on balance, had a salutary effect), it is nevertheless the case that a great deal of political experience around the world since Madison's time supports the view that direct democratic consultation holds dangers, at least on occasion, of majority tyranny. The referendum was used by Napoleon to provide the appearance of popular legitimacy. It was later used by Nazis and other fascists for the same purpose.[16] Clearly, a great deal of care must be taken with the social context of referenda: how they are proposed and with what motives, and what opportunities are offered for serious public education on competing sides of the issue. Some of the American experience in the Western states where referenda are common also raises issues of "faction" aroused by passions apparently adverse to the rights of others. A good example might be Proposition 187 in California, which was intended, in 1994, to deny access of illegal aliens to schools and medical care.

The conundrum seems to turn on the fact that mass democracy brings with it the limitations of the mass public. Individual citizens in the large-scale nation-state are typically inattentive and uninformed due to the incentives for rational ignorance. Candidates and policy advocates who would persuade them, often find it advantageous to treat them as consumers who might be swayed by advertising rather than as citizens who might deliberate. And they have all the vulnerabilities that worried the Founders about being aroused by passions or interests that might be adverse to the rights of others.

One caveat is worth noting to this dispiriting picture. There may be rare historical occasions when all three of our principles are, in fact, realized simultaneously in the large-scale nation-state. Bruce Ackerman's theory of the American Constitution offers a compelling picture of "constitutional moments." At times of great national crisis it is possible for the entire country to be aroused in serious deliberative discussion. Ackerman claims that this has happened at least three times in American history – the founding, Reconstruction and the New Deal. On those occasions, there is something approaching a kind of "deliberative plebiscite." The substance of the issues is joined in a great national debate, in which various institutions play a role in raising arguments and counter-arguments, until a new consensus on constitutional principles is reached and then institutionalized.[17]

Modern Deliberative Microcosms

But the exceptional character of Ackerman's constitutional moments only helps reinforce the point that under most circumstances most of the time, we can expect that mass consultation will fail to yield anything like mass deliberation. Indeed, Ackerman uses the term "normal politics" for the conjunction of mass inattention and elite-dominated interest-group politics that provides the rule – to which the great occasion of a "constitutional moment," once in many generations, provides the exception.

The difficulty, in other words, is that most of the time, under normal conditions, the three principles we have specified pose fundamental conflicts. If we try to implement political equality through mass consultation, we will encounter the limiting conditions of rational ignorance and the danger that the public will only be aroused by passions or interests of the sort the Founders feared when they constructed their original "indirect" system – a system we have progressively abandoned over the years as we have made our institutions increasingly direct, increasingly sensitive to the "mirror" rather than the "filter." Furthermore, American democracy is not, of course, alone in this move to increasingly direct consultation. Referenda, opinion polls and other forms of mass consultation have become common in every democracy around the world. And elites everywhere have found themselves forced by public pressure to defer to mass opinion, once it is measured and publicized by the media. From the standpoint of political equality, this may well be a good thing, but from the standpoint of deliberation, it is clearly a problem. The quest for realizing both values at the same time (without also impinging on the non-tyranny condition) remains.

Largely lost in the dust of history, the Athenian solution remains as a viable alternative. If a statistical microcosm of the citizenry is gathered together, it can do so under conditions where real deliberation is possible, where its members are effectively motivated to overcome rational ignorance and behave more like ideal citizens. Both deliberation, for this microcosm, and political equality can be achieved. The Athenian solution was to select the participants by lot – giving each citizen an equal random chance of being decisive. Such a solution comports with the root notion of political equality mentioned earlier.

Modern social science experiments have demonstrated the viability of this idea, at least as an institution that might serve an advisory function for public policy. In various efforts, given different names in different countries, representative microcosms of the citizenry have been gathered to deliberate about important public issues. Some of these experiments have gone so far as to use scientific random sampling, the modern extension of the ancient Athenian lot, to select the participants. The most ambitious efforts, combining scientific random sampling of entire nation-states with deliberations lasting several days, fall under the heading of "Deliberative Polling." I will confine these remarks to Deliberative Polling, but the same points apply, to varying degrees, to efforts termed "citizens juries" (in Britain and the US), to "consensus conferences" (on scientific issues in Denmark and Britain), to "planning cells" (in Germany and Switzerland).[18]

Deliberative Polling begins with a concern about the defects likely to be found in ordinary public opinion: the incentives for rational ignorance applying to the mass public and the tendency for sample surveys to turn up so-called "non-attitudes" or non-existent opinions (as well as very much "top of the head" opinions that approach being non-attitudes) on many public questions. The public does not like to admit that it does not know and may well make up answers on the spot in response to survey questions.[19] These worries are not different in spirit from the Founders' concerns about mass public opinion, at least as contrasted to the kinds of considered judgments that might result from the filtering process of deliberation.

At best, ordinary polls offer only a snapshot of public opinion as it is, even when the public has little information, attention or interest in the issue. Such polls are, of course, the modern embodiment of the mirror theory of representation, perfected to a degree never contemplated by the Anti-Federalists. But Deliberative Polling is an explicit attempt to combine the mirror with the filter. The participants turned up by random sampling, who begin as a statistical mirror of the population, are subjected to the filter of a deliberative experience.

Every aspect of the process is designed to facilitate informed and balanced discussion and, eventually, a considered judgment of the issue in question. After taking an initial survey, participants are invited for a weekend of face-to-face deliberation; they are given carefully balanced and vetted briefing materials to provide an initial basis for dialogue. They are randomly assigned to small groups for discussions with trained moderators, and encouraged to ask questions arising from the small group discussions to competing experts and politicians in larger plenary sessions. The moderators attempt to establish an atmosphere where participants listen to each other and no one is permitted to dominate the discussion. At the end of the weekend, participants take the same confidential questionnaire as on first contact and the resulting judgments in the final questionnaire are usually broadcast along with edited proceedings of the discussions throughout the weekend.[20] In every case thus far, the weekend microcosm has been highly representative, both attitudinally and demographically, as compared with the entire baseline survey and with census data about the population. In every case thus far, there have also been a number of large and statistically significant changes of opinion over the weekend. Considered judgments are often different from the "top of the head" attitudes solicited by conventional polls. The evidence of these experiments is that deliberation does indeed make a difference. Informed and engaged public opinion would be different in its conclusions from what we normally find in the mass public.

But what do the results represent? The respondents are able to overcome the incentives for rational ignorance normally applying to the mass public. Instead of one vote in millions, they have, in effect, one vote in a few hundred in the weekend sample, and one voice in fifteen or so in the small group discussions. The experiment is organized so as to make credible the claim that the opinions of each participant matter. They overcome apathy, disconnection, inattention and initial lack of information. Participants from all social locations change their opinions in the deliberation. From knowing that someone is educated or not, economically advantaged or not, one cannot predict change in the deliberations. We do know, however, from knowledge questions, that becoming informed on the issues predicts change on the policy attitudes. In that sense, deliberative public opinion is both informed and representative. As a result, it is also, almost inevitably, counterfactual. The public will rarely, if ever, be motivated to become as informed and engaged as these weekend microcosms.

The idea is that if a counter-factual situation is morally relevant, why not do a serious social science experiment – rather than merely engage in informal inference or armchair empiricism – to determine what the appropriate counter-factual might actually look like? And if that counterfactual situation is both discoverable and normatively relevant, why not then let the rest of the world know about it? Just as John Rawls's original position can be thought of as having a kind of recommending force, the counterfactual representation of more thoughtful and informed public opinion identified by the Deliberative Poll also recommends to the rest of the population some conclusions that they ought to take seriously. They ought to take the conclusions seriously because the process represents everyone under conditions where the participants could think. Deliberative Polling is meant to uncover representative and deliberative conclusions – considered judgments that embody deliberation, political equality and, presumably, non-tyranny.

The Deliberative Poll appears to function as what John Stuart Mill called a "school for public spirit," a social context where ordinary citizens can come to consider the public interest on its merits. Mill thought the jury system functioned in that way and he had the same hope for public voting (for voting in which one publicly affirmed one's choice). Mill thought that when the private citizen participates in public functions, "He is called upon, while so engaged, to weigh interests not his own; to be guided in case of conflicting claims, by another rule than his private partialities; to apply, at every turn, principles and maxims which have for their reason of existence the general good. . . . He is made to feel himself one of the public and whatever is in their interest to be his interest."[21]

This kind of increased sensitivity to the public interest can be seen in Deliberative Polls on environmental matters, in which the respondents were repeatedly willing to make modest sacrifices of self-interest for the public good by agreeing to be charged more on their monthly utility bills to promote a clean environment (through investments in energy conservation, and renewable energy as opposed to fossil fuels).[22] The Deliberative Polling experiments are filled with other examples as well in which participants find common ground on contentious issues such as crime or welfare reform and where, after deliberation, they evince a clear willingness to modulate their pursuit of self-interest for some collective benefit for the entire community. In a way, the very process of deliberating public problems together helps create a social context for shared concerns, a public space for public opinion in which what Madison called "the cool and deliberate sense of the community" (*Federalist*, no. 63) can be discovered. Under these conditions participants are interested in solving public problems together rather than in taking away the rights of some for the benefit of others. While more empirical work is needed, the record thus far supports the notion that statistical microcosms of the people can be brought together to realize all three principles: deliberation, political equality, and the avoidance of tyranny of the majority.

The Role of Representatives

Efforts to revive the Athenian solution, at least in an advisory form, suggest how the three principles can be embodied explicitly in new kinds of democratic institutions. But even without new institutions, deliberative public opinion may influence politics and policy provided that representatives and citizens regard it as morally relevant. When Madison claimed that representatives should "refine and enlarge the public's views" it is arguable that he was claiming they should consider what their constituents *would* think about an issue if they were better informed and could deliberate about the issue.[23] This gloss on Madison suggests a middle ground in the common account of the dilemma often facing representatives.[24] Should representatives follow the polls? Or should they vote their own views of what is best for the country (or their state or district)? This simple dichotomy dominates the discussion about how members of Congress and other legislators should approach their task, yet each of these two basic possibilities has difficulties. If members of Congress follow the polls, then they can be dismissed as leaderless weathervanes for the shifting winds of public opinion. Given how ill-informed the public tends to be on most policy issues, the blind would literally be doing the leading. On the other hand, if they follow their views of the substantive merits when their constituents disagree, then they can be criticized for imposing their personal value judgments on an electorate that thinks otherwise.

The middle position, between following public opinion as it is, and following one's personal views on the merits, is so obvious that it hardly requires explicit statement. It is easily overlooked and only occasionally articulated. Representatives can take account of what they think their constituents would think about an issue, once they were well informed and got the facts and heard the arguments on either side and had a reasonable chance to ponder the issues. This view of a representative's role provides grounds for resisting the pressure of polls on issues that the representative knows the public knows little about. On the other hand, this position is not the same as just the representative's own views on the issue in question. The representative may know that his or her values differ from those of constituents on a given question or that constituents would never accept a particular policy, even with a great deal more information and discussion. The representative may also know his or her constituents well enough to have some idea of what they would accept, if only they had the information. This deference to the counterfactual deliberating public provides a way of thinking about the representative's role that avoids the difficulty of following the public's uninformed views, on the one hand, and of following the representative's more informed but (perhaps) merely personal views, on the other. While this point may seem only common sense, it has large implications. Once it is granted that counterfactual but deliberative public opinion is something that representatives should pay attention to, it becomes possible to implement at least some modest elements of deliberative democracy without requiring a wholesale transformation of current representative institutions. Deliberative democracy is not a merely utopian ideal; it is also something we can move towards in modest ways. Other reforms that might encourage the media to treat voters as citizens rather than as consumers of advertising and that might encourage better civic education might also be considered to promote movements toward deliberative democracy.[25] Experimentation with new institutions, such as revivals of the Athenian solution for certain policy contexts, should be continued as well.

Compared with other forms of democracy, deliberative democracy gives a prime role for the public's *considered* judgments – for opinions that people arrive at after they have had a chance to consider competing arguments and opposing points of view. If democracy is to mean anything, it is hard not to prefer deliberative forms of democracy to those in which the public is inattentive, ill-informed, or manipulated. If preferences are more meaningful once they have had the benefit of deliberation, then so should the collective decision processes that employ them. However, since most citizens most of the time under most circumstances do not deliberate, many of the key questions about deliberative democracy focus on its reconciliation with political equality (since this principle would require counting everyone's preferences equally, even the preferences of those who are not deliberating) and non-tyranny (since this principle would require that unjust outcomes be avoided, even if they seem to result from procedurally correct democratic processes). We have seen that these principles can, in fact, be reconciled and that deliberative democracy is an ideal that can actually be realized, at least to some degree. However, this ideal provides for a novel agenda of change and experimentation, an agenda that has only recently become prominent again, despite the fact that the questions at the core of deliberative democratic theory are as old as democracy itself.

Notes

1 For more on Athenian democratic practices, see the excellent account offered by Mogens Herman Hansen, *The Athenian Democracy in the Age of Demosthenes* (Oxford: Basil Blackwell, 1991).

2 James Madison, *Notes of Debates in the Federal Convention of 1787 Reported by James Madison*, with an Introduction by Adrienne Koch (New York: Norton, 1987), p. 40.

3 Jack N. Rakove, "The Mirror of Representation," in *Original Meanings: Politics and Ideas in the Making of the Constitution* (New York: Vintage Books, 1997), p. 203.

4 Herbert Storing (ed.), *The Complete Anti-Federalist* (Chicago: University of Chicago Press, 1981), vol. II, p. 265.

5 As Rogers Smith notes: "when restrictions on voting rights, naturalization, and immigration are taken into account, it turns out that for over 80 per cent of U.S. history,

American laws declared most people in the world legally ineligible to become full U.S. citizens solely because of their race, original nationality or gender. For at least two-thirds of American history, the majority of the domestic adult population was also ineligible for full citizenship for the same reasons." Rogers Smith, *Civic Ideals* (New Haven: Yale University Press, 1997).

6   See Jonathan Still, "Equality and Election Systems," *Ethics* (April 1981), for an overview of this literature that is still very useful. "Equal probabilities" is more demanding than a closely related criterion such as equal shares and less demanding than anonymity or majority rule.

7   See John G. Geer, *From Tea Leaves to Opinion Polls* (New York: Columbia University Press, 1996), for an excellent account of how politics has changed for political leaders as they have learned to assess public opinion more systematically.

8   This account has obviously been influenced by Robert Dahl's discussion of Madison and the problem of tyranny in democratic theory in his *A Preface to Democratic Theory* (Chicago: University of Chicago Press, 1956). For a fuller account of this view of "tyranny of the majority," see my *Tyranny and Legitimacy: A Critique of Political Theories* (Baltimore, MD: Johns Hopkins University Press, 1979).

9   When decision makers are in a blind-alley situation such that no matter which option they choose, terrible consequences will result for at least some people, it hardly seems appropriate to use such a severe term as "tyranny." Rather, they are in a situation that might better be characterized as "tragic choice."

10   "Rhode Island's Assembly Refuses to Call a Convention and Submits the Constitution Directly to the People," in Bernard Bailyn (ed.), *The Debate on the Constitution*, Part II (New York: The Library of America, 1993), p. 271.

11   "The Freemen of Providence Submit Eight Reasons for Calling a Convention," in Bailyn (ed.), *The Debate*, p. 280.

12   See Rakove, *Original Meanings*, ch. V.

13   See Anthony Downs, *An Economic Theory of Democracy* (New York: Harper and Row, 1956).

14   See Michael X. Delli Carpini, and Scott Keeter, *What Americans Know about Politics and Why It Matters* (New Haven: Yale University Press, 1996). For an excellent overview, see Robert C. Luskin, "From Denial to Extenuation: Political Sophistication and Citizen Performance," in James H. Kuklinski (ed.), *Thinking about Political Psychology* (New York: Cambridge University Press, forthcoming, 2001).

15   I say "on a consistent and continuing basis" so as not to rule out the possibility that, episodically, there may be a crisis that produces what Bruce Ackerman calls a "constitutional moment." See below.

16   For a good overview, particularly of European experience, see Vernon Bogdanor, "Western Europe," in David Butler and Austin Ranney, *Referendums Around the World* (Washington, DC: AEI, 1994).

17   Bruce A. Ackerman, *We the People*, vol. 1: *Foundations* (Cambridge, MA: Harvard University Press, 1991), for the basic idea, and *We the People*, vol. 2: *Transformations* (Cambridge, MA: Harvard University Press, 1998), for detailed evidence. The "deliberative plebiscite" claim is made on p. 83 of volume 2.

18   While all of these efforts share a root idea, the citizens juries typically involve too small a number (12 or 18, the size of a modern jury) to be statistically representative; the consensus conferences employ self-selected samples recruited from newspaper adver-

tisements; the planning cells employ only a series of local random samples. For more on these differences see James S. Fishkin and Robert C. Luskin, "The Quest for Deliberative Democracy," *The Good Society*, vol. 9, no. 1 (1999), pp. 1–9.

19   See the seminal essay by Phil Converse and the enormous literature it stimulated (which I cannot review here): Philip Converse, "The Nature of Belief Systems in Mass Publics," in David E. Apter (ed.), *Ideology and Discontent* (pp. 206–61) (New York: Free Press, 1964). For a more recent take on this literature see John Zaller, *The Nature and Origins of Mass Opinion* (Cambridge: Cambridge University Press, 1992).

20   For more on how this works, see James S. Fishkin, *The Voice of the People: Public Opinion and Democracy* (New Haven: Yale University Press, 1997). See also the essays collected in Maxwell McCombs and Amy Reynolds (eds.), *A Poll with a Human Face: The National Issues Convention Experiment in Political Communication* (Mahwah, NJ: Lawrence Erlbaum Associates, 1999).

21   J. S. Mill, *Considerations on Representative Government* (New York: Prometheus Books, 1991), p. 79.

22   See James S. Fishkin, *The Voice of the People: Public Opinion and Democracy* (New Haven: Yale University Press, 1997), pp. 200–3.

23   See Joseph M. Bessette, *The Mild Voice of Reason: Deliberative Democracy and American National Government* (Chicago: University of Chicago Press, 1994), pp. 35–7, for this interpretation of Madison.

24   For a classic statement of the dilemma, see Hanna Pitkin, *The Concept of Representation* (Berkeley: University of California Press, 1967), ch. 7.

25   See Fishkin, *The Voice of the People*, ch. 5, for more on these strategies.

Bibliography

Ackerman, B. A. (1991). *We the People*, vol. 1: *Foundations*. Cambridge, MA: Harvard University Press.

——(1998). *We the People*, vol. 2: *Transformations*. Cambridge, MA: Harvard University Press.

Bessette, J. M. (1994). *The Mild Voice of Reason: Deliberative Democracy and American National Government*. Chicago: University of Chicago Press.

Delli Carpini, M. and S. Keeter (1996). *What Americans Know about Politics and Why It Matters*. New Haven: Yale University Press.

Elster, J. (ed.) (1998). *Deliberative Democracy*. Cambridge: Cambridge University Press.

Fishkin, J. S. (1991). *Democracy and Deliberation: New Directions for Democratic Reform*. New Haven: Yale University Press.

——(1997). *The Voice of the People: Public Opinion and Democracy*. New Haven: Yale University Press.

——and R. C. Luskin (1999). "The Quest for Deliberative Democracy." *The Good Society*, 9: 1–9.

Madison, J., A. Hamilton, and J. Jay (1987). *The Federalist Papers*. New York: Penguin Books (originally published 1788).

Manin, B. (1997). *The Principles of Representative Government*. Cambridge: Cambridge University Press.

McCombs, M. and A. Reynolds (eds) (1999). *The Poll with a Human Face*. Mahwah, NJ: Lawrence Erlbaum Associates.

Mill, J. S. (1991). *Considerations on Representative Government*. New York: Prometheus Books (originally published 1861).

Rakove, J. N. (1996). *Original Meanings: Politics and Ideas in the Making of the Constitution*. New York: Vintage Books.

Chapter 11

Citizenship and Pluralism

Daniel M. Weinstock

My intention in this essay is to canvass some of the major developments which have occurred within contemporary political philosophy as a result of the greater attention which writers have devoted to the issue of *social pluralism*. More specifically, I will be focusing on the various ways in which our understanding of what it means to be a *citizen* of a liberal democracy has been altered by the myriad phenomena which fall under the rubric of pluralism.

The essay will be divided into five parts. First, I will attempt to bring some order to our understanding of the principal concepts involved, namely pluralism and citizenship. Getting clear on these concepts will give us a clearer sense of the range of topics that need to be addressed. Next, I will discuss the question of whether a greater appreciation of the cultural pluralism of most modern societies requires that we extend the range of *rights* associated with the status of citizenship beyond the core of individual rights identified most famously by T. H. Marshall to include various kinds of *collective* rights. Third, I will discuss changes wrought by pluralism in our understanding of the characteristic *practices* of citizenship. What kinds of *activities* are characteristic of a plausible ideal of citizenship in a pluralist social context, and what norms should govern these activities? Reflecting on these questions will lead me to consider two distinct, but ultimately related questions: What norms should we impose upon citizens involved in the practice of democratic deliberation? And in a fourth section: What should be the relationship between the norms of the liberal democratic state and those of the free associations which make up the sphere of civil society?

Finally, I will address the vexed question of how the role of citizen should ideally inform our identities, the range of our affections, and the traits of character which determine how we comport ourselves in the public arena. Should our psychological economies be such that the role of citizen which we share with our *concitoyens* habitually trumps other, more particularistic aspects of our identities? Or is it appropriate in the context of a pluralist society for those aspects of our identities which bind to all of our fellow citizens to joust with more particularistic allegiances? And if the latter is the case, how can modern societies come to possess the kind of "social cement" required to sustain a minimal commonality of purpose?

These are the questions to which I will be turning my attention in the next few pages. Two caveats are in order before I begin: first, I will not try to provide an objective and exhaustive survey of all that has been written on the topic of pluralism in the past twenty years or so. Rather, I will engage critically with what I take to be the most important contributions to the area, and will not shy away from putting forward my own positions. My hope is that the reader will better be able to find her feet in these debates by encountering a (necessarily incomplete) episode of the debates rather than by being confronted with a hands-off description of the debates which have taken place. Second, the agenda set forth in this introduction, while copious enough, does not address all of the normative questions involved in a complete understanding of citizenship in the context of pluralist societies. In particular, I have had to omit a discussion of the normative principles surrounding the *acquisition* of citizenship. What principles can a polity justifiably invoke to distinguish members and non-members, and how should these principles respond to the social and political processes which have made modern societies as pluralistic as they are? There is much to say about the problems of immigration, naturalization, and the granting of refugee status, but it will have to await another occasion.[1]

I

The theory and practice of liberal democracy have been profoundly affected over the course of the past generation by the greater attention which theorists have devoted to the *pluralism* of modern societies. While this claim has become something of a truism for students of contemporary political philosophy, there is still something paradoxical about it. After all, it can be argued that liberal democratic theory received its original impetus from an appreciation of the great variety of interests and beliefs present in society, combined with a growing desire to manage this diversity in a peaceful manner. Many liberal theories, from Hobbes to Rawls and beyond, have for instance employed the device of the social contract as a way to dramatize the plurality of views and interests present in societies, and to justify the terms of political association to all citizens, regardless of their particular sets of beliefs and desires, provided only that they are rational. One of the problems which for example leads Hobbes to the conclusion that human beings will only be able to find peace and security by alienating their personal sovereignty to a Leviathan has to do with the fact that in the state of nature, core evaluative terms such as "good" and "evil" are defined subjectively by individuals as a function of their varying desires, appetites, hates and aversions (Hobbes, 1996, p. 35). And even liberals who were not drawn to the justificatory device of the contract, such as John Stuart Mill, viewed liberal institutions as primarily justified by serving as a bulwark against conformity and allowing individuality to flourish (Mill, 1982). Thus, it would seem, far from being of recent vintage, an appreciation of diversity has been at the heart of liberal democratic theory from its very inception. In what sense then can we really speak of a *new* appreciation of pluralism among liberal democratic theorists?

This observation, which will seem banal to anyone familiar with the liberal-democratic philosophical tradition, forces us to sharpen our understanding of the specific ways in which pluralism has been understood by contemporary thinkers. Two things seem relatively new about the present concern with pluralism. First, many contemporary thinkers have come to appreciate that the *cultural* diversity of modern polities poses problems for theories of justice and citizenship which have been understudied by previous generations of philosophers. This cultural diversity is a result of (at least) four processes. First, immigration, primarily, but not exclusively, to the societies of the "New World," has created societies of often quite staggering ethnic diversity. Second, colonialism has placed descendants of European colonists in contact with indigenous societies, both on the colonized territories, and increasingly as a result of the decolonization processes of the twentieth century, within the erstwhile colonial metropolises themselves. Third, the vagaries of state formation in the modern era have thrown different national groups together in multination states, either, as in the case of the United Kingdom, as a result of complex processes of conquest and treaty, or as in the case of many African states, as a consequence of the division of spoils by colonial powers. Fourth, and perhaps most controversially, there is a growing awareness, both among citizens and among theorists, that cultures are not necessarily *ethno*-cultures. Identities form and communities organize around quite different aspects of people's lives, to do (for example) with sexual preference, gender, and handicap.

All four of these processes are now, moreover, rightly perceived as giving rise to considerable problems for our traditional understanding of justice and citizenship. Gone is the assumption that immigrants can unproblematically be subjected to a process of assimilation and integration based solely upon the interests and cultural self understandings of the receiving society. Philosophers and politicians are now attempting to understand what can as a matter of justice be expected of immigrants; and they are also spelling out ways in which the receiving society itself must adapt to the fact of immigration, most importantly by putting forward a conception of shared citizenship which does not depend upon the kinds of "thick" shared understandings which are characteristic of communities with deep historical roots (see, e.g., Bader, 1997). The relationship of native communities to the societies formed as a result of (primarily European) colonialism and immigration is now viewed as a matter not (solely) of raw power but of justice. The question of the restitution owed to native communities for wrongs committed in the past is now part of the political agenda of many countries. And perhaps most significantly, the assumption that natives would in time simply assimilate into mainstream society, which informs such policy documents as Canada's assimilationist *White Paper*, no longer finds many advocates (Government of Canada, 1969). In its place, we find the idea, still far from realized, that the continuance of societies born of European expansion in places like Canada, New Zealand, and Australia must be compatible with meaningful institutions of self-government for native peoples, an idea which has found expression in the *Mabo* decision in Australia, the Nisga'a treaty in Canada, and the Waitangi tribunal in New Zealand. See, for example, Cook and Lindau (2000), Sharpe (1997), and Tully (1995). And the search for principled grounds upon which to base relations between nations within multination states has of late taken on particular urgency, both because geopolitical realities make for the full realization of the "nationalist principle," according to which each nation should ideally be able to form its own state, and because there is a growing recognition of the fact that federal arrangements between partially self-governing political communities represents a plausible political response to the increasingly continental and global economic and informational processes, one that avoids the dystopia of a world-state. John Stuart Mill's assertion in *Considerations on Representative Government* that a shared national culture is required as a condition of the viability of institutions of democratic representation today seems completely out of tune with the resolutely multicultural nature of many (most?) modern societies (Mill, 1991). Finally, some citizens whose identities are bound up with their membership in non-ethno-cultural groups have come to believe that if immigration and multinationality warrant that highly unified accounts of citizenship be modified to reflect recognition of ethno-cultural difference, than it should also be altered so as to reflect, as it were, different forms of difference (Isin and Wood, 1999; Young, 1990).

A recognition of the relevance of cultural pluralism to normative theorizing about citizenship and justice has thus contributed significantly to renewing political philosophy's agenda. A second important change on the landscape of political philosophy has had to do with *value pluralism*. There has been an increased appreciation of the fact that there are a number of incommensurable values and corresponding ways of life which are all legitimate objects of human aspiration, and that different citizens can make different, but equally legitimate choices within that set. Individual achievement vs. loyalty to community, spirituality vs. materialism, political involvement vs. the private sphere, all of these rival pairs present values which are only compossible to a limited degree, and yet Reason does not univocally incline for one or the other sides of these dualities. It is, moreover, a signal achievement of the institutions of freedom which liberal democracies have created that citizens feel increasingly empowered to come up with their own specific ways of ordering the range of incompatible values which presents itself to them – to engage freely in what John Stuart Mill called "experiments in living."

Why should an appreciation of value pluralism alter the task of political philosophy? After all, it at first glance resembles the kind of problem already noticed by Hobbes, and which on his estimation called for the establishment of the Leviathan, namely that we all define good and evil according to our own personal idiosyncrasies, but that peaceful and secure communal existence requires that we arrive at a shared enforceable conception of these terms.

The difference, to put matters bluntly, is that theorists now doubt what had been an assumption of social contractarians, namely that there is a shared conception of reason which can be repaired to in order to set the terms of political life, and which cuts across citizens' quite different conceptions of their own individual good (Rawls, 1993; D'Agostino, 1996; Gray, 2000). At its deepest level, value pluralism tells against the assumption that conceptions of rationality are ever completely value-free. Supposedly neutral conceptions of rationality which one encounters in the contractarian constructions of theorists from Hobbes to Rawls actually incline toward some – and away from other – conceptions of the good life. So legitimating discourse – the kind of argument which is supposed to reconcile all citizens, through reason, to the principles and institutions of liberal democracy – cannot be thought of as had previously been done. If liberal democracies are to be presented as legitimate from the point of view of all reasonable conceptions of the good, it will have to be by reference to something other than a supposedly neutral conception of human rationality. The most important theoretical task to which value pluralism gives rise is thus to find a way of legitimating a liberal-democratic political order to individuals and groups whose conceptions of the good are based upon defensible orderings of the various values in function of which human beings typically orient their lives, ones that nonetheless incline them away from liberal democracy.

In sum, political philosophers have deepened their construal of social pluralism in at least two ways. First, they have recognized that cultural pluralism is a permanent feature of most modern liberal democracies, and that it renders suspect conceptions of citizenship and of justice premised upon an (often unspoken) assumption of cultural homogeneity. Second, many political philosophers have come to realize that value pluralism poses a deeper problem for the legitimacy and justification of liberal-democratic norms than had previously been appreciated, in that it forces us to reconsider whether there exists a shared conception of rationality with which we might neutrally broker the conflicts and differences to which the differing conceptions of the good life present in society give rise. How do these changes in our philosophical understanding of pluralism affect our conception of citizenship? Before we can answer that question, we must get a clearer sense of citizenship's semantic field: just what does the term traditionally denote?

Few concepts in politics are as vulnerable to the risk of conceptual overload as that of citizenship (Kymlicka and Norman, 1994, 2000). As some contemporary commentators have noted, the term has come to mean all things to all people. A perusal of some recent writing on citizenship makes an emotivist analysis of the concept tempting: in the same ways as A. J. Ayer once argued that describing an action or an agent as good is simply a way of expressing our (non-rational) approval of it, some contemporary authors, in claiming that such and such a policy or practice is vital for citizenship, simply seem to mean that they think well of it. Use of the term sometimes seems to have no other purpose than to add normative weight to a policy, institution or practice that could just as aptly be described without reference to citizenship.

The concept of citizenship therefore needs to be disciplined. I propose to do so, first of all, by identifying five semantic fields with which the concept of citizenship seems to be inextricably tied. First, and perhaps most fundamentally, citizenship denotes a *status*. To be a citizen is to be a member of a political community. There is, if not today, at least at the historical inception of the concept, a *contrastive* dimension to the notion of citizenship. My status as citizen confers upon me a dignity and standing which non-citizens do not possess. In the modern era, this status has been identified most closely with a second dimension of citizenship: those bundles of *rights* which citizens enjoy *as* members of a particular political community. One of the principal responsibilities of the liberal-democratic state is, on the modern understanding, to protect its members in their enjoyment of these rights. In T. H. Marshall's canonical formulation, these rights are of three kinds: civil rights, which protect citizens against the potentially tyrannical use of state authority; political rights, through which all members of the community are allowed to participate in democratic self-government; and socio-economic rights, which guarantee a minimal level of welfare for all citizens, and in the absence of which the granting of the aforementioned civil and political rights would be empty.

While they are, in the modern understanding, connected to the secure possession of rights, the dignity and standing which attach to citizenship have historically also been connected to a third dimension to which the concept of citizenship is conceptually connected: that of self-government. Citizens are political *actors*, rather than merely passive subjects of political authorities. *Any* political community can confer membership, and can thus distinguish between insiders and outsiders. But only free, self-governing polities can make *citizens* of subjects, for only they can give members a share in self-government. Thus, the idea of citizenship seems to be conceptually connected to that of *democracy*.

This aspect of citizenship's semantic field is tied in to a fourth. Citizens, as opposed to subjects, are *active* in the definition and administration of a common good. And so, there must be a range of *practices* characteristic of citizenship through which members manifest their active status. Members are citizens not only through what they *are*, but through what they *do*.

Fifth, and finally, citizenship denotes an *identity*. To be a citizen means to have a set of psychological dispositions which binds one to one's fellow citizens, and an ensemble of psychological dispositions or "virtues" which facilitate one's daily interactions with them. To be a citizen is to *identify* to at least some degree with the political community to which one belongs, and to be disposed to behave toward one's fellow citizens in ways which promote the stability and unity of the community.

I do not pretend that this list is exhaustive. But it does provide us with a sense of the *density* of the concept of citizenship. It denotes (at least) an individual's status as a *member* of a *self-governing* political community, one which protects the individual in her enjoyment of *rights*. It also points to characteristic *practices* of citizenship, and to dispositions and traits of character which are in play in these practices. Finally, it refers to an important aspect of individual *identity*.

A second preliminary clarification: though rooted in institutional and political reality, the concept of citizenship possesses an inescapably *normative* dimension. True, we can ask ourselves what conception of citizenship is at work in the laws, institutions, and practices of different societies. The rights of citizens, and the conditions which individuals must satisfy in order to count as citizens of a given society, are given in the positive law of the societies in question. Moreover, one can fruitfully inquire empirically into the extent to which citizenship informs the identities of individuals in different societies (for example, see Johnston Conover, 1995), and into the ways in which citizens of a particular society engage in practices through which they evince their practical commitment to the common good (for example, see Wuthnow, 1998). What's more, purely normative theorizing about citizenship risks irrelevance if it is not grounded in institutional reality. More than other political ideals, such as equality and freedom (though, I would argue, for those as well), citizenship is realized in and through concrete institutions, rather than being a disembodied ideal floating above these institutions. So normative reflection about citizenship must be continuous with a more pragmatic, institution-based form of reasoning (Bauböck, 1994; Carens, 2000). Nonetheless, citizenship also functions in our conceptual repertoire as an ideal, as a goal toward which both democracies and individuals must aspire. Thus, we can also ask what rights a democratic community *ought* to grant its citizens, or how it *ought* to grant membership (e.g., to non-member residents), if it is to realize the values intrinsic to the ideal of democracy. And we can also ask ourselves what virtues and dispositions of character ought to be displayed by citizens when they interact with one another in the public sphere, or what practices they ought to engage in, in order to satisfy the norms of the "role-morality" of citizenship. Though the present essay will be focused predominantly on such normative questions, I will attempt not to lose sight of the institutional questions which also necessarily arise in any discussion of citizenship.

This overview provides us with a clearer view of the range of questions which should be addressed in order to get a fix on the impact which pluralism has had on our understanding of citizenship. Our inquiry should ideally touch on the ways in which both cultural and value pluralism have impacted both on the institutional reality and on the ideal conceptions related to the multiple dimensions of citizenship, including the rights and practices which citizenship involves, the virtues of character to which it refers, and the share which citizens should have in self-government. This essay only scratches the surface of the vast agenda to which this brief statement points, but I hope that it will provide the reader with a fair idea of the work which lies ahead.

II

Liberal political philosophers have traditionally thought of rights as attaching to individual agents, and as justified by reference to the fundamental interests of individual agents. According to Ronald Dworkin's influential formulation, rights function as "trumps" against actions of a government which, while they might be justified from a consequentialist standpoint which considers only how laws and policies affect a collection of individuals considered as an aggregate, are incompatible with the fundamental interests of *some* members of society (Dworkin, 1977). According to this view, rights protect individuals against the risk of the "tyranny of the majority" (Mill, 1982).

In recent years, this quasi-orthodoxy has been shaken by an argument which was first formulated by Joseph Raz, but which finds its most complete expression and systematization in the work of Will Kymlicka (Raz, 1986; Raz and Margalit, 1990; Kymlicka, 1987, 1995). The argument holds that some fundamental individual interests can only be realized if individuals have secure membership in groups, and holds further that this security of membership can only be ensured if the groups in question are granted significant self-government rights. The fundamental interest at stake is one to which liberal political philosophers have traditionally attached signal importance. Indeed, the argument claims that we have a fundamental interest in being autonomous rational choosers, capable of arriving at a rational life-plan, and of revising it if need be, but that this interest can only be satisfied through membership in a secure, viable "societal culture," one which provides the individual with a range of options across the full range of fields of human endeavor, and with an evaluative grid on the basis of which to ascertain the value of these options.

Now, for most people, these cultural conditions for the exercise of the capacities involved in autonomous choice are easily satisfied. Members of the majority national culture of most modern states automatically gain access to the requisite cultural resources of their societal culture. But this is not the case for members of minority cultures. They face the assimilationist pressures which being part of a minority group in a larger social whole almost inevitably involves. What's more, the attitude of members of the majority culture toward them is typically one of (at best) benign neglect, and (at worst) overt hostility. Fairness thus requires that members of such cultures be able to adopt special measures to allow their members to avail themselves of the cultural resources required to realize their potential as autonomous choosers just as members of the majority culture can. But, the argument runs, such measures cannot be cashed out simply in terms of individual rights. Individuals acting alone cannot ensure the viability of the institutional infrastructure required to keep a societal culture alive. Thus, the argument, if successful, shows that members of minority societal cultures require for the satisfaction of their fundamental interest in being able to act as autonomous choosers that the *groups* to which they belong be granted collective rights. And it does so in a way which should seem unobjectionable to liberals, that is, by identifying an *individual* interest taken to be sufficiently fundamental to warrant its satisfaction being immunized from the impact of majoritarian political procedures and other sociological forces which might generate assimilationist pressures.

Kymlicka's work has been subjected to a great deal of critical scrutiny, which I do not want to rehearse in the context of this essay.[2] I want instead to show that arguments such as Kymlicka's are perched uncomfortably between two quite different positions, both of which leave a number of questions to do with the form which citizenship should take in pluralist democracies unanswered.

Note, to begin with, that an argument linking group rights to individual interests in autonomous choosing via the notion of societal culture, if successful, would involve attributing such rights to a fairly narrow range of groups. Indeed, only societal cultures, that is cultures that already function to a significant degree as self-standing societies, with an adequate range of economic and political institutions, qualify. What's more, only societal cultures that *promote autonomy* meet the justificatory test which Kymlicka's theory sets forth. Presumably, minority cultural groups which passed the "societal culture" hurdle, but which (for example) set significant obstacles in the path of women who aspire to non-traditional lives, would lack the normative justification which the argument imposes upon aspirants to group rights. In effect, therefore, it justifies granting self-government rights to fully formed national minorities such as those which one finds in Quebec, Catalonia, and Corsica, and to a handful of other minority national cultures that find themselves associated to other, larger national groups within multination states.

There are reasons to oppose limiting the argument to societal cultures as morally arbitrary. Many different kinds of groups have played quite significant roles in providing their members with the wherewithal required for autonomous choice. For example, it is plausible to claim that the existence of gay associations of various kinds have made a gay lifestyle more readily "choosable," and have (among other things) sheltered gays from the self-loathing and self-doubt that comes from taking on the evaluations which the broader society imposes. Kymlicka seems to restrict the range of groups to which group rights can be attributed because of two unwarranted elisions: first, the assumption that group rights are necessarily *self-government* rights, which only groups possessed of significant institutional infrastructure can in fact exercise. In fact, there are a full range of group rights which do not require such powers, including, for example, exemption from specific laws in the broader society (Levy, 1997). And second, the assumption that because only societal cultures *in fact want* to exercise self-government rights, only they *ought* to be able to (Carens, 2000).

What I want to focus on however, is the strong perfectionist basis of the argument. Groups are valuable, and merit protection, if and only if they are structured in a way that promotes autonomy. This means that groups which, in non-coercive ways, encourage their members to adopt (say) traditional ways and not to value the full range of options available in the broader society and the capacities involved in being able to choose among them, should in principle not be able to claim group rights. Indeed, the perfectionist basis of the argument could be made to support a stronger argument, to the effect that a broader, autonomy-promoting culture could be warranted in taking steps to *eliminate* such ways of life from the repertoire from which citizens can draw.

Some perfectionists are willing to bite this perfectionist bullet (Raz, 1986; Hurka, 1994). It sits uncomfortably, however, with Kymlicka's own professed espousal of the importance of state neutrality (Kymlicka, 1989). And more generally, it is incompatible with a commitment towers value pluralism. If there are really a number of different, equally acceptable ways of ordering the values which legitimately lay claim to individuals' allegiances, then organizing the affairs of the state in a manner which privileges one such ordering is problematic. Thus, it would seem that an argument designed to accommodate cultural pluralism falls foul of the strictures which value pluralism seems at first glance to impose.

If we are unwilling to follow the perfectionist route, one option that is open to us is to broaden our understanding of the value of group membership. Groups matter to individuals because they allow them to realize a number of different fundamental interests. An argument of this kind can be found in the writings of various authors who have defended some form of what has come to be called "identity politics." I will focus my remarks on Iris Marion Young's important book, *Justice and the Politics of Difference* (though see also Minow, 1990).

Young claims that group identity is constitutive of human individuality. Whether we acknowledge it or not, we are (to employ a Heideggerian phrase) "thrown" into roles, implicit meanings and evaluations which our group membership foists upon us. Group identity poses a problem for a just society because, when it is unacknowledged, dominant groups will impose what are in the end one group's values upon society as a whole, and will tend to view these values not as partial and perspective-bound, but as "impartial" and "universal," and thus as appropriate to the public sphere, and will relegate the values and self-understanding of other groups to the "private" sphere. Ascribing rights to groups is a way of righting this systematic bias which would otherwise infect the body politic. If group membership ineliminably shapes our identities and our values, then a concern for equality and fairness would allow *all* groups to influence the public sphere. For Young, this would mean, among other things, group representation in legislative assemblies and group vetoes (Young, 1990: 184).

What interests me in the present context is that Young's conception of social groups is fluid and expansive. She imposes no substantive constraint on which groups "count" from the point of view of a theory of justice. She recognizes that group formation in a given society will depend in large measure upon the vagaries of social interaction within that society. And she argues that group membership is a function not of objective criteria but of a mutual sense of affinity and of subjective identification (ibid.: 172). Thus, on the face of it, her conception of group rights allows us to reconcile the demands of cultural pluralism as well as those of value pluralism. If it is the case that group membership is of fundamental importance to human beings, to the point that they ought to be protected in their membership through the attribution of group rights, then we ought not, absent a convincing argument to the contrary, impose *a priori* limitations on the kinds of groups to which rights can legitimately be attributed.

What should we make of this argument? Let me make three observations about it. First, there is an incompatibility between two claims which partisans of identity politics such as Young are wont to make (Miller, 2000a). On the one hand, they claim that individual identities in conditions of pluralism are fluid and complex. Members of modern societies belong to a number of different groups, and their identities reflect the multiplicity of their attachments. What's more, they are not irredeemably wedded to any one group. Conditions of social pluralism tend to encourage them to move between groups. Citizens of modern pluralistic societies are, on a view such as Young's, de facto what arguments like Raz's and Kymlicka's would have them be de jure, that is, autonomous, unrooted choosers.

But legal and political instruments such as rights presuppose less fluidity. Rights must be attributed to identifiable bodies (representing women, gays, single parents, racial minorities, etc.). And by their very nature, such bodies will be much less fluid and complex than the members they will then claim to represent. The alternative seems to be the following: either limit the attribution of rights to individuals, as liberals have traditionally insisted, and allow individuals freely to concoct their identities out of the various cultural materials at their disposal in civil society, or else attribute rights to groups, which will be much more monolithic than individual identities tend to be, and therefore just as unrepresentative of the real complexity of individual life as the "impartial public sphere" decried by partisans of identity politics had supposedly been.

Second, and relatedly, the acknowledgment that group membership is a fundamental interest of individuals, one that warrants the attribution of group rights, does not imply that just *any* group right will be justified on the basis of the argument from an individual's interest. If the foregoing arguments have merit, it follows that individuals have an interest *both* in being able to belong to groups, *and* in being able to exit groups as they see fit. Rights which would secure the former, but not the latter interest, would thus not be based on a complete understanding of the full range of interests which individuals have with respect to groups. Now, rights can appropriately be termed *group* rights for a variety of different reasons: first, individuals can claim and exercise weakly collective rights *as* members of groups; secondly, collective agents mandated by the members of a group can claim *moderately collective* rights which are then to be exercised by individual members of the group; thirdly, collective agents can both claim and exercise *fully* collective rights on behalf of their members (Bauböck, 1994). The problem which stems from the gap between the fluidity and complexity of individual identities and the comparatively greater fixity and homogeneity of groups can be at least in part circumvented by limiting the legitimate range of group rights to those drawn from the first two categories just sketched, for only they reliably preserve the optional character of group membership, which, I have claimed, also reflects a fundamental interest of individuals.

Third, it has been claimed that the recognition by the state of group rights risks fragmenting the public sphere and undermining the viability of democratic institutions. The fear of faction has been a concern of democratic theorists at least since Rousseau. The claim is that if we are members of particular groups first, and *citizens* second (if at all), then the commonality of purpose which should bind citizens of a democratic polity becomes impossible. The functioning of democratic institutions on this view requires that disputed questions be resolved from the point of view of the common good, rather than from the perspective of this or that sectional interest (Miller, 2000b). For many contemporary theorists, this implies that, above and beyond their particular allegiances, citizens of a political community should share a *national identity* (Miller, 1995; Tamir, 1993).

Attention to the full range of conceivable group rights allows us to ally these concerns at least to some degree. Rights which grant groups significant degrees of autonomy and self-government with respect to the broader society might have this effect. That is, they may encourage groups to withdraw from the affairs of the broader society to create more or less autarkic enclaves. This is most likely to occur through the granting of what I have above termed *fully* collective rights, as they are most likely to provide collective agents with the institutional wherewithal to create pockets of sovereignty within the broader society.

Yet many group rights which, on their face, exempt members of groups from norms which apply in the broader society, might have the opposite effect, namely, of fostering a feeling of greater inclusion and stakeholding. To invoke a Canadian case, exempting Sikhs from the norms which govern the headgear of members of the Royal Canadian Mounted Police facilitates and promotes a greater sense of inclusion on the part of minority groups. It conveys the message that they are welcome into the public institutions of the broader society, and that they need not abandon their particular identities in order to be considered full citizens. Similarly, and as I will argue more fully below, allowing members of religious groups to make arguments in the public arena based on their "comprehensive conceptions of the good" is likely to lessen their sense of alienation from the broader society. In general, allowing particularities to manifest themselves in the public arena need not give rise to social fragmentation. On the contrary, it can encourage a sense of belonging.

This is not to say that it is never justified to grant fully collective rights to some groups. Many political communities incorporate a plurality of "political cultures of self-determination" to borrow Anna Moltchanova's helpful phrase (Moltchanova, 2001), that is, cultures whose members think of themselves as constituting an autonomous and self-standing political entity. Though fate and political circumstance may have thrown them in with other such cultures within the confines of the same state, the members of such cultures think of their political identities as defined in the first instance by their political culture. Their allegiance to the broader state is primarily instrumental: they identify with it to the degree that it provides a congenial political context within which to exercise self-determination. In such cases, concerns about the fragmenting effects to which fully collective rights give rise are out of place: the members of such groups *already* think of themselves as separate. The challenge for states that encompass them is not to make them abandon their political identities in favor of an identity focused on the broader state. History shows that "nation-building" of this kind can only be carried out by flagrantly illiberal means, involving, for example, the prohibition of schooling in local languages, and that its achievements are always fragile, as has dramatically been demonstrated in recent years by nationalist stirrings in some regions of France, a country which is traditionally thought of as among the most unitary in the world. Rather, the challenge is to strengthen the *instrumental* tie which binds such cultures to the state, by creating an institutional setting and a political culture which is likely to foster the sense that members of such groups will be more likely to exercise meaningful political self-determination within the broader state than outside of it. This is another way of saying that *federalism* is a solution well-suited to multination states wanting to stem the centrifugal force of nationalism without resorting to the illiberal policies which have traditionally been used by nation-builders.[3]

The attribution of fully collective rights poses greater problems with respect to groups of (in Jeff Spinner's useful phrase) "partial citizens" (Spinner, 1994). Such groups do not seek to establish complete systems of law parallel to those of the broader society. Rather, they seek sovereignty over selected aspects of community life, either to shelter themselves from laws and institutions of the broader society that offend against fundamental beliefs (for example, some ultra-orthodox Jewish communities have asked for the right to have their own para-medical teams respond to medical emergencies within their own communities, so as to ensure that the care of bodies will conform to Jewish norms), or to resist assimilationist pressures exercised by the broader society (as in the famous *Yoder* case in which an Old Amish family requested that their children be exempt from laws governing length of school attendance obtaining elsewhere in the United States).

No single principle exists that would allow liberal-democratic societies to adjudicate such cases. Decisions as to whether or not to recognize such "semi-sovereignties" must be taken within the context of a plurality of relevant but conflicting norms which do not always have the same weight across all cases. On the one hand, if liberal democracies really want to create a context conducive to a variety of different "experiments in living" and responsive to the truth (if it is one) of value pluralism, then they will have to provide communities organized around conceptions of the good which stand in some tension to the values traditionally associated with liberal democracy with the requisite institutional means. A commitment to pluralism is empty lip-service if it is not accompanied by a willingness to allow groups to set their own rules on questions which they deem central to their survival (Spinner, 1994). On the other hand, liberal democracies have a responsibility toward *all* their citizens to uphold their fundamental rights. Some group norms stand in tension, and in some cases flatly contradict, such norms. The right to bodily integrity is such a right, and so practices such as female circumcision must be opposed, even if they are deemed central to group identity by some. But many cases cannot be dealt with in such a black and white way. The family and property laws which obtain in some communities are not in line with liberal-democratic norms of sexual equality. Should they be systematically over-ridden by the laws of the broader society, or should judges affirm community law (Réaume, 2000a, 2000b; Levy, 2000)? Is there a threshold in the spectrum of rights beyond which group norms must be overridden? And if so, how do we set out to define it? Is an "unforced consensus on human rights" (in Charles Taylor's helpful phrase) possible?

Another relevant normative parameter has to do with fairness across the whole society. It is felt by some writers that the exemptions and powers which some groups claim as a condition of the viability of their ways of life cannot be justified from a point of view which would consider the interests of all citizens equally. Jeremy Waldron has argued, for example, that the land claims made by aboriginal groups as a way of correcting past injustices stand in tension with norms of dis-tributive justice. The resources of the political community as a whole should in his view be distributed in a way which benefits all members of society (Waldron, 1992). And there has been growing resentment in recent years against ultra-orthodox Jews being exempted from military service in Israel. Military security, it is felt, is a precious public good, one which the ultra-orthodox benefit from, but to which they do not contribute.[4]

In sum, the decision to grant group rights to "quasi-citizens" raises complex questions which cannot be resolved by invoking a single "master principle." Con-siderations of pluralism, basic right and fairness will always bear on such cases, but the weight which should be attributed to one or another of these considerations will vary from case to case. Normative discussion of group rights in such cases will thus necessarily be deeply contextual (Carens, 2000).

Let me summarize the main themes that have emerged from this somewhat mean-dering discussion. The question which has guided my inquiry in this section has been the following: Should a consideration of social pluralism lead us to recon-sider the canonical Marshallian trinity of civil, political and social rights to include *group* rights? A consideration of Will Kymlicka's influential work led to the con-clusion that if we do consider group membership as representing an individual interest sufficiently fundamental to warrant the attribution of group rights, we must do so in a way which does not privilege autonomy-promoting groups. A discussion of Iris Young's more expansive conception of group membership led us to refine our view of the complex interests which individuals have with respect to groups. They have an interest in belonging, to be sure, but they also have an interest in being able to view their belonging as *optional*. Reconciling these inter-ests would involve limiting the extension of *fully* collective rights which empower collective agents to take decisions *for* their members, and attempting to secure the goods of community through what I termed "weakly" and "moderately collec-tive" rights. Finally, we considered cases in which the extension of fully collective rights of self-government seems legitimate: first, and most obviously, they are justified both morally and prudentially in the case of multination states. And second (and more problematically), more limited fully collective rights covering some aspects of community life can in certain contexts be appropriate in the case of communities of "quasi-citizens."

Some of the themes which will be at the center of our attention in the following sections of this essay have already been broached. First, the question of the degree of unity required to sustain democratic institutions has been raised via the concern, voiced *inter alia* by David Miller, that the granting of group rights risks fragmenting the public sphere to an unacceptable degree. We will take up in Section V the question of whether "liberal nationalists" such as Miller have been right to insist upon a high degree of national unity as a condition of the viability of liberal-democratic institutions. Second, we have also broached the issue of whether or not it is appropriate for citizens engaged in democratic deliberation in a pluralist society to do so in the terms of their comprehensive conceptions of the good. Section IV will thus lead us to a consideration of the arguments of present-day "deliberative democrats." Before that, however, I want to consider the question of what the characteristic practices of citizenship might be in conditions of social pluralism. In particular, I want to examine the advantages and disadvantages of an active conception of citizenship focused on participation in the institutions of *deliberative democracy.*

III

What are the distinctive *practices* which can be associated with a conception of citizenship appropriate to modern pluralistic mass societies? Traditionally, they have been of two kinds. The role of "citizen" involves deliberating with fellow citizens about the laws and policies which will govern their common affairs, and acting so as to promote a common good.

The paradigmatic activities of citizenship can obviously not simply mimic the ideal (or idealized) view of citizenship which comes down to us from the thinkers of the ancient Greek *polis* and from the writers of the Italian Renaissance. Theirs were small-scale political communities, whose full-fledged members probably only numbered a small fraction of the overall population. Women, slaves and servants, metics, peasants and others were excluded from the prerogatives and responsibilities of citizenship. The remaining male notables who made up the bulk of the citizenry of Greek *polei* and Renaissance city-states were beset by neither of the principal obstacles to effective active citizenship which characterize most modern societies. They had to deal neither with the challenge of number, nor with that of pluralism. The size of city-states, coupled with the substantial restrictions on citizenship which they tended to impose, meant that the affairs of the city could be dealt with on a face-to-face basis. And it is plausible to suppose that, despite their competition and rivalries, citizens of such city-states were not as deeply divided on questions of the good life as citizens of modern societies are.

How is effective citizenship possible in modern, pluralistic mass societies? How can citizens participate effectively in the administration of a common good despite the anonymity which appears to be an unavoidable correlate of size? And how can they deliberate about the laws and policies which are to regulate their affairs when their perspectives on key issues are informed by such different worldviews?

Many theorists have in recent years been tempted by an answer to the first question which accords great importance to the role played in modern mass democracies by the institutions of *civil society*. As understood by these writers, civil society is made up by the vast array of "intermediate bodies," lying as it were "between" the state and the individual, in which citizens freely associate around an issue of common concern, and act politically in order to realize a shared interest. These associations include trade unions, neighborhood associations, environmental groups, philanthropic associations such as the Shriners or the Elks, and a wide variety of others.

Though republican thinkers such as Rousseau have viewed them with suspicion as encouraging faction, the thinkers of liberal democracy have in general viewed them as performing essential functions for the health of society. Alexis de Tocqueville praised the thriving civil society which he saw blossoming in early nineteenth-century America, for in his view the organizations of civil society are "schools for democracy" (de Tocqueville, 1981). Among more recent authors, Hannah Arendt (1950) argued that free associations lying as it were "between" the state and the individual are a vital bulwark against totalitarianism. When individuals become atomized and withdrawn into the private sphere, they are on her view easy prey for the seductive rhetoric of totalitarian leaders.[5]

Simplifying and systematizing somewhat, let me point out a number of distinct functions which civil society is taken to perform in the context of modern democracies, as well as some dangers and drawbacks that have also been associated with it. First, and most obviously, the associations of civil society represent for the vast majority of citizens the only possible focus for active, effective citizenship. Only through their participation in smaller-scale associations will citizens be able to act concretely in association with their fellows in the pursuit of *a* common good. What's more, a thriving civil society rife with associations organized around a plurality of different goods gives concrete expression to the good of pluralism: if we think it important that individuals be able to choose between a wide range of life options, it is essential that they be able to avail themselves of a wealth of associations bringing together like-minded individuals. Through associations, options gain concreteness. Thus, to the extent that there are goods which individuals can only achieve through participation of this kind, civil society performs a crucial role as a means to *individuals'* good.

Second, the organizations of civil society can perform a number of functions crucial to the functioning of the broader society. De Tocqueville thought that participation in the associations of civil society would wrench individuals from privatism, and instill virtues of public-spiritedness and cooperation crucial to the viability of democratic societies as a whole. He has been followed by a number of recent writers (see e.g., Macedo, 1996) in stressing the *educative* function of civil society.

Third, some have argued that civil society is crucial to the successful design and implementation of public policy (Habermas, 1996; Cohen and Rogers, 1995). When previously voiceless individuals associate, they can give expression to needs which would otherwise have gone undetected by even well-intentioned public policy designers. They can also perform an important function in the successful *implementation* of public policy. Indeed, as we know from bitter experience, public policy motivated by the most morally admirable motives can run aground for lack of appropriate *context-sensitivity* (Scott, 1998). Partnerships between the state and civil society can help to alleviate this unfortunate tendency of public-policy implementation.

Fourth, as Nancy Rosenblum (1998) has recently argued, even organizations of civil society whose members join together in the name of values and beliefs that run counter to liberal-democratic norms – that might indeed be viewed as threats – may end up contributing to the overall health of liberal democracies. Indeed, such organizations can in certain cases channel destructive, anti-liberal energies in relatively benign ways.

Thus, civil society can provide individuals with the goods of association, and can provide them with concrete options embodying different values, interests and ways of life. It can contribute to effective public-policy design and implementation by articulating needs and allowing for context-sensitive application. And it can channel potentially destructive passions so as to minimize the risk that they will manifest themselves in deleterious ways.

On the other hand, there are risks attached to a thriving civil society from the point of view of the overall health of society. De Tocqueville's optimism about civil society, that the virtues of cooperation and public-spiritedness acquired by associating with others in small-scale association will transfer smoothly to the larger society, is based upon an assumption which does not seem entirely justified, namely, that the increased *ability* to cooperate with others will be matched by an increasing *willingness* to do so. Yet there is the risk that, as one's identity and interests become increasingly wrapped up with a particular group in civil society, one will come to see policy issues which bear on the interests of all one's fellow citizens through the narrower prism constituted by one's group identity. Public policy needs to be assessed from a point of view that encompasses – and adjudicates between – all relevant social interests, and there is no guarantee that participation in civil society will encourage the development of the virtues of character that would incline one to take up this point of view. On the contrary, there are risks that too divided and fractured a civil society will for any policy proposal give rise to quite partisan responses (Young, 2000).

What's more, as Kymlicka and Norman have noted, many civil-society associations will tend to give rise to traits of character and dispositions which are in considerable tension with the values of liberal democracy. Whereas liberal democrats tend to encourage equality and freedom of individual conscience, many associations are built around subservience and authority. So on the face of it, it would seem that at least some segments of civil society promote virtues which are directly antithetical to those which liberal democracy requires.[6]

Finally (and here we touch upon a set of questions which were already broached in Section II), some organizations in civil society embody illiberal *norms*, both by restricting membership in ways which seem unacceptable from the standpoint of liberal values (the much-discussed case of the US Jaycees' ban on female membership comes to mind in this context), and by imposing unjust norms *among* members (think of the bar which many organized religious groups place upon the right of women to occupy various positions, or that which the Boy Scouts in the United States impose upon the ability of Gays to serve as Scout leaders).

Especially given the tendency which some groups in civil society have of offending against core liberal-democratic values such as equality and autonomy, should the liberal-democratic state be in the business of *regulating* civil society, most notably by adopting various more or less coercive measures designed to promote liberal-democratic values *within* groups? As had been the case with the question of whether or not the state ought to extend group rights or not, this question does not admit of a simple answer. Various normative considerations seem relevant, and they do not weigh in exactly the same way from case to case. Obviously, the liberal-democratic state's commitment to values such as equality and autonomy rings hollow if it is not at times willing to stand up for them in cases of egregious violation. What's more, the invocation which some might be inclined to make of the public/private distinction in order to justify state inaction (on the view that the state should only uphold liberal-democratic values in the *public* sphere, whereas civil-society associations are better classed as belonging to the *private* sphere) would not bear much critical scrutiny. We now recognize that rights can be violated in the private arena in ways which warrant state intervention (it is now no longer considered contradictory to claim that a man can rape his wife), and civil-society associations do not cleanly fit either side of the public/private dichotomy in any case. Membership in organizations like the Jaycees has an impact on the distribution of opportunities, and so properly falls under the purview of a theory of justice. A final argument for the regulation of civil society by the state has been provided by Cohen and Rogers: if we value civil society because it permits the articulation of needs that would otherwise go unheeded, the state should positively *encourage* the creation of groups in particularly disenfranchised and voiceless segments of society (Cohen and Rogers, 1995).

On the other hand, freedom of association, surely a cornerstone of liberal-democratic societies, must to some degree imply the freedom of associations to define terms of membership, and the right to some latitude in the organization of internal affairs. And to the extent that liberals value pluralism, and the ability to choose among a wide array of options, they must accept that not all associations will be microcosms of liberal-democratic society as a whole. Perhaps, as Jeff Spinner (1994) has argued, liberal democrats should view values such as freedom and equality as sufficiently protected by the important place they occupy in the broader society, by the fact that they inform the backdrop for all the associations of a liberal-democratic public sphere, and by the assurance of a substantial right of exit for all members of groups within civil society.

The natural conclusion of the foregoing remarks is that the state should step in to regulate civil society in cases of egregious violation of liberal-democratic norms, but should refrain from doing so otherwise. Just where the threshold of egregiousness is located is, however, a vexed question which, thankfully, lies beyond the scope of this essay.

IV

Regardless of the precise place where this line gets drawn, it remains the case that, in the context of mass societies characterized by a plurality of different views of the good life, the obstacles to citizenship which pluralism and number represent can only be overcome by participation in the free associations of civil society. Surely, though, this participation does not exhaust what it means to be a citizen. One of the central dimensions of citizenship has traditionally had to do not with *action* but with talk. Being a citizen means taking an interest in public affairs, and deliberating upon issues of common concern with one's fellow citizens in a public-spirited manner. The Greek *agora* and the New England town hall are privileged sites of the practice of citizenship, for it is in fora such as these that citizens attempt to overcome their differences in order to arrive at common laws and policies.

There has, moreover, probably never been as much philosophical attention devoted to the norms which should govern the practices of deliberation as there has been in recent years. This is due to the impact that value pluralism has had upon one of the principal theoretical aspirations of liberal philosophers. From Locke and Kant onwards, liberal political philosophers have attempted to show that the political and legal principles underpinning a liberal order could attract the *rational consent* of all those who fall within its ambit. Value pluralism, taken seriously, would appear to put paid to this hope. For the liberal project depends upon there being a range of interests and values which rational agents can be taken to share, regardless of the particular "conception of the good" to which they give their allegiance.

In recent years, John Rawls (1971) has most famously made an argument of this kind: in his view there exists a range of "primary social goods" which all people can be taken to need, regardless of what they want, and there exists a uniquely rational way of *ranking* these goods. These two assumptions, taken together, allow him to show that the principles of what he calls "justice as fairness" could be shown to be justified from the point of view of all rational individuals.

Rawls has famously come to reject these assumptions, arguing that the "fact of pluralism" should now be seen as a "permanent feature" of modern liberal democracies. It is unclear, however, that he has taken the full measure of the pluralism he now recognizes. A liberal doctrine can still in his view be shown to be justified, but now not because reason univocally inclines toward it, but because it can be inferred from the intellectual and institutional traditions of actually existing liberal democracies. As I have argued elsewhere (Weinstock, 1994), however, this does not so much confront as sidestep the problem of value pluralism: it is unclear that the traditions of *any* liberal democracy can be read in as univocal a manner as Rawls suggests; what's more, if the "fact of pluralism" is as deep and pervasive a problem as Rawls claims, then it is entirely likely that there will be citizens who on any non-circular account should be classed as "reasonable" whose political views will not spontaneously incline them toward the political ethic of liberalism.

This brings us back to deliberation: the intuition shared by the many authors who today defend a version of "deliberative democracy" is that, in the absence of any shared conception of practical reason, or of what ultimately matters in life, the justification of a liberal political order cannot be achieved by a philosophical justification logically linking these shared values with political principles. Rather, citizens and their representatives in deliberation must, in the words of a recent book on the topic, "make it up as they go along," that is, they must talk to one another across their doctrinal differences and achieve consensus in this manner. The assumption is that value pluralism does not make consensus impossible; it simply makes it impossible to achieve in the usual manner. Monological reflection is, given the fact of pluralism, insufficient, but dialogue, it is hoped, can be effective in forging principles of political agreement.

Of course, no one expects that agreement on principles will emerge from just *any* process of political discussion. The log-rolling and pork-barreling which goes on in many legislatures, and the heated, alcohol-fueled arguments which occur in cafés and student dorms cannot be expected to yield justified outcomes. Rather, justified political consensus depends upon the *deliberation* of citizens. Deliberative democrats distinguish deliberation from the threats, blackmail, rhetoric and naked emotional appeals that often characterize the public spheres of liberal democracies by emphasizing the importance for the achievement of justified political agreements of the exchange of *reasons*. When citizens and their representatives enter the political arena with their interests and political preferences pre-formed, and simply do battle on behalf of these interests with whatever political means are at their disposal, outcomes might reflect the balance of forces and the distribution of political savvy, but they will not be justified on grounds of principles. However, when they allow the exchange of reasons with their fellow citizens partially to inform and define their interests and preferences, and when they approach the procedures of reason-exchange in a public-spirited manner, then they can legitimately aspire to justified outcomes.

On the deliberative democratic view, the talk which citizens engage in democratic fora must therefore be disciplined and constrained by appropriate norms. But what should those norms be? Two broad families of answers have been provided to this question. *Weak deliberativists*, as I shall be calling them, argue that deliberators ought to restrict themselves in debate to the exchange of *reasons*, that is, of utterances bearing cognitive content (rather than, say, merely express-ing an individual or group preference) from which inferences can be drawn, which possess the requisite level of generality, etc. What's more, they must observe *procedural* constraints which will make it as likely as possible that the outcome of deliberation will reflect the weight of the better argument (rather than, for example, certain participants' greater rhetorical skill or social power). Thus, they will insist upon rules ensuring fairness in agenda-setting, turn-taking, and the like.[7] But they will impose no constraints upon the *content* of participants' utterances. As long as they put forward reasons and respect the relevant procedural norms, citizens can legitimately make reference to their particular conceptions of the good, even when they know that these conceptions are not shared by their fellow citizens.

Strong deliberativists go one step further by imposing *substantive* constraints upon the reasons which can properly be put forward in deliberation. They argue that citizens must restrict themselves to reasons which might conceivably be shared by their fellow citizens. This means, negatively, that they must abstain from making reference to their own partisan conceptions of the good, and positively, that they must restrict themselves in deliberation to the conceptual resources of "public reason."[8] (As a first approximation, public reason makes reference to the obliga-tions and rights which characterize a liberal political order, and avoids aretaic and teleological talk. Public reason refers to the right, not to the good.)

Should citizen deliberators be weak or strong deliberators? Before we can answer this question, let me throw a pair of variables into the mix. First, deliber-ation can have a variety of different goals. Most importantly, it can aim at *con-sensus* or *compromise*. When consensus occurs in deliberation, there is agreement in principle. The parties to the consensus become convinced that the views with which they had started off were mistaken, or rather only embodied a partial view of the issues at hand. When compromise is reached, however, the parties remain convinced that their original position was, abstractly considered, the best, but they recognize that what has been agreed to represents the best that can plausibly be achieved in a context in which others continue to disagree. Parties to a compro-mise agree to "split the difference" in the name of social peace and continued cooperation (Benjamin, 1990).

Second, deliberation can occur at different levels in the decision-making process. Most obviously, deliberation occurs, or should occur, in legislative bodies and courts. Here, officials are mandated explicitly to deliberate for the common good. But, one can imagine a political culture in which deliberation is, as it were, pervasive, that is, where the deliberation that goes on in courts and legislatures is *continuous* with that which goes on in the media, in parliamentary commissions and task forces, and in public squares and cafés. On this view, the norms which govern deliberation in official arenas must therefore, to some degree, pertain to citizens as well.

If the "fact of pluralism" is as deep and pervasive as Rawls and others claim it is, then compromise is a more appropriate goal for deliberation than consensus is. This is so for principled reasons as well as for pragmatic ones. As far as principle is concerned, public-policy debates on hotly contested issues will be those around which the different legitimate rankings which citizens will ascribe to the values which bear on the decision will become most salient. Pragmatically, the insistence on consensus tends to be counter-productive: setting consensus as a goal tends to discredit and devalue compromises. Where consensus is the aim, compromise can come to appear to participants as an undesirable second-best. The thirst for consensus makes the legitimacy and dignity of compromise difficult to ascertain (van Gunsteren, 1998).

Moreover, if our vision of the good society is one in which citizens fulfill the roles and take part in the paradigmatic practices of citizenship, rather than being mere private consumers protected from one another and from the state by a barrier of rights, then the responsibility of deliberation belongs to citizens rather than merely to legislators and judges.

So a normatively attractive conception of citizenship appropriate to conditions of pluralism will include a conception of deliberative democracy that aims at compromise, and that pervades society, rather than being restricted to politicians and judges. Should such a view of deliberative democracy be, in the terms defined above, weak or strong? It seems clear that, though it is appropriate to insist that citizens engaged in deliberation exchange reasons, and that they respect procedural norms ensuring fairness, the requirements of strong deliberation are excessive (Weinstock, 2001). Let me briefly provide three grounds for thinking that deliberation ought to be governed by weak norms only. First, the requirement that citizens deliberate in a way that abstracts from their deepest convictions is psychologically implausible. These convictions will continue to inform people's positions and political preferences, and their use of public reason will only superficially occlude this fact. The resources of public reason are sufficiently plastic to allow expression of most policy preferences. For example, those who favor the public funding of religious schools can always speak of a parent's "right to choose." True, the "public reason" requirement will preclude the expression of truly egregious positions. Even when citizens are insincere in their use of public reason, the constraint which they impose on themselves by speaking in its terms will inform what they can say. Jon Elster has written in this context of the "civilizing force of hypocrisy" (Elster, 1995). On the other hand, a conception of democracy which preserves the causal role of people's deepest convictions in shaping their political interventions while shielding these convictions from view makes it less likely that these convictions will *themselves* be shaped and altered by discussion with others.

And surely, what we want is not merely that people not be able to *express* the more illiberal or intolerant aspects of their conceptions of the good, but rather more deeply, that their *beliefs* be challenged by discussion.

Second, the expression by citizens of their deepest convictions in deliberative contexts when these convictions inform their political positions has *epistemic* value. Political positions which might have seemed irrational, unreasonable or unintelligible to others when expressed in abstraction of their roots in such convictions can be revealed as legitimate (though not necessarily as shareable) when they are considered as of a piece with convictions about the good. For example, certain exemptions claimed on religious grounds might seem bizarre to the uninitiated were those religious grounds not made clear.

Third, it must not be forgotten that the roles which democratic deliberation performs in a healthy democracy cannot be *reduced* to its decision-making function. People deliberate not only to reach decisions that reconcile the various values and interests in play. The process of deliberation is important to the health of democracy, even when considered independently of the results of deliberation. That citizens converse with one another about matters to do with the common good matters. Norms of deliberation will therefore among other things have to ensure that the conversation will continue. They should therefore promote civic friendship (Blattberg, 2000).

Now, though this is an empirical point, it seems to me that this function of deliberation will better be achieved if citizens are allowed to discuss their conceptions of the good in deliberative fora. Citizens are more likely to want to engage in conversation with their fellows when they feel that, though they may be required to make compromises when decisions need to be arrived at, they do not have to compromise *themselves* in the process. What's more, conversation in a pluralist society probably also depends upon citizens not remaining completely opaque to one another. Though citizens of a diverse society should not, as we have seen, aspire to consensus and sameness, they should as a condition of the viability of their deliberations aim for *understanding*. And it seems plain that we cannot understand that which systematically shields itself from view.

For these reasons and others, I argue that deliberation in pluralist societies ought to be constrained by norms of weak deliberation. Some would argue, however, that even *weak* deliberative norms are excessive. Conversation among citizens should in their view not be restricted to the exchange of reasons, where reasons are understood narrowly as propositions putting forward reasons for or against specific policy proposals. Language is also *expressive*, through it citizens ought to be able to express *who they are* rather than simply *what they want* (Blattberg, 2000). What's more, there are modes of expression, such as story-telling, which serve crucial expressive functions, especially for some cultural groups, but which do not as such put forward *reasons*. A true appreciation of pluralism, which would include a pluralism of modes of expression, would invite these modes of expression into democratic deliberation (Young, 2000). Thus, on this view, even weak deliberativists impose excessively rigid norms.

I have already conceded some of this objection in my criticism of strong deliberativists. In putting forward their policy preferences *as well as* the deepest grounds
underlying these convictions, citizens make plain – express – to each other the
essential aspects of their identities. But we must be keenly sensitive to the conditions which make possible a sustained conversation among citizens of radically different ethnic, religious and cultural perspectives. Modes of expression which have
no other function than self-expression risk functioning as conversation-stoppers
rather than as invitations to pursue discussion. Narratives which do not provide
radically different citizens with something to latch onto in conversation may run
this risk. We must be wary of excessively unanimist or consensus-oriented conceptions of deliberation, especially in contexts of pluralism. But we must also
remember that conversation has its conditions, and among these might be the
commitment by all participants to foster the give-and-take which characterizes
discussion. A commitment to reason-giving seems well-suited to this role.

V

I want in closing this overview of the debates to which a renewed attention to
pluralism has given rise to consider a problem which has thus far been held in
abeyance, but which has in a sense hovered above the discussion from the outset.
It has been an unspoken assumption of this essay that pluralism poses a *problem*
for traditional theories of citizenship, one to which theorists of citizenship should
respond by adopting less unitary conceptions of citizenship. Among other things,
as we have seen, we ought perhaps to be more willing to accept that different
groups of citizens might be granted different sets of rights, some of them exercised by the group understood as a corporate body rather than merely by individual members of the group, depending on the particular needs, values, beliefs,
etc., of the group in question. We should be more open than some republican
theorists (Rousseau is the paradigmatic example here) have been to the associations of civil society as appropriate loci of active, participatory citizenship. And we
should accept that when citizens take part in debates over matters of common
concern, they will do so as bearers of "thick" identities, rather than as citizens
sharing a common identity.

But perhaps the problem is not so much with citizenship as with pluralism.
Rather than inflecting our conception of citizenship so as to accommodate the
claims of pluralism, perhaps we ought to question the normative importance
accorded to pluralism. A healthy democracy requires patriotism on the part of
citizens, a sense of allegiance to a truly common good (Taylor, 1989). Yet giving
up too much ground to pluralism erodes the requisite sense of common purpose.
Rather than modifying our conception of citizenship so as to incorporate pluralism, perhaps liberal democracies ought to take measures to instill a sense of patriotism and belonging. They might do this for example through the educational

system: creating citizens, and patriotic ones at that, ought perhaps to be a goal of our schools.[9]

In recent years, the concern that citizens be animated by a sense of common purpose has taken the form of a renewal of interest in nationalism. Many authors now feel that, in the modern world characterized by the continued pre-eminence of the nation-state, a chastened, liberal nationalism can provide the "social cement" required to offset the centrifugal forces which our diverse identities set in motion.

There has been a veritable explosion of scholarly writing on the question of whether, despite the horrors which have been committed in its name in the twentieth century, a duly constrained nationalism might still be warranted to prevent the erosion of political communities beset by the increasingly complex, conflicting claims of culture, religion, race, sexual orientation, and the like.[10] I will, however, focus primarily on arguments which have in recent years been put forward by David Miller.

Miller's rehabilitation of nationalism is grounded upon what might be termed an "immanent critique" of the kind of purely procedural, somewhat disembodied liberal-democratic theory which has become prevalent in Anglo-American writing. There is in Miller's view a tension in many liberal views, one that can only be resolved if the nationalism tacitly presupposed by liberals is fully acknowledged. Liberals writing in a Rawlsian vein have tended to be ethical universalists. Their arguments purport to address the interests of human agents as such, rather than citizens of this or that concrete polity. Famously, John Rawls had argued that we ought to reflect upon the terms of just political association from a perspective that he calls the "original position," in which we abstract from the particularities which happen to characterize us, but which should be viewed as arbitrary from the "moral point of view." Yet they also suppose that citizens have obligations in the first instance toward their fellow citizens, rather than toward humanity at large. But how do we account for these particularistic obligations from a universalistic moral perspective? Miller's argument is that we cannot. We must eschew universalism and acknowledge more fully that nations, far from being arbitrary from the moral point of view, represent significant moral contours in the ethical landscape. More than this, we must recognize that the fact that the better-off are inclined to recognize distributive obligations toward the less well-off reflects not so much their espousal of a universalistic ethic, but rather a sense of solidarity born of shared nationality. Liberal democrats therefore attack nationalism at their peril, for they risk undercutting the cultural conditions required to account for the very redistributive obligations for which their theories argue.[11]

So rather than attempting to hide the nationalist underpinnings of liberal-democratic commitments from view, liberal democrats should find ways to promote a national identity, lest they undercut the very conditions which make citizens inclined to fulfill the obligations which a liberal-democratic ethos would impose upon them. But what are the components of national identity? According to Miller and Tamir, it incorporates both objective and subjective conditions.

Members of a nation must, subjectively, *believe* that they form a nation, and that the distinctive objective traits they share have some kind of ethical import. These objective traits, in turn, include such things as a shared sense of history, a sense of place, and a national character, which, on Miller's account, includes such things as political beliefs, shared mores governing everyday transactions and dealings such as queuing, and, perhaps, religious and cultural commitments (e.g., to the preservation of a language).

In order to promote a national identity, therefore, a liberal democracy must on the liberal nationalist view promote a sense of belonging among its citizens, as well as a sense of sharing in an historical narrative, and being rooted in a specific place, and it must also foster the conditions for the emergence and maintenance of a national character. Various levers are at the disposal of states wishing to do so, the most obvious of which is the educational system.

It is important to emphasize that liberal nationalists such as Miller and Tamir are *liberal* nationalists. They seek to walk a fine line between the kind of cultural neutrality and disembodiment they perceive in much contemporary political philosophy, and the kind of exclusive and xenophobic view of politics that has marred nationalism's history, especially in the twentieth century. And so, it is important that the objective traits they see as lying at the heart of a chastened national identity be *shareable*. It must be psychologically plausible for all members of society to adhere to them without undue hardship.

To simplify matters somewhat, therefore, liberal nationalists mount a two-pronged argument against cultural neutralists, and *a fortiori*, against those pluralists and multiculturalists who would respond *positively* to the demands for differentiated citizenship put forward by groups within society. First, they argue that the position is self-defeating, because the demands of multiculturalists are only intelligible given an assumption that national identity matters even to them (why would they care about the recognition or lack thereof of their fellow citizens if they did not also view them as *compatriots?*), and because liberal democracy itself, to the extent that it expects citizens to observe redistributive obligations toward their less fortunate fellows, is underpinned by the kind of solidarity that only nationalism can ensure. I will refer to this as the *empirical argument*. And secondly, they argue that the state should, while avoiding exclusivist excesses, promote a national identity. I will refer to this as the *normative argument*.

What are we to make of these two arguments?[12] I believe that they both face insuperable obstacles. The empirical argument ignores a much simpler answer to the question of why people seem both to be more disposed to help their fellow citizens, and to care more about their recognition. This answer is an institutional one: as it happens, people are thrown together, whether they want to be or not, into the ambit of the institutions of the state. These institutions make more *salient* the need of fellow citizens, and most obviously, through the taxes that they levy, they make it more difficult to avoid. Also, since the welfare of those people joined together in common is greatly interdependent, they care more about whether those with whom they are assembled under common state institutions will be well-disposed toward their (sometimes group-specific) interests, because they are in a position greatly to *affect* those interests. Thus we do not need to assume some mysterious national bond in order to account for the puzzles liberal nationalists raise. Institutional reasoning solves them as well, and does it much more economically.

Institutions have an impact on the obligations people recognize. Rather than assuming that institutions also fix the obligations that they *ought* to recognize, I would argue that this latter question needs to be settled independently, and institutions should be designed which will incline people to recognize the obligations they ought.[13]

What of the normative argument? I lack the space to deal even in passing with each of the elements which, according to Miller and Tamir, make up national identity. But let me briefly discuss one, which has to do with the shared sense of historical continuity. In multicultural societies, especially those that receive great numbers of immigrants, and/or that incorporate distinct nations, the argument that history should be taught in a way that fosters attachment is caught in a bind. Briefly stated the problem is this: if history is to serve to cement a national identity, then it will have to be sanitized and moralized. According to Miller, history will serve its socializing function by reassuring us as to the historical reality of our nation, and by providing models of "the virtues of our ancestors" which we should strive to emulate (Miller, 1995: 36). Let's focus on the first of these functions. Teaching a history attempting to serve the first function will necessarily be untrue to immigrants and their children, who though they might very well *learn* about the history of the place to which they have immigrated, will not have an identity stake in this history. It is implausible to expect that a young Vietnamese immigrant to Québec learning about the Battle of the Plains of Abraham will feel that it is *her* community that was already in a sense there at the time. Insisting that she should risks having an alienating effect, rather than fostering belonging.

The alternative is to teach history realistically, and to make clear the conflicts, fractures and discontinuities which are the lot of all real-world societies. But then, the teaching of history will not have the desired effect as regards the building of a cohesive national identity.

Does this mean that we cannot do anything to resist the fragmentation which multiculturalism and pluralism risk causing if unchecked? The first thing to note is that nationalists exaggerate the dangers to which the social fabric is prey.[14] What is needed is not so much that people be bound to each other in such a way that, had they happened not to find themselves under constitutions, they would have chosen to do so anyway; what is required instead to offset fragmentation is that people *lack* good reason to put into question the political unions in which they already find themselves thrown. In other work (Weinstock, 1999b), I attempted to define a kind of relationship between citizens which I termed "trust." This relationship obtains when citizens rightly feel that their fellow citizens are not ill-disposed toward the satisfaction of their interests, including their group-specific interests. I also attempted to indicate ways in which institutions can foster trust among citizens. I cannot go into the detail of that discussion now; suffice it to say that citizens that trust one another despite their differences are unlikely to fall away from one another in the manner suggested by the nationalist argument. On the contrary, they are more likely to *stay* together if they view the political association they are in as congenial to their interests as holders of diverse beliefs and as bearers of different identities, than they are if they are subjected to nation-building projects.

Conclusion

The pluralism of value and culture which has become (and perhaps has always been) constitutive of mass societies rightly inflects and informs our conceptions of justice and of citizenship. The diversity of views and of ways of life cannot simply be relegated to the private sphere in the name of a culturally homogenized and sanitized public sphere. This is because citizens' values inform the positions that they take on issues of *common* interest, and because their very diverse ways of life in part determine the interests which they have. The challenge for political philosophers is to continue to imagine ways in which the values and virtues intrinsic to the conception of citizenship we have inherited from our political culture can be adapted to changing circumstances both internal to existing polities, and increasingly, in the relations between citizens of *different* polities. We must therefore articulate the practices, virtues, rights and institutions both of a differentiated citizenship and of a cosmopolitan citizenship. I hope to have contributed modestly to the first of these tasks.

Notes

1   See, *inter alia*, Carens (1987), Brubaker (1989), Bauböck (1994), Schwartz (1995), and Castles and Davidson (2000).
2   I have discussed Kymlicka's work in greater detail in Weinstock (1998).
3   I have discussed the federalist option in more detail in Weinstock (forthcoming). For skeptical considerations concerning federalism's capacity to halt the secessionist logic which the granting of fully collective rights of self-government sets in motion, see Kymlicka (1998).
4   For a fascinating discussion of multiculturalism in the Israeli context, see Gavison (1999).
5   For recent overviews of debates around civil society, see Cohen and Arato (1992), Ehrenberg (1999), Keane (1998) and Seligman (1992).
6   Though one should keep in mind another observation of de Tocqueville's concerning American society, namely that the discipline and self-abnegation which (most notably) religious organizations promote act as a salutary counterweight to the license which the democratic way of life might itself promote.

7   Though they differ on points of detail, weak deliberativists include Habermas (1996), Bohman (1996) and Chambers (1996).

8   The paradigmatic work here is that of Gutmann and Thompson (1996, 1998). See also John Rawls (1998).

9   For different views on this question, see Fullinwider (1996), Brighouse (1998).

10 See *inter alia*, Miller (1995), Tamir (1993), Canovan (1996), McKim and McMahan (1997), Couture et al. (eds.), Moore (1998).

11 Miller (2000a) mounts a similar immanent critique of the differentialist claims made in the name of "identity politics." In Miller's view, the fact that partisans of identity politics demand recognition of their identities from their fellow citizens means that the recognition of their fellow citizens *matters* to them more than that of people with whom they do not share national bonds. And so, "the politics of recognition" in a sense presupposes the tacit belief by partisans of identity politics in what Miller terms "the principle of nationality."

12 I have discussed these issues at greater length in Weinstock (1996) and Weinstock (1999a).

13 Though I lack the space to go into this in any detail, this argument disposes of an argument made by Miller against cosmopolitan citizenship. He argues (Miller, 1999, and Miller, 2000) that cosmopolitan citizenship is impossible because there are no cosmopolitan institutions to act as a focus for accountability to rival those which the nation-state provides. If my argument is on the right track, we need to figure out whether we have cosmopolitan obligations, and then imagine what institutions might be designed to realize them.

14 For an interesting argument to this effect in the case of the US, see Hall and Lindholm (1999).

Bibliography

Arendt, Hannah (1950). *The Origins of Totalitarianism*. New York: Harcourt, Brace and Co.

Bader, Veit (1997). "The Cultural Conditions of Transnational Citizenship." *Political Theory*, vol. 25, no. 6: pp. 771–813.

Bauböck, Rainer (1994). *Transnational Citizenship: Membership and Rights in International Migration*. Aldershot: Edward Elgar.

Benjamin, Martin (1990). *Splitting the Difference: Compromise and Integrity in Ethics and Politics*. Lawrence: University of Kansas Press.

Blattberg, Charles (2000). *From Pluralism to Patriotic Politics*. Oxford: Oxford University Press.

Bohman, James (1996). *Public Deliberation*. Cambridge, MA: The MIT Press.

Brighouse, Harry (1998). "Civic Education and Liberal Legitimacy." *Ethics*, 108: 719–45.

Brubaker, Rogers (ed.) (1989). *Immigration and the Politics of Citizenship in Europe and North America*. Lanham, MD: University Press of America.

Callan, Eamonn (1998). *Creating Citizens*. Oxford: Oxford University Press.

Canovan, Margaret (1996). *Nationhood and Political Theory*. Cheltenham: Edward Elgar.

Carens, Joseph H. (1987). "Aliens and Citizens: The Case for Open Borders." *Review of Politics*, vol. 49, no. 2: 251–73.

——(2000). *Culture, Citizenship, and Community: A Contextual Exploration of Justice as Evenhandedness*. Oxford: Oxford University Press.

Castles, Stephen and Alastair Davidson (2000). *Citizenship and Migration: Globalization and the Politics of Belonging*. London: Routledge.

Chambers, Simone (1996). *Reasonable Democracy*. Ithaca: Cornell University Press.

Cohen, Jean and Andrew Arato (1992). *Civil Society and Political Theory*. Cambridge, MA: The MIT Press.

Cohen, Josh and Joel Rogers (1995). *Associations and Democracy*. London: Verso.

Cook, Curtis and Juan D. Lindau (2000). *Aboriginal Rights and Self-Government*. Montreal: McGill-Queens' Press.

Couture, Jocelyne, Kai Nielson, and Michael Seymour (eds.). *Rethinking Nationalism* (*Canadian Journal of Philosophy Supplementary Volume 22*).

D'Agostino, Fred (1996). *Free Public Reason: Making It Up as We Go*. Oxford: Oxford University Press.

de Tocqueville, Alexis (1981). *De la démocratie en Amérique*. Paris: Garnier-Flammarion.

Dworkin, Ronald (1977). *Taking Rights Seriously*. Cambridge, MA: Harvard University Press.

Ehrenberg, John (1999). *Civil Society: The Critical History of an Idea*. New York: The NYU Press.

Elster, Jon (1995). "Strategic Uses of Argument." In K. Arrow et al. (eds.), *Barriers to the Negotiated Resolution of Conflict*. New York: Norton, pp. 236–57.

Fullinwider, Robert (1996). "Patriotic History." In R. Fullinwider (ed.), *Public Education in a Multicultural Society*. Cambridge: Cambridge University Press.

Gavison, Ruth (1999). "Can Israel be Jewish and Democratic?" *Israel Studies*, 5: 44–77.

Government of Canada (1969). *Statement of the Government of Canada on Indian Policy*. Ottawa: Department of Indian Affairs and Northern Development.

Gray, John (2000). *Two Faces of Liberalism*. New York: The New Press.

Gutmann, Amy and Dennis Thompson (1996). *Democracy and Disagreement*. Cambridge, MA: Harvard University Press.

——(1998). "Why Deliberative Democracy is Different." *Social Philosophy and Policy*, 17: 161–80.

Habermas, Jürgen (1996). *Between Facts and Norms: Contributions to a Discourse Theory of Law and Democracy*. Cambrdige, MA: The MIT Press.

Hall, John A. and Charles Lindholm (1999). *Is America Breaking Apart*. Princeton: Princeton University Press.

Hobbes, Thomas (1996). *Leviathan* (ed. J. C. A. Gaskin). Oxford: Oxford University Press.

Hurka, Thomas (1994). "Indirect Perfectionism: Kymlicka on Liberal Neutrality." *Journal of Political Philosophy*, vol. 2, no. 3.

Isin, Engin and Patricia K. Wood (1999). *Citizenship and Identity*. London: Sage.

Johnston Conover, Pamela (1995). "Citizen Identities and Conceptions of the Self." *Journal of Political Philosophy*, vol. 3, no. 2 (June 1995): 133–65.

Keane, John (1998). *Civil Society*. Stanford: Stanford University Press.

Kymlicka, Will (1987). *Liberalism, Community and Culture*. Oxford: Oxford University Press.

——(1989). "Liberal Individualism and Liberal Neutrality." *Ethics*, vol. 99: 883–905.

——(1995). *Multicultural Citizenship*. Oxford: Oxford University Press.

——(1998). "Is Federalism a Viable Alternative to Secession." In Percy Lehning (ed.), *Theories of Secession*. London: Routledge.

Kymlicka, Will and Wayne Norman (1994). "The Return of the Citizen: A Survey of Recent Work on Citizenship Theory." *Ethics*, vol. 104, no. 2: 354–81.

——(2000). "Citizenship in Culturally Diverse Societies: Issues, Contexts, Concepts." In Kymlicka and Norman, *Citizenship in Diverse Societies*. Oxford: Oxford University Press.

Levy, Jacob (1997). "Classifying Group Rights." In Ian Shapiro and Will Kymlicka (eds.), *Ethnicity and Group Rights*. New York: The NYU Press.

——(2000). *The Multiculturalism of Fear*. Oxford: Oxford University Press.

Macedo, Stephen (1996). "Community, Diversity and Civic Education: Toward a Liberal Political Science of Group Life." *Social Philosophy and Policy*, vol. 13, no. 1: 240–68.

McKim, Robert and Jeff McMahan (eds.) (1997). *The Morality of Nationalism*. Oxford: Oxford University Press.

Mill, John Stuart (1982). *On Liberty*. Harmondsworth: Penguin.

——(1991). *Considerations on Representative Government*. Albany, NY: Prometheus Books.

Miller, David (1995). *On Nationality*. Oxford: Oxford University Press.

——(1999). "Justice and Inequality." In A. Hurrell and N. Woods (eds.), *Inequality, Globalization, and World Politics*. Oxford: Oxford University Press.

——(2000a). "Group Identities, National Identities and Democratic Politics." In David Miller, *Citizenship and National Identity*. Oxford: Polity Press.

——(2000b). "Citizenship and Pluralism." In David Miller, *Citizenship and National Identity*. Oxford: Polity Press.

——(2000c). "Bounded Citizenship." In David Miller, *Citizenship and National Identity*. Oxford: Polity Press.

Minow, Martha (1990). *Making All the Difference: Inclusion, Exclusion and American Law*. Ithaca: Cornell University Press.

Moltchanova, Anna (2001). "The Basic Principle of the International Legal System and Self-Determination of National Groups." Ph.D. thesis, Department of Philosophy, McGill University.

Moore, Margaret (ed.) (1998). *National Self-Determination and Secession*. Oxford: Oxford University Press.

Rawls, John (1971). *A Theory of Justice*. Cambridge, MA: Harvard University Press.

——(1993). *Political Liberalism*. New York: Columbia University Press.

——(1998). "The Idea of Public Reason." In *Collected Papers*. Cambridge, MA: Harvard University Press.

Raz, Joseph (1986). *The Morality of Freedom*. Oxford: Oxford University Press.

Raz, Joseph and Avishai Margalit (1990). "National Self-Determination." *The Journal of Philosophy*, 87.

Réaume, Denise (2000a). "The Legal Enforcement of Social Norms: Techniques and Principles." In A. Cairns et al. (eds.), *Citizenship, Diversity and Pluralism: Canadian and Comparative Perspectives*. Montreal: The McGill-Queens' Press.

——(2000b). "Legal Multiculturalism from the Bottom Up." In R. Beiner and W. Norman (eds.), *Canadian Political Philosophy: Contemporary Reflections*. Oxford: Oxford University Press.

Rosenblum, Nancy L. (1998). *Membership and Morals: The Personal Uses of Pluralism in America*. Princeton: Princeton University Press.

Schwartz, Warren (1995). *Justice in Immigration*. Cambridge: Cambridge University Press.

Scott, James (1998). *Seeing Like a State: How Certain Schemes to Improve the Human Condition have Failed*. New Haven: Yale University Press.

Seligman, Adam (1992). *The Idea of Civil Society*. Princeton: Princeton University Press.

Sharpe, Andrew (1997). *Justice and the Maori*. Oxford: Oxford University Press.

Spinner, Jeff (1994). *The Boundaries of Citizenship: Race, Ethnicity, and Nationality in the Liberal State*. Baltimore: The Johns Hopkins Press, 1994.

Spinner-Halev, Jeff (2000). *Surviving Diversity: Religion and Democratic Citizenship*. Baltimore: The Johns Hopkins Press.

Tamir, Yael (1993). *Liberal Nationalism*. Princeton: Princeton University Press.

Taylor, Charles (1989). "Cross-Purposes: The Liberal–Communitarian Debate." In N. Rosenblum (ed.), *Liberalism and the Moral Life*. Cambridge, MA: Harvard University Press.

Tully, James (1995). *Strange Multiplicity: Constitutionalism in an Age of Diversity*. Cambridge: Cambridge University Press.

van Gunsteren, Herman R. (1998). *A Theory of Citizenship*. Boulder: Westview.

Waldron, Jeremy (1992). "Superseding Historical Injustice." *Ethics*, vol. 103: 2–28.

Weinstock, Daniel M. (1994). "The Justification of Political Liberalism." *Pacific Philosophical Quarterly*, vol. 75: 165–85.

——(1996). "Is there a Moral Case for Nationalism?" *Journal of Applied Philosophy*, vol. 13: 87–100.

——(1998). "How can Collective Rights and Liberalism be Reconciled?" In R. Bauböck and J. Rundell (eds.), *Blurred Boundaries: Migration, Ethnicity, Citizenship*. Aldershot: Ashgate.

——(1999a). "National Partiality: Confronting the Intuitions." *The Monist*, vol. 82: 516–41.

——(1999b). "Building Trust in Divided Societies." *The Journal of Political Philosophy*, vol. 7, no. 3: 287–307.

——(2001). "Saving Democracy from Deliberation." In Ronald Beiner and Wayne Norman (eds.), *Canadian Political Philosophy*. Oxford: Oxford University Press.

——(forthcoming). "Toward a Normative Theory of Federalism." *International Social Science Journal*.

Williams, Melissa (1998). *Voice, Trust and Memory*. Princeton: Princeton University Press.

Wuthnow, Robert (1998). *Loose Connections: Joining Together in America's Fragmented Communities*. Cambridge, MA: Harvard University Press.

Young, Iris Marion (1990). *Justice and the Politics of Difference*. Princeton: Princeton University Press.

——(2000). *Inclusion and Democracy*. Oxford: Oxford University Press.

Chapter 12

The New Enlightenment: Critical Reflections on the Political Significance of Race

A. Todd Franklin

In the allegory of the cave, Plato uses the imagery of the difficult physical and psychological process of freeing oneself from the perceptual misconceptions resulting from a life lived in the illusory world of an underground cavern to illustrate the critical project of freeing oneself from cognitive misperceptions about the world and life. As Plato describes it, the cave is inhabited by prisoners who have been chained there since childhood. Moreover, they are chained in such a way that they face the far wall of the cave and are unable to turn to see those chained beside them or the opening that lies behind them. Interposed between the prisoners and the opening of the cave is a fire and between them and the fire is a short wall. Behind this wall, men carry representations of various animals and objects that cast shadows on the cave wall below. Unable to see anything other than these shadows and their own, the prisoners consider these distorted images indicative of reality.

Symbolically, these prisoners represent the vast majority of people whose conceptions of the world are skewed by "their own passions and prejudices and by the passions and prejudices of other people as conveyed to them by language and rhetoric."[1] Although these people are steeped in error, they are so habituated to their so-called "reality," that they are extremely reluctant to forsake it, for as Plato describes it, to do so would be as painful and bewildering as suddenly emerging from darkness and being temporarily blinded by the brightness and glare of the light.[2] However, if one of the prisoners does somehow break free and grow accustomed to the light, he will see that those things that were once considered realities are merely coarse distortions.

In its broadest sense, the allegory of the cave exemplifies Plato's epistemology. More specifically, however, it serves the practical purpose of illustrating a process of enlightenment that the political leaders of the State must undergo if they are going to develop a critical knowledge and understanding of the values, principles, and social realities that will allow them to successfully serve and promote the good of the State. Focused on freeing themselves from the prejudices and sophistry that hold sway in the proverbial cave, Plato's ideal political leaders are those who commit themselves to critically assessing received views in an effort to grasp things in a true light. More precisely, these enlightened leaders are those who actively endeavor to recognize and overcome the perverse social and political effects of distorted conceptions of self, personal or self-interested passions and prejudices, and shared passions and prejudices that are reified by language and rhetoric. Following in the spirit of this Platonic ideal, this essay constitutes an attempt to hasten the dawn of a new Enlightenment that breaks free of the gross distortions that hamper a clear understanding of the political significance of race.

Focusing more specifically on the relationship between race and the dominant political theory of liberalism, I explore the ways in which liberal theory fails to adequately grasp the social reality of race, and I go on to argue that a true appreciation of the political significance of race challenges theorists to reconceptualize social justice in accordance with a more enlightened view of race as a constitutive element of individual political identity. Proceeding in the mode of critical theory, the goal of this essay is to develop a reflective analysis of race that clarifies its meaning, history, and deployment within the context of liberalism. Broadly construed, critical theory denotes a philosophical enterprise aimed at combating the ideological inculcation of systemic forms of domination and oppression by identifying ways in which the political significance of the concrete specificity of human subjectivity and a host of other contextual determinants of social relations and political structures are routinely unrecognized, unacknowledged, and unappreciated. Thus, the committed goal of this essay is to foster a greater critical awareness of and sensitivity to the fact that considerations of race are crucial to the development of political theories and principles that articulate and serve the interests of social justice.

In keeping with this aim, I begin with an account of the historical emergence of the political theory of liberalism that focuses on its connection to Western European Enlightenment. Highlighting liberalism's faith in the efficacy of reason, the first section details the nature of liberalism as a political ideal that emerges in concert with the development of Western European Enlightenment. In the second section I go on to develop a brief genealogy of the concept of race that contextualizes its historical transformation and subsequent intersections with early expressions of liberalism. Drawing upon the genealogy of the previous section as a point of entry, the third section offers a critical assessment of liberalism's failure to acknowledge the political significance of race and spotlights its subsequent complicity in the perpetuation of racial oppression and domination. In the fourth and final section, I conclude by sketching the features of an enlightened liberalism infused with a heightened racial consciousness and therewith a more comprehensive political conscience.

From Modernity to Enlightenment: The Historical Emergence
of Liberalism

In order to fully understand the character of liberalism it's best to begin by acquainting oneself with the intellectual currents that led to its genesis. Emerging in the eighteenth century, liberalism is in essence the political expression of the ideology, ideas, and principles that define what is loosely described as the Western European Enlightenment. Given the intellectual convergence of these two traditions, the first task is to examine the historical emergence of the broader tradition of Western European Enlightenment and the second is to detail the way in which liberalism constitutes its political embodiment. Highlighting the main factors and features that prefigure the Enlightenment, and therewith liberalism, the following begins by drawing attention to the rise of modernism.

Modernism emerges in the seventeenth century as a profound shift in the nature and focus of European thought. Up until the seventeenth century, European intellectualism was largely the purview of Christian theologians, many of whom served as university professors. Although a number of these theologians made noteworthy contributions to speculative metaphysics (e.g., Aquinas, Scotus, Ockham), the majority of pre-modern, or medieval, philosophers were devoted to the development of theologically refracted commentaries on the canonical works taught in the universities and the development of scholastic treatises aimed at elucidating received truths. Thus understood, pre-modern philosophy is distinguished by a devotion to canonical tradition and a subservience to theology that manifests itself as a persistent tendency to interpret everything in direct relation to God. In contrast, modernism is marked by the emergence of original and independent thinkers who reject the theocentrism of the medieval period and pursue philosophy as a purely autonomous branch of study.

In general, the shift to modernism occurs during a period of religious disillusionment and intellectual frustration. Plagued by the religious strife exemplified by the various reformations and dismayed by the epistemic deficiencies of scholasticism, the shift to modernism is marked by a shift to a more naturalistic focus and the development of new methodologies that are more conducive to the attainment of certainty. By and large, the philosophers of the modern period were the products of a burgeoning educated and cultured secular class. Operating outside of both the Church and the University, modern philosophers enjoyed a material and social independence that facilitated an eruption of original and creative philosophy unbeknownst to Europe since the time of the Greeks. Notable among the early modern philosophers were people like Sir Francis Bacon (1561–1626) and René Descartes (1596–1650). Frustrated by the methodological shortcomings of mediaeval thought, Bacon and Descartes contributed to the development of the modern methodologies of empiricism and rationalism respectively. Although distinct insofar as empiricism focuses on sensory observation and induction while rationalism focuses on mathematical forms of deduction, both methodologies are premised on a bold new confidence in the human mind's ability to develop a clear and certain understanding of natural phenomena without recourse to canonical or divine authority.

Broadly construed, seventeenth-century modernism can be characterized as an intellectual movement that produces three profound shifts. The first is a shift in intellectual autonomy. Transformed into a secular enterprise, the study of philosophy emancipates itself from the tutelage of theology and distinguishes itself as an independent discipline. In the process, it forsakes appeals to canonical and divine authority and becomes self-validating. The second is a shift in focus from theological issues to naturalistic phenomena. And the third is a shift from a scholasticism that focuses on the clarification of received truth to the speculative methodologies of empiricism and rationalism.

In contrast to the profound intellectual shifts witnessed in the seventeenth century, the eighteenth century is a relatively stable period in the history of Western European thought. Widely referred to as the period of European Enlightenment, the eighteenth century represents a continuation of the intellectual currents of modernism. In particular, it is a period that maintains the focus on natural phenomena and continues to employ unencumbered empirical and rationalistic methodologies in the pursuit of knowledge and truth. Furthermore, given the apparent success of the speculative natural sciences, the European Age of Enlightenment also marks a growing optimism concerning the efficacy of corresponding speculative applications of reason to the science of humanity.

Punctuating the success of modernism's approach to natural science, Sir Isaac Newton (1642–1727) combined the use of speculative reason with mathematics to produce a theory of gravity that would serve as one of the rudiments of physics for more than two centuries. Newton's theory, set forth in his magnum opus *Principia Mathematica* (The Mathematical Principles of Natural Philosophy), reasoned that all bodies, both celestial and terrestrial, move through mutual attraction. Demonstrating this relationship mathematically, the theory defined the force of gravity as proportional to the inverse square of the distance between two bodies, and in doing so, laid the groundwork for a host of scientific and technological achievements.

Steeled by the success of Newton's program of rational and unbiased investigation as applied to the physical world, enthusiastic exponents of the enlightenment project felt that it was only a matter of time before they would develop an equally clear understanding of the nature of humanity, and derivatively, a clear understanding of the ideal orders of the moral, social, and political spheres of life. Although the eighteenth century would go on to give rise to a variety of different philosophical accounts of the nature of humanity, none would achieve the certainty and stability of Newtonian physics. Nevertheless, a constant theme uniting all of the enlightenment theories focusing on the human condition was the abiding conviction that human rationality would eventually successfully serve as the fount of self-understanding and normative objectivity.

In his famous essay "What is Enlightenment?" Immanuel Kant (1724–1804) gives further voice to the Enlightenment's enthusiasm for reason. Critical of what he perceives as a pervasive docility and subservience to external authority regarding all facets of life, Kant describes the Enlightenment as an intellectual movement committed to rational self-determination:

> Enlightenment is man's leaving his self-caused immaturity. Immaturity is the incapacity to use one's intelligence without the guidance of another. Such immaturity is self-caused if it is not caused by a lack of intelligence, but a lack of determination and courage. . . . Sapere Aude! Have the courage to use your own intelligence! Is therefore the motto of the enlightenment.[3]

Although Kant claims that courage is the key to enlightenment, he concludes that practically speaking:

> All that is required for this enlightenment is *freedom*; and particularly the least harmful of all that may be called freedom, namely, the freedom for man to make *public use* of his reason in all matters.[4]

Moreover, Kant argues that the opportunity to exercise one's reason in the development of free thought fosters greater intellectual maturity. In addition, he goes on to close the essay by claiming that eventually, the upsurge in rational free thought would also foster the development of a politically enlightened state.

Exemplifying the spirit of such enlightened reflection, liberalism emerges as a philosophical tradition that centers around a commitment to rationally derived political principles that respect and promote free thought and self-determination. Thus understood, liberalism denotes a political commitment to formal justice, i.e., a commitment that is typically referred to as a commitment to "the priority of the right over the good." Moreover, as Michael Sandel aptly describes it, liberalism exemplifies the view that:

> society, being composed of a plurality of persons, each with his own aims, interests, and conceptions of the good, is best arranged when it is governed by principles that do not *themselves* presuppose any particular conception of the good; what justifies these regulative principles above all is not that they maximize the social welfare or otherwise promote the good, but rather that they conform to the concept of *right* [i.e., justice], a moral category given prior to the good and independent of it.[5]

Although prefigured in the political philosophy of John Locke and codified in the political declarations of eighteenth-century liberal-democratic regimes, the belief in the absolute priority of the *right*, i.e., formal justice, enjoyed the status of a conviction, but lacked the certainty guaranteed by independent justification. Recognizing this shortcoming, Kant sets out to establish the absolute priority of the *right* as an objective and universal law of reason.

To this end, he draws a distinction between practical principles that reflect particular conceptions of the good and principles of justice that are independently derived. In contrast to practical principles that are subjective with respect to particular conceptions of the good, and therewith, potentially coercive or oppressive when applied to all, principles of justice are completely undetermined and unconditioned by conceptions of the good and are thus regarded as consistent with human freedom. However, having characterized principles of justice as stemming in no way from conceptions of the good, on what else can such principles be based? Kant's response: the basis for principles of justice lies not in some particular end or object of the will, i.e., in some notion of the good, but rather in the autonomous will that constitutes our ability to rationally reflect upon and choose between ends independently of our phenomenal particularity.[6] Shifting the justificatory focus from the ideality of political ends to the ideality of rational autonomy, Kant introduces a new approach to the speculative project of articulating and grounding the principles of social justice. An approach, moreover, that continues to serve as one of the central paradigms of contemporary liberal political thought.

A Genealogy of Race and its Intersections with Early Expressions of Liberalism

Negro, Homo pelli nigra, a name given to a variety of the human species, who are entirely black, and are found in the torrid zone, especially in that part of Africa which lies within the tropics. In the complexion of negroes we meet with various shades; but they likewise differ far from other men in all the features of their face. Round cheeks, high cheek-bones, a forehead somewhat elevated, a short, broad, flat nose, thick lips, small ears, ugliness and irregularity of shape, characterize their external appearance. The negro women have the loins greatly depressed, and very large buttocks, which give the back the shape of a saddle. Vices the most notorious seem to be the portion of this unhappy race: idleness, treachery, revenge, cruelty, impudence, stealing, lying, profanity, debauchery, nastiness and intemperance, are said to have extinguished the principles of natural law, and to have silenced the reproofs of conscience. They are strangers to every sentiment of compassion, and are an awful example of the corruption of man when left to himself.

The foregoing excerpt from the 1798 American edition of the *Encyclopedia Britannica* exemplifies the historical tendency to link various human qualities to the biological notion of race. Moreover, in this case, the view is that the Negro race is marked by certain physical features such as black skin, flat noses, and thick lips that in addition to ugliness and physical irregularity, connote moral corruption and intellectual deficiency as well.

Although long regarded as an Aeterna Veritas, the biological concept of race has a curious origin. One way of understanding this origin is to think in terms of the Nietzschean notion of a process of interpretive imposition. In aphorism 58 of *The Gay Science*, Nietzsche writes:

> This has given me the greatest trouble and still does: to realize that what things are called is incomparably more important than what they are. The reputation, name, and appearance, the usual measure and weight of a thing, what it counts for – originally almost always wrong and arbitrary, thrown over things like a dress and altogether foreign to their nature and even to their skin – all this grows from generation unto generation, merely because people believe in it, until it gradually grows to be a part of the thing and turns into its very body.

At base, Nietzsche's paradigm connotes a temporal process of transformation. Drawing an initial distinction between something's original character and prevailing notions of "what it counts for," Nietzsche highlights the fact that over time, rhetoric and rationalizations can overpower and transform reality.

In the case of race, the interpretive transformations primarily responsible for its eventual emergence as a biological concept connote gross distortions of pre-modern political, religious, and scientific schemes of classification.

Widely regarded as the progenitors of modern democratic thought, the Greeks subscribed to a scheme of classification that drew hierarchical distinctions between individuals on the basis of a political conception of human telos or purpose. For the Greeks, life was considered a precarious struggle against the forces of time and circumstance. Subject to both the caprice of nature and the eminence of their own mortality, the Greeks viewed politics as the ideal means of raising oneself above the temporal order of natural necessity. Moreover, they believed that through politics, one could establish one's immortal significance and worth as an active contributor to the creation of a flourishing and well-ordered society. Drawing upon this view, Aristotle devises a hierarchical scheme of classification that roughly divides human beings into those who are civilized, i.e., those who actively participate in and are governed by a rationally ordered state, and those who are barbarians, i.e., those who live according to either natural instincts, or passively accepted traditions, customs, and habits. Notably, however, the distinction between the civilized person and the barbarian is based strictly on the possession or lack of capacities and dispositions that are peculiar to individuals as opposed to distinct hereditary groups.[7]

In contrast, the distinction between civilized and barbarian takes on a decidedly biological character when it is later invoked in the sixteenth century. Precipitated by the success of the European voyages of discovery, and the resulting increase in contact with peoples who appeared strikingly different both in form and in custom, the distinction between civilized and barbarian becomes interpretively transformed into a distinction between peoples, or races. Arguing that as a people, Native Americans were by nature wild, savage and servile, the renowned Aristotelian scholar Gines de Sepulveda appealed to Aristotle's claim that civilized people were justified in enslaving natural barbarians, who were incapable of controlling and governing themselves. Neglectful of the fact that Aristotle rejects the idea that natural barbarism is hereditary, Sepulveda's argument proves to be woefully unfaithful. Nevertheless, its articulation contributes to the popularity of the notion of an essential racial character.

Corresponding to the shift from a dominant Greco-Roman political order to a new theocentric order, the pre-modern religious scheme of classification originates as a simple dichotomy between those who were recognized as belonging to God (the Hebrews) and those who were estranged from God (the Gentiles). In contrast to the Greeks, who distinguished people on the basis of the degree to which they possessed and employed a capacity for rational self-governance, the Hebrew distinction was based on one's belief in and devotion to the patriarchal divinity of Yahweh. It is against this background that the Jewish historian Flavius Josephus (37–95 CE) appeals to the biblical story of Ham to explain the historical dispersion of the world's population.

According to Josephus' account, after the great flood, the population of the world was divided into three parts: the first were the inhabitants of Europe, who were the descendants of Noah's eldest son Japhet, the second were the inhabitants of the Middle East, who were the descendants of his second son Shem, and the third were the inhabitants of Africa, who were the descendants of his youngest son Ham. Although all lines of descent could be traced back to Noah, the line of Ham was marked by a curse that stemmed from an act of impiety. As Josephus writes:

> [Noah] offered sacrifice, and feasted, and being drunk, he fell asleep and lay naked in an unseemly manner. When his youngest son saw this, he came laughing, and showed him to his brethren; but they covered their father's nakedness. And when Noah was made sensible of what had been done, he prayed for prosperity to his other sons, but to Ham, he did not curse him, by reason of his nearness in blood, but cursed his posterity. And when the rest of them escaped that curse, he inflicted it upon the children of Canaan.[8]

On Josephus' account, the curse visited upon Ham's posterity is the curse of estrangement. In response to the prayer of his faithful son Noah, God disowns the children of Ham. However, insofar as Ham effectively estranged himself from his father by acting impiously, the curse that is visited upon his children merely reciprocates the consequence of Ham's initial actions.

Although initially understood as the story of a horrific curse that divides humanity into those who enjoy a relationship with God and those who are estranged from Him, the story of Ham prominently re-emerges in the sixteenth century as an explanation of racial difference, or more precisely, an explanation of blackness. In his *True Discourse of the Three Voyages of Discoverie* (1578), the Englishman George Best rejects the view that blackness is a product of heat exposure and claims instead that it is a product of a natural infection that proceeds by lineal descent.

Invoking the story of Ham, Best maintains that the infection was originally a product of the Hamitic curse. Moreover, as Ivan Hannaford points out, Best's account goes on to describe the accursed descendants of Ham as "marked with a black badge to symbolize loathsomeness and banished to the cursed and degenerate voids of Africa, where they lived as idolators, witches, drunkards, sodomites, and enchanters."[9] Despite its misguided focus on physical and dispositional inheritances, biological readings of the story of Ham proliferated and enjoyed popular acceptance well into the nineteenth century.

Finally, a third major locus of interpretive transformation centers around the scientific concept of biological classification. Widely hailed as the father of biological classification, Aristotle set out to classify living things in accordance with their nature and independently of superficial resemblances or variations. Examining a variety of different specimens of numerous organisms, he created a *scala naturae* that ordered living things on a continuous scale of creatures increasing in complexity and perfection from plants to man. Relying mainly on embryological criteria, Aristotle classified creatures into genuses according to their embryonic form and ordered them according to the level of developmental maturity exhibited at birth. Thus among the blooded animals, i.e., the vertebrates, those who laid eggs that changed in size, shape or form once outside of the female were grouped together in the genus of reptiles and amphibians while those who laid fully formed eggs were grouped together in the higher genus of birds. Lastly, those who gave birth to live young were grouped together in the penultimate genus of mammals.

Within each genus, Aristotle also drew further hierarchical distinctions in terms of species. Thus within the genus of mammals, cows and apes were considered distinct species, that were each lower than the species of humans on the scale of nature. Ultimately, however, it is here at the level of species that Aristotle's scheme of differentiated subordination ends, for although he recognized differences between members of the same species, he believed that such differences failed to warrant further differentiation on the *scala naturae*.[10]

Although Aristotle's philosophy differentiates between human beings in a variety of different contexts, his biological system of classification de-emphasizes morphological differences insofar as it regards all humans as members of the same species. In contrast, however, the natural historians of the eighteenth century considered morphology a crucial determinant of human differentiation on the great scale of being. Linking differences in skin color, hair, and facial features to differences in character and disposition, the famous naturalist Carolus Linnaeus (1707–78) transformed superficial morphological differences into a substantive basis for subdividing the human species into four distinct races: *Homo Europeaus*, *Homo Asiaticus*, *Homo Americanus*, and *Homo Afer*. At the top of the hierarchy, *Homo Europaeus*:

European. White, Sanguine, Brawny. Hair abundantly flowing. Eyes blue, Gentle, acute, inventive. Covered with close vestments. Governed by customs.

At the bottom of the hierarchy, *Homo Afer*:

> African. Black, Phlegmatic, Relaxed. Hair black, frizzled. Skin silky. Nose flat. Lips tumid. Women's bosom a matter of modesty. Breasts give milk abundantly. Crafty, indolent. Negligent. Anoints himself with grease. Governed by caprice.[11]

Although later eighteenth-century theorists would go on to develop different accounts of definitive racial characteristics and their causes, all would regard race as a correlate to character, and therewith, a basis for drawing hierarchical distinctions between humans.

With the science of natural history now adding its voice to a chorus led by political and religious schematizations that proclaim the reality and significance of human difference in terms of race, the creation and reification of the modern biological concept of race is effectively complete. Given the pre-eminence of this concept during the age of Western European Enlightenment, it should come as no surprise to see early expressions of liberalism intimately involved in the intellectual dynamic that defined the socio-political significance of race.

Long regarded as progenitors of liberalism, John Locke and Immanuel Kant develop philosophies that herald the enlightenment commitment to human liberty and equality. In his famous *Second Treatise on Government*, Locke declares that all men are naturally in:

> *a state of perfect freedom* to order their actions, and dispose of their possessions and persons, as they think fit, within the bounds of the law of nature [i.e., reason], without asking leave, or depending on the will of any other man.
>
> A state also of *equality*, wherein all the power and jurisdiction is reciprocal, no one having more than another; there being nothing more evident than that creatures of the same species and rank, promiscuously born to all the same advantages of nature, and the use of the same faculties, should also be equal one amongst another without subordination or subjection. (Section II, par. 4)

Similarly, Kant formulates a supreme principle of morality that aims to guarantee universal respect for the intrinsic autonomy and equal worth of all: "Act so as to treat man, in your own person as well as in that of anyone else, as an end, never merely as a means."[12] From the foregoing, it would appear that both men are philosophically committed to an idea of human equality that transcends race. Unfortunately this proves not to be the case.

In order to clearly understand the relation in which each of their philosophies stands to the notion of race, you have to resist the temptation to read them anachronistically. If successful, the careful reader will find that both philosophies are structured so as to accommodate subordinating racial discriminations. Both philosophies rely on what seem to be non-racial, or more broadly, non-discriminatory philosophical anthropologies. In Locke's case, however, notice the fact that although his philosophy clearly postulates equality and prohibits "sub-ordination or subjection," it does so only for "creatures of the same species and rank," which for Locke means those who are "industrious and rational."[13] Analogously, despite Kant's insistence that all men be regarded as ends in themselves, the actual concern is for man qua "rational being" as opposed to humans in toto. In sum, each philosophy employs a notion of humanity that is defined in terms of specific threshold conditions, conditions that warrant racial exclusions.

The fact of such warrant proves undeniable when each philosopher's specific views of racial difference are properly taken into account. As David Goldberg points out, Locke's particular view of racial difference reflects "widely held European presuppositions about the nature of racial others," and is largely a consequence of his nominalistic conception of human identity.[14] In contrast to metaphysical views that consider particular properties essential to the constitution of an object, Locke contends that objects are best understood in terms of "nominally essential properties," i.e., the contingent properties of an object that the speakers of a language conventionally designate as essential. Thus construed, essence is a function of collective perception. And in the case of race, Locke himself points out that color serves as a nominally essential property of humans insofar as empirical observations give rise to the consensus that color is correlated to rational capacity. Given this consensus, he concludes that conceptions of humanity could rationally fail to include racial others among "creatures of the same species and rank."

Like Locke, Kant also accepts the consensus view that racial differences correlate to differences in rational capacity. Noting David Hume's remarks about the inferiority of the Negro, Kant writes:

> Mr. Hume challenges anyone to cite a simple example in which a negro has shown talents, and asserts that among the hundreds of thousands of blacks who are transported elsewhere from their countries, although many of them have been set free, still not a single one was ever found who presented anything great in art or science or any other praiseworthy quality, even though among the whites some continually rise aloft from the lowest rabble, and through superior gifts earn respect in the world. So fundamental is the difference between the two races of man, and it appears to be as great in regard to mental capacities as in color.[15]

Moreover, as Cornel West points out, Kant's commitment to the view that racial differences are indicative of differences in rational capacity is further evidenced when he disparages a black man's advice to a Father Labat, by noting that although the man's advice may contain some elements worthy of consideration, the fact that "this fellow was quite black from head to foot" served as "a clear proof" that, by and large, what he had to say was stupid.

> And it might be that there was something in this which perhaps deserved to be considered; but in short, this fellow was quite black from head to foot, a clear proof that what he said was stupid.[16]

In line with their outlooks, both philosophers accepted slavery as an acceptable consequence of racial difference. As an investor in the slave trade and a contributor to the drafting of the Carolina colony's slave constitution, Locke was an active supporter of the institution of slavery. Although Locke's acceptance of slavery is most often couched in terms of his notion of a just war, he also warrants slavery on the basis of racial inferiority. Notice once more that for Locke, respect of freedom and equality are the natural rights of "creatures of the same species and rank." However, insofar as certain races, such as Native Americans, are clearly inferior in terms of "industriousness and rationality," they lack the requisite rank and thereby fail to count as creatures worthy of equal respect. Similarly, Kant condones slavery for much the same reasons. Dismissing Native Americans as completely unredeemable (and by implication, worthy of genocidal eradication), he goes on to offer the following comments about Negroes:

> The race of the Negroes, one could say, is completely the opposite of the Americans; they are full of affect and passion, very lively, talkative, and vain. They can be educated but only as servants (slaves), that is they allow themselves to be trained.[17]

Highlighting Kant's ideological complicity in the institution of slavery, Christian Neurgebauer points out that Kant also counsels those who engage in the "training" of African servants or slaves to beat them into submission using a "split bamboo cane instead of a whip" so as to inflict the greatest degree of pain and suffering possible without causing death.[18]

Although Locke's and Kant's philosophies are continually celebrated as classic and paradigmatic expressions of liberalism, rarely are they viewed more broadly in terms of the obvious ways in which their underlying philosophical anthropologies intersect with the biological concept of race. However, once appreciated, these intersections clearly reveal that in its earliest forms, liberalism sanctioned racial exclusions and oppressions and hence reified the concept of race as politically significant.

Contemporary Egalitarian Liberalism and the Marginalization of Race

In contrast to classic expressions of liberalism that consider race constitutive of identity, and therewith, an important political consideration, contemporary expressions of liberalism dismiss race as essentially irrelevant. Unlike classical expressions of liberalism, which sanctioned and perpetuated various forms of human subjugation and subordination by relying upon a dubious philosophical anthropology that reified biological notions of substantive human difference, contemporary theories vigilantly regard each and every human individual as equal irrespective of the specific characteristics that are constitutive of his or her identity. In his landmark work, *A Theory of Justice*, John Rawls regards race as nothing more than an accidental feature of human identity that has no bearing on one's essential character. Focusing exclusively on a universal human capacity for reason, he views considerations of human particularity, e.g., gender, age, religion, class, as well as race, antithetical to the creation of principles of justice dedicated to equal regard for all. In its less extreme forms, egalitarian liberalism marginalizes race by turning a blind eye to its normative social significance and focusing instead on procedural constraints aimed at creating equitable distributions of social goods and positions.

In both cases, the impetus for the marginalization of race stems in large part from a well-meaning commitment to social justice.

In general, egalitarian liberalism considers universality and impartiality fundamental to the political project of establishing and preserving social justice. Faced with the difficult task of reconciling and balancing the diverging and sometimes competing interests manifest within a society comprised of a diverse plurality of persons, contemporary theorists embrace universality and impartiality as constitutive characteristics of any ideal theory of justice. In particular, they consider universality the hallmark of a theory that both encompasses and applies to all and impartiality an effective guarantee that its principles and dictates will afford everyone an equal measure of consideration and respect.

Following in the tradition of the European Enlightenment, egalitarian liberalism considers reason, or more precisely, a capacity for reason, central to both universality and impartiality. However, in contrast to early expressions of liberalism, contemporary versions reject the idea that differences in race correspond to differences in rational capacity and unequivocally extend the notion of human equality to all. In particular, egalitarian liberalism strives to establish universal respect and impartial political regard for everyone by designing principles of justice that fairly distribute rights, duties, benefits, and burdens among all members of the society. In an effort to derive these principles in accordance with a fundamental respect for human autonomy, John Rawls creates a hypothetical original position that allows the rational members of a society to engage in impartial deliberations aimed at producing fair principles of justice.

In Rawls's original position, the parties engaged in deliberations concerning the principles of justice are sequestered behind a "veil of ignorance," that deprives them of knowledge of their particular race, sex, social position, talents, abilities, convictions, desires, and overall goals. Although they know that they do have specific interests and aims in life, the veil of ignorance forces them to determine the principles of justice independently of them. Thus situated, the individuals behind the veil are effectively reduced to nondescript rational agents. Stripped of all knowledge of their own particular needs, interests, and aims, all parties consider it prudent to select principles of justice that promote common interests and treat people equally and fairly regardless of their actual constitution and circumstance.

Despite its obvious advantages over early expressions of liberalism in terms of its genuine commitment to human equality, Rawlsian liberalism's antiseptic notions of universality and impartiality prove to be dangerously unrealistic and insensitive to the constitutive importance of race. In its zeal to theoretically provide and safeguard universal respect and regard for all members of society, Rawlsian liberalism reduces the human individual to an emaciated self. According to Rawls, only the capacity for reason is essential to human identity; everything else that commonly attaches to personhood is accidental and ascriptive. Moreover, following Kant, Rawls considers "moral personality," i.e., our nature as free and equal human beings, "the fundamental aspect of the self."[19] Given this view, human equality becomes manifest as a self-evident truth. Unfortunately, however, such conceptions of the self secure a universal regard and respect for all human beings at the expense of everything constitutive of individuality.

Critics of this philosophical anthropology charge that it belittles all of the substantive features of character and individuality that are constitutive of our identity as persons. Emphasizing this point with respect to race, Lucius Outlaw writes:

> For me, raciality and ethnicity (and gender) are constitutive of the personal and social being of persons, thus are not secondary, unessential matters: they make up the historically mediated structural features of human life-worlds and inform lived experience. Further, they have both absolute (i.e., in themselves) and relative (i.e., in relation to other racial, ethnic, gender groups) value *to the extent that, and for as long as, persons take them to be constitutive of who they are.* It is here that the philosophical anthropology of the Enlightenment [and of Rawlsian liberalism] comes up short. A theory of society that sets itself the task of understanding, scripting, and producing revolutionary social transformation while disregarding these basic "social facts" is, in my judgment, seriously deficient.[20]

At base, critics such as Outlaw and others are troubled by the fact that a narrow and presumptuous characterization of human beings as rational creatures capable of substantive self-reflection and self-determination independent of character and circumstance demeans the concrete concatenation of facts, features, and facets that are intrinsic to who we are. Distinguished in terms of varying endowments of talents and abilities that contribute to their sense of self-worth; united by the affections, affiliations, and shared experiences that define them as members of various collectivities; intertwined within a historically mediated nexus of social, political and economic relations that contextualize their interactions; and emboldened by the aims and attachments reflectively informed by their particular situations and perspectives, human beings are undoubtedly creatures whose individual identities are inextricably rich and complex.

By and large, current expressions of egalitarian liberalism reject the presumptive practice of making reductive metaphysical claims about human identity. In fact, Rawls himself later qualifies his own view in an effort to disavow any earlier invocations of the Kantian noumenal self.[21] Nevertheless, despite its recognition of the constitutive importance of particularity with respect to human identity, egalitarian liberalism remains complicit in the marginalization of race. In particular, egalitarian liberalism fails to adequately appreciate and address the constitutive importance of race with respect to social norms. Committed to the view that race should play no role in the determination and realization of an individual's prospects for life, egalitarian expressions of liberalism devise a variety of institutional dictates and initiatives aimed at creating a society that extends rights and opportunities equally to all of its citizens regardless of race. Unfortunately, however, these dictates and initiatives are insufficient to stem the tide of racial discrimination.

Sensitive to this fact, egalitarian liberalism endorses additional corrective measures such as affirmative action. Although many people view affirmative action as a program whose special concern for certain groups and races is antithetical to a commitment to disregarding race, egalitarian theorists argue that affirmative action measures are actually consistent with this stance when viewed in terms of the broader scope of their mission. Recognizing the social virtues of affirmative action, Ronald Dworkin argues that race-based preferential-treatment programs aimed at increasing the numbers of underrepresented groups in socially strategic positions and professions are justified in virtue of their viability as means of reducing the degree to which a society is racially conscious.[22] Thus construed, the goal of affirmative action is to neutralize race and thereby render it socially and politically insignificant. Unfortunately, this normative commitment to the marginalization of race fails to appreciate its pervasive significance within the social order.

Focusing in particular on the absence of certain racial groups (and women) from various positions of privilege and distinction, affirmative action calls on institutions to curb social injustice by adopting formal procedures that provide members of these groups greater access to opportunities and positions that influence an individual's range of life-plans and prospects for success.[23] Unfortunately, however, the procedural focus on greater access in no way addresses the underlying social conditions that bear heavily on a person's chances for success. Given a pre-established and rigidly entrenched corporate, professional, or institutional "culture," a person's success depends not on whether or not they gain access, but on whether or not they can adapt to the "culture" and win acceptance by living up to its norms. Highlighting this situation in relation to African Americans, David Cochran writes:

> Equality of opportunity integrates some African Americans into white institutions, but it does little to change the informal sources of power, rooted in an institution's culturally structured norms and practices, that still privilege white members. It may shuffle social positions, but it does little to address underlying social relations.[24]

More broadly, egalitarian liberalism's theoretical focus on equality of opportunity relies on the belief that racial discrimination is aberrant and that once the formal impediments to opportunity are removed, individuals will be measured only in terms of impartial norms and standards. Unfortunately, however, norms and standards are never impartial, for as Iris Young writes:

> Where group differences in capacities, values, and behavioral or cognitive styles exist, equal treatment in the allocation of reward according to rules of merit competition will reinforce and perpetuate disadvantage. Equal treatment requires everyone to be measured according to the same norms, but in fact there are no "neutral" norms of behavior and performance. Where some groups are privileged and others oppressed, the formulation of law, policy, and the rules of private institutions tend to be biased in favor of the privileged groups, because their particular experience implicitly sets the norm.[25]

In sum, Young highlights the troubling fact that egalitarian liberalism's failure to fully acknowledge and address the fundamental significance of race actually results in the unintended perpetuation and exacerbation of social injustice.

The New Enlightenment: Race Consciousness in the Service of Social Justice

Commenting on what he would do if he had an opportunity to teach children victimized by the systemic social and economic effects of racial discrimination, James Baldwin writes:

> I would try to teach them – I would try to make them know – that those streets, those houses, those dangers, those agonies by which they are surrounded are criminal. I would try to make each child know that these things are the results of a criminal conspiracy to destroy him. I would teach him that if he intends to get to be a man, he must at once decide that he is stronger than this conspiracy and that he must never make peace with it. And that one of his weapons for refusing to make his peace with it and for destroying it depends on what he decides he is worth. I would teach him that there are currently very few standards in this country which are worth a man's respect. That it is up to him to begin to change these standards for the sake of the life and health of the country.[26]

Embedded within Baldwin's poignant account of his own pedagogical aims is an apt description of the difficulties and challenges wrought by invidious institutional forms of racism. The first thing that Baldwin notes is an array of desperate material and social conditions that disproportionately befall people of color. Characterizing the failure to address these conditions as "criminal," he attributes the creation and reproduction of identifiable patterns of racial discrimination to what is best described as a conspiracy of unjust institutional structures, processes, and practices. In the face of this conspiracy, he challenges its victims to dedicate themselves to creating a healthy society by affirming their own self worth and changing the pernicious standards and norms that disparage it. Echoing Baldwin's charge, many critics believe that insofar as egalitarian liberalism is dedicated to the creation of a healthy, and therewith equitable, society, it must also recognize the incumbent need to facilitate the transformation of institutional standards and norms in the name of social justice (Mills 1998; Outlaw; West; Young). Moreover, the consensus among these scholars is that egalitarian liberalism must move beyond the focus on equitable patterns of distribution and broaden its mission to include the goal of equitable institutional structures, i.e., procedural and organizational constraints, that are responsive to the underlying conditions that produce and reproduce racial discrimination.

Standing out as one of the most obvious and efficacious means of realizing this goal is a shift from a sweeping philosophical commitment to universality and impartiality that marginalizes race as well as other forms of human specificity to a more enlightened commitment to plurality and deference that embodies a greater sensitivity to the political significance of group-specific differences. Popularly known as the politics of difference, the idea is to break the social cycles of domination and oppression by diversifying the institutional power structures that determine the norms, standards, and policies of the socio-political order.

In concert with this new approach, enlightened liberalism reconceptualizes affirmative action as more than just a means of promoting equal access to socially significant positions and professions. Recognizing the biases inherent in the norms, policies and procedures that structure social institutions, enlightened liberalism endorses affirmative action as a means of promoting the internal transformation of these institutions in ways that better accommodate diversity. Thus deployed, the goal of affirmative action is to ensure not only that marginalized social groups are represented within various social institutions, but that they are effectively represented at all levels of those institutions and within the decision-making bodies that govern them as well.

Thus conceived, however, affirmative action alone is insufficient to achieve enlightened liberalism's broader end. For example, consider a public university's large all white department of literature that adds two or three faculty of color in compliance with the school's state-mandated policy of affirmative action. Devoid of any real commitment to racial and ethnic diversity, the prevailing attitude of the existing members of the department is that its curriculum, standards, and practices are fine as they are and that it's OK if "these" people come in and teach "their" courses so long as they don't disrupt the current intellectual order. Given such a situation, it seems highly unlikely that the faculty of color will be able to work within the system to successfully diversify the department in substantive and meaningful ways.

Recognizing this difficulty, enlightened liberalism includes additional procedural components that compel institutions to substantively recognize social-group differences. Drawing upon Young's notion of an ideal democratic public, enlightened liberalism calls for structural changes that create mechanisms that guarantee that "the distinctive voices and perspectives" of those who are oppressed or disadvantaged are afforded due consideration.[27] Moreover, it demands that the society as a whole commit itself: (1) to supporting the development of group-specific organizations that allow marginalized social groups to discuss and define their collective needs and interests; and (2) to the development of institution-specific policies that require decision-making bodies to demonstrate that their deliberations "have taken group perspectives into consideration."[28] Thus, in the case of public policy, enlightened liberalism demands that issues that directly, and sometimes uniquely, pertain to marginalized groups are included on the local, state, and national agendas that frame public discourse. In the case of non-political institutions, enlightened liberalism demands that the voices and perspectives of the oppressed factor into the policies, procedures, and decisions that determine the ways in which they operate.

One of the principal benefits of these procedural constraints is the way in which they encourage the development of an enlightened self-consciousness. Here again, Young's account of an ideal democratic public proves instructive. Highlighting the virtues of guaranteeing political recognition of the voices of difference, Young stresses the fact that a polity that is structurally respectful of difference "asserts that oppressed groups have distinct cultures, experiences, and perspectives on social life with humanly positive meaning."[29] Furthermore, she points out that in making such assertions, a polity not only validates the identity of the oppressed in the eyes of others, it also encourages members of the oppressed to recognize the positive aspects of their particular group identity and break free of the self-denigrating forces of assimilation. Additionally, Young also notes that the public recognition of oppressed groups forces dominant groups to become conscious of their own specificity. And that more importantly, it undermines the pretense that their perspectives and values are objective and hence unbiased.

Coupling the procedural constraints of political recognition together with programs of affirmative action, enlightened liberalism creates a powerful dynamic for institutional change. At the structural level, the procedural constraints of political recognition effectively ensure that the needs, concerns, and perspectives of marginalized groups factor into institutional decision-making processes. Against this backdrop, the members of formerly excluded social groups who occupy positions within institutional power structures – positions that were made more accessible by affirmative action – enjoy conditions that enhance their ability to serve as effective agents for change.

Consider once again the example of the recently "integrated" literature department. With the addition of procedural constraints that force the department to recognize and consider a variety of different racial and ethnic voices and perspectives, monochromatic discussions of the character, content, and aims of the department's curriculum become infused with color. Furthermore, insofar as the white protectorate is now faced with having to justify the status quo to racially and ethnically distinct others, the contrivances and contingencies that give rise to the standards, styles, and objectives that it takes for granted as norms are more likely to be unmasked and thrust to the fore. Working within this environment, the faculty of color serve as an ever-present check against failures to adhere to the procedural demands of social justice. In addition, the faculty of color are guaranteed a formal opportunity to make a case for various forms of institutional change. And insofar as these demands serve the interests of social justice, they can take solace in the fact that they can no longer be denied without reasons that both reflect the due consideration of diverse perspectives, and are in keeping with a socio-political commitment to equal respect and regard for all.

In the end, it is a liberalism informed by the politics of difference that serves as the best response to the demands of social justice. Sensitive to the existential and political significance of race, as well as other forms of social-group specificity, such enlightened forms of liberalism transcend the limits of a mantra of universality and impartiality which perpetuates the institutional forms of discrimination that leave many people socially and psychologically trapped within invidious cycles of domination and oppression. Cognizant of the social and political realities of these pernicious cycles, an enlightened liberalism actively promotes the recognition of human specificity as a means of combating the hegemony of oppressive monolithic determinations of normativity.

Notes

1 Nettleship, *Lectures on the Republic of Plato*, p. 260.
2 Plato, *Republic*, 515c.
3 Kant, "What is Enlightenment?" translated by Carl J. Friedrich. In Friedrich (1949).
4 Kant goes on to describe the public use of one's reason as the exercise of one's reason outside of one's function in accordance with the demands of one's civic post or office.
5 Sandel, *Liberalism and the Limits of Justice*, p. 1.
6 Kant develops this argument in the *Groundwork of the Metaphysics of Morals*. The present summary is indebted to the lucid recapitulation developed by Michael Sandel in his *Liberalism and the Limits of Justice*.
7 Aristotle, *Politics*, 1254b and 1255b. Sadly, however, the Greeks considered women naturally lacking in the capacities and dispositions requisite of active political life.
8 Quoted in Hannaford, *Race: The History of an Idea in the West*, p. 91.
9 Ibid., pp. 166–7.
10 Ibid., p. 52.
11 Quoted in West, "A Genealogy of Modern Racism," p. 56.
12 Kant, *The Philosophy of Kant*, edited by Carl J. Friedrich, p. 178.
13 Locke, *Second Treatise on Government*, Section V, par. 34.
14 Goldberg, *Racist Culture*, p. 27.
15 Quoted in West, "A Genealogy of Modern Racism," pp. 62–3.
16 Quoted in ibid., p. 63.
17 Quoted in Eze, "The Color of Reason," in *Race and Enlightenment*, p. 215.
18 Ibid.
19 Rawls (1971), p. 563.
20 Outlaw, *On Race and Philosophy*, p. 174.
21 See Rawls, *Political Liberalism*, Lecture I, §4 and §5.
22 See Dworkin (1977), "Why Bakke Has No Case."
23 For a useful summary of the historical account of affirmative action see John D. Skrentny's *The Ironies of Affirmative Action*.

24   Cochran, *The Color of Freedom*, p. 62.
25   Quoted in ibid., p. 62.
26   Baldwin, "A Talk to Teachers," p. 685. James Baldwin (1998) *Collected Essays.*
27   Young, *Justice and the Politics of Difference*, p. 221.
28   Ibid.
29   Ibid., p. 204.

Bibliography

Appiah, K. A. (1992). *In My Father's House: Africa in the Philosophy of Culture.* New York: Oxford University Press.

——and Gutmann, A. (1996). *Color Conscious: The Political Morality of Race.* Princeton, NJ: Princeton University Press.

Baldwin, James (1998). *James Baldwin Collected Essays*, New York: The Library of America.

Banton, M. P. and J. Harwood (1975). *The Race Concept.* New York: Praeger.

Barker, E. (1948). *The Politics of Aristotle.* London, England: Oxford University Press.

Boxhill, B. R. (1984). *Blacks and Social Justice.* Totowa, NJ: Rowman & Allanheld.

Cochran, D. C. (1999). *The Color of Freedom: Race and Contemporary American Liberalism.* Albany, NY: State University of New York Press.

Dworkin, Ronald (1977). "Why Bakke Has No Case." The New York Review of Books, November 10, 1977. In John Arthur (ed.) (1981). *Morality and Moral Controversies.* Englewood Cliffs, NJ: Prentice Hall Inc.

Eze, E. C. (ed.) (1997). *Race and the Enlightenment: A Reader.* Cambridge, MA: Blackwell.

Feagin, J. R. and C. B. Feagin (1978). *Discrimination American Style.* Englewood Cliffs, NJ: Prentice-Hall.

Friedrich, C. J. (ed.) (1949). *The Philosophy of Kant: Immanuel Kant's Moral and Political Writings.* New York: The Modern Library.

Goldberg, D. T. (1993). *Racist Culture: Philosophy and the Politics of Difference.* Cambridge, MA: Blackwell.

Gray, J. (1986). *Liberalism.* Minneapolis, MN: University of Minnesota Press.

Hamilton, E. and C. Huntington (eds.) (1961). *Plato: The Collected Dialogues.* Princeton, NJ: Princeton University Press.

Hannaford, I. (1996). *Race: The History of an Idea in the West.* Baltimore, MD: The Johns Hopkins University Press.

Kymlicka, W. (1990). *Contemporary Political Philosophy: An Introduction.* New York: Oxford University Press.

Macpherson, C. B. (ed.) (1980). *Second Treatise on Government.* Indianapolis, IN: Hackett Publishing Co.

Mills, C. W. (1997). *The Racial Contract.* Ithaca, NY: Cornell University Press.

——(1998). *Blackness Visible: Essays on Philosophy and Race.* Ithaca, NY: Cornell University Press.

Nettleship, R. L. (1955). *Lectures on the Republic of Plato*, 2nd edn. London, England: Macmillan.

Outlaw, L. T. (1996). *On Race and Philosophy.* New York: Routledge.

Rawls, J. (1971). *A Theory of Justice.* Cambridge, MA: Harvard University Press.

——(1993). *Political Liberalism.* New York: Columbia University Press.

Sandel, M. J. (1989). *Liberalism and the Limits of Justice.* New York: Cambridge University Press.

Skrentny, J. D. (1996). *The Ironies of Affirmative Action: Politics, Culture, and Justice in America.* Chicago, IL: The University of Chicago Press.

Snowden, F. M. (1983). *Before Color Prejudice.* Cambridge, MA: Harvard University Press.

West, C. (1982). "A Genealogy of Modern Racism." In C. West, *Prophesy Deliverance! An African-American Revolutionary Christianity.* Philadelphia, PA: The Westminster Press.

Young, I. M. (1990). *Justice and the Politics of Difference.* Princeton, NJ: Princeton University Press.

Chapter 13

Religion and Liberal Democracy

Christopher J. Eberle

In 1992, Bill McCartney, then head coach of the University of Colorado football team and subsequent founder of "Promise-Keepers," held a news conference in which he asserted that homosexual lifestyles are an "abomination of almighty God" and on that basis urged his fellow Coloradans to amend their state's constitution. "Amendment 2" would have repealed existing laws in Colorado that prohibit work- and housing-related discrimination against homosexual citizens and would have forbidden the passage of any comparable law elsewhere in that state. McCartney's public advocacy of Amendment 2 turned out to be critically important, as it energized an otherwise moribund petition drive to put Amendment 2 on statewide ballot. Ultimately, however, McCartney's extremely controversial crusade came to naught. Although passed with a slight majority, Amendment 2 was struck down by the United States Supreme Court on grounds that it violates the Equal Protection Clause.

McCartney's advocacy of Amendment 2 raises a number of important questions. Not the least of those questions has to do with the *moral merits* of Amendment 2, e.g., is it morally appropriate for the state to force a landlord who believes that homosexuality is an abomination to let an apartment to homosexual applicants? There are a number of distinct, but no less important, questions that McCartney's advocacy of Amendment 2 raises – questions that have to do, not with the moral merits of Amendment 2, but with the *manner* in which a citizen ought to evaluate the merits of Amendment 2. Specifically, the following question has received considerable attention from liberal theorists: Is it appropriate for a citizen to support a law on the basis of her religious convictions?[1] Was it appropriate for McCartney to urge his fellow Coloradans to amend their state's constitution by appealing to the claim that homosexual relations are an abomination to God? Given that the citizens of Colorado adhere to widely divergent moral, metaphysical and religious commitments, was it morally proper for McCartney to advocate for Amendment 2 on so sectarian a basis?

Note that this question is not a *legal* one: no liberal theorist disputes the claim that each citizen has a legal right to support a law on religious grounds. Indeed, the question at hand is not really a matter of *moral rights*: presumably each citizen has a moral right to support her favored laws on pretty much whatever basis she pleases. But a citizen can exercise her moral and legal rights in an irresponsible manner. (Even if the rich have a legal and moral right not to give of their excess to the starving, their failure to do so might very well be reprehensible.) The question that has exercised many liberal theorists is whether a citizen is *morally criticizable* for exercising her moral and legal rights in a certain way, viz., by supporting her favored laws on religious grounds.

Note that there are two importantly different ways to formulate this question. First, is it morally appropriate for a citizen such as McCartney to support his favored laws on the basis of his religious convictions? Second, is it morally appropriate for McCartney to support his favored laws on the basis of his religious convictions *alone*? It is one thing for McCartney to support Amendment 2 on non-religious grounds, thereby addressing his non-religious compatriots, yet *also* to support Amendment 2 on *corroboratory* religious grounds. It is quite another matter – a much more troubling matter, given its sectarian overtones – for McCartney to support Amendment 2 for no reason other than a religious reason. Given its particularly troubling nature, recent discussions among liberal theorists have tended to focus on the latter kind of religious support, as shall I. So, then, here is the focal point of this essay: may a citizen support a law *solely* on religious grounds or, to the contrary, ought she insure that she enjoys a rationale that *includes* (even if it is not limited to) a non-religious rationale?

Justificatory Liberalism

Many prominent liberal theorists are committed to some blend of *justificatory liberalism*: in spite of significant disagreements, liberal theorists as diversely committed as John Rawls, Amy Gutmann, Charles Larmore, Gerald Gaus, and Robert Audi have defended that position or some close cousin thereof.[2] And it is in virtue of their commitment to justificatory liberalism that Rawls, et al., affirm the following position: that each citizen should insure that she has a suitable non-religious rationale for her favored coercive laws, such that a citizen who supports a coercive law solely on religious grounds is morally criticizable for so doing. (The pertinent discussions typically focus on *coercive* laws – and I will narrow my focus accordingly.[3])

What is justificatory liberalism? First, justificatory liberals are committed to a suitable selection of particular policies and practices. Most centrally, they believe that each citizen should enjoy an adequate scheme of *rights*: to free speech, to free association, to religious freedom, to vote, to due process, etc. Adherence to such substantive commitments, given wide latitude for alternative specifications, is a necessary condition of adherence to justificatory liberalism – it is what makes the justificatory liberal a *liberal*. But adherence to such substantive commitments is nowhere nearly sufficient for adherence to *justificatory* liberalism; one can be fully committed to such policies and nevertheless reject justificatory liberalism. A second, further commitment distinguishes justificatory liberalism from other species of liberalism, viz., the *norm of public justification*: that a citizen ought to provide a public justification for her favored coercive laws. The clarion call of justificatory liberalism is that each citizen ought to support only those coercive laws that she sincerely takes to be *justifiable* to each member of the *public*.

The norm of public justification will be a central focus of attention in this essay, just as it has been a focal point of recent liberal political theory generally, and just as it has been a focal point of recent discussions of the more specific issue of the proper role of religion in liberal politics. But what, exactly, is a public justification? Proposals vary widely; the concept of "public justification" is exceptionally slippery and has been articulated in a dizzying variety of alternative and often conflicting ways. Nevertheless, given even its diverse specifications, the basic notion is fairly straightforward. A public justification is an *other-directed* rationale: a citizen's rationale must be convincing not only to her, given her distinctive point of view, but to other citizens as well given their respective points of view. A public justification isn't just a rationale that its proponents regard as plausible, but is also one that its proponents expect that their compatriots will, or at least can, take to be plausible.

The claim that a citizen should provide a public justification for her favored coercive laws has an immediate bearing on the proper role of religious convictions in liberal politics. How so? A religious rationale is *paradigmatically* non-public. Given the highly pluralistic nature of a contemporary liberal democracy such as the United States, any religious rationale will be utterly unconvincing to many citizens: McCartney's rationale for Amendment 2 is a case in point. And even though a high proportion of United States citizens are theists, millions are not and so will reject McCartney's rationale for Amendment 2. Consequently, McCartney's rationale does not count as a public justification. Since there is nothing special about the kind of religious rationale McCartney offered for Amendment 2, we may generalize: *no* religious rationale by itself suffices for a public justification. Consequently, according to the justificatory liberal, a citizen who enjoys only a religious rationale for a favored coercive law ought to withhold her support from that coercive law. The position, then, that a citizen ought to refrain from supporting coercive laws solely on religious grounds is a direct implication of the norm of public justification and is, therefore, a non-negotiable feature of justificatory liberalism.

Justificatory vs. Mere Liberalism

The heart of justificatory liberalism, the commitment that distinguishes it from other species of liberalism, is a claim about the kinds of reasons a citizen may employ as a basis for coercive laws. Since what distinguishes the justificatory liberal from other species of liberal is a matter of the sort of justification required for coercive laws, rather than a matter of the specific laws the justificatory liberal affirms, it is possible to *reject* justificatory liberalism without thereby rejecting *any* of the substantive commitments characteristically associated with a liberal polity. It is possible, in short, to reject justificatory liberalism and nevertheless to affirm *mere liberalism*, where a necessary and sufficient condition of commitment to mere liberalism is commitment to characteristic liberal policies. Thus, for example, Elijah can affirm the right to religious freedom, he can affirm that right solely on religious grounds, yet he can deny that he should refrain from supporting that right, absent a public justification. In that case, Elijah adheres to a fundamental liberal commitment – to religious freedom – but eschews the norm of public justification. He is, we may assume, a mere, but not a justificatory, liberal.

This distinction between justificatory liberalism and mere liberalism enables us to clarify three important points. First, as indicated by the fact that Elijah can coherently affirm the right to religious freedom solely on religious grounds, commitment to religious freedom is distinct from commitment to the norm of public justification. These two commitments arise at different levels of discourse: the right to religious freedom is a substantive policy for which a citizen might have all manner of reasons whereas the norm of public justification is a constraint on the sort of reasons a citizen ought to have for her favored policies.

Second, it is possible to reject justificatory liberalism and nevertheless be *rationally justified* in accepting characteristic liberal commitments (such as to religious freedom). This possibility is a function of constitutive differences between rational and public justification. Put crudely and dogmatically, rationality of belief formation is a function of the manner in which a citizen employs *his* cognitive capacities in reflecting on the reasons available in *his* epistemic environment in reaching conclusions that make sense from *his* perspective, whereas a public justification is a function of a citizen's being able to articulate a rationale that *others* do, or can, regard as convincing. Given appropriately different epistemic environments, rational justification and public justification can diverge. For example, we may assume that, given the evidence available in his epistemic environment, Socrates rationally believed that the sun revolves around the earth; that, given the evidence available in our epistemic environment, we moderns rationally deny that the sun revolves around the earth; and that, given the relevant differences between our respective epistemic environments, Socrates would have been unable to articulate a rationale for his geocentric convictions that we moderns regard as even remotely convincing. In that hypothetical case, Socrates would enjoy a rational, but not a public, justification for his geocentric convictions. And, of course, this truth about matters astronomical is equally true for matters political: Elijah can be rationally justified in affirming the right to religious freedom given the evidence available in his epistemic environment but be unable to articulate a rationale for that right that will, or even can, be convincing to those ensconced in sufficiently different epistemic environments. Rational justification is one thing, public justification quite another.

Third, it is possible to reject the specific constraint on reasons that justificatory liberals advocate and nevertheless to endorse any number of alternative constraints. For example, it is plausible to suppose that a citizen ought to support only those coercive laws that she rationally takes to be morally defensible. But given that rational and public justification can diverge, one can accept that fairly burdensome constraint and nevertheless reject the norm of public justification. In short, to reject the norm of public justification does not commit one to the claim that *anything goes* by way of the manner in which a citizen may support her favored coercive laws.

We are now in a position to focus narrowly on the most contentious aspect of justificatory liberalism. There is nothing particularly contentious about the justificatory liberal's advocacy of *religious freedom*: both the justificatory liberal and her critics are free to agree that each citizen enjoys that right. There is nothing particularly contentious about the claim that a citizen should have *good reason* for her favored coercive laws: both the justificatory liberal and her critics are free to concur that a citizen may support only those coercive laws she rationally takes to be morally defensible. And there is nothing particularly contentious about the claim that a citizen should obey *restrictions on the reasons* she employs as a basis for her favored coercive laws: both the justificatory liberal and her critics can agree that each citizen should abide by some such restrictions, e.g., that each citizen should withhold support from coercive laws, absent rational justification. Rather, the main point of contention has to do with the *specific restrictions* on reasons the justificatory liberal endorses: she claims that each citizen should enjoy a public justification for her favored coercive laws and thus should not support coercive laws solely on religious grounds, whereas many critics have found that restriction indefensible.

Why Public Justification?

Why reject the norm of public justification and its correlative strictures on religious grounds? Surely one of a citizen's most important obligations is to treat her compatriots in accord with the dictates of conscience. A citizen acts in accord with her conscience only if she treats her compatriots in ways that she sincerely believes to be morally appropriate. So one of a citizen's most important moral obligations is to treat her compatriots in ways that accord with what she sincerely takes to be morally appropriate. But the norm of public justification requires of each citizen a willingness to violate this fundamentally important obligation. Consequently, we should reject the norm of public justification.

The crucial premise here is the claim that the norm of public justification requires of each citizen a willingness to refrain from treating her compatriots in accord with the dictates of conscience. And why believe that premise? As we have seen, the norm of public justification is a restriction on the reasons a citizen is permitted to employ to support a coercive law. And it is possible that a citizen who abides by that restriction concludes that the balance of *permissible* reasons provides insufficient support for a coercive law that she regards as morally obligatory when judged from the point of view of both *permissible* and *impermissible* reasons. Consider Rachel, whose religious convictions provide essential support for the claim that a fetus is a person, and thus that aborting a fetus is morally reprehensible, and thus that the state ought to criminalize abortion. Rachel believes that aborting a fetus is morally reprehensible but would not do so were it not for her religious commitments. In that case, the norm of public justification counsels Rachel to refrain from supporting any law that criminalizes abortion and thus forbids her to support a coercive law that she sincerely believes to be mandated by moral truths of obvious importance. And although Rachel need not ever find herself so unfortunately circumstanced, she should recognize that she *might* find herself so circumstanced and that, if she is, obedience to the norm of public justification requires her to exercise restraint. So a citizen who commits to the norm of public justification must be *willing* to violate the dictates of conscience even if she need not ever do so.

Given the importance of a citizen's obligation to treat her compatriots in accord with the dictates of conscience, it would seem that each citizen has powerful moral reason to reject the norm of public justification. Moreover, given the peculiar nature of religious commitment, it seems that religious citizens have even further reason to reject the norm of public justification. For religious citizens typically regard their obligation to obey God as *overriding* – as their most important and weighty obligation. And they often take adherence to their religious practices as essential to their identity as persons and thus to a *meaningful* existence. Given these facts about religious commitment, the strictures imposed on religious citizens by the norm of public justification are extremely burdensome. And so it seems that religious citizens have particularly powerful reason to reject the norm of public justification.

The Argument from Respect

This argument is far from conclusive. After all, there are some contexts in which a citizen ought to abide by restrictions that are similar in structure to the norm of public justification. For example, a citizen on a jury ought to refrain from considering reliable but inadmissible evidence in her deliberations. But there are powerful reasons why the members of a jury ought to abide by such restrictions. And the burden on the justificatory liberal is to provide considerations that override what seems a powerful presumption against the kind of restriction constitutive of the norm of public justification.

The *argument from respect* is by far the most common argument for the norm of public justification, of which Charles Larmore's is perhaps the clearest and most compelling. Larmore's argument begins with a claim about human personhood. A person has her own perspective on the world: she has a set of cares and concerns in virtue of which things matter to her. A person also has the capacity to reflect on those cares and concerns, to employ her reflective capacity to change her perspective on the world and therefore to alter what matters to her. In that essential respect, persons differ from non-persons – from rocks, trees, and pieces of lint. Such non-persons have no cares and concerns, and so nothing matters to them, and so they have no perspective on the world that can be altered by reflection.

These facts about personhood have an important bearing on how a citizen ought to treat her compatriots: because persons care about what happens to them and, in particular, are typically deeply averse to being treated as the object of another's whim, a citizen ought not merely manipulate her compatriots, as she may pieces of lint and other non-persons. More generally, a citizen ought not treat her compatriots *merely* as means to her ends, as she is permitted to treat non-persons. Rather, she ought to treat persons as ends in themselves – not *just* as ends in themselves, but *also* as ends in themselves.

This general principle has an important implication for our topic. If a citizen ought not treat her compatriots solely as means to her ends, then she ought to refrain from getting her compatriots to submit to her demands only by coercing them. Larmore writes:

> Now forcing people to comply with principles of conduct is to treat them as means: their compliance is seen as conducive to public order or perhaps to their own reformation. In itself the use or threat of force cannot be wrong, for otherwise political association would be impossible. What is prohibited by the norm of respect is resting compliance only on force. For the distinctive feature of persons is that they are beings capable of thinking and acting on the basis of reasons. If we try to bring about conformity to some political principle simply by threat, we will be treating people solely as means, as objects of coercion. We will not be treating them as ends, engaging directly their distinctive capacity as persons.[4]

If a citizen ought not countenance the employment only of force to insure compliance to some law, then how ought she to insure compliance? By addressing her compatriots on the basis of their capacity to reflect on what matters to them. Her obligation to respect her compatriots requires a citizen to commit herself to bring about conformity to her favored coercive laws by means of rational discourse: she will try to *convince* her compatriots that her favored coercive laws are morally appropriate by addressing them with *reasons* rather than depending solely on the threat of punishment.

A citizen committed to bringing about conformity to her favored coercive laws by means of rational discourse will abide by the canons of rational discourse. And the canons of rational discourse oblige a citizen to articulate arguments that her compatriots, given their distinctive perspectives on the world, can accept. If Jill rejects Jack's rationale for coercive law L, and if Jack is committed to a rational resolution of their dispute over L, then he will not simply insist on repeating, in mantra-like fashion, his rationale for L. Rather, he will retreat to *neutral, common,* or *public* ground.

> In discussing how to resolve some problem (for example, what principles of political association they should adopt), people should respond to points of disagreement by retreating to neutral ground, to the beliefs they still share in order either to (a) resolve the disagreement and vindicate one of the disputed positions by means of arguments that proceed from this common ground, or (b) bypass the disagreement and seek a solution of the problem on the basis simply of this common ground.[5]

In order rationally to resolve a given disagreement, the interested parties must rely on common ground, premises contained in each of their respective evidential sets. And their retreat to common ground enables them to resolve the relevant disagreement in either of two ways. First, they can rely on common ground to resolve their disagreement in favor of one party, e.g., they can resolve a dispute over the morality of abortion by employing whatever common ground they enjoy to vindicate a particular position on abortion. This strategy is unlikely to succeed in most cases and so the parties engaged in rational discourse over disputed laws must find some other way to resolve their disagreement. And there is a second way: they can agree to disagree on the specific issue at hand but then employ the remaining claims they share to determine what ought to be done in spite of that disagreement, e.g., they can agree to bypass their dispute over the morality of abortion by agreeing to abide by the results of popular referenda on abortion-related policies.

Of course, whether citizens resolve their disputes in one or the other of these ways is not as important to Larmore as is his proposed constraint on the manner in which citizens ought to resolve their disputes. Given that a citizen's obligation to respect her compatriots forbids her to treat her compatriots merely as means to her ends, and given that a citizen's obligation to refrain from treating her compatriots merely as means to her ends implies that she ought to retreat to common ground, it seems that each citizen should commit to resolve political disagreements on the basis of common ground – by supporting only publicly justifiable resolutions of disagreements. And of course this conclusion has direct implications for our topic: since a citizen who enjoys only a religious rationale for coercive law L thereby does not enjoy the desired public justification for L, she ought not to support L.

Evaluation of Larmore's Argument from Respect

Larmore's version of the argument from respect is, I think, unsound. In order to see why, we need to distinguish between the claim that a citizen ought to *exercise restraint* and the claim that she ought to *pursue public justification.*[6] The claim that a citizen ought to exercise restraint, or as I shall say, *the doctrine of restraint*, is the claim that a citizen ought to withhold her support from any coercive law for which she lacks a public justification. The doctrine of restraint lays down a constraint on the policies a citizen is permitted to support: a citizen is permitted to support a coercive law L *only if* she enjoys a public justification for L. The "only if" implicit in the doctrine of restraint provides that doctrine with its critical edge: a citizen who lacks public justification for L *should not* support L. By contrast, the claim that a citizen ought to pursue public justification, or as I shall say, *the principle of pursuit*, is the claim that she ought to do what she can to insure that her compatriots have what each regards as adequate reason to support L. So the principle of pursuit is a claim about what a citizen should *aspire* to achieve.

Although distinct, both the principle of pursuit and the doctrine of restraint are embedded in the norm of public justification: that a citizen should *provide* a public justification for coercive law L, as the norm of public justification requires, is ambiguous as between the claim that she should *try* to provide a public justification for L and the claim that, if she *fails* in her attempt, she should withhold her support from L. That the doctrine of restraint and principle of pursuit are distinct is indicated by the fact that the former comes into play only after a citizen has failed in her pursuit of public justification. A citizen can do everything that can reasonably be expected by way of attempting to discern a public justification, and thus have *satisfied* her obligation to pursue public justification, without being *successful* in the attempt. We try but do not invariably succeed; we strive but all too often fail to achieve our aspirations. That a citizen ought to pursue public justification for L provides her with no guidance at all as to what she should do in a case where she fails in that aspiration: that she ought to pursue public justification, pretty obviously, provides no guidance in answering the question, "What should I do in the event that, *having discharged my obligation to pursue public justification*, I nevertheless find myself without the desired justification?" Perhaps she should cease and desist from supporting that policy. That is as it may be, but we need a different argument for that claim than for the claim that she ought to pursue public justification.

It to me seems that Larmore's version of the argument from respect vindicates the principle of pursuit: in Larmore's idiolect, respect requires the *aspiration* to decide political matters by retreating to common ground. And that is no mean achievement: that a citizen ought to obey the principle of pursuit forbids her to conduct her political deliberations and advocacy entirely within the ambit of her parochial convictions. Rather, she ought to exit her perspective on the world and enter the respective mindsets of her compatriots, in order to articulate some rationale for her favored coercive laws that her compatriots find convincing. And, of course, the principle of pursuit has direct implications for religious citizens: a citizen must exit her *religious* perspective on the world and attempt to articulate some rationale for her favored coercive laws that her compatriots might find convincing.

Although his is a very important conclusion, Larmore intends to vindicate not just the principle of pursuit but also the doctrine of restraint. As with justificatory liberals generally, Larmore wants religious citizens to refrain from engaging in certain activities: he wants McCartney to refrain from supporting Amendment 2 if McCartney enjoys only a religious rationale for Amendment 2. In fact, this restrictive aim seems much more central to the justificatory liberal's project than does the principle of pursuit. But Larmore does not succeed in vindicating his restrictive aim. Why?

If Larmore is correct, each citizen has an obligation to resolve disagreements over some coercive law L by retreating to common, neutral, or public ground. But it is a contingent matter whether there actually is common ground to which the parties who disagree over L can retreat. For any given dispute, it is possible that the parties to that dispute lack common ground that is sufficiently rich as to enable them either to resolve that dispute directly or to determine what to do given their inability to resolve their dispute. The case of abortion seems to fit this characterization: we find ourselves at loggerheads not just over the moral propriety of abortion but also over what to do given our interminable disagreement over that issue, e.g., whether we should allow the issue to be settled by popular referendum or by the dicta of the United States Supreme Court.

Given that there might be no common ground to which we can repair in order to reach a publicly justifiable resolution of our continuing disagreement over coercive law L, it is quite misleading to claim that we ought to retreat to common ground. That claim assumes that there will be common ground to which we can retreat. Since, however, there might not be any such ground, it would seem more accurate to claim that we have an obligation to retreat to common ground *so long as common ground is available*. After all, we cannot be obliged to do the impossible, viz., to retreat to a place that does not exist.

Suppose, then, that each citizen, out of respect for her compatriots as persons, ought to retreat to such common ground as exists. This conclusion immediately raises the question: What ought a citizen to do if she has done all that she feasibly can to discover or forge the desired common ground but cannot discern that common ground? Granted that she has done her level best to retreat to common ground, what does respect for her compatriots require her to do when the ground she shares with her compatriots is insufficient to resolve their disagreement? It seems to me that Larmore's argument provides no guidance whatsoever as to how we ought to answer that question. From the claim that a citizen ought to *try* to resolve her disagreements with her compatriots on the basis of common ground, nothing follows regarding what she ought to do if, having pursued common ground, her pursuit ends in failure.

Thus, for example, suppose that Bill McCartney had sincerely attempted to discern a widely convincing rationale for his conviction that homosexual relations are morally wrong, but failed in his attempt. The central question for McCartney is: What should McCartney do if he finds himself so circumstanced? Granted that he has attempted to vindicate Amendment 2 by retreating to common ground, and granted that he has failed in his attempt, may he persist in his support for Amendment 2? Larmore wants to claim that he may not – McCartney should cease and desist from supporting Amendment 2. But once we distinguish between the claim that McCartney should pursue public justification and the claim that he should exercise restraint, it seems clear that Larmore's argument establishes no such conclusion.

It might still seem that Larmore's argument has some life in it. After all, it might seem that a citizen who persists in supporting a coercive law absent a public justification fails to treat her compatriots as ends in themselves. After all, she does indeed coerce her compatriots against their respective wills, regardless of whether she has done what she can to avoid that condition.

This response is inadequate, and the distinction between pursuing public justification and exercising restraint enables us to see why. The moral heart of Larmore's argument is that a citizen who respects her compatriots ought not to treat her compatriots as means *only*, but she is not forbidden from treating them as means *at all*. But a citizen who pursues public justification for her favored laws does not treat her compatriots *only* as a means: she attempts to address her compatriots on the basis of their respective capacities to form their respective points of view regarding her actions. She attempts to reason with her compatriots, to convince them that her favored policies are appropriate. That she does not meet with success, and thus regards herself as conscience bound to support coercive laws absent a public justification, does not obviate the fact that she accords significant weight to the fact that her compatriots are persons and allows that fact to constrain the manner in which she supports her favored laws. Pretty clearly, a citizen who is committed to pursuing public justification but who refuses to exercise restraint treats her compatriots *both* as means *and* as ends in themselves.

A General Problem for the Argument from Respect

The doctrine of restraint is both central to, and yet the most contentious aspect of, the justificatory liberal's project: although few religious citizens will object to the principle of pursuit, many will find the doctrine of restraint intolerably burdensome. And as I see the matter, no appeal to respect for persons suffices to vindicate the doctrine of restraint. In fact, so long as religious citizens affirm the principle of pursuit, they take the argumentative wind out of the rhetorical sails of the argument from respect. How so? The argument from respect targets citizens (e.g., Bill McCartney) who intend to coerce their compatriots solely on the basis of their parochial convictions without concerning themselves at all with the fact that their compatriots lack reason to affirm their favored coercive laws. *That* kind of callous indifference to the fate of their compatriots is supposed to indicate that citizens who refuse to exercise restraint thereby disrespect their compatriots. But a citizen who persists in coercing her compatriots absent a public justification *need not* be callously indifferent to their fate. Consequently, it seems implausible to suppose that a citizen who insists on supporting her favored laws absent a public justification, and even solely on religious grounds, thereby fails to respect her compatriots.

This point is best made by considering a concrete case. Suppose that Elijah surveys what he sincerely and rationally takes to be all of the reliable evidence relevant to coercive law L. He abides by the relevant norms of rational justification and so, for example, he is willing to analyze critically the various considerations for and against L, to evaluate alternatives and amendments to L, to subject his preliminary convictions about L to the critical analysis of his peers, etc. He concludes, after all, that the case for L is compelling. Moreover, the case for L that he takes to be compelling is religious in nature. He realizes, of course, that that rationale will be unconvincing to many of his compatriots. So out of a deep aversion to coercing his compatriots against their better judgment, Elijah attempts to articulate a rationale for L that will be convincing to his compatriots and that, therefore, does not depend on his religious convictions. But he learns as a consequence of many hours of vigorous argument that he cannot do so: his pursuit of a public justification for L ends in failure. Given that he is rationally convinced that the case for L is compelling, Elijah persists in supporting L. He refuses to exercise the kind of restraint the justificatory liberal advocates, not out of a gleeful exercise of power over his compatriots, but with a sense of tragedy: he is conscience bound to impose L on his compatriots even though his compatriots have, as they see the matter, no reason at all to support L.

Does Elijah fail to manifest respect for his compatriots? I can't see that he does. In fact, I think that it is obvious that he does not disrespect his compatriots. Respect for persons requires a citizen, not to withhold her support from coercive laws absent a public justification, but to do what is within her power to avoid putting herself in the unfortunate condition that she lacks a public justification. A citizen who rationally believes that coercive law L is morally appropriate, who is therefore conscience bound to support L, and who assiduously pursues a public justification for L, does just that and *thereby* manifests the appropriate respect for her compatriots. So, it seems, a citizen who refrains from supporting coercive laws absent a rational justification and who pursues public justification, thereby respects her compatriots *irrespective* of her willingness to exercise restraint. And this conclusion has a direct bearing on our topic: since a citizen who supports L solely on religious grounds can fully commit both to withhold her support from coercive laws absent a rational justification and to pursue public justification, it follows that a citizen who supports her favored coercive laws solely on religious grounds need not disrespect her compatriots.

The Argument from Religious Warfare

The argument from respect to restraint has a decidedly deontological tone: although the justificatory liberal expects obedience to the doctrine of restraint to have all manner of salutary effects, the argument from respect does not depend for its soundness on any such claim about consequences. Given the demise of the argument from respect, perhaps a *consequentialist* rationale for the doctrine of restraint has a better chance of carrying the day. And justificatory liberals have not been loath to avail themselves of consequentialist considerations. Consider in this regard the *argument from religious warfare.*

Religious wars have played a defining role in the history of liberal democracy: the liberal commitment to freedom of religion was formulated and defended in direct reaction to an appalling series of events: a century and a half of wars fought to "resolve" religious disagreements. Given the defining, if dubious, role that religious warfare has played in the history of liberal democracy, the specter of religious warfare lingers on in the self-understanding of many liberal theorists: the bleak history of religious warfare motivates an extreme wariness regarding the intrusion of religion in politics. And, in some cases, that wariness motivates the justificatory liberal to endorse the doctrine of restraint. But why does the specter of religious warfare mandate citizens to obey the doctrine of restraint?

Here is one way to formulate the argument. Religious wars are morally abhorrent: military conflicts guided by religious aims are purely destructive, extraordinarily vicious and utterly without redeeming value. A widespread repudiation of restraint has a realistic prospect of engendering religious warfare: if religious citizens rely solely on their religious convictions to direct state coercion, such citizens might attempt to enlist the power of the state to force conversion and persecute heretics, an attempt that would likely be met with determined resistance. Given that a widespread repudiation of restraint has a realistic prospect of generating religious conflict, each citizen should obey the doctrine of restraint. In short, adherence to the doctrine of restraint is a crucial bulwark protecting us from confessional conflict.

Although very popular, this argument fails to vindicate the doctrine of restraint. Why? The argument is dystopian: it recommends that we should take seriously in our practical deliberations a possibility that has no realistic prospect of actualization under current or foreseeable conditions. Although it is no doubt logically possible that a widespread repudiation of restraint will result in religious warfare, conditions in a contemporary liberal democracy such as the United States render that possibility too remote to vindicate the doctrine of restraint. But why is the prospect of religious warfare so remote? What is it about the early twenty-first-century United States in virtue of which we can safely dismiss the prospect that we will be engulfed by a religiously generated war like that which afflicted, say, mid-seventeenth-century England? What has changed in the meantime? Simply put, we now have in place measures that effectively protect us from religious warfare, measures that are effective irrespective of obedience to the doctrine of restraint. Let me explain.

Liberals learned two crucially important lessons from the religious wars that wracked sixteenth- and seventeenth-century Europe. First, they learned a lesson about the *conditions* in which religion plays a role in causing warfare: religion plays a role in generating warfare when some agency (the state in particular) employs coercion to compel citizens to worship in accord with a religious creed they reject, punishes citizens for heterodox religious practices – in short, when the state employs coercion in order to achieve religious ends. *That* use of the state's coercive power naturally results in resistance: coerced religious communities might very well defend themselves – by force of arms if necessary. Thus, John Locke: "it is not the diversity of Opinions (which cannot be avoided) but the refusal of Toleration to those that are of different Opinions (which might have been granted) that has produced all the Bustles and Wars, that have been in the Christian World, upon account of Religion."[7] According to Locke, it is the forcible compulsion to assent to orthodoxy, the use of coercion to achieve religious uniformity, that causes religious war. Again:

> No body, therefore, in fine, neither single Persons, nor Churches, nay, nor even Commonwealths, have any just Title to invade the Civil Rights and Worldly Goods of each other, upon pretence of Religion. Those that are of another Opinion, would do well to consider with themselves how pernicious a Seed of Discord and War, how powerful a provocation to endless Hatreds, Rapines, and Slaughters, they thereby furnish unto Mankind. No Peace and Security, no not so much as Common Friendship, can even be established, so long as this Opinion prevails, That *Dominion is founded in Grace*, and that Religion is to be propagated by force of Arms.[8]

Second, liberals learned that the state must leave whatever religious convictions a citizen accepts and whatever religious practices he pursues entirely "to the Conscience of every particular man."[9] The state ought to accord each citizen a right to worship as he sees fit without being subject to punishment for the way he exercises that right. In so doing, the state does all that is necessary to insure that religious disagreement does not escalate into religious warfare. Thus, John Noonan: "that religion has caused many acts of violence and perpetuated many hatreds is a datum of history. . . . For the evils, at least for most of the evils that religion brings, a sovereign remedy exists – free exercise."[10]

Religious warfare is not a realistic prospect in the contemporary United States, then, because we have learned how to insure that it does not occur and have taken the appropriate measures: the proper prophylactic for religiously generated strife is a legal and constitutional one, viz., effective protection of religious freedom. We need nothing more, and nothing less, to insure that religious disagreement does not escalate into inter-religious conflict. So we need not worry that a repudiation of restraint risks religious warfare. It is commitment to religious freedom that really matters: so long as citizens are firmly committed to religious freedom, their willingness to support coercive laws solely on religious grounds has no realistic prospect of engendering religious warfare.

Of course, it is logically possible that citizens in the United States will flag on a massive scale in their commitment to religious freedom. But that's beside the point. The question is whether there is a plausible story that takes us from our current state to some condition in which large numbers of citizens are intent on employing state power to compel their compatriots to adhere to some religious creed or to participate in some religious practice. And there is no such story; at least, I've never heard it told. Perhaps in part because of the effectiveness of religious freedom in precluding religious warfare, the vast majority of citizens in the United States are fully and firmly committed to the right of their compatriots to worship freely, if at all. There is, no doubt, quite a bit of disagreement – often acrimonious – as to the proper application of the right to religious freedom in specific cases. Nevertheless, only small numbers of citizens, located at the extreme fringes of the political spectrum, are willing to deny their compatriots the right to religious freedom.

Not only is there no reason to believe that we face a realistic prospect of religious warfare, there are at least two reasons to deny that, even if there *were* a realistic prospect of religious warfare, a widespread repudiation of restraint holds out that prospect. This is particularly important for the following reason. We are interested in the argument from religious warfare only insofar as it provides support for the doctrine of restraint. As a consequence, only if a repudiation of restraint regarding religious convictions has a realistic prospect of generating conflict do citizens have reason to exercise restraint. By contrast, even if religion does have a realistic prospect of generating conflict, so long as we have no reason to believe that a repudiation of restraint holds out that realistic prospect, then citizens have no reason to obey the doctrine of restraint. So why deny that a repudiation of restraint regarding religious convictions has a realistic prospect of engendering religious warfare?

First, recall that, since the right to religious freedom and doctrine of restraint have to do with distinct levels of discourse, affirmation of religious freedom is entirely consistent with rejection of the doctrine of restraint. The doctrine of restraint constrains the *reasons* a citizen employs as a basis for her political commitments. The right to religious freedom is a *substantive political commitment* for which a citizen might have all manner of reasons. Given that the doctrine of restraint constrains the reasons a citizen employs as a basis for her political commitments, but is silent regarding the political commitments she ought to support, it is entirely possible for a citizen to reject the doctrine of restraint but to affirm the right to religious freedom. In fact, it is possible – indeed likely for members of the dominant faith traditions in the United States – that citizens will affirm religious freedom *for* religious reasons.

Second, citizens who reject the doctrine of restraint have special reason to *affirm* religious freedom. Why? Effective protection of religious freedom makes for a political framework in which religious citizens can "crusade" to transform the laws that govern the United States without thereby initiating the sort of religious strife that bedeviled the sixteenth and seventeenth centuries. Public affirmation of the right to religious freedom, and, more importantly, zealous defense of that right, exhibits a commitment to refrain from pursuing an agenda that has proved terribly destructive in the past: the forcible imposition of orthodoxy. This commitment to religious freedom allows citizens who reject the doctrine of restraint to employ the moral resources of their respective religious traditions to mold and shape the laws that govern the United States free from the stigma that rightly attaches to those who would attempt to employ the power of the state to punish heretics, impose religious orthodoxy, etc. Commitment to religious freedom frees the citizen who repudiates restraint to engage in the democratic process on equal footing with her compatriots: by supporting her favored coercive policies as her conscience dictates.

In short, we have reason to believe neither that we face a realistic prospect of religious warfare nor that, even if we did, repudiation of restraint would hold out that prospect. The move from the deontological argument from respect to the consequentialist argument from religious warfare does not forward the justificatory liberal's case.

The Argument from Divisiveness

But not so fast. The central problem with the argument from religious warfare is that the consequences it associates with a repudiation of restraint have no realistic prospect of actualization. But there are many other possible consequences of a widespread rejection of restraint. In particular, many citizens express considerable concern, frustration and even alienation at the intrusion of religious considerations into politics. A cursory perusal of recent history indicates that, even if the intrusion of religion into politics does not engender religious warfare, such intrusion is *divisive*. McCartney's advocacy of Amendment 2 is a representative case in point. Given that the intrusion of religion into politics polarizes already contentious political disputes, conscientious citizens will, it seems, obey the doctrine of restraint. This *argument from divisiveness* is fairly straightforward: frustration, alienation, marginalization, in short, divisiveness, are morally undesirable states of affairs; a widespread refusal to obey the doctrine of restraint is divisive; consequently, citizens ought to obey the doctrine of restraint.

What should we make of this argument? In order to evaluate it properly, we need to clarify the moral status of "divisiveness." A citizen who engages in divisive behavior does not *necessarily* act in a morally inappropriate manner: a citizen who engaged in the Civil Rights movement – the Freedom Rides, for example – acted in ways she had to know would be divisive and yet is rightly *commended* for her actions. Again, a citizen who performs *extremely* divisive actions does not necessarily behave in a morally inappropriate way: sometimes extremely divisive actions

are necessary to achieve goals of utmost moral importance. Clearly, the justificatory liberal must show more than that a refusal to exercise restraint is divisive or
that it is extremely divisive. But what must she show? Something like the following: if we take into consideration all of the morally relevant consequences both
of obedience to the doctrine of restraint and of rejection of that doctrine, we
are better off, morally speaking, when citizens obey the doctrine of restraint than
when they do not. That is, the justificatory liberal must engage in that complex
"weighing process" characteristic of consequentialist arguments of the sort under
discussion: she must identify the morally desirable and morally undesirable
consequences that would result were either of the two alternatives to materialize,
"add" up the morally desirable consequences of both alternatives, "subtract" from
each sum the morally undesirable consequences of each alternative, and then determine on the basis of those calculations which of the two alternatives is morally
preferable "on balance."

In spite of the considerable division generated by the religious advocacy for
coercive laws, it seems doubtful that that division is sufficiently weighty as to vindicate the doctrine of restraint. Three reasons in particular undermine the move
from divisiveness to restraint.

First, although there can be no doubt that religious advocacy for coercive laws
is very divisive, much of the division generated by religious advocacy does not
count in favor of the doctrine of restraint. Why? Here it is crucial that we recall
what the doctrine of restraint forbids and what it does not forbid. The doctrine
of restraint does *not* forbid a citizen to support coercive laws on religious grounds;
rather, it forbids her to support coercive laws on religious grounds alone. But then
only the division generated by a citizen's supporting a coercive law solely on religious grounds counts in favor of the doctrine of restraint: since the justificatory
liberal has no objection to religious support for coercive laws, the division generated by religious support for coercive laws can hardly count in favor of the doctrine of restraint. Now it seems that, as a matter of fact, very few citizens have a
general practice of supporting coercive laws solely on religious grounds. Why?
Simply, a citizen who supports her favored coercive laws on religious and non-
religious grounds stands a much better chance of gaining her compatriots' support,
and therefore of achieving her political aims, than does a citizen who relies solely
on religious grounds. So the division generated by much, if not most, religious
advocacy will not count in favor of the doctrine of restraint.

Second, as I have argued above, each citizen ought to pursue public justification for her favored coercive laws out of respect for her compatriots as persons.
Now it seems that a widespread refusal to pursue public justification for coercive
laws would generate considerable frustration, alienation and division: citizens who
refuse to pursue public justification thereby disrespect their compatriots, which in
turn warrants legitimate *resentment* on the part of the disrespected citizens. But
given the distinction between the principle of pursuit and doctrine of restraint,
none of the division, alienation and exclusion that results from a refusal to pursue
public justification may be adduced in favor of the doctrine of restraint. Rather,

only the division generated by citizens who have assiduously pursued public justification, who have failed in their pursuit, and who persist in supporting their favored coercive laws, counts in favor of the claim that a citizen ought to withhold support from coercive laws absent a public justification. As with the prior point, this dramatically reduces the amount of divisiveness that the justificatory liberal may adduce in favor of the doctrine of restraint.

Indeed, it seems to me that a proper appreciation of the distinction between the principle of pursuit and doctrine of restraint considerably weakens the argument from divisiveness. So long as we fail to bear that distinction in mind, we are likely to *overestimate* considerably the morally undesirable consequences of a widespread repudiation of restraint (by counting the divisiveness generated by a refusal to pursue public justification in favor of the doctrine of restraint). But keeping that distinction in mind dramatically *reduces* the amount of division to which the justificatory liberal may appeal in her attempt to show that a refusal to exercise restraint makes us worse off, morally speaking, than does exercising restraint. This is important since the argument from divisiveness, in accord with its consequentialist nature, unavoidably involves us in a numbers game: given that the central question raised by that argument is whether refusing to exercise restraint puts us further in the "moral black" than the alternative, anything that dramatically reduces the "debit" side of the ledger is obviously of crucial importance.

Of course, nothing I've said indicates that repudiation of restraint generates no division: undeniably, some citizens take considerable umbrage at their compatriots' refusal to exercise restraint. As a consequence, it is important to identify morally undesirable consequences of *obedience to* the doctrine of restraint of such magnitude that they can "outweigh" the division generated by repudiation of the doctrine of restraint. And it is not difficult to identify the ill consequences that might result from the effective enforcement, by means of social stigma, of the expectation that citizens exercise restraint regarding their religious convictions.

Religious citizens will very likely take considerable umbrage at the expectation that they obey the doctrine of restraint. (It is helpful to focus on theistic citizens, since the vast majority of citizens in the United States are theists of one sort or another.) Theists do not typically regard their religious convictions as a set of preferences on the order of a desire to vacation in exotic locations. Rather, they take themselves to be obliged to obey God. As I argued earlier, the doctrine of restraint requires that theistic citizens be willing to disobey what they have good reason to believe are God's demands. Given the nature of theistic commitment, many theists will regard that expectation as extremely alienating. And we must factor that resentment and alienation into our consequentialist calculation.

One further point is essential. As I have noted, the argument from divisiveness is a consequentialist argument and therefore depends on the exact quantities of morally good and morally bad consequences likely to be generated by the relevant alternatives. Successful prosecution of the argument from divisiveness depends on a numbers game: *How much* alienation is likely to be generated by the repudiation of restraint? *How many* citizens will find restraint offensive? Etc. But the vast majority of citizens in the United States are theists. And many will regard the kind of restraint the justificatory liberal advocates as quite burdensome. Given the large quantity of theistic citizens, and given their likely aversion to the doctrine of restraint, it seems very doubtful that we will find ourselves further in the moral black by imposing on citizens the expectation that they exercise restraint than by imposing on them a much weaker and commensurately less objectionable set of constraints, viz., that they genuinely and sincerely pursue public justification for their favored coercive laws but that they need not restrain themselves from supporting their favored coercive laws when their pursuit of public justification ends in failure. The argument from divisiveness, as with the argument from respect, counsels citizens to obey the principle of pursuit but not the doctrine of restraint.

What Is Public Justification?

Up to this point, our discussion has focused almost exclusively on the question: *Why* ought a citizen to refrain from supporting her favored coercive laws absent a public justification? That question raises another: What, exactly, is a public justification? To be sure, a religious rationale is not a public justification: justificatory liberals unanimously agree on that point. Even so, the justificatory liberal must provide some principled justification for this evaluation of religious grounds: she can't just provide us with a laundry list of non-public grounds, on which religious grounds are prominently displayed, and expect us to take her word on the matter. Failure to provide some principled demarcation between public and non-public grounds opens the justificatory liberal to a (commonly expressed) charge of arbitrariness: she advocates restraint regarding religious grounds without advocating restraint regarding all manner of considerations that seem similar to religious grounds in relevant respects. In short, the justificatory liberal must articulate a conception of public justification that, in a principled manner, gets the right results regarding religious grounds.

Moreover, she must articulate a conception of public justification that is satisfactory in other essential respects. Most particularly, that conception must not be so demanding that citizens are unable to articulate a public justification for central liberal commitments: although her favored conception of public justification must be strong enough to forbid a citizen to rely solely on religious grounds, it must be weak enough for citizens to be able to provide a public justification for characteristic liberal policies. Otherwise, justificatory liberalism is deeply incoherent: its justificatory component would undermine commitment to characteristic liberal policies, in which case we no longer have justificatory *liberalism*. So the justificatory liberal seems obliged to perform a challenging balancing act: she must articulate a conception of public justification that is demanding enough to get the right results regarding religious grounds, but relaxed enough to allow citizens to rely on an array of considerations sufficient to articulate a successful public justification for characteristic liberal policies.

I'll briefly review some of the justificatory liberal's options with an eye toward identifying a very significant obstacle she must overcome in articulating a defensible conception of public justification. And a natural place to begin is to note the constraints the justificatory liberal's rationale for the doctrine of restraint imposes on the available conceptions of public justification. Briefly: since the central rationale for the doctrine of restraint is an appeal to respect for persons, and since a citizen's obligation to respect her compatriots is an obligation to respect them as they are rather than as she wishes them to be or as they would be under radically altered conditions, then it seems most natural for the justificatory liberal to adopt a *populist* conception of public justification. That is, it is most natural for her to adopt a conception according to which a public justification is a function of what the actual citizens in a given liberal democracy actually find convincing. Thus it seems natural for the justificatory liberal to defend:

(1) rationale R counts as a public justification for coercive law L only if each citizen affected by L *actually accepts* R as a basis for L.

(1) has a number of attractive features. First, (1) provides a principled basis for determining whether some rationale counts as a public justification: what makes for a public rather than a non-public justification is a function of the position the members of the public take toward that rationale – whether they accept it or reject it. Second, (1) gets the desired result regarding religious grounds: many citizens will reject any particular religious rationale, and so no religious rationale, according to (1), counts as a public justification. In spite of these attractive features, however, (1) is utterly implausible. Regrettably but undoubtedly, some citizens in any given liberal democracy are cognitively inept and so are unable to accept even minimally complex arguments. And since (1) requires a public justification to enjoy the actual imprimatur of *all* affected citizens, then no minimally complicated rationale will count as a public justification. But this is disastrous for justificatory liberalism. For in that case, even basic liberal commitments will not be amenable of public justification: even so highly regarded a liberal commitment as the right to religious freedom will require a slightly complex rationale for its justification.

(1) is easily modified to avoid this problem. All the justificatory liberal needs to do is to restrict membership in the public to cognitively adept citizens. So suppose she proposes:

(2) rationale R counts as a public justification for coercive law L only if each *cognitively adept* citizen affected by L accepts R as a sufficient basis for L.

(2), quite reasonably, does not require a public justification to be accepted by children, the insane and other cognitively inept citizens. Given this minor modification, does (2) constitute a defensible conception of public justification? No, (2) is still far too restrictive. Given the millions of citizens in a large-scale liberal democracy such as the United States, and given their freedom to decide for themselves what to believe about the coercive laws to which they are subject, it beggars credulity to suppose that we are able to articulate some rationale for characteristic liberal commitments, such as the right to religious freedom, that will be convincing to each of our cognitively adept compatriots. Although a natural candidate for the justificatory liberal, (2) founders on the undeniable reality there will inevitably be some cognitively adept citizens who object to almost any rationale for political commitments of moment.

As with its predecessor, (2) is easily modified. Consider the following conception:

> (3) rationale R counts as a public justification for coercive law L only if each cognitively adept citizen affected by L *can* accept R as a sufficient basis for L.

(3) weakens (2) rather dramatically: (3) requires only the *possibility* that R is accepted by the members of the public rather than, as with (2), that R is *actually accepted* by the members of the public. But in what sense must it be possible for the members of the public to accept R? Surely not in the sense of logical possibility: were we to interpret the modal term "can" in (3) as requiring only logical possibility, (3) would not get the right result regarding religious convictions, since it is logically possible for even the most hard-bitten atheist to assent, for example, to McCartney's rationale for Amendment 2.

Are there more promising candidates? Undoubtedly. Without cycling through a tiresome menu of options, consider the following: A citizen can accept some rationale in the relevant sense only if accepting that rationale would not require her *drastically* to alter her fundamental convictions. Thus, Bill McCartney's rationale for Amendment 2 is not acceptable in the relevant sense just because, if his atheistic compatriots were to accept his claim that homosexuality is an abomination to God, they would have to convert to theism and so would be rationally compelled to alter their metaphysical commitments, presumably, in quite a thoroughgoing manner. So far as (3) goes, McCartney's atheistic compatriots *cannot* accept his rationale for Amendment 2.

Even though (3) weakens (2) considerably, it is still too demanding. How so? Some citizens in the United States not only reject the liberal commitment to religious freedom, but they find that commitment so alien that its acceptance would oblige them to alter their core commitments in fundamental respects. Thus, for example, some citizens in the United States are *Christian Reconstructionists* and so believe that the United States ought to be governed by the laws encoded in the Old Testament. And given their commitment to the abiding authority of Old Testament law, Christian Reconstructionists advocate that we revoke the civil rights of non-Christians, that we stone adulterers, etc. Surely, acceptance of the liberal commitment to religious freedom would require a rather thorough reworking of the Christian Reconstructionist's creed. But in that case, there is no prospect that we are in any position to articulate a rationale for the right to religious freedom that satisfies (3). Consequently, (3) is too strong for the justificatory liberal's purposes. The highly pluralistic nature of a modern liberal democracy such as the United States – which makes likely the existence of fringe groups like Christian Reconstructionism – renders (3) utterly utopian under current and foreseeable conditions.

At this point, justificatory liberals have been inclined to make the same basic move with Christian Reconstructionists as they make with regard to the cognitively inept: that we adopt constraints on membership in the public that obviate the necessity of articulating a rationale that is, or can be, convincing to such "fanatics." Perhaps the most popular proposal of this sort, associated with John Rawls, has been to restrict membership in the public to *reasonable* citizens. Thus, we might modify (3) as follows:

(4)   rationale R counts as a public justification for coercive law L only if each cognitively adept and *reasonable* citizen affected by L can accept R as a sufficient basis for L.

What makes for a reasonable citizen? For Rawls, the "reasonable" is a moral, rather than an epistemic concept: the mark of reasonableness is a willingness to seek, propose and obey fair principles of social cooperation. "Reasonable persons . . . desire for its own sake a social world in which they, as free and equal, can cooperate with others on terms all can accept."[11] The phrase "on terms all can accept" is crucial: the only citizens to whom a prospective public justification must be acceptable are those committed to the project of proposing and obeying coercive laws acceptable to all.

It seems obvious that Christian Reconstructionists are unreasonable in their insistence that the United States ought to be governed by Old Testament law: they can expect little else but that non-Christian citizens will find their theocratic project shockingly repugnant. Given that they are unreasonable, (4) permits us to ignore their protestations in determining whether we enjoy a public justification for the right to religious freedom.

Have we arrived at a defensible conception of public justification? No: the restriction to reasonable citizens is too weak to exclude Christian Reconstructionists from membership in the public, in which case (4) is still too demanding. Briefly put, the Christian Reconstructionist's repudiation of religious freedom need have nothing to do with an unwillingness to seek, propose and obey social terms that all can accept and have everything to do with adherence to ordinary empirical claims about the consequences of religious freedom. Thus, for example, suppose the Christian Reconstructionist assents to the venerable claim that *social order depends on agreement regarding fundamentals*, and in particular, on agreement regarding religious matters. According to this staple of pre-modern political wisdom, in order to avoid social anarchy, citizens must agree on religious matters, and in order to approximate religious uniformity, the state must employ its coercive force to compel religious uniformity. Now imagine the justificatory liberal proposing that the state accord each citizen a right to religious freedom: what she purports to propose as a policy *all* can accept, the Christian Reconstructionist regards as a recipe for social disaster! Pretty clearly, the liberal's advocacy of religious freedom is just as objectionable *to the Christian Reconstructionist* as the Christian Reconstructionist's denial of religious freedom is *to the liberal*. And the Christian Reconstructionist's rejection of religious freedom need have nothing to do with her unwillingness to seek, propose and accept fair terms; rather, it will depend on her, quite understandable, rejection of any proposal that ensues in social chaos. The disagreement between the liberal and the Christian Reconstructionist results not from a deficit of reasonableness on the latter's part but from a disagreement about fact: about the likely consequences of religious freedom. But since Christian Reconstructionists need not be unreasonable, the exclusionary move embodied in (4) will do nothing to obviate the problem Christian Reconstructionists pose for (4): there will remain reasonable citizens for whom any rationale for religious freedom is simply *unacceptable*, in which case we will be stymied in our attempt to articulate a rationale for religious freedom that satisfies (4).

Here again, the justificatory liberal is not without options. The obvious difficulty of articulating a satisfactory populist conception of public justification under conditions of manifold pluralism motivates many justificatory liberals to articulate an *epistemic* conception of public justification. In contrast to populist conceptions, which require that a rationale be actually acceptable in some robust sense to the members of the public, epistemic conceptions require that a rationale enjoy some epistemic property in virtue of which that rationale merits acceptance *in spite of* the fact that members of the public reject that rationale. There are many epistemic conceptions on offer; in fact even a cursory familiarity with the literature on the proper role of religious convictions in politics will acquaint the reader with a healthy dose of references to "critical rationality," "intelligibility," "common human reason," "criticizability," "accessibility," "replicability," and the like. I'll discuss only one epistemic conception.

Consider that, although Christian Reconstructionists need be neither cognitively inept nor unreasonable, they are most certainly misinformed. How so? The last several centuries have provided ample empirical refutation of the pre-modern commonplace undergirding the Christian Reconstructionist's rejection of religious freedom: it just isn't true that social order depends on agreement on fundamentals, whether religious or not. The Christian Reconstructionist might believe otherwise, but she's just wrong about that.

Even if the Christian Reconstructionist is rationally justified in believing that social order requires agreement on fundamentals, the justificatory liberal proposes that we take into consideration the fact that that claim is false in determining whether the right to religious freedom is amenable of public justification. After all, it seems unduly constraining to suppose that, in order for some rationale to count as a public justification, that rationale must be convincing to the members of the public, *irrespective of how ignorant or benighted they are*. Surely, a successful public justification need be convincing only to adequately informed citizens. Thus, some justificatory liberals have endorsed:

(5)   rationale R counts as a public justification for coercive law L only if each cognitively adept, reasonable and *adequately informed* citizen affected by L can accept R as a sufficient basis for L.

(5) is afflicted with a number of very serious problems. I will focus on two. First, consider McCartney's rationale for Amendment 2. McCartney's rationale for Amendment 2 assumes that God has authored the Bible, such that the Bible is a repository of reliable information about, among other things, God's express convictions about all manner of moral claims. (McCartney's claim that homosexuality is an "abomination of almighty God" is an allusion to Leviticus 18:22, viz., "You shall not lie with a male as one lies with a female; it is an abomination.") Since McCartney believes that the Bible is a reliable source of information about God's moral convictions, it is entirely natural for him to conclude that an adequately informed citizen will be aware of that fact. After all, how could McCartney's compatriots be adequately informed about homosexuality if they are ignorant of one of the most important facts about homosexuality, viz., that an omniscient moral authority has expressly condemned homosexual relations? McCartney will, no doubt, claim that non-believers think otherwise because they are *inadequately* informed: to be unaware of an omniscient being's express moral judgments is to be desperately ignorant. It seems, then, that (5) is too weak to get the desired results regarding religious convictions: even if McCartney accepts (5), he has no reason to withhold support from Amendment 2 solely on the basis of his religious rationale for Amendment 2.

Of course, the justificatory liberal is free to propose constraints on what counts as adequate information so as to disallow McCartney from concluding that adequately informed citizens would be aware that his theological commitments are true. But it is entirely unclear on what *principled* basis the justificatory liberal can provide for such a restriction and, of course, providing some such principled basis is essential to the justificatory liberal's case. Moreover, I am unaware of any extant attempt to do so.

Second, (5) seems disjoint with the justificatory liberal's rationale for the doctrine of restraint. Consider the argument from respect (although the same point holds for both the argument from religious warfare and the argument from divisiveness). As I have noted, the argument from respect articulates most naturally with a populist conception of public justification: since each citizen has an obligation to respect her compatriots as they are, rather than as she wishes them to be or as they ought to be, and if respect requires something by way of public justification, then it seems most natural for the justificatory liberal to claim that a citizen ought to provide a rationale for her favored coercive laws that is acceptable to her compatriots more or less as they are. By contrast, it strikes me as utterly unnatural for the justificatory liberal to claim that respect requires a citizen to articulate a public justification that satisfies (5). In fact, it seems utterly mystifying why a citizen who obeys (5) exhibits respect for her compatriots. After all, a citizen's rationale for some coercive law can satisfy (5) even though it is thoroughly repugnant to the actual citizens subject to that law. That their counterfactual counterparts in some – perhaps *very* distant – possible world would find a given rationale acceptable is cold comfort to the flesh-and-blood citizens who are not so favorably circumstanced with respect to that rationale and thus who find that coercive law highly objectionable.

The demise of (5) by no means closes the books on the justificatory liberal's search for a defensible conception of public justification. More generally, this short discussion by no means establishes that justificatory liberals are unable to articulate a defensible conception of public justification. But it does illustrate a serious problem for the justificatory liberal, viz., to articulate a conception of public justification that is *strong* enough to mandate restraint regarding religious convictions, but *weak* enough to enable citizens to articulate a public justification for characteristic liberal commitments. My judgment is that justificatory liberals have not successfully performed this balancing act, although none of these general comments establish that conclusion. In order to do that, we would need to engage in a detailed analysis of the many proposed epistemic conceptions.[12] But at least we can spy where the trouble lies.

Conclusion

According to some liberal theorists, religion should be excluded in its entirety from liberal politics. Thus, for example, Richard Rorty advocates a thoroughgoing privatization of religion: "contemporary liberal philosophers think that we shall not be able to keep a democratic political community going unless the religious believers remain willing to trade privatization for a guarantee of religious liberty."[13] Rorty's concern for the very existence of liberal democracy motivates his suggestion that we aspire to make "it seem bad taste to bring religion into discussions of public policy."[14] But this much-discussed and oft-criticized policy of privatizing religion is extreme and extremely implausible.

There are more plausible positions in the general area. Justificatory liberals have advocated a much more plausible position: rather than excluding religion entirely from liberal politics, religious citizens are free to support their favored coercive laws on religious grounds so long as they complement their religious grounds with a public justification. But even this conciliatory position faces quite formidable obstacles. I have identified two.

First, it is not clear that a citizen ought to refrain from supporting coercive laws absent a public justification. To be sure, each citizen should *pursue* public justification for her favored coercive laws – respect for her compatriots as persons

requires at least that. But it is not clear that, if a citizen pursues public justification for a given coercive law and fails in that attempt, she should also withhold
her support from that law – particularly if she is rationally justified in believing
that that law is morally appropriate. So far as I can tell, no justificatory liberal has
shown that she should exercise restraint under those conditions.

Second, even if a citizen ought to refrain from supporting coercive laws absent
a public justification, justificatory liberals have provided no compelling reason to
conclude that a citizen who enjoys a religious rationale thereby lacks a public justification. Indeed, the claim that a citizen should exercise restraint regarding her
religious convictions smacks of arbitrariness: the justificatory liberal advocates
restraint regarding religious convictions whilst helping herself to considerations
that are no less controversial and no more epistemically respectable than are religious grounds. This arbitrariness casts the doctrine of restraint even further into
doubt.

It seems that even the conciliatory approach defended by justificatory liberals
is too strong. An even weaker position seems appropriate: that a citizen should
attempt to articulate a widely convincing rationale for her favored coercive laws,
but need not withhold her support from coercive laws for which she lacks a widely
convincing rationale. So religious citizens should be willing to attempt to meet
their compatriots on what Larmore calls common ground and therefore should
be willing to do what they can to articulate reasons for their favored coercive laws
that do not depend essentially on their religious convictions. Respect for persons
counsels each citizen to refrain from an intransigent parochialism; religious citizens shouldn't conduct their political deliberations entirely within the ambit of
their theological commitments. But a citizen whose religious convictions counsel
her to support some coercive law, and who cannot provide a rationale for that law
that her compatriots find convincing, is not thereby morally criticizable for per-
sisting in her support for that law. In fact, her willingness to persist might very
well be morally admirable such that we should commend her for doing so.

Notes

1 For simplicity's sake, I understand a religious ground to be a reason that has *theistic*
content, e.g., the claim that the Bible is inspired by God, that some religious authority has been appointed to speak for God, and the like.
2 I have taken this term from Gerald Gaus, who coined it in his *Justificatory Liberalism*
(Cambridge: Cambridge University Press, 1996), although my use of the term is quite
a bit broader than Gaus's.
3 Some theorists, e.g., John Rawls and Charles Larmore, focus their attention even more
narrowly – to constitutional matters and matters of basic justice. But as I see the matter,
nothing essential hangs on that difference.
4 Charles Larmore, "Political Liberalism," in *The Morals of Modernity* (Cambridge: Cambridge University Press, 1996), p. 137.
5 Ibid., pp. 134–5.

6   For more on this distinction, see Christopher J. Eberle, "Why Restraint is Religiously Unacceptable," *Religious Studies*, 35/3 (September 1999): 247–76.
7   John Locke, *A Letter Concerning Toleration*, ed. James Tully (Indianapolis, IN: Hackett, 1983), p. 55.
8   Ibid., p. 33.
9   Ibid., p. 55.
10 John Noonan, *The Lustre of Our Country: The American Experience of Religious Freedom* (Berkeley, CA: University of California Press, 1998), p. 2.
11 John Rawls, *Political Liberalism* (New York: Columbia University Press, 1993), p. 50.
12 I have evaluated a large number of epistemic conceptions in "Liberalism and Mysticism," *Journal of Law and Religion*, 13/1 (1996–98): 189–238.
13 Richard Rorty, "Religion as a Conversation-Stopper," *Common Knowledge*, 3/1 (1994): 3.
14 Ibid., p. 2.

Bibliography

Audi, Robert (2000). *Religious Commitment and Secular Reason*. Cambridge: Cambridge University Press.
——and Nicholas Wolterstorff (1997). *Religion in the Public Square: The Place of Religious Convictions in Political Debate*. Lanham, MD: Rowman and Littlefield.
Carter, Stephen (1993). *The Culture of Disbelief*. New York: Basic Books.
Greenawalt, Kent (1988). *Religious Convictions and Political Choice*. Oxford: Oxford University Press.
——(1995). *Private Consciences and Public Reasons*. Oxford: Oxford University Press.
Perry, Michael (1991). *Love and Power: The Role of Religion and Morality in American Politics*. Oxford: Oxford University Press.
——(1997). *Religion in Politics: Constitutional and Moral Perspectives*. Oxford: Oxford University Press.
Rawls, John (1993). *Political Liberalism*. New York: Columbia University Press.
Weithman, Paul (ed.) (1997). *Religion and Contemporary Liberalism*. Notre Dame, IN: University of Notre Dame Press.

Select Bibliography

The select bibliography includes recent and contemporary titles that may be of special interest to readers of this collection. This bibliography makes no claim to be exhaustive. However, in the editor's judgment the titles selected not only provide background or development of themes, positions, or arguments that have been especially influential to the development of recent social and political philosophy but also are relevant to the argument of more than one of the essays in the collection. While most of the entries listed also appear in the bibliographies following each essay, several do not. These additional entries provide comprehensive treatments of topics relevant to the material covered in this volume in their own right. The select bibliography does not include books and articles by the contributors to this volume since their current views are developed in their essays. However, relevant books and articles by the contributors to this Blackwell Guide are listed in the bibliographies following each chapter.

I General Surveys and Analyses

Bowie, Norman E. and Simon, Robert L. (1998). *The Individual and the Political Order*. Lanham, MD: Rowman and Littlefield.

Hampton, Jean (1997). *Political Philosophy*. Boulder: Westview.

Kymlicka, W. (1990). *Contemporary Political Philosophy: An Introduction*. New York: Oxford University Press.

II Specialized Studies of Selected Topics

Appiah, K. A. and Amy Gutmann (1996). *Color Conscious: The Political Morality of Race*. Princeton: Princeton University Press.

Audi, Robert (2000). *Religious Commitment and Secular Reason*. New York: Cambridge University Press.

Barry, Brian (1995). *Justice as Impartiality*. New York: Oxford University Press.

——(2001). *Culture and Equality*. Cambridge, MA: Harvard University Press.

Buchanan, A. (1982) *Marxism and Justice: The Radical Critique of Liberalism*. Totowa, NJ: Rowman and Littlefield.

Cohen, G. A. (1978). *Karl Marx's Theory of History: A Defense*. Princeton: Princeton University Press.

Dworkin, Ronald (1977). *Taking Rights Seriously*. Cambridge, MA: Harvard University Press.

Feinberg, Joel (1984). *Harm to Others*. New York: Oxford University Press.

Gauthier, David (1986). *Morals By Agreement*. New York: Oxford University Press.

Gutmann, Amy and Dennis Thompson (1996). *Democracy and Disagreement*. Cambridge, MA: Harvard University Press.

Hart, H. L. A. (1963). *Law, Liberty, and Morality*. Stanford: Stanford University Press.

Jaggar, Alison (1983). *Feminist Politics and Human Nature*. Totowa, NJ: Rowman and Littlefield.

Kittay, Eva Feder (1999). *Love's Labor: Essays on Women, Equality, and Dependency*. New York: Routledge.

Kymlicka, Will (1995). *Multicultural Citizenship*. New York: Oxford University Press.

Nozick, Robert (1974). *Anarchy, State, and Utopia*. New York: Basic Books.

Nussbaum, Martha C. (1999). *Sex and Social Justice*. New York: Oxford University Press.

Okin, Susan Moller (1989). *Justice, Gender, and the Family*. New York: Basic Books.

Outlaw, L. T. (1996). *On Race and Philosophy*. New York: Routledge.

Pateman, C. (1979). *The Problem of Political Obligation*. Berkeley: University of California Press.

Rawls, J. (1971). *A Theory of Justice*. Cambridge, MA: Harvard University Press.

——(1993). *Political Liberalism*. New York: Columbia University Press.

Raz, J. (1986). *The Morality of Freedom*. Oxford: Oxford University Press.

——(ed.). (1990). *Authority*. New York: New York University Press.

Sandel, Michael (1982). *Liberalism and the Limits of Justice*. New York: Cambridge University Press.

Scanlon, T. M. (1998). *What We Owe To Each Other*. Cambridge, MA: Harvard University Press.

Walzer, Michael (1983). *Spheres of Justice*. New York: Basic Books.

Young, Iris Marion (1990). *Justice and the Politics of Difference*. Princeton: Princeton University Press.

Index

Page numbers in bold type indicate a main or detailed reference.